Lucifer's Labyrinth:

Individualism, Hyper-Abstract Thinking, and the Process of Becoming Civilized From the Middle Ages to the Guilded Age

by

Bruce Lerro

www.amazon.com/author/brucelerro

Printed by Kindle Direct Publishing in the United States of America.

First printing, 2019.
ISBN: 978-0-9974670-3-1

Editing and Design by Red Dress Press.
www.reddresspress.net

Preface

<u>Genesis of this book</u>

This book was born of abundance. The original manuscript, *Forging Promethean Psychology* was 443 pages with ten-point font. One reviewer gently commented that the manuscript was too big. I took it to heart and thought about how I could cut the manuscript in two, anticipating another book. As it turned out. *Forging Promethean Psychology* was "slimmed down" to 489 pages in the standard twelve-point font. I thought what I had left was a 300-page book. But in a pattern that is too satisfying to break, as I wrote what has now become *Lucifer's Labyrinth I* incorporated new books to the point where it totals over 550 pages in its own right. There is so much to say and so many disciplines to cover to say it!

In the old days, *Lucifer's Labyrinth* would have become the second volume of *Forging Promethean Psychology.* But in the publishing business, we no longer see authors referring their books as Volume I and II and so forth. Also, these days it is presumptuous to expect readers to commit to reading two books to understand the full power of an author's argument. So, *Lucifer's Labyrinth* is a *companion* book to *Forging Promethean Psychology*, meaning they can each be read separately.

As for the title, the original meaning of Lucifer was the bringer of light, but this is not light of love and harmony. It is the bringer of light by a rebel who refused to serve God. Lucifer brings light to humanity by seeking the truth through the Tree of Knowledge. So much of Western history, from the Middle Ages to the Gilded Age, deals with humanity setting its own course for better or worse. In a way, it is a rebellion against any spiritual or material authority who claims to guide us. The word 'labyrinth' is defined in the dictionary as a complicated, irregular network of passages through which it is difficult to find one's way out. By the end of the nineteenth century, in the Gilded Age it is safe to say that western humanity was in danger of losing its way. But all along the way there have been patterns of conflict within the western tradition that are similar to the story of *Faust*.

In the Preface to *Forging Promethean Psychology,* I named twenty-two dialectical tensions that have permeated western history, with more tension flaring up in some periods, and then dying down in others. From these tensions I will select only those that are directly connected to this book.

<u>The wicked concoction in Lucifer's labyrinth</u>

1) *Nature is malleable, and subject to evolution and the intervention of humanity.* This was opposed to the idea of nature as a finite closed system, prevalent in the Middle Ages.

2) *Biophysical nature can be understood best as having discrete parts which are measurable, quantitative, and mathematical.* This was the foundation of mechanistic science. This way of thinking challenged the organic conception of nature in which relations were qualitative substances such as fire, water, earth, and air. The manipulation of these substances was the basis the high magical traditions in the Renaissance. It was also an organic (as opposed to a mechanistic) depiction of nature.

3) *Society is evolving.* It is possible for human beings to engineer social organization and change it for the better. This was opposed to the notion in the Middle Ages of society being static, and of always having been more or less the same.

4) *Capitalism is the greatest economic system for assuring wealth and prosperity to humanity.* It wasn't until the Enlightenment that this way of thinking gained favor.

5) *A linear sense of time, in which the future—whether society or the individual—will be better than it was in the past*. This was an overlay on the cyclic sense of time which predominated not only in the Middle Ages, but all the way to the eighteenth century.

6) *The value of individualism*. There is a tension between individualism and collectivism. A fiercely held value in the west (especially by the eighteenth century) was the commitment that the individual has value and should be treated as an end in itself. This was opposed by collectivism, which was most prominent in the Middle Ages.

7) *The individual is capable of self-development*. This ran opposite to the temperament theory prior to the eighteenth century, in which a person is born with a certain configuration of body fluids which made fixed our identity once and for all.

8) *Metropolitan life in the cities is the space in which individuals are most likely to thrive*. When peasants ran away from the manor to the towns and cities long before the industrial revolution, the aristocrats could not get them to return. There is some truth in the saying that 'city life makes you free.' The reason is because cities are in the crossfire of many cultures from around the world, and these spaces provide exotic opportunities and constantly challenge the roles and situations that keep individuals habituated.

9) *The body must be controlled either by becoming civilized (the upper middle class or middle class) or disciplined (the working class)*. Becoming civilized requires the cultivation of hindsight, insight, and foresight in order to navigate dense social situations. Before the seventeenth century, according to Norbert Elias, no culture in Europe

was civilized. Of course, they were socialized, obeyed the authorities and conformed to their social class norms. But being civilized is something else.

10) *Self-reflection is a highly-valued quality.* This follows from the process of becoming civilized, but it also applies to identity (individualism), cognition, and emotion. Until the eighteenth century, most people were practical, action-oriented, and not very psychological at all.

11) Cognitive processes work best through a process what I call 'hyper-abstract' thinking. This includes deductive logic, inductive logic, abductive logic, and statistical thinking which includes probability and chance. This is a far cry from the more moderate abstraction of reasoning described by Stephen Toulmin.

<u>My literary resources</u>

Psychologically, the authors whom I've learned the most from who inform the entire book include Lev Vygotsky, Alexander Luria and A. N. Leontiev. Carl Ratner is the most uncompromising Vygotskian in the United States that I've encountered, and I've learned a great deal from his three books, which are listed in this work's bibliography. Marshall Berman's great book, *All That is Solid Melts into Air* gave me a literary grounding from the nineteenth century about what it means to be modern.

As I review the authors chapter by chapter who have given me the richest material, my main inspirators for individualism prior to the Reformation include Aaron Gurevich, Alan MacFarlane, and C.B. MacPherson. For individualism from the Reformation forward to the nineteenth century, Charles Taylor's *Sources of the Self* shows deep understanding of European culture through the nineteenth-century Victorian self.

When I turned my eyes westward, what I found most striking was how long it took individualism to really take hold in the United States. Barry Alan Shain was most responsible for this in his book *The Myths of American Individualism*. J.E. Crowley's book *This Sheba Self* very carefully showed that capitalism was very slow in convincing Puritans that Adam Smith's invisible hand was a way to organize an economy. When we finally get to the types of individualism in the nineteenth century, I owe most to Peter Berger, Erich Fromm, David Reisman, Allen Wheelis, and Richard Sennett.

In terms of chapter five (on the evolution of geography), humanistic geographer Yi-Fu Tuan opened up a whole new world for me with his distinction between 'places' from 'spaces.' He showed how the two evolved from the Middle Ages forward, into the modern world, and connected them to the organization of houses, and even the theatre. Robert David Sack demonstrated very convincingly what 'spaces' have to do with cities and capitalism. In the case of time, Richard Nisbett's *History of the Idea of Progress* was a steady guide.

My chapter on ontogenesis was the last new chapter I wrote and it is still simmering. Poor Erik Erikson is raked over the coals by the work of Philippe Aries, Roy Baumeister, and Lawrence Stone. I struggled through Jonas Langer's dry-as-dust *Theories of Development* in order to be grounded the controversies within developmental psychology between Piaget, Vygotsky, and Heinz Werner. I toast Klaus Riegel, who first got me thinking about human development from a dialectical materialist viewpoint.

What it meant to become 'civilized' was first inspired by Norbert Elias and Pieter Spierenburg. The idea of civilized behavior as being for the upper classes, while becoming disciplined was for the lower classes is my own distinction. Thank goodness for Stephen Mennell, a careful and ambitious student of Elias, who raised and answered the question of to what extent (if at all) could Elias' work by applied to the United States. Mennell made some useful distinctions between Northern and Southern cultures, but it was Colin Woodard who really got specific about the differences between the eleven regions in the United States. While generalization from eleven regional cultures to one big 'American culture' is too much, the regions of New England, New York, and Virginia did give me a basis of what it means to an American with which to apply Mennell's work.

My initial guides for the distinction between reason and rationality, as well as their evolutionary interaction, owe most to Stephen Toulmin's books, *Cosmopolis* and *Return to Reason*; Chaim Perelman's book *The New Rhetoric;* and later, John Dewey in his book *Quest for Certainty.* When I turned to the quantitative side of thinking—to gauging probabilities and chance—my guides were Ian Hacking and Lorraine Daston (affectionately known by my partner as 'my girlfriend' because I gobbled up three of her works in a year). Both authors combine breadth, clarity, and comprehensibility in their writings.

My chapter on cognitive evolution starts with the description of the *ontogenetic* development by the master, Jean Piaget. However, it was C.R, Hallpike's work that first made me think that perhaps Piaget's stages of cognitive development only emerged at certain points in history. Furthermore, it took certain kinds of social institutions to bring them into full operation. Despite the slings and arrows leveled upon Hallpike by cultural relativists, I found support for him from the arena of cognitive evolution, in the work of Jack Goody, Walter Ong, and (of late) David Olson.

For the grand sweep of Western history I owe most to Alfred Crosby in his book *The Measure of Reality*, and William Mc Neil's great *Rise of the West*.

In fact the cover of this book draws it's inspiration from Pieter Bruegel's painting "Temperance". I will quote at length the description of the painting from the Introduction of my last book:

"In his wonderful book, The Measure of Reality, Alfred Crosby sets out to explain how the West developed the way it did. Crosby points out how the painting Temperance by Netherlandish Renaissance painter, Pieter Bruegel, captures the essence of the western tradition. Crosby interprets the Bruegel painting in the following way: at the top-center of the painting is an astronomer teetering on the North Pole as he measures the angular distance between the moon and some neighboring star. Just below are an array of measuring devices; a compass, a mason's square and a plumb bob.

The upper right of the painting is devoted to the weaponry of the musket, the crossbow and artillery. The use of these weapons is carried out, not by aristocrats clashing on horseback, but by foot soldiers who learned to perform mechanically, marching in step and who were controlled by officers using tables of square roots to guide their operations. In the lower left there is a flurry of calculation; a merchant counts his money and an accountant calculates their accounts receivable and accounts payable.

Temperance herself occupies the center of the picture. In her left hand she holds spectacles as a material device of scientific exploration beyond the naked eye. It could just as well have included the telescope and the microscope. In her right hand are reins that lead to a bit in her mouth, representing self-restraint. Spurs on her heels indicate control over great power and a snake knotted around her waist as a belt represent evil passions under control. She stands on the vane of a post windmill, medieval Europe's greatest single contribution to power technology.

Generally, most of the figures in the painting are engaged in one way or another in visualizing the stuff of reality. Today many authors have connected the rise of these Promethean projects with the rise of vision. But one of the angles Crosby brings to light is how things are envisioned. Things are quantified and measured. Crosby believed that breaking things down and mathematizing them held the key to western success in science, technology and economics."

My appreciations

Thanks to the staff of Red Dress Press, Liz, Chris and Em for their enthusiasm, integrity, timeliness, and flexibility in working with me. Not much time has passed since my previous book, so my personal appreciations extend mostly to the same sources. In my *History of Psychology* course, my students at

Dominican University in San Rafael were stuck with an ever-expanding lecture notes packet. I regret that just as I had the manuscript ready to be published, I was bumped out of the course by full-time faculty because of budget cuts. Ah, yes...education under capitalism. My scholarly fellow travelers included my best critic, Gene Anderson, and Kosta Bagakis.

Best of all, to my partner Barbara MacLean for her steadiness, warmth, appreciation, and respect for all my projects, writing and otherwise.

Lucifer's Labyrinth:
Individualism, Hyper-Abstract Thinking and the Process of Becoming Civilized From The Middle Ages To The Gilded Age

Detailed Table of Contents

Chapter 9 Becoming Civilized in Yankeedom: How the Upper Classes Got 'Class'

Part IV: Luciferian Hyper-abstract Thinking

Chapter 10 From Reason to Rationality: How Rationality Lost Its Way

Chapter 11 From Rationality to Reason: How Reason Lost and Regained Its Balance

Chapter 12 Quantitative Rationality: Theories of Probability and Chance From the Middle Ages to the Eighteenth Century

Chapter 13 Quantitative Rationality: Application to Law, Economics, State Politics, and Mental Illness in the eighteenth and nineteenth Centuries

Chapter 14 Cognitive Evolution: Amplification of Concrete Operations in Early Modern Europe

Introduction

I feel my power growing
As if I'd drunk new wine, I'm glowing
I feel courage to plunge into the world
To bear all of earthly grief, all earthly joy
To wrestle with the storm, to grapple and clinch
To enter the jaws of the shipwreck and never to flinch

Goethe, from Faust

What it means to be modern: welcome to the maelstrom

A better way to start might be to ask: what does it mean to be *pre-modern*? To be pre-modern is to be pre-objective and pre-subjective. To be pre-objective is to understand the world as inseparable from local customs and the cultural values that go with it. There is no attempt to compare cultures or to see one's situation historically. To be objective means to strive for universality, not particularity. To be objective means to see the world truthfully as it really is, neutrally; not as how we would like it to be. To be objective also means to understand one's place relative to world history in the making.

To be pre-subjective means that an individual's wishes, hopes, and fears are inseparable from those of the *group*. All psychology is group psychology. On the other hand, to be subjective means to take one's psychological life seriously. This means to be introspective about one's life and the relationship between what has been done to us and what we intend to do in the future. Secondly, subjectivity means communicating this psychological life to others, and expecting the other person to do the same.

To be modern does not mean one is necessarily anti-religious, but it means that for better or worse the modern world is the creature of *collective humanity*. Furthermore, we are not just creatures of the world, but co-creators of it. Subjectivity is deeper and more intensely developed than in pre-modern times. Yet the products of this subjectivity—goods and services—appear in an alien form. The experience of things constantly changing for better and for worse, at the same time encapsulates the experience of being modern. In his book on sociologist Georg Simmel, David Frisby says:

> Simmel is the first sociologist of modernity...in the sense given to it originally by Baudelaire as the ephemeral, fugitive, the contingent in modern life. The artist of modernity is the painter of the passing moment who captures the newness of the present and is able to distill the eternal from the transitory in city life, fashions, gestures. Simmel declares that "the psychological foundation of the metropolitan personality type is the increase of nervous life, which emerges out of the rapid and unbroken change in external and internal stimuli." (40)

To be modern is to accept living a life of contradiction. This turbulence has many sources: the discoveries that the earth is not the center of the solar system; that humans evolved from apes; and that the bulk of human life is now in cities. This is just the tip of the iceberg!

In Berman's book *All That is Solid Melts into Air*, he breaks modernity into three phases—the eighteenth, nineteenth, and twentieth centuries. In the eighteenth century, there were simply people learning to grapple with modernity. There was no reflection upon it. In the nineteenth century, thinkers were both enthusiasts and enemies of modern life. They all believed that modern individuals had the capacity to both understand their fate and fight it. According to Berman, the twentieth century could not hold both at once. Choices were flattened out to either:

- blind, vapid enthusiasm for modernity, as seen in the theory of progress
- a dismissal of modernism leading to a crypto- romanticism; our vision of modern life tends to split into material and spiritual planes

Goethe's *Faust*

According to Berman, one of the most original and fruitful ideas in *Faust* is the relationship between economic development on the one hand and psychological *self*-development on the other. Yet human power is not advanced by any lightness and love, but rather through wrestling with the powers of darkness, either economic or psychological.

The Faustian project will draw on nature's own energy and organize it into fuel for new collective human purposes. They are concrete operational plans for harnessing the sea for human purposes: man-made harbors and canals to move ships full of goods and men; dams for large-scale irrigation. The key to his achievement is a visionary intensive and systematic organization of labor (62). Walking the earth with the pioneers of his new settlement, Faust feels far more at home than he ever felt with the friendly but narrow folk of his home town. (66)

Baudelaire: modernism in the streets

According to Berman, Baudelaire did more than anyone in the nineteenth century to make men and women of his century aware of their modern selves. He accepted modern man in his entirety, with his weaknesses, his aspirations, and his despair. Modern life has an authentic beauty in spite of its anxiety and misery. Part of this is that in modern cities it is possible to be in private *publicly,* such as with two lovers happily gazing into each other's eyes, a still point in the maelstrom of passing strangers.

Then Baudelaire asks:

What if the multitudes of men and women who are terrorized by modern traffic could learn to confront it together as they did in the days of the Commune in 1871 and again in St Petersburg in 1905 and 1917, Berlin in 1918 and Barcelona in 1936?

People stop and overturn the vehicles in their path...They incorporate the wreckage they have created into rising barricades. (163)

<u>Dostoevsky, Gogel, Biely's Saint Petersburg</u>

When we think of the origins of modern life, most of us would not include Russia on our list. Russia's role throughout the nineteenth century was to be the vanguard of European counter-revolution. But one would never have known it because, in the span of barely two generations, it produced one of the world's great literatures.

Saint Petersburg developed a reputation as a strange and wonderful place which was brought to life by Gogel and Dostoevsky, and especially Nevsky. Berman points out:

All existing classes came together—from nobility whose palaces and town houses graced the street at the Winter Palace to poor artisans and prostitutes, derelicts and bohemians who huddled in the wretched taverns near the railroad station. Then Nevsky brought them together whirled them around in a vortex and left them to make their own experience (195)

From Andrei Biely's novel *Petersburg*. Berman says:

Its planes of vision, like those in cubist and futurist painting are shattered and askew. Even Biely's punctuation goes wild, sentences break off in midair, while periods, commas, question marks and exclamation points float along in the middle of the page, lost in empty space. He is forcing us to experience the dazzling but mystifying atmosphere in which the people of Petersburg were forced to live. "Petersburg is the fourth dimension that is not indicated on maps." (256)

The nineteenth-century modernists show how humanity can hold themselves together despite everything else, and create new economic and psychological worlds. This book comes out of this cautious optimism of the nineteenth century rather than from either the blind optimism of 'progress' or the crypto-romanticism of the twentieth century.

Plan of the book

The book is divided into five parts. The first four chapters are about what I call 'the Luciferian self.' The first two chapters trace the evolution of individualism in Europe from the Middle Ages to the end of the nineteenth century. Chapters three and four switch the focus from Europe to what I call 'Yankeedom.' Chapter three addresses the spiritual, economic, and political foundations of individualism in the United States. Chapter four specifically involves types of individualism that developed from the beginning to the end of the nineteenth century.

Part two takes on socially-perceived space and time parameters. In chapter five I discuss Luciferian geography, and how the evolution of the built environment impacts people's psychology in three areas: how housing was organized, how cities evolved, and how the relationship changed between the performers onstage and the audience. All this is traced from the Middle Ages to the Gilded Age. In chapter six the focus switches from how *space* is conceived in the evolution of social *time*. One highlight is the change from cyclical to linear time. If Chapter six is about the evolution of *macro* time, chapter seven is about *micro* time: how childhood, adolescence, and adulthood have changed during the same 800-year period.

What does it mean to be 'uncivilized?' Being civilized has something to do with manners, the arts, literacy, speaking skills, clothing, and personal hygiene. But isn't that just being socialized? Yes and no. Part three has two chapters on the process of becoming civilized. Chapter eight deals with Europe and chapter nine with the United States.

Part four is the longest part in the book, addressing what I call 'hyper-abstract' cognition. Chapters ten and eleven come to terms with two kinds of qualitative thinking: rationality and reason. Chapter ten discusses how rationality lost its way when it was misapplied to areas which were more appropriate for reason. Chapter eleven is about how the limits of rationality were reached, and how reason returned to favor. If chapters ten and eleven address qualitative cognition, Chapters twelve and thirteen address quantitative thinking. There are two kinds of quantitative rationality: probability and chance. These two ways of thinking are traced from the Middle Ages to the eighteenth century in Chapter twelve. In Chapter thirteen I show how each changed in the nineteenth century. Chapter thirteen applies probability and chance to law, economics, the state, and mental illness.

Chapters fourteen and fifteen of part four take on the controversial question of whether there is cognitive evolution in history. I argue that Piaget's stages of concrete operations and formal operations are both amplified by the evolution of technological, economic, and political institutions between the Middle Ages and the end of the nineteenth century. Chapter fourteen discusses the impact that double entry bookkeeping, the use of Hindu-Arabic algebra, and written musical scores had on the complexification of concrete operations. In chapter fifteen I argue that formal operations could not have developed without the seventeenth revolution in scientific methodology, statistics, and capitalism in the nineteenth century.

The concluding chapter examines how individualism, becoming civilized, hyper-abstract thinking all reinforced and amplified each other. I also summarize the pros and cons of Lucifer's journey through the labyrinth of the western world. Its pluses and minuses are weighted *relatively* in terms of its impact on various social classes and *absolutely* for western civilization as a whole.

Overview of each chapter

By what process did Western cultures become individualists? What historical landmarks can we point to? In Chapter one, I demonstrate how individualism first manifested itself artistically, spiritually, politically, philosophically, and economically from the Middle Ages up to the Protestant Reformation. In chapter twol discuss what the scientific revolution, the capitalist revolution, the Enlightenment, and Romanticism had to do with individualism. At the end of Chapter two, I identify seven elements of individualism.

On the surface it might seem that individualism in the United States goes all the way back to the first settlers. But as I show in chapters three and four, American individualism only really emerges in the early nineteenth century. As it turns out, Puritans and Republicans went *against* individualism. Furthermore, it took a great deal to convince Americans that Adam Smith's invisible hand of the market was really a way to conduct business. In chapter four I contrast four kinds of individualism in the nineteenth century. The utilitarianist individualism (later called 'character') is contrasted with the expressive individualism of the late nineteenth century (later called 'personality'). Secondly, the spiritual individualism of Emerson and Whitman is contrasted with the entrepreneurial individualism of capitalist social Darwinists.

Among other topics, the field of environmental psychology studies the attachment of human beings to objects. In addition, environmental psychology studies the impact of the physical environment on people. Examples include the height and design of buildings, the organization of rooms in houses, and the impact of interior design on the perception and cognition of individuals.

In chapter five we find that humanistic geographers make a useful distinction between places and spaces, arguing that each calls forth a different part of the human psyche. Places are areas that are designed to provide comfort, continuity, and order in a person's life. Spaces are created to provoke and change discontinuity and adventure in human beings. In medieval cities, street life was dominated by places. Between the end of the Middle Ages and the end of the nineteenth century, spaces expanded and places contracted. What social forces were instrumental in making this change? Chapter five also addresses why Western cultures evolved to prefer spaces *over* places. I draw the psychological implications.

In chapter six, the Promethean geographical concept of space finds its temporal partner in linear theories of social change, specifically diagnosing this change as 'progress' in the history of human societies. Theories of progress hold that the later in time we go social evolution the better things get for humanity in terms of scientific knowledge, leisure time, quality of life, happiness, and morality.

In chapter seven, on ontogenesis, I ask whether or not individuals go through predicable stages of development that can be characterized as 'progress' (as some historians claimed for social evolution). Erik Erikson is famous for his eight stages of psycho-social development. But how well do these stages hold up when we examine them historically? Do children in the Middle Ages go through Erikson's stage of 'autonomy versus shame and doubt'? Do they experience 'initiative versus guilt?' Do adolescents in the Middle Ages have role confusion as teenagers? Erikson's stages do not hold up very well, according to the more historical psychologists like Roy Baumeister, Phillipe Aries, and Lawrence Stone. What we will find is that most of his stages of development were either present in a weak form in earlier historical periods, or they didn't exist at all.

There are two social mechanisms by which individuals learn self-control: becoming civilized or becoming disciplined. Becoming civilized is what happens to the middle classes and becoming disciplined is the process by which working-class people are hammered into shape by class society. I covered the topic of discipline in my book *Forging Promethean Psychology.* In chapters eight and nine of this book, we will study what it means to be civilized.

According to Norbert Elias, when the merchants defeated the European nobility the king extended the nobles a place in his court as a peace offering. For this old warrior class, life at court was quite an adjustment. They had to compete with other aristocrats in establishing a pecking order, but they could not afford to become violent. They had to learn to be mannerly; become astute at reading body language; practice self-control; and possess foresight, insight, and hindsight. Norbert Elias called this process 'becoming civilized.' At first, merchants of the Enlightenment mimicked the aristocracy but then broke away from the court to create their own notions of what it meant to be civilized. They called this 'cultured.' Lastly, in the nineteenth century, we probe the artistic romantic revolt against becoming civilized. Early Romantics were passionate and hopeful, but by the end of the nineteenth century these dandies, bohemians, and aesthetes had become more cynical.

Does it make a difference to the civilizational process that the United States had a frontier and Europe didn't? Did the superior literacy of the United States make Americans more civilized than Europeans? Did the existence of the 'wild west' in the states help or hurt the American civilizational process? In chapter nine I ask the question how well can Elias' 'civilizational process' apply to the United States? I begin with Colin Woodard's contention that the eleven rival regional cultures make it impossible to do justice to any generalizations. However, the regions of New England, New York, and Virginia were the most powerful in defining America. It is these areas that are compared to Europe.

Is there a difference between being reasonable and being rational? Science philosopher Stephen Toulmin argues that there is. Tracing the origins of what is reasonable in the rhetorical tradition to the Sophists and Aristotle in ancient Greece, Toulmin argues that what was reasonable continued into the Renaissance but 'lost its balance' in the seventeenth century, losing out to mathematical rationalism. The result has led to some of the darker and more dangerous currents in the Promethean tradition that surfaced in the nineteenth century. This is the subject of chapter ten.

How did rationality become 'unhinged'? In the first half of the seventeenth century, the religious wars between Catholics and Protestants were also epistemological wars over certainty. These wars (combined with the witch craze, the Little Ice Age, the London Plague of 1655, and the almost constant warfare between states) led some scholars to call this the 'Crisis of the seventeenth century.' European hunger for certainty began to pervade the secular world of science. The philosophical understandings of Descartes and Hobbes and the revolutionary findings of Galileo and Newton were all based on mathematics. This encouraged the middle classes to hope that all true knowledge might be mathematical and rational.

People in the middle classes were not the only ones who needed reassuring. In chapter eleven, we find the Catholic Church and European kings joining forces, using baroque painting as propaganda, to contain doubt and skepticism among the lower classes. With its exaggerated scale, majesty, and pomp and circumstance, the counter-reformation hoped to sweep the lower classes off their feet.

Chapter ten is about how the preoccupation with rationality got carried away, simply transferring the religious demand for certainty to the secular world. Toulmin defines reason as practical problem solving, argumentation, and judgment based on probability in particular times and places under conditions of uncertainty. Rationality was judgment based on formal logic, judgments based on when all the information given is certain. Between 1750 and World War I, the citadel of rationality began to fracture. The chapter shows evidence from the fracturing in areas of natural science, psychology, economics, philosophy, and literature.

Chapter eleven focuses on the return of reason in the Enlightenment and in the nineteenth century. The shortcomings in the use of rationality came out because biological scientists discovered the self-organizing power of organisms. This threw a monkey wrench into the mechanistic view of nature in science. At the end of the nineteenth century, the rational deterministic orientation in physics was rocked by quantum mechanics and Einstein's special relativity theory. Freud was far from alone in questioning the rational nature of human beings. Novelists' cultivation of the 'double' exposed the darker side of humanity. Marx and Veblen's research revealed the irrational nature of capitalism.

If you flip a coin three times in a row and it comes up heads all three times, what are the chances it will come up heads again? Aren't tails 'due' to come up? The evolution of what I call 'random-ness' in the West now distinguishes between two types of thinking: probability and chance. Probability is the *degree* of confidence a person has that an event is likely to occur regardless of subjective confidence levels. Chance is the objective statistical *likelihood* that events will occur regardless of subjective confidence or doubt. Interest in the study of chance goes all the way back to game-playing in tribal societies, but it really became a science beginning in the seventeenth century. Why then? What international economic risks did the seafaring bourgeoisie face that might have encouraged them to understand statistical laws? How might statistical records be used by a state to control its population? Chapter twelve covers these two topics, between the Middle Ages and the Enlightenment.

In chapter thirteen I follow the twists and turns of probability and chance as they are applied to law, annuities, games, and attempts by the state to control its population. In the seventeenth century, when Dutch merchants went on the high seas to ply their trades, they had to face the prospect that their cargo could be stolen by pirates. In order to protect their goods they took out annuity policies at home. But how could they calculate a fair insurance rate when they set sail? Did the season of the year matter? Did the weather conditions matter? Did the state of the international economy matter? How was it possible to systematize these calculations? While the subject of probability and chance was discussed before the seventeenth century in the areas of games and law, the economics of a growing global capitalist system created an urgency to solve this problem.

In the same period, courts of law faced the following questions: first, was it possible to quantify various degrees of proof between a claim and its evidence? And was it possible to set up a system of degrees of confidence that the witness is telling the truth?

As states set up surveillance systems for disciplining their populations, they began taking a census. As part of their surveillance, they had to understand patterns of birth and death rates. As they gathered statistics, they also had to interpret what the statistics meant. Risk assessment was crucial. The ability to gage probabilities and chance in everyday life assumed importance by the end of the nineteenth century. We also take probability and chance up through the end of the nineteenth century when, as Ian Hacking puts it, chance went from being 'wild' to being 'domesticated'.

Chapters fourteen and fifteen attempt to historicize Piaget's stages of cognitive development. Cognitive research supports Piaget's theory that, over the course of a lifetime, an individual moves through four stages of cognitive development: sensory-motor, pre-operational, concrete operations, and formal operations. But do these stages of cognition organically unfold inside the individual, *regardless* of economic, political, or technological inventions? Or do the stages blossom only under specific historical circumstances?

In chapter fourteen I ask whether or not the invention of cartography, clocks, double-entry bookkeeping, algebra, and written musical scores impacted the cognitive processes that people used in the High Middle Ages and early modern Europe. The chapter addresses these issues as I argue that Piaget's concrete operations were amplified by these inventions.

Is it possible that the development of the scientific method, the understanding of chance and probability, and the development of capitalist currency changed nothing in the cognitive thinking processes of adults? In Chapter fifteen I argue that it was the institutions of the West, specifically the West's technology, economics, politics, and science, that amplified people's opportunities to use formal operational reasoning. As Piaget demonstrated, formal operations required thinking deductively (the rationality described in chapters ten and eleven) and inductively (gauging the odds as described in chapters twelve and thirteen). The ability for formal operations spread among the upper middle classes as an adaptation strategy for working in the fields of science, economics, and law. It is these social practices that demand ontogenetic development in individual cognition. I argue against Piaget's formal operations being present in all people regardless of time, place, and circumstance. Research on Piaget's theory has shown that most adults even in twentieth-century western society do not develop formal operations.

Lucifer's Labyrinth contains the following devil's ingredients:

- individualism
- geographical spaces
- linear time
- becoming civilized
- quantitative rationality (probability and change)
- qualitative rationality
- qualitative reason
- complex concrete operational thinking
- complex formal operational thinking

In my conclusion, I show how these ingredients snap, crackle, and pop together in the labyrinth. Once these new psychological processes came into being, they mutually forged and intensified *each other* in creating the Promethean Western identity.

Also, in my conclusion I remind the reader that it was the institutions of the West, specifically the West's technology, economics, politics, and science, which drives psychological development. This chapter will allow us to take a deep breath, climb to the top of the mountain, and examine Lucifer's labyrinth at a distance for both its perils and its promises. Its material institutions and its psychology will be examined in terms of the quality of material culture and the psychological life of society *as a whole*. Then the same material institutions and psychological processes will be probed *relatively* in terms of their impact on the poor and working classes as well as for the middle classes. We'll ask if living out of Lucifer's labyrinth myth is a blessing, a curse, or maybe something else.

Theoretical perspectives

Psychohistory

In the Introduction into my previous book, I went into detail about the different ways to understand the relationship between western history, its social institutions and psychology. This book is a direct challenge to a school of thinking called 'psychohistory.' We need to divide psychohistory in general from *psychoanalytic* psychohistory.

The psychoanalytic field of history focuses on four areas (Szaluta, 1999): the biographies of political leaders (Luther, Jefferson, Napoleon, Hitler, and Nixon); group dynamics; the history of childhood; and the history of the family. Psychoanalytic historians argue that the impact of the unconscious motives—how well the Oedipal complex was resolved, or which defense mechanisms were used—will tell us a great deal about what really happened in history. Psychoanalytic historians suggest the personal ups and downs of a great leader's psychological life *drives* historical events. Had the major inventors and architects of western history (Galileo, Kepler, Leibniz, or Goethe) had good or bad parents or whether or not their motives were conscious or unconscious has a great deal to do with the time, place, or even whether historical events would have taken place.

The scientific basis of psychoanalytical history has been subjected to acidic criticism by David Stannard in his book *Shrinking History.* He argues that while some psychohistory such as Erikson's *Young Man Luther* is better than others, little (if any) psychohistory is good history. To begin with, psychoanalytic theory, even as a school of personality and therapy (let alone its historical application), has all sorts of problems. For one thing, its population is not a representable sample. Stannard says:

> The patients were mostly white, women, predominantly Jewish, relatively young, exceptionally affluent, highly educated and very well informed as to the nature of analytic therapy. (37)

Secondly, their method of collecting data consisted of case studies rather than far more reliable statistical studies. Thirdly, analysts used the memory of *adults* to recall their childhood problems. Knowing the unreliable nature of memory, this is hardly a sound gathering procedure. Fourth, the therapists did not write down in systematic detail what their patients' memories were. We are asked to trust the *therapists'* memory of what their patients said.

According to Stannard, *theoretical* psychoanalysis relies on weak evidence and builds its interpretation on shaky grounds. It also violates the Occam's Razor principle which advises that interpretations should be simple, and complexity should not be added unnecessarily. Psychoanalysis is filled with far-fetched interpretations which wind up putting more heat on events than shedding light. In understanding causes, it repeatedly blurs the relationship between correlation and cause (committing the post hoc, ergo proper hoc fallacy).

Lastly, psychoanalysis does not make its claims falsifiable. It doesn't state the conditions under which it could be proven wrong. We have temporarily had to separate psychoanalysis as a theory of behavior and a method of healing in the present from history, because when psychoanalysts decide to study history they use the theory and practice of psychoanalysis *in therapy* to assist them. How do psychohistories do as histories by *historians'* standards? Not very well.

In the first place, it is clear that psychohistorians have a version of the 'great-man' theory of history, or history 'from the top down.' Psychohistorical biographies are not equally distributed among all social classes but are instead focused on leaders with great wealth. Secondly, psychoanalytic historians are guilty of 'presentism,' meaning consciously or unconsciously projecting the conditions of the present back into time when these conditions didn't ever exist. For example, it is questionable whether the Oedipus complex could exist in the Middle Ages or Early Modern Europe, where extended families were the norm. Thirdly, most psychohistorians are cross-culturally parochial. They have not followed anthropological research seriously, and superimpose their own theories. For example, in Freud's interpretation of the life of Leonardo, he was unaware of Italian cultural traditions in Leonardo's time that would have better explained what Leonardo was up to, rather than far-fetched psychoanalytic interpretations. Anthropologist Anthony Wallace, who was sympathetic to psychoanalysis, throws up his hands:

Anthony Wallace who thinks that the reason that empirical investigations has failed in its efforts to confirm psychoanalytic theory is rooted in labyrinthian intricacies of that theory. 'They are so fantastically complex and so protracted that empirical observation cannot record a sufficient number of relevant dimensions. (*Shrinking History*, 104)

At this point, we need to separate the psychoanalytic theory of history from psychological approaches to history. For example, both behaviorism and cognitive psychology are far more psychologically grounded than psychoanalysis. There is no reason they couldn't be applied to history. However, the deeper issue is this: any theory that tries to incorporate psychology into history has to answer the question of what is the causal relationship between the micro world of psychology and the macro social world of technology, economics, and politics. What drives what? My position in this book is that macro-historical forces drive people's psychology, rather than the other way around. Individuals were born in certain historical periods which allowed them to do some things and not others. Neither Galileo, Newton, Kepler, nor Copernicus could have done their work in the Middle Ages because the social institutions that supported them were not present. It would not matter what their childhood was like nor whether they were married or divorced. It is not primarily great individuals that make society or history. Rather it is history and society that make individuals.

History of mentalities

Closer to home for me is the 'history of mentalities'

school. Here I will quote from my previous book, *Forging Promethean Psychology*:

There have been historians (more likely social historians and macro sociologists) who do make interdisciplinary connections between science, economics, politics and philosophy but they are not usually interested in drawing out the psychological implications. Macro-sociologists such as Norbert Elias, Pieter Spierenburg and social history authors like Schivelbusch are the exceptions.

The "history of mentalities" is part of the Annales school founded by Fernand Braudal. The work of Lucien Febvre, Marc Bloch, Robert Mandrou, Jacques LeGoff, and Alain Corbin are innovative for at least four reasons:

1) They move away from "great men" histories and "great events" history to track "great social movement processes" such as the Renaissance and the Reformation.
2) They describe history less as large historical events and more how the everyday life of people changed. What people ate, where they slept and how their houses were built
3) They developed a "history from below" outlook, with focus on the everyday life of artisans and peasants rather than the upper classes.
4) The topics discussed also touch a psychological topics such as how the use of the senses has changed historically as well as how childrearing practices have changed as well as attitudes towards death.

What is missing is a clearer explanation of how the macro-historical forces (capitalism, the scientific revolution) get inside individuals and change how they remember things; how they reason or how they assess risks or what kinds of pathology they develop. (xxxviii-xxxix)

The history of Mentalities school is weak in terms of *the*

mechanisms by which social structures get inside of people's psychology. Lev Vygotsky and his followers provided that mechanism.

Vygotskian socio-historical psychology as my theoretical perspective

Lev Vygotsky is currently 'hot stuff' in the field of American psychology. But, as in the case of Freud, his work becomes truncated and sanitized once it crosses the Atlantic. Many American psychologists who praise the work of Vygotsky as the 'father of cooperative learning' or discuss his zone of proximal development in how people learn either don't know or actively suppress the reality that Vygotsky was a Marxist who wanted to build a communist psychology. As a Marxian psychologist in the Soviet Union he set out to answer the question of what a communist psychology would look like

Famously, Vygotsky's work showed that all higher psychological processes do not begin *inside* of people, the way Piaget or Heinz Werner may claim. Rather they begin in the structured, meaningful, recursive, and cooperative relations *between* children and adults as they play and work. It is only later that the skills they learn become internalized. He called this first stage the zone of *proximal* development for a reason.

But what is ignored in his work is that he also believed that *whole societies* can go through a zone of proximal development. Though Vygotsky didn't do research on this subject, his colleague Alexander Luria did. Luria did a study to test the psychological changes that some of the peasants in Russia went through during the Russian revolution. He found that as peasants moved from the farmlands to the cities, their psychology changed. As they went to school and worked in factories, their perception, cognition, and identity and categorization processes became more abstract and universalistic. His point was to show that Vygotsky's zone of proximal development could be applied to *all* the people undergoing a rapid industrialization. The purpose of this book and the previous one to is to show a *slow-motion* process of the social zone of proximal development that occurs over the 800-year period of this book.

This socio-historical zone of proximal development goes through the following transformations:

- technological, economic and political changes in European society from the Middle Ages to the Guided Age provided the scene in which cooperative learning *occurs on the job* (zone of proximal development)
- people then internalize what they've learned on the job and possess these learning skills independently for their private use as their subjective skills
- these same workers than apply them to non-work social settings such as play, child-rearing or religious practices

In other words, the movement goes from social, to psychological, and back again to social. However, society is not static:

- ecological, demographic, economic and political crises require new forms of technology, economic exchange and politics meet the crisis
- this requires new kinds of social institutions which invite new kinds of work
- as people learn new work habits, new tools to use, new symbol systems to manipulate, there is a new zone of proximal development
- this leads to new internalization processes—a repeat of the aforementioned internalization, except on a higher level
- after these skills have been internalized, we will see a change in child-rearing, game playing and religious practices that reflect these new work habits

Lucifer's Labyrinth is the story of how psychological processes that we might consider private actually evolved but they are driven by social and historical processes.

CHAPTER 1

European Individualism from the Middle Ages to the Reformation

Orientation: Personality Structures—do they change over the course of history?

If you are like most people, you imagine that, though people may have had different problems during the Middle Ages or the Renaissance, the structure of their personalities was the same: either extroverted or introverted, a sensation seeker or a planner. How do you think people living in during the Middle Ages or the Renaissance would have answered the following questions:

- How important is geographical or class mobility to personality?
- Did people always think the sources of their conflicts came from *inside* of them?
- Did people always introduce themselves at gatherings by the kind of work they did?
- What differences might there have been in who were claimed to be sources of personality problems?
- Generally, we are trained to think that whatever is new is good, as exemplified in slogans such as 'new and improved'; 'a change will do us good' or even Obama's call for 'change.' Have people always felt this, that the latest was always the greatest?

- Did people always feel that 'appearances' can be deceiving?
- Like it or not, many personalities today are deeply affected by the clothes they wear and the fashions they follow. How far back into history does expressing oneself in fashion go?

- Today it seems that even when we don't want to, there is pressure from authorities, groups or romantic partners to 'improve' oneself. Did people in the Middle Ages care about improving their personalities?
- What differences might exist in whether people express or suppress their emotions? In what ways has this changed since the Middle Ages?
- Most of us agree that to get anywhere in life we need to have some semblance of a plan. How important is the ability to make plans to the forming and sustaining of personality? What would it do to a personality to live in a society when virtually no one made any plans?
- To what extent are class and gender socialization understood as affecting how your personality turns out? Did people in the Middle Ages think this was important?
- If you were given a choice as to who knows more about your personality, you or other people, you'd probably claim you know more about yourself than others know about you. Did people always have such confidence in their own judgments?
- What criteria did you use to pick your current romantic partner? Good looks? Common interests? What other criteria might have existed in the Middle Ages?
- Psychologist Erik Erikson and many others have argued that personality *needs time* to unfold as we age. How did people prior to the Enlightenment feel their personality changing over time?
- What is the relationship between the roles you play during the day and your personality? Are they *masks* which hide the real you? How did persons in different historical periods feel about how roles effected their personality?

By the end of this book you may have some interesting answers to these questions, and you will have many more questions answered which will lead you, hopefully, to more and deeper questions.

The heart of this chapter aims to show how the

individualist self emerged from the collectivist self in Europe through radical changes in technology, economics politics, spirituality, and intellectual movements. If these historical social institutions can change something seemingly as private as one's identity, then that means that historical institutions set the parameters for the kinds of personality that are possible at any historical period. The trouble starts when we project this individualist self on to personalities which are rooted in social formations which have collectivist identities. This not only keeps us from understanding the collectivist personalities in the European Middle Ages, but also understanding people in Africa, Asia and Latin America today, most of whom still have collectivist identities.

Collectivism vs individualism

Differences between collectivism and individualism

In the first chapter of my previous work, *Forging Promethean Psychology,* I distinguished between collectivism and individualism. Collectivists have an *organic* understanding of the relationship between the individual and society. This means that individual members of society are interdependent on each other in such a way that they cannot imagine themselves outside society. For collectivists the group is primary and the individual is a derivative and society is understood as a whole which is more than the sum of its parts.

Individualists, on the other hand, understand society as an aggregate, a voluntary association which people can enter or leave voluntarily, and society is no more than the sum of the actions of individuals.

Whereas collectivists see the individual society and spiritual presences as overlapping and porous, individualists compartmentalize society, nature and the spiritual world as separate with strong boundaries. The third major distinction is that, for collectivists, society is ruled by customs and traditions, while individualist societies are governed primarily by constitutions and natural laws.

Cross-cultural psychologists have pointed out the around the world how collectivism has been prevalent while individualism is a late starting phenomenon, peculiar to Western Europe and the United States. But in the next three chapters, I will show that collectivism existed in Europe for *most* of its history. More surprising still is how that citadel of individualism, the United States, had collectivist beginnings. I am not speaking about native Americans, but Puritan Americans. This chapter and the next will discuss how individualism emerged in Europe. In chapters three and four I will discuss how individualism emerged in the United States.

The seven aspects of individualism

Again, in Chapter 1 of *Forging Promethean Psychology,* I identify seven aspects of individualism. We will find that these seven aspects do not appear historically at the same time. Rather, they emerge and then mutually amplify each other over an eight-hundred-year period from the Middle Ages to the Gilded Age. The seven characteristics are:

- Equality at birth
- Autonomy
- Privacy
- Self-development
- Self-reflection
- Self-control
- Uniqueness

The King's two bodies in the Middle Ages: how political and religious contradictions opened up space for individualism

Signs of collectivism in the Middle Ages

There are a number of indicators which show the low ebb of individualism in the Middle Ages:

- All punishment was *collective* punishment. It made no difference how many innocent people suffered. The primacy of the corporate group was the key factor in judicial decisions.

- The writings of scholars and pamphleteers was all *anonymous.*

- There was a *lack of individuality in handwriting.* Copying had an impersonal character which in retrospect was an imitation of the letters of printing blocks.

- The *absence of majority principle of one person, one vote in corporate voting procedures.* Political decisions were qualitative majorities, rather than quantitative. They did not take into account exact numbers of people voting. The greater weight went to those voters who had a higher authority, greater knowledge, and more learning experiences. It was not the individual casting his vote that counted but the value which he had to the corporate body. Only when all the voters had the same office, the same standing, was the qualitative majority replaced by a quantitative numerical principle.

<u>Lack of state centralization in the Middle Ages</u>

Many scholars have argued that ecological and geographical conditions in Europe acted to inhibit the formation of a single centralized European state. The mountainous terrain of Europe made communication and transportation difficult. Centralized states emerged in many other regions of the world for the initial purpose of building and managing large-scale irrigation systems. Europe's adequately rain-watered agriculture did not require the development of centralized irrigation systems, and so this functional legitimation for large and centralized states was lacking. The absence of a centralized state after the fall of Rome has implications for the study of personality, because state centralization is most often accompanied by vertical collectivism (caste or status hierarchies), while a system composed of smaller and more competitive states may facilitate individualism.

In short, I will map out the processes by which the individual developed from a subject of a king to a citizen of a state. In the early Middle Ages, the individual had a submissive relationship to God with the Ecclesiastical authorities and the king as mediators between themselves and God. With the development of high feudalism the individual won some autonomy through the introduction of the Magna Carta in England, along with the social-contractual relations between lords and vassals. I will be drawing from the work of Walter Ullman (1966) To discuss these developments.

Authoritarian kingship: rule from the top down

According to Christian theory, with the coming of Christ, the individual ceased to be a man of nature, a man of flesh. He became a spiritual being, at the bottom of a spiritual hierarchy. The Christian individual maintained his place by obeying the law of earthly authority's sanction by the Divinity. Faith was the foundation of obedience. There was no reciprocity between the individual and God. Prayers were either answered or not answered.

Correspondingly, the king's power over his people was *not derived from the people but from divinity*: by the grace of God. Behind all demands for obedience stood the *concept of the office* which made possible the distinction between superior and the inferior. *Doing the will of the people had nothing to do with the office of kingship*. Its source was an emanation of the *divine* good will from the king. Unction was the one concrete element which lifted the king out of the mass of all his subjects, because unction was the means by which God's grace entered the king's body. Without the grace of the king, the individual subject had no standing in public. Unction is the benevolent protection which a father affords to a child or a pastor to his parishioners.

Furthermore, there was no such thing as equality before the law. An inferior could never legitimately bring any accusations against a superior, nor could they invoke the help of a law court against a superior. There was simply no right of resistance to a superior authority. To do would be a rebellion against divinity itself, meriting eternal punishment for the subject. Individuals did not have a right to demand action or to carry out petitions. Certain members of society were not even permitted to write or receive letters within the public sphere. Subjects had none of the rights which even the lowest classes have enjoyed since the Enlightenment.

Cracks in the hierarchical order

All Christian ideology of the unity and seamlessness of divine kingship aside, the King's rule in the Middle Ages was objectively weak and did not penetrate the lower classes. Apart from paying proper homage to King and aristocrats, the daily life of the lower classes was largely self-governing. The villain, cotter, crofter, plowman, bailiff, and miller were able to conduct their business with little intervention by those above them. Within these orders, members elected their own officers, made their own regulations, and managed their own affairs. Villages arranged the times of plowing, tilling and cultivating the soil, the time of harvesting and the manner of managing the fields.

Furthermore, there was self-government in the towns. Merchants, journeymen, and artisans were practically untouched by divine kingship. The problem for the authorities was that the theocratic pomp and circumstance from above floated unconnected to the secular self-governing tendencies in the towns and the villages below. It was this self-governance at the collective level of the group independent of the king that later sowed the seeds for the individual to break free from the king. In other words, sub-group rebellion was a necessary condition for individual rebellion.

An inter-role conflict within kingship provides leverage for aristocrats

Kingship is divided into two parts. One part is being king by the grace of God. However, every medieval king *was also a feudal lord*. Feudalism was first forged by military and social necessity, as a bulwark against tribal invasions during the Dark Ages in Europe. It was later consolidated by the oath of fealty between a feudal lord and feudal vassal. This was a legal relationship which involved two individuals in a contract. The relationship between lord and vassal became increasingly contradictory to the relationship between king and subject. The feudal function was diametrically opposed to the theocratic function.

On one hand the king owed his sovereignty to *divine* sources, not to the people. Nevertheless, as a feudal king he had entered into *contractual* relations of an individual nature with his tenants-in-chief (the lords) and thereby had become one of them. *In this feudal capacity,* the king did not stand above the kingdom, but was a member of the feudal community. Within the feudal function of kingship, law was arrived at by counsel and consent. As might be expected, kings tried to shirk their obligations as a feudal lord by claiming divine right. However, the barons (as equal feudal lords) could claim things from the king that they couldn't expect if they were seen as subjects of the king. What the barons wanted was not the king's law but the law of the land. This law of the land became the Magna Carta.

In contrast to the *descending* theme of government where the *permanent one-way relationship* constituted the essential ingredient between king and his people, the vassal relationship between king and lords was a *contractual* relationship between individuals. For the lords there was now a legal means of resistance. Treason against the highness of the king by a *subject* was treason, but the repudiation of the same king in his role as a feudal lord by another lord was not treason. In other words, a vassal was not a subject and could not be treated by the king in the same way.

Dual nature of kingship sows the seeds for the Magna Carta

The aristocrats, in a constant state of resistance against the king's attempted control over their local domains, seized the opportunity to weaken the king's power by insisting on having dual governing power. Secularly, the king was just another feudal lord, only a 'first among equals.'

The divine right of kings was based on Roman Law or private law. Under the challenging Magna Carta, public law or English common law, the king lost his divine right and now had only *prerogatives*. Common law blocked the divine right of kings. It stated that no freeman could be captured, imprisoned, outlawed or exiled except by a lawful tribunal of his *peers* and by the law of the land. The Magna Carta contained in embryo the principle of due process. At his coronation, the king must promise to lead the community of the realm.

Marc Bloch, in his book *Feudal Society*, thinks the clearest legacy of feudalism for modern societies is the emphasis placed upon the notion of a political *contract*. The common lawyer mediated between the abstract Latin logic of the schoolmen and the concrete needs of the unschooled. The twelfth and thirteenth centuries formed the period in which the seeds for future constitutional development occurred, when the largely private character of feudal relations became the province of public law. At least in England, from late thirteenth century the individual gradually emerged as a full-fledged citizen. The promotion of a positive and concrete contractual element might be considered a preparatory step towards the full contract theory of a later age. Table 1.1 shows the tensions involved in the dual nature of kingship.

Table 1.1 Dual Nature of Kingship

As King	Category of comparison King's Role	As Feudal Lord
Divine sources: office	**Source of sovereignty**	Contractual relations with individuals
Above the kingdom	**Place of king in the kingdom?**	In the kingdom
Through God's grace	**How is rule justified?**	Through counsel and consent
Subjects	**Nature of ones ruled?**	Vassals
Treason	**How is dissent from below categorized?**	No treason
Roman Law	**Type of law**	Magna Carta (common law)
Divine right	**Rights of king**	Prerogatives
Whim of king	**How are offenders judged?**	Judged by peers of the same estate (judged by other lords)
Private law	**Is the law private or public?**	Public law
King promises nothing to the population	**Obligations of the king?**	Coronation promises of the king—community of the realm
Latin	**Language used**	English

The secularization of politics

According to Ullman, the birth of the science of politics occurred in the thirteenth century. It was Aristotle and Saint Thomas that supplied the solvent that was to release the inferior subject from his superior's tutelage to become a citizen of the state. For Saint Thomas Aquinas, a citizen's role was as a constituent member of the State. This citizen is part of natural man. Furthermore, Dante stresses the human element in the concept of civilitas. Humans pursued a twofold aim as Christians: an other-worldly supernatural aim of attaining salvation and the natural aim of being citizens.

In summary, before an individual could be seen as separate from society, there first needed to be open conflicts between aristocrats and king. In England, the victory of the aristocrats was embodied in the Magna Carta. There also needed to be a conflict within the king's role in receiving his authority from the divine on the one hand and secular sources on the other. His secular role was that of being one of several feudal lords. These estate conflicts are the preconditions for the politicization of individual rights which leads eventually to full blown individualism.

The development of individualism in Medieval Europe

Better crops and more labor specialization

According to Colin Morris (2000), social conditions in Europe between 1050 and 1200 CE made individualism more likely to spread beyond the aristocracy. Improved agricultural techniques allowed the cultivation of wastelands and the clearance of forests, making it possible to grow more crops and to feed more people. A larger population in turn allowed for more specialization and new types of occupations. While there was an incipient individualism among the aristocrats of ancient civilizations, what was new in Western Europe was the spread of individualistic personalities to other social classes. This tendency increased in the fourteenth century as a shortage in agricultural labor emerged. Peasants ran away to the towns to try their hand at a new life. Both craft production and trade demanded more initiative and rational activity than agriculture, and more individualism.

Demographic and economic growth coincided with a managerial revolution in both the State and the Church. Both needed skilled lawyers and literate clerks. As cathedral schools and universities emerged to meet these needs, the middle classes had a wider range of choices of vocations—teacher, monk, administrator and scholar-lawyer. These new choices both promoted individualism and raised anxiety. This situation made people uncertain about the roles and the rules of their new professions. Consensus about morality and ethics decreased. The resulting anxiety often stimulated either other-worldly renunciation (monasticism) or a newfound optimism about the future (Morris 2000).

Upheavals within the church

Between 1050 CE and 1200 CE the Church underwent a number of reforms that Europeans could not help but find unsettling. The organization and texts of the Church became increasingly anachronistic. Morris points out that:

> For the early Church, to become a Christian was a deliberate personal choice, involving both an interior change (repentance) and an exterior one (baptism)...Service of Christ thus consisted of both an individual decision and membership in a close community...Neither of these experiences could be meaningful to the men of the tenth century. It required no personal choice to become a Christian nor did the believer find himself to be part of a community distinct from society as a whole. (Morris 2000: 24)

This resulted in a shift from the New Testament teachings of Saint Paul to the Old Testament doctrines of King David. More disturbing for the individual was the fact that authorities did not always agree on the interpretations of biblical texts. The truthfulness and reliability of the Scriptures were called into question with the rise of a new class of educated church bureaucrats.

Another development was an interesting shift in the Church's attitude toward salvation. According to Morris, until the eleventh and twelfth centuries salvation was understood as the salvation of mankind. After this time there was more concern with the salvation of the individual through acts of personal piety:

> Earlier eschatology had kept a balance...between an individual and a corporate expectation. The particular person might look forward to his own release, but he did not normally count upon the perfection of his happiness until the renewal of the creation at its final perfection in the general resurrection...[But later] the whole strength of eschatology now became attached to the individual...attention was concentrated upon one's personal answer and personal hope of heaven, if necessary, after a stay in purgatory...the destiny of the individual was becoming the center of attention, and the theme of the renewal of all things was slipping into a secondary place. (Morris, 147-148)

The ancients were not individualists

Because the psychology of people who lived hundreds of years ago is difficult to study empirically, we must rely on documentary evidence for clues as to changes in the social self. Most of us find it hard to believe that the uniqueness of individuals was not always a feature of human identity. But according to Morris (2000), the notion of individual uniqueness was quite rare in the ancient world (e.g. Saint Augustine, Marcus Aurelius, Seneca) and it only became more frequent in Europe in the late-eleventh century. According to Aaron Gurevich (1995), words with the prefix 'self' (e.g. self-aware, self-support) that indicate a focus on a unique self, have expanded widely only since the Protestant Reformation. Early instances of individualism were not usually associated with the notion of uniqueness. For example, though some of the people in classical Greece were certainly individualists (e.g. the nature philosophers, Plato, Socrates, and Aristotle), individuality was not normally conceived of as uniqueness.

Autobiography, confession and meditation

Gurevich argues that self-reflection and individual uniqueness were rarely found in pre-modern societies:

> The inner psychological essence of the human being in the Greek world was not the object of tenacious quests and investigations. In Ancient Rome the position was slightly different. Certain writers manifested a tendency to engage in self-examination (Seneca, Marcus Aurelius) but the genuine breakthrough to psychological introspection...was that undertaken by Saint Augustine (Gurevich, 1995,91).

Most of these early thinkers were not interested in the qualities that made individuals different from one another. Even in Medieval Europe, originality or idiosyncrasy was often interpreted as grounds for the charge of religious heresy.

Art is another arena in which individuality was not understood as uniqueness. Greek sculptures, like those of other ancient civilizations, were not portraits of particular individuals, but were rather embodiments of universal principles and expressions of the social status of individuals. According to Gurevich:

> It was not customary to look hard at an individual's facial features...something which becomes a habit for people who use mirrors...[Thus] in those conditions, people do not acquire sensitivity to details of physiognomy (Gurevich, 1995, 247).

Gurevich also contends that paintings which attempted to render a faithful likeness of a particular individual were very rare before eleventh century Europe.

St. Augustine was one of the first to suggest that individuals were responsible for their situations. In contrast to the conceptions of Fate or Necessity of the Greeks, Augustine declares that it's the 'I'—not Fate, not Destiny, not the devil. This is an extraordinary statement because it is closer to modern individualism than any writer until the Italian poet Petrarch one thousand years later in the fourteenth century.

In the Middle Ages, we can see a number of individualistic tendencies that are nested in the bosom of the Catholic church. These include personal confessions, mystical visions, autobiographical writings, individual meditation, personal atonement, and the importance of intention. All these had proto-individualistic elements, but those tendencies had to fight an uphill battle against the forces of authority and group pressure: subordination to God, to one's extended family, to the village, or to one's vocation. People were also supposed to emulate archetypes such as heroes of the pagan past, or figures from the Gospels.

Although biography exists in the classical world (e.g. Plutarch's Lives), the first experiments in autobiography appeared in the tenth and eleventh centuries, and occurred more frequently in the literature of the twelfth and thirteenth centuries. Yet these first autobiographies did not cover the whole of an individual's life but only up to the point where they reach their spiritual goal. Medieval autobiography was not a self-generating activity for its own sake, but instead a means for attaining spiritual enlightenment.

While few people wrote down their autobiographies, it was a practical requirement of every Christian to make a confession to a priest once a year. Confession required self-analysis over a relatively long stretch of time before confession. Visions were another vehicle through which individuals were allowed to tell their story, with visions as stages of conversion. Through these forms, feelings of fear, depression, and suppressed desire could be expressed, all safely smuggled in the service of some higher purpose.

Another sign of individualism was the growth in the spiritual practice of meditation and the ritual receiving of sacraments by individuals. Peter Abelard's ethic shifted the attention of moral judgment away from deed to the intention than lay behind it. The medieval penitential theory and practice began to stress contrition (genuine sorrow for sins) over external acts of penance and mindless, superstitious ritual. In monasteries, monks strove to see others objectively, independent of their needs, and they understood being open to the feelings and views of others as a virtue.

Troubadours, lyric poetry and heroic individualism

Let us also look at the growth of individualism outside the Church. Morris notes that the Church did not value marriage as a sacred experience in itself. It supported and validated marriages for religious or social purposes. Divorce was not possible according to the Church. But as individuals began to free themselves from loyalties to institutions, they formed relations with others based on personal choice rather than on kinship authority. While marriages were usually arranged by parents to strengthen political and economic alliances among families, the troubadours propagated their notion of romantic love outside of marriage. This made more room personal relations based on individual choice (at least for the aristocracy).

Landed aristocrats, knights, merchants and artisans were most likely to express individualistic tendencies than the peasantry. The life of a knight at times took him far from home, which weakened loyalty to clan and family:

> In battle a knight had to rely primarily on his own strength and valor, for he was usually fighting on his own rather than among other fighting men. He was protected not by a compact battle formation, but by chain mail or armor, the speed of his own reactions and his mount's training. On horseback, a knight resembled a self-contained mobile fortress. (Gurevich, 178-179)

The troubadours were champions of romantic love, who wrote lyric poetry based on revelations of personal experiences as opposed to epic poetry which is about the trials, tribulations and victories of heroes in the service of the gods. Medieval troubadours advocated the virtues of fidelity, prowess, joy, and courtesy. They developed an ideology of romantic love that challenged the institution of religiously sanctified marriage based on considerations of politics and property. But while the monks tried to develop an appreciation of the unique qualities of others, the troubadours paid this less attention. The point of courtly love and romance was to develop an understanding of one's own emotional life and the thoughts they inspired and the passions they evoked:

> The poet showed little interest in their ladies' character. The twelfth century felt a persistent attraction for the legend of Narcissus and the symbol of the mirror, which were used to describe 'the birth of self-consciousness through love...' (Morris, 2000, 118-119)

According to Gurevich, Scandinavians had a more advanced form of individualism than did those in Western Europe because they were unhampered by accusations of sin and pride, or the need for humility perpetuated by the Church. For example, the hero in Scandinavian mythology identified more with great deeds rather than blind loyalty to family. His extraordinary feats lived on in the minds of individuals through his reputation.

But here also there were limits to individualism. The hero's source of identity was not a mental attunement with a spiritual world (the way it would have been for Saint Augustine or Plato) but rather through physical deeds. Intentions and moods were not reflected on but rather were revealed through actions. The conflicts that might have existed within the personalities of the epic heroes were projected as being between individuals. This does not mean that the hero had no loyalty to his clan. It only means that since his actions were determined by Fate his clan would forgive him no matter what he did. And because the hero's actions were determined by Fate, there was no conscience, no weighing of pros and cons or consideration of different viewpoints before deciding:

> The concept of conscience is hardly appropriate here, demanding as it does moral self-control on the part of the individual who independently formulates moral precepts and evaluates these. In a society where clan traditions hold sway and where personality emerges as clan personality, moral issues regarding the individual could not yet have acquired any substantial importance. (Gurevich, 1995, 38)

It is important to realize that just as human societies do not evolve in a unilinear way, neither does the self. By most standards the Greek philosophers and Saint Augustine are stronger exemplars of modern individualism than any individual from the Middle Ages. We might say they had the self-reflective, developmental and self-managing ingredients of individualism. In the Middle Ages the troubadour and the warrior break free from collective responsibility.

Yet within the Middle Ages it was becoming easier for more than exceptional persons to develop an individual identity.

Merchants, travel, and quantitative calculation

If the tools of knightly individualism were military, the tools of the merchant were commercial—the abacus and the ledger for accounting. Engaging in commercial operations demanded not only attention to detail but also an ability to take entrepreneurial risks, to anticipate future needs, and a capacity for reasoned calculation of costs and benefits that were somewhat independent of loyalty to specific groups. The nature of risk-taking created in the merchant a unique combination of rationality regarding the processes he could control along with an acceptance of the power of chance.

> Confidence in themselves and in their abilities was to be found side by side with 'melancholy'

> in the minds of merchants and financiers, side by side with visions of destiny as an all-powerful and capricious force that would bring either sudden success or just as easily, unexpected disaster... The image of Fortuna, tirelessly turning her wheel, on which people of various social estates first climb aloft and then inevitably fall, became very popular in the twelfth and thirteenth centuries. (Gurevich, 194)

Here is a summary list of the activities of Medieval individualists:

- Writing autobiographies
- Confession
- New occupations
- Mystical visions
- Meditation/ introspection (vs public penance)
- Importance of intentions (vs. actions)
- Troubadours and romantic love
- Lyric poetry (as opposed to Epic poetry)
- Merchants abacus, ledger

Revolution in the arts and sciences

What followed was a revolution in the arenas of the arts and sciences which helped to produce individualist selves. In the visual arts, there was a broader change from Gothic, otherworldly art to naturalistic realism and landscapes. In portraiture, paintings of individuals contained images which did not conform to classical ideals but rather to actual flesh and blood individuals, as expressed by Giotto. Architecture and sculptural works were entrusted to lay people rather than those working for the Church. Literature was translated out of Latin into the vernacular, where the motives and emotions of individuals were easier to describe. The fourteenth century saw the beginning of personal diaries and the cultivation of epistolary style. The rediscovery of Aristotle brought practical, empirical, and observational methods to science, which challenged the methods of syllogistic rationality of the Schoolmen.

The origins of Individualism in thirteenth-century England

The traditional story of England

England, like all other European societies in the Middle Ages, was a small-scale peasant society. From this there was a slow but steady economic growth. Fueled by the Protestant Reformation and two waves of commercial and industrial capitalism, a new economic individualism emerges. New agricultural methods and technologies disrupted peasant life and led to enclosures, commercial farming (the wool industry), and later the emergence of industrial capitalism in the second half of the eighteenth century. One problem is that according to MacFarlane (1978) there was no peasantry in England in the later fourteenth and fifteenth centuries! Let us now turn directly to his work.

Types of farmers: peasants versus yeomen

All farming in the Middle Ages was stratified and dominated by aristocrats with a weak state, depending on the country. Eastern Europe, Russia, India and China had peasants who worked the land on subsistence agriculture and turned over a most of their produce to the nobles. However, MacFarlane argues that farmers in England at least as far back as the thirteenth century were yeomen, not peasants. What does this mean? Yeomen had more control over their land than peasants. Class inequalities were more the result of competition between farmers for resources and tools, in hopes of increasing the chances of productive harvests. Furthermore, yeoman farming was not just production for subsistence's sake. A certain percent went to investments in commercial farming products, like fruit and hops. Less than one-fourth of their produce would have been consumed directly.

Property within families

Property in England was not family property but individual property. One son was a joint holder with his father.

In addition, this property was a gift from father to son. It wasn't automatically inherited by his first son. It was legal for a father to sell his holdings to his sons. A father could sell his holdings to a stranger over his son. Only about half the total number of transactions between 1280-1300 CE were within the family, in some cases less than half. Here is one of the many ingredients for individualism in England.

Care of the elderly

If children had little right to property, the favor was returned to the parents in their old age. Co-habitation with their parents was not given by sons or daughters, but was merely the result of a lengthy written contract or maintenance agreement drawn up. From Richard Smith's analysis of the largest collection of medieval maintenance contracts ever assembled, three quarters of them contained clauses which suggested separate residence and semi-independent economic behavior for the two generations. When aged parents did live with their children, they were often treated as 'lodgers.' There are examples of children charging their aged parents for bed and board. Even by the thirteenth century, mothers and fathers could not depend on their children's good will. Without legal guarantees, parents had no rights whatsoever. It was as if parent and child were two strangers bargaining.

Stratification mobility of yeoman farmers

In terms of stratification, there was more stratification in yeoman farmers between families than among peasant farmers who occupied most of Europe. Among these peasants there was cyclical mobility though generations. This means that if a family succeeded in one generation and became rich, it had more children. But resources had to be partitioned amongst a large number of sons. This would lead to a decrease in resources, and their wealth would shrink. On the other hand, poor families would coalesce, limiting their size and gradually helping to accumulate wealth. The family moved up or down in the class hierarchy as a group. If one brother grew wealthy, they all did. But among yeoman farmers there was no cyclical mobility, but rather intergenerational polarization. An eldest son who became richer was not expected to help his siblings economically. Consequently, younger sons and daughters became poorer. Different branches of the same family rose and fell simultaneously. Both upper and lower families were much less community-oriented.

Women's rights

In typical feudal societies, peasant women could not be landowners. She could not draw up a will, sell property, inherit property or enter into contracts on her own. In most peasant societies women remained under the authority of their parents until marriage, then passed into the control of their husbands and later, as widows, to that of their own sons. When women married out they might have taken a dowry of movables, but the land normally stayed with the men. Very few women did not remarry. There were few 'old maids.'

Yeoman women, on the other hand, had rights to one third of her husband's estate, including goods, while she was a widow. After the Norman conquest, an adult female was a fully competent person for all purposes of private law. She could make a will or sell property. After her husband's death, the property passed into her private hands and she could enter contracts on her own account. Furthermore, a married woman would sometimes appear as her husband's attorney and the guardian of her children. In contrast to female peasants, large number of yeomen women left with estates and did not remarry.

Summary

Unlike the rest of Europe, England was not a feudal society. It was a system whose wealth was based on trade rather than land. Its economy, property rights, family life, legal system, geographical and class mobility approximated Hobbes's market society (which will be discussed shortly). Furthermore, this difference from the rest of Europe did not originate with the Protestant Reformation or from the rise of capitalism, as it is often proposed. Its individualism developed in England at least as early as the thirteenth century. See the table below for a full contrast between England and full-fledged feudal societies on the continent.

Table 1.2 Origins of English Individualism

European Continent 13th-17th century	Country	England-13th-17th century
Peasants Subsistence farming No commercial farming Production for use value Little or no money circulated Village barter No wage labor	**Type of farmer Political economy**	**Yeoman** Less subsistence farming More commercial farming Production for use value and exchange value Money circulated in villages Wage labor hired
Family property Sons work the land with their fathers Parents, married children and their spouses and grandchildren work land plus adopted children No servants	**Domestic economy**	Individual property Sons apprentice themselves to other farmers About one-half of sons and daughters leave home by ages 10-18 Husband and wife hire wage laborers for help Some servants
Extended family Women marry in their teens Few women are single or remain single after marriage	**Family life**	Nuclear family (4.75 average) Women don't marry until in their mid-twenties More women are single or remain single after marriage
Little - If they move, they move as a block	**Geographical mobility**	More - If they move, they do not move as a family unit
Cyclical mobility	**Stratification**	Intergenerational polarization
Roman law Peasant cannot alienate land without heir's consent Wills unknown and disliked	**Property rights**	**English common law** Yeoman can alienate land or labor Active land and labor market Wills are common with chattels and real estate involved
No rights under public law No rights under private law Women cannot be landowners Cannot make a will or sell property Women cannot inherit property (subordinate intergenerationally to father, husband, and her son) Cannot enter into contracts of her own	**Women's rights**	No rights under public law Some rights under private law Have rights to one third of her husband's estate Can make a will and sell property After husband's death property can pass into private hands Can enter contracts of her own account
Children have automatic rights to their parents' goods Either land distributed to all sons or distributed to the first son	**Children's rights**	Children do not have automatic rights to their parents' goods Father can sell sons' rights
Children take care of parents	**Care of Elderly**	Cohabitation only after a lengthy written contract Parents treated as lodgers and charged bed and board
Collectivist self	**Type of self**	**Individualist self**

Humanism and the Italian Renaissance

> I created you as a being neither heavenly nor earthly, neither mortal nor immortal, so that you may freely make and master yourself and take on any form us choose for yourself. He can degenerate to animality or be reborn towards divinity.
> *-Dignity of Man*

Myths and realties about Renaissance individualism

When people think of the Renaissance, they think of a group of independent thinkers (literary men, painters, philosophers) who rebelled against the otherworldly nature of the Catholic church. In extreme cases they may be looked at a neo-pagans who wanted to revive the traditions of Greece and Rome. But In his book *Renaissance Thought*, Paul Kristeller points out that when pagan gods, heroes and allegories were used, no one thought seriously of reviving them to oppose the Church. In fact, the Church even incorporated them. As I pointed out in *Forging Promethean Psychology*, all Renaissance high magical traditions considered themselves Christians (with the possible exception of Bruno).

As Peter Burke points out in *The Italian Renaissance*, it is true that paintings became more secularist, but only moderately. A sample study suggests that the proportion of Italian paintings that were secular in subject rose from five percent in 1420 to twenty percent by 1540.

Two stages of the Renaissance

According to Lauro Martines (*Power and Imagination*, 1979) the Renaissance formed in two stages. The first was from 1100 CE to1300 CE. In this first stage, social energies went into economics, politics, and an increase in population. Later, Nicholas of Cusa argued that, in this period, lay knowledge about weighing and measuring was respectable. This knowledge was present in the everyday skills of buyers and sellers as they engaged in price setting, haggling, and handling various currencies involved in translocal trade.

The second phase from the late thirteenth century to late sixteenth century involved the governing class being deeply implicated in clerical abuse and the neglect of parishes. There was a slow spread of disdain for active trade. Eventually, Italians were so displaced by the Atlantic trade, they became conquered by Spain politically. Seen in this light, the 'High Renaissance' of Leonardo and Michelangelo was at least partly a cultural attempt to show in painting, sculpting, architecture and lyric poetry all that Italians had lost in politics and economics. In addition, the sixteenth century demoralization narrowed the wide lens of the earlier period, at least as far as politics went. As Martines proposes, in the sixteenth century, political thinkers understood it in terms of dualisms between idealism and realism: reason and passion; man and beast; rich and poor; civil society and our anarchistic nature; order and disorder; virtue and fortune; elites and multitudes; and law versus violence.

According to Agnes Heller in *Renaissance Man*, the individual was embedded in three forms of loyalty: as a member of an estate (in relation to other estates); a member of the Christian community (as opposed to heretics and infidels) and as a member of a city-state (Florence, as opposed to Genoa or Venice). Especially in the latter form we see a breaking away from Medieval collectivism when love and friendship was treated and *more important* than blood relations, or even the marriage bond. The family was no longer the foundation of support.

Artisans and Humanists

In the early Renaissance, there were three kinds of practitioners. The artisans, painters, and sculptors, who were the children of shopkeepers and family businesses. They worked full-time and belonged to guilds for protection. Burke identified five functions of the guilds:

- To regulate the standards of quality and relation between clients, masters, journeyman and apprentices
- To collect money for subscriptions and requests
- To lend or give money to members who were in need
- To organize festivals in honor of the patron of the guild
- To maintain standards and fair prices by calling on artists to evaluate the work of others in cases of disputes

between other artists and clients

Artists and their patrons fought over many things:

- What materials were used: gold, lapis, or bronze or marble for sculpture
- The price, including the type of currency, and whether they were paid on installment or up front
- The delivery date—whether it was vague or precise
- The size of the painting (which often was not specified)
- How many assistants one was allowed
- The content of what went into the picture

According to Burke, these artisans were not respected for three reasons: they worked with their hands; the guild involved itself with retail trade; and they lacked learning in the classics and in theology.

On the other hand, the writers (Humanists) were the children of professional men. They did not belong to guilds, and they worked part-time. They were in the employ of princes, and their professional life was more tenuous. Humanists became interested in nonreligious intellectual interests such as rhetoric, ancient poetry, grammar, history, and literature of original texts. They loved the work of Homer, Virgil, Horace, Seneca and Ovid. While they liked the Church fathers, they loved the rhetorical studies of Cicero and Quintilian more. Humanists developed new techniques for studying original manuscripts for textual and historical criticism by comparing them.

These men of the Renaissance were called humanists because they saw untapped potential of human beings that was being buried by the preoccupation with sin and preparation for the next world. Humanism put the human species at the center of its morality and ethics. Renaissance humanism was a cultural and educational program more than it was a philosophy. It emphasized Greek and Latin classics in secondary education, against the demands for a more practical and more scientific training.

In spite of these noble goals, it would be a mistake to think of humanists as serious reformers, let alone revolutionaries. Their criticisms of princes and oligarchies were not done in the name of dissent, but rather what was good for the constituted authorities. Humanists sought to turn political men into better statesmen (Machiavelli) and statesmen into moral men. Humanists sought to increase the civility of the ruling groups and to soften the worst kinds of blatant attachment to money.

The emergence of humanism in the European Renaissance was linked to the development of individualism. Some medieval humanists dealt optimistically with the anxiety of living in a rapidly changing society, and others pessimistically. Some humanists became satirists, attacking the Church for its corruption, or for its exclusion of critics (Erasmus' *Praise of Folly*). Others such as Petrarch saw in humanism the birth of a new world.

According to Richard Sennett (1990), in the ancient world, fortune was understood as impartial, made by the gods. But by the time of the Renaissance, fortune was wedded to chance that were both made *by humanity.* This is one of the first signs that while individual lives may remain uncontrollable, the external forces responsible were no longer understood as cosmic or natural, but rather as *social and historical*. In B*eing Between Angels and Animals,* Giovanni Pico argued that humans alone were capable of change. The derivation of architectural proportions from the human body implied that human beings had enough dignity to be a standard of measurement for building dimensions.

Petrarch was an early proponent of a humanist tradition that did not unhinge individual consciousness from its immediate social connections but expanded intersubjectivity beyond everyday life. In addition, he cultivated an appreciation of the deep past and distant future. For example, he did not rely on a mentor from his own time. Instead he chose Saint Augustine, who lived a thousand years earlier, to be his intimate teacher, as well as Cicero. Gurevich says of Petrarch:

> He used to rise while it was still dark and leave the house as the first rays of sunlight appeared: he would contemplate, read, write and consort with his friends. Yet, who were his friends? They were not only the individuals with whom he came into contact in his day-to-day life, but also those who

> had died centuries before and who were known to him only through their works. 'I assemble them from any place and any age...I am happier to converse with them than with those who imagine themselves to be alive...'(Gurevich, 233). Petrarch sees himself as belonging to 'extended time': he is able with infinite ease to move from era to era feeling at home wherever he goes... (Gurevich, 233). Petrarch is clearly anxious not just to be a man of his times but...to be a man of the classical past, which he is bringing back to life...and at the same time to be able to link himself with the future. (Gurevich, 236)

Beyond Humanism: the science of the real—Leonardo

In his book *The Individual and Cosmos in Renaissance Philosophy,* Ernst Cassirer says that the work of Leonardo represented a force beyond humanism. Unlike the humanists, Leonardo said that mathematics, rather than natural language, contained the key to understanding the world. Secondly, he said that the true nourishment of the mind did not lie in the writings of others, in the translators and commentators, but in the discovery new things in nature, in their experience as discoverers. But even here, true object was not these experiences themselves, but rather the *mathematics that lay behind* these experiences. Instead of going back in time to seek human regeneration, Leonardo encouraged dealing with contemporary problems which were concrete, technical, and artistic as the basis for forming a theory.

Revelation would occur through studying works in nature, not in the study of words. For Leonardo, science was the second creation of nature brought about through reason. The notion that man could conquer something from nature, creating from primary nature a second nature, dates from the Renaissance, according to Heller. The path of Leonardo led directly to Galileo and the seventeenth-century scientific revolution. Leonardo called this path the 'reason of the real' (for him, through painting and inventions). For Leonardo, the connection between nature on the one hand and freedom on the other was the order of proportion. This proportion could be found not only in numbers and measurement, but in tones of music. Although nature was inexhaustible and infinite, that infinity could be captured in mathematics.

Renaissance individualism

In understanding individualism in the Renaissance, it is useful to distinguish three meanings of the term:

- *The degree of self-consciousness.* This is what Jacob Burckhardt noted when pointing to the autobiographies, diaries and journals written in first person. This would also be applicable to the work of Petrarch.
- *Self-assertiveness and the craving of fame, glory, honor along with the envy and shame of failure.* This search for fame and glory is discussed by Machiavelli, and in Vasari's book on Italian artists. There was an aristocratic love of display. Italians admitted concern with controlling themselves and manipulating others (Machiavelli, Guicciardini). We should understand that this individualism was extroverted and heroic, not inward and contemplative. They were motivated by hatred, envy and jealousy of all those who were more successful. The Renaissance man was an individual because he externalized himself in his creations, with the result being financial success.
- *Uniqueness.* There was a development of a personal style of painting or writing. Still, there are some misunderstandings. For example, the signing of paintings was *not* good evidence of individualism. According to Burke, all this meant was that the work met the standards of the shop. Still there was a gradual rise in the social status of artists, from guilds to academies. Artists were becoming more like poets and less like carpenters. The arts became increasingly independent from the practical function of their crafts. The arts also became more independent of each other. For example, music ceased to be dependent on words, and sculpture emerged independent from architecture.

What Renaissance individualism was not

Individualism in the Renaissance valued neither privacy nor solitude.
The poetry of Dante is never private, never turning away from the public. And at least for the artisan, being a member of a clan or sworn association was essential. Without this, he was friendless, weak and subject to manipulation. Neither were artists independent of patrons. While Renaissance artists may have had more freedom in *technique*, in terms of subject matter (as Burke notes) they did what they were told.

Contrary to Burckhardt's assertion, the heart of individualism was *economic*—to be found in the expanding effects of cash and credit mechanisms of urban merchants, rather than in aristocratic politics. Lastly, there is not a hint of romanticism in Renaissance art. 'Genius' was not what subjectively motivated the individual. The criterion for genius was what was produced objectively and how successful it was. The results mattered more than the process.

The Protestant Reformation and Individualism

The Protestant Reformation was a revolt against what it perceived as the decadence of the Catholic Church. While it is well-known that when Luther attacked the Church for selling indulgences for the supposed purposes of shortening the time of suffering in Purgatory in the next life, that was just the tip of the iceberg. These first reformers attacked the Church not only for its corrupted involvement with power and wealth, but also for its spiritual doctrine and its practices.

Against pomp and circumstance

According to Luther, the Gospel did not dictate how religious services should be enacted. Sacraments, candles, and elaborate vestments were all props which got in the way of the primary relationship between the individual and God. The saturation of the senses through stain glass windows, dramatic organ music, incense, statues, and relics, were really magical techniques for altering states of consciousness. Protestants felt that this undermined the sobriety and seriousness of Christian life. Confession and absolution were avoidances of the self-discipline and control, required of true Christians at all times. Reliance upon intermediary spiritual beings in the next life (whether saints or angels) were distractions from the ultimate relationship with God.

Anti-Authoritarians

Protestants were radical individualists. No human being was more expert than others in knowing how to live a spiritual life. The authority of the Pope, the cardinals, and the bishops was undercut. At best, Protestants took counsel from pastor elders. Like the Jews and the Catholics, the Protestants believed that the nature of the relationship between God and man was *a contract,* a covenant rather than any immanent or necessary relationship. However, for Catholics, an individual could only fulfill their contract and be redeemed through membership in a collective institution—the Church. According to Lukes (1978), Catholicism is the incarnation of the principle which sociologist Tonnies called “community”. The whole is before the parts, an organic unity. The whole (the Church) exuded sympathy for part, the person (even the poor) and the unconditional love of God.

The emergence of sincerity

Beginning in the sixteenth century there was a decisive increase in the rate of social mobility. Previous systems of deference in the Middle Ages now co-existed with scheming and plotting among the middle and upper classes, as the aristocrats battled the merchants for power. Feigning and pretense were the order of the day, as Machiavelli pointed out. Dante, representing the Medieval synthesis, assigned those accused of scheming to the worst part of his Inferno. Out of this disgust with behind-the-scenes manipulation came a new psychological virtue: sincerity.

‘Sincerity’ is one of those psychological states which is tempting to imagine as being a universal psychological characteristic that has always existed. While we might say that some individuals are more sincere than others, surely a significant number of individuals in any society, in any point in history, have been sincere. However, in his book *Sincerity and Authenticity*, literary critic Lionel Trilling argues that the word has an origin in history. Before the sixteenth century, the word 'sincere' referred to a material substance such as a liquid or metal that existed in pure or unadulterated state. The word used to describe individual *psychological* characteristics only appeared in the last third of the sixteenth century.

Typically, a phrase that promotes sincerity is 'To thine own self be true.' What does that mean? Compared to what other 'self'? What are the conditions of insincerity? These conditions could be:

- choosing to deceive oneself so that one's true nature cannot be made explicit
- deceiving others
- engaging in fantasy or ritual cynically with bad intentions

Prior to the rise of sincerity, humanity did not have an awareness of what historian Georges Gusdorf called "internal space." We did not imagine ourselves in more than one role, standing outside or above our personality. Trilling defines sincerity as the expression to others of our own feelings without any sugar-coating. Where sincerity is present, individualism is already in place, because expressing true feelings assumes a *true self which is separated from the roles one plays* in normal social interaction. To be sincere means to unburden one's heart regardless of appearances, role, situational constraints or costs. For the sincere self, roles are a burden, a mask which hides one's true self. Sincerity expresses *in words* either what is in one's heart (Calvin) or temperament (Montaigne). According to Trilling, the heart emerges at the center of one's identity in the first third of the sixteenth century.

Sincerity is about creating a transparent relationship between one's feelings and one's words. But Medieval monasticisms were also interested in a harmonious relationship between inner states, verbal communications and actions which they called our Concordia. But for monasticism, the expression of one's heart was simply a microcosm of any individual with the cosmic whole.

Sincerity for the Protestants differed from Concordia in a number of ways. Sincerity was an expression of emotions of an *individual* with a *unique* heart. And because Protestants had a more transcendental conception of God, what was in the individual heart was not in any way connected to God because humanity was sinful. For the Protestants, an individual's expression of feelings (usually suffering) was an exemplary project on the road to salvation.

Table 1.3 Catholic and Protestant Sincerity

Medieval Monasticism	**Historical setting**	**Protestant reformation**
Concordia	**Type of individual virtue**	Sincerity
Proper interplay between outer words and deeds	**Relationship between inner states, words and deeds**	Proper interplay between inner states and words
Realists Dante, Ficino	**Representatives**	**Nominalists** theologians, Luther
Agreement of one person with other people in relation to God	**Relation of individual to society and God**	No harmony with God or with other peoplee Humans are fundamentally sinful
Humans are similar to God	**Human relation to God**	Human is radically individualist
Heart is a microcosm of the greater whole	**Place of the heart**	Heart is an individual identity
Porous Can be invaded by the devil or spirits	**Boundaries of Self**	**Focused** Considered porous, self-superstitious

Democratic religious associations

While it is probably fair to say that for Protestants the religious formula to spiritual harmony is the individual, God and the Bible, I would overstate things by saying the Protestants were against community. The first Protestant Congregations were some of the most democratically run organizations in Europe. In John Calvin's time, ministers and elders were in charge of separate congregations, and general religious controversies were decided by representative assemblies consisting of both ministers and laymen. While the Protestants had a congregation, it was governed by the principle of *association.* The parts (the individual) came before the whole (the Congregation). Ultimately the individual was on their own.

There was little sympathy for the poor Protestants as God helped those who helped themselves. Puritan doctrine treated poverty as a mark of moral shortcoming. Unemployment was due to moral depravity of the individual, not merchant capitalism. There was a similarity between the view of the poor and Calvinist view of the position of the non-elect. The non-elect are not full members of the Congregation sharing in the government of the church, but members enough to be subject to its discipline.

Another indicator of the flattening of collectivist hierarchies was the change in the language of the services. While Church masses were performed in Latin, Protestant services were done in local vernacular. In short, Protestants wanted to close the gap between religious organizations and the laity. They wanted to close the Catholic monasteries and return the priests and nuns to secular life.

In terms of biblical focus, the Protestants (at least the Calvinists) were closer to the Jews than the Catholics. The Protestants roused their congregations through the fire and brimstone of the Old Testament. The Catholic emphasis on the New Testament, with the meek inheriting the earth, absolved individuals from sin and working on themselves in this life. The Protestants exploited the emergence of the printing press to make propaganda against the Church and mass-produce their interpretations of bibles in the vernacular (rather than Greek or Latin).

The Protestant work ethic

Unlike the Catholics, according to the Puritans God had predestined who would be saved and who would be damned. So how was salvation to be known while we were still on earth? For the Church, salvation was achieved by good works. For Protestants, faith alone was required. However, in this age of anxiety we can still look for signs as indicators. One of the greatest indicators was how Protestants handled their vocation.

The word 'vocation' in Latin means 'calling from God.' While Saint Thomas certainly saw work as a noble activity, Catholics made no connection between how someone worked as being a possible indicator of whether they were saved or damned. According to Max Weber, the Protestants transformed Catholic otherworldly aestheticism to 'this-worldly' aestheticism, which included the virtues of seriousness, industry, and frugalness at work. The purpose of this-worldly aestheticism was to lead an alert, intelligent life through vigilance, prudence and the destruction of spontaneous impulsive tendencies. Wasting time was the deadliest of sins. A loss of time through sociability, idol talk, luxury, inactive contemplation, recreation, feasting, sport (unless for health reasons), theatre, and the arts all distracted one from the calling.

The aesthetic tendencies of the monks were to be sublimated into ascetic ideals not in monasteries but in mundane occupations. As Weber says, the Protestants substituted the spiritual aristocracy of predestined saints of God *within* the world for spiritual aristocracy of monks outside and above the world.

However, it was not just the *process* of good vocational habits that was an indicator of salvation. It was also the *results*. Material success in worldly affairs was the highest form of moral activity. It is tempting to jump from this to conclude that Luther and Calvin advocated the accumulation of capital and the unlimited consumption of commodities. This would not be fair to either Luther or Calvin. For one thing neither one sanctioned disloyalty to one's estate nor social climbing.

What might be new with Calvinism is that Calvin sanctioned *several* callings provided you were faithful to each one. Furthermore, the successful pursuit of worldly goods was *not seen* as an end-in-itself, but rather as an indicator that one was saved. According to Weber, what might be directly connected to the rising merchant class was the call to a restless, continuous, systematic work, while consuming only the necessary and practical things that was the most powerful sign for the spirit of capitalism. After all, at least at the dawn of capitalism, merchants did have to work hard to compete with the aristocracy while navigating through the obstructions thrown at them by monarchies and emperors.

CHAPTER 2

European Individualism from the Capitalist Revolution to Proto-Romanticism

Orientation

In chapter one, we focused on three time periods—the Middle Ages, the Renaissance, and the Reformation. We considered how autonomy, privacy and self-control were the most prominent of the seven elements of individualism.

In this chapter, we will examine European movements from the sixteenth century through the French revolution, including the capitalist revolution, the scientific revolution, the Enlightenment, and the beginnings of Romanticism. In chapter one, the elements of individualism were derived from changes in politics (decentralization based on conflicts between the king and the aristocrats), art (Renaissance), and religion (the Reformation). In this chapter new elements of individualism—individual rights, self-development, self-reflection and uniqueness—are more prominent as a result of the rise of capitalism, the scientific revolution, and the Enlightenment.

Capitalist revolution and its impact on individualism

Capitalist mythology: Opulence and Public Order through individualist self-interest

Most of us are familiar with the quips and explanations for how capitalism justifies itself:

- capitalism unleashes the creative spirit of innovation
- capitalism produces unprecedented wealth
- capitalism is the most efficient means of circulating goods and services
- capitalism has always existed
- people are naturally greedy; capitalism is a means to harness that greed in a productive manner
- people are naturally ambitious; capitalism is a

means of harnessing ambition

- people are naturally envious; capitalism is a non-violent means of channeling that envy
- people are naturally lazy, and any planned production would pander to that laziness

Capitalist theorists on human nature divide people into two kinds. On the one hand, most individuals are greedy pleasure-seekers and envious of what others have but are too lazy and lack the ambition necessary to work and have more than others. On the other hand, there are ambitious individuals (capitalists) who are capable of shrewdly assessing a social situation for potential markets and possessing the self-discipline for saving, planning, delaying gratification, and working hard. This sets them apart from lazy hedonists. Capitalists compete with other capitalists, and the competition between capitalists produces expanding wealth for society. The lazy, pleasure-seeking, and envious sector of humanity goes to work for capitalists as wage slaves because they have no other choice.

Capitalist economists such as Adam Smith and von Hayek are fascinated by the opulence produced by apparent self-interest. These unintended social benefits are far beyond what any state planning could ever accomplish. How did this way of thinking about human nature and social relations come to be? How did the buying and selling of commodities, services, banking, and profit-seeking which are so respectable today become so, especially after being condemned by many as greed and avarice in the Middle Ages and the Renaissance?

Passions, avarice, and ambition in the Middle Ages

The passions of honor and glory

The longstanding concern throughout the Middle Ages was the passions, specifically honor and glory (virtues of the ruling aristocracy). According to Albert Hirshman, even as far back as the early Middle Ages, St. Augustine condemned lust for possessions and money as one of the three sins of fallen humanity, along with lust for power and sex. Augustine hoped that one passion might *check* another, and he mildly endorsed seeking glory. In the Middle Ages, glory was seized on by spokesmen for the chivalric aristocratic ideal of honor and glory as the touchstone of a man's virtue and greatness, in contrast to the purely private pursuit of riches. In the Renaissance, the pursuit of honor expanded as the power of the Church receded. But how do we make sense of the passions?

Ever since the end of the Middle Ages, as a result of the increasing frequency of interstate warfare and civil wars in the sixteenth and seventeenth centuries, there were efforts for new rules of conduct and mechanisms which would impose much needed discipline and constraints on both rulers and those they ruled.

Avarice and Ambition

Max Weber claims that capitalistic behavior and activities were originally the indirect and unintended result of a desperate search for individual salvation. Weber suggests that Calvin's doctrine of predestination did not lead to fatalism among his followers. Neither was it driven by a frantic search for pleasures. Rather, it was a methodical activity informed by purpose and self-denial in order to attain salvation. Without realizing it, Calvinists were developing the beginning of capitalist rationality.

Proto-money

In his book *Reason in the Middle Ages*, Alexander Murray points out that in the early Middle Ages property was distributed by authority of the king or the aristocracy by law or gift. This exchange happened mostly in-kind, say cereal for wine, with local coins used to make up the difference. There was scarcity of coins, so there were limitations to the degree to which coins and goods could be mixed.

With proto-money, the symbol of money is unstable. On the one hand, it symbolizes something not immediately present, but on the other hand the symbol itself has use value. For example, some money could be eaten (bags of grain or pepper, for instance). Coins that stood for money could be smelted into ornaments, such as chalices. The choice of the type of money used would vary with the contexts. For example, pepper was used as money on long journeys because of its durability, lightness, ease of transport, and acceptability to other cultures. Livestock could be used as money in local exchanges because the owner was more likely to be known and trusted.

Low status of money

An example of the lack of high status attributed to coined money can be seen in the record of how wealth was tracked. This list went from the most important to the least important: farms, serfs, serving maids, horses,
oxen, enjoyment of hounds and hawks, abundance of things to wear, implements, corn, wine, oil weapons. Silver, gold, and gems come only *at the end* of this list. In Flanders, gold and silver are listed first but are treated more as an adornment to wealth rather than the substance of it.

The unavailability of coined money was a problem for a number of reasons:

- the difficulty of acquiring bullion (Silver was more available than gold, but it was hoarded by the Catholic Church)
- the lack of skill of minting the bullion
- the lack of commitment from a central authority to mint the coin (Charlemagne was supportive of building a currency, but he started serious currency reform late in his life)
- the commercial demand was too low to justify the investments in discovering and extracting the metal
- the lack of international trade discouraged monetary circulation (Compared to Islamic civilization which linked north-west India, Mesopotamia and Egypt, Europe had nothing to offer but a handful of barbaric luxuries whose market was too narrow and too sporadic to create substantial monetary circulation)

To show how little money was valued in the Early Modern Europe, the word pecuniary, which we take to have something to do with money, in those days meant land, buildings, or animals.

The word rich did not mean economically wealthy but meant *politically* powerful. However, by 1000 BCE the *economic* meaning of money started to become more prominent.

Reification of money

Beginning in the tenth century the European market began to grow, and with its expansion coins became more necessary to use as barter became impractical. In addition, labor became quantified into a price (wage labor). On the positive side wages more widely accepted currency led to an increase in travel and traveling gangs of builders spread more uniform styles of architecture. However, the presence of money also worked against the worker and society.

One of Murray's deeper analyses is the parallel he draws between the circulation of money and the circulation of people throughout society. As money begins to circulate, it wraps itself around and through the people who use it, so that the characteristics of people begin to resemble the movement of money. Just as money moves freely from hand to hand with no obstruction, so too, with the development of wage labor, humans become more interchangeable on the job and not determined by linguistic or religious loyalties. Secondly, just as money travels beyond the local region, so too men travel from their village and weaken the ties within the home base of the village. Third, just as a lot of coins can be concentrated into a treasure chest, so too people can be herded together into a town, like coins in a chest. Fourth, just as money is infinitely storable and not subject to spoil, the exchange value produced by workers is invested in machines which live on beyond the generation of workers who "spoil" and die. Just was there is liquidity in money there is liquidity in people. Workers are used up and replaced by other workers.

The weakening of loyalty to village, language, and religion changes people's psychology, creating two new psychological characteristics in people desiring class mobility: avarice and ambition. Avarice is the desire of infinitely acquiring more and more money. Ambition is the desire to climb the social hierarchy to attain power.

Table 2.1 How Money Moves People

Characteristics of money	Category of comparison	Characteristics of humanity
Money moves freely from hand to hand with less consideration for who the exchanges are with, or what the occasion is for exchange	**Decline of mediating influences**	Through wage labor, humans become interchangeable on the job with less consideration for religious or linguistic loyalties
Money travels across borders	**Spatial reach**	Workers travel away from villages
Money can be divided into infinitely small units	**Divisibility**	The division labor is creating increasingly specialized work
Money can be easily concentrated in one place	**Centralization**	People are herded into towns, like coins in a chest
Money can be left to pile up without suffering natural vicissitudes	**Duration**	Social wealth is concentrated in machines which endure beyond the life and death of individual workers
The circulation of money makes for easier distribution across classes	**Circulation**	Humans to hoping to accumulate wealth (avarice) and cross social classes (ambition)

Avarice

But how do we know people in the Middle Ages became more preoccupied with acquiring more and more money? Murray provides five sources of evidence for avarice:

- the relationship between patterns of crime and the growth of the use of currency
- the trends in the appointment of church offices
- the plight of the Jews
- literary evidence of satire
- literary evidence of homily

The very characteristics which make coined money more attractive than proto-forms of money are the very qualities that make coined money the most tempting of all property to steal. In terms of theft, the portability of money means it can be easily carried and exchanged at a recognized value without anyone knowing where the coins came from. Furthermore, coins can be gotten rid of as evidence when they are exchanged, especially for concrete goods. Murray sees a relationship between the increasing use of coined money and the pillages by other societies in Western Europe by the Magyars from 880 to 955 CE, the Sarcens pirates in Italy and southern France in the tenth century, and the attacks on England by the Vikings at the end of the tenth century.

The second piece of evidence for the increasing interest in the accumulation of money is the rise of simony—the appointment to church offices for a price—which occurred about the same time as an increasing circulation of currency. It arose first in northern Italy and then spread to Germany and France. The third piece of evidence is the changed perception of the Jews who were the main money lenders. At the start of the eleventh century there was little reported about persecution of the Jews. But by 1100 things had changed.

Murray points out that in non-commercial regions, what

trade exists is entrusted to a foreign people, those whom ethnic relations theorists call middle-man minorities. Then, once commercial relations are established within the region, the native traders compete with these foreigners:

> Jewish social structure and traditions... helped them adapt with exceptional speed to the finer skills of money-making, not least, that of finance at interest...their new wealth enabled them to enlarge Jewish religious institutions...to the point where Christians felt threatened. (69)

The pogroms of the 1090's CE could be understood as a case of the native merchants ousting the Jews and using the preaching of the Crusades to fire-up the peasants against them. The source of peasant hatred of Jews was as moneylenders, an easily visible target.

The fourth piece of evidence is in satire and parody:

> The 11th century has seen a sporadic increase in money-satire generally from Egbert of Liege *Ship of Plenty* (1025) down to satires of Sextus Amaricus. In the generation just before and after the year 1100, money-satire emerged as a literary sub-category on its own. (72)

Lastly, unlike satire and parody, homily affords chronological comparison. Throughout the tenth and eleventh centuries, vices and virtues were symbolized in art. The total number of dateable examples show an *increase* in the number of representatives of avarice from the ninth to the thirteenth century. Even the religious Scholastics had a positive attitude toward certain categories of business pursuits.

In the early modern world, torn as it was by religious wars which were thought to be caused by human passions, the vice of avarice seemed tame by comparison. With the expansion of capitalism in the seventeenth century, all heroic virtues were exposed as masks for self-preservation by Hobbes or self-love by La Rochefoucauld. The search for glory was seen as a vane and frantic escape from real self-knowledge by Pascal. The passions were seen as demeaning by Racine and denounced as foolish by Cervantes.

On the other hand, commercial exchange by comparison came out smelling like a rose. Montesquieu thinks that the spirit of commerce itself brings a spirit of "frugality, economy and moderation". As long as this spirit prevails, the riches it creates will not have any bad effect. Montesquieu also notices the constancy and persistence of the passion of accumulation. He says "it is almost a general rule that wherever the ways of man are gentle, there is commerce and wherever there is commerce, there the ways of men are gentle." (*Reason In the Middle Ages*, 60) For much of the eighteenth century, in both England and France, the dominant appraisal of the love of gain was positive, if somewhat disdainful. 'Sweetness', 'softness', 'calm' and 'gentleness' are some of the most common terms used. It was thought that avarice itself could never get out of control. Capitalism was supposed to accomplish exactly what many today point to as its worst feature.

Ambition (Desire to climb up the social scale)

In the eleventh century, for ascetic Christians, ambition was a sin, a particular instance of pride, and it remained at the top of the diabolic pantheon right through the Middle Ages. But among more materialistic Christians, things were different. While avarice is an important quality to cultivate in people if they are to acquire more money, one needs ambition if one hopes to rise in the structures of power. Gaining power is necessary in order to *sustain* money's flow over time. What institution might promote the promise of rising in the social hierarchy? State-building and church-building.

The political activities of the state depend on money. But, in order to find people to build the state, the state must promise something beyond selfless devotion, such as class mobility. In the early Middle Ages, obstacles to rising within the military were illiteracy and ancestry. But in the central Middle Ages, men who were not noble in birth were admitted. In Germany, state ministers began as serfs and by working efficiently could rise in social status. So too, a commoner efficiently carrying out of the church's business could buy benefices. Murray points out that the sight of someone else winning rank and honor tends to spark off hope and desire in others. He suggests that ambition made a man busy—externally active and pressed for time.

From passions to interests

What Albert Hirschman does in his book *The Passions and the Interests* is not to examine justifications for capitalism *after* it attained power, but to ask by what process it justified itself *before* it became the dominant economic system. The justification for capitalism before its triumph was that it promised to repress the passions—lust for power, sex and glory—with 'interests.' While passions were rash, immoral, and unpredictable, following one's interests in trade made the individual plan and calculate for the long-term. It also made him more even-tempered, more benign, and more predictable. What Hirshman does is take us through the evolution of how capitalism justified itself through the transformation of human nature from passions to interests from the Middle Ages to the eighteenth century. In the Forward to Hirshman's book, Sen provides us an example of how a violent action could be subdued by enlightened self-interest:

> Consider a situation in which you are being chased by murderous bigots who passionately dislike something about you—your skin, the look of your nose and the nature of your faith...As they zero in on you, you throw some money around as you flee and each of them gets down to the serious business of... collecting the notes. You will be impressed by your own good luck that the thugs have such benign self-interests.

In this example, the passionate pursuit of perceived enemies is undermined by the prospect of an increase in wealth.

There was a 200-year historical process by which 'interests' were once seen as merely one of a number of passions, before the term finally came out of its shell and subordinated the rest of the passions to it. At first, when faith in the aristocratic hero had declined, the long-maligned trader did not correspondingly rise to prestige immediately. The idea that he was mean, grubby, and uninspired lasted a long time. People became indifferent to the pursuit of glory and greatness, but not because interests were held in high esteem by the second half of the eighteenth century.

It is tempting to think that the defense of interests against the passions was initiated by Adam Smith. But, actually, Smith had many predecessors. According to Hirshman, long before the disciplines of political science or economic disciplines were in place, philosophers and political economists prior to the triumph of capitalism speculated about the likely consequences of commercial expansion. For example, Montesquieu says that even though passion may prompt people to be wicked in the moment, they have a longer-term *interest* in not being so. Sir James Steuart claims that interests are the most effectual bridle against the folly of despotism. Even before then, Vico, Hobbes, and Locke all added pieces to the theory.

Strategies for dealing with the passions

There were three strategies for dealing with the passions: *coercing* them through Church or State repression advocated by Augustine and then Calvin. The second was to *harness* the passions. For example, Vico argued that ferocity, avarice, and ambition could be harnessed productively for commerce and politics, thereby strengthening the republics of the day and causing civil happiness. The third strategy was to *countervail the passions with other passions*. Mandeville in his famous *Fable of the Bees* turns private vices for luxury and emulation into material goods for public benefits. For Mandeville, when humanity is driven by their private, selfishness in playing passions against each other, the inadvertent result is economic prosperity. Private vices will be transformed into public benefit.

Assigning which passions are wild and which are tamable underlies the Hobbesian system: the aggressive pursuit of riches, glory and dominion is overcome by passions that include the desire for peace and the fear of death. Hume argued that the passions are imperviousness to reason. Nothing can oppose passion but a *contrary* passion. Although luxury is evil, according to Mandeville, it is a lesser passion than sloth. Can the love of pleasure be countered by the love of gain? In other words, is it not possible to discriminate among the passions and fight fire with fire?

The rise of interest and the depreciation of the passions

The roots of the use of the word interest do not originate as a replacement for *individual* passions. According to Hirshman, the old association of interests was with money-*lending* and had a special affinity with rational calculation. Interests were the benefits to be derived from the *predictability* of human conduct. Because of the larger number of actors, the opposition between interests involved in trade could not be nearly as devastating as the results of conflicting passions. The roots of interests were also associated with political statecraft. The state must look after its long-term interests and engage in diplomacy rather than start wars it cannot finish. Just as in individual life, so in matters of the state, one must not let oneself be guided by disorderly appetites (passions) which make us undertake tasks beyond our collective strength.

Interests start out as just another tame passion that is assigned a challenging function. One set of passions—greed, avarice or love—could be used to oppose other passions, like ambition, lust for power, or sexual lust. But once money-making was connected with interests it was given the job of holding back the passions. Bacon and Spinoza, in turn, brought interests down from the macro world of politics to the micro world of individual psychology.

Interests, expanded time and perseverance

The difference between passions and interests are also related to the speed at which they are satisfied. Passions are generally understood as impulsive, and mercurial, ebbing and flowing. Interest required reflection and calculation. The desire for wealth derived from avarice does not carry with it an *intensity* of desire, but a kind of delayed gratification, a willingness to pay a high price initially to achieve even higher benefits. Yet rational calculation of interest was not as slow moving and abstract as the high order reasoning of the scholastics, Descartes or Spinoza. Rather, it was short-term calculating rationality of Weber. A calm desire is thus defined as one that acts with calculation and rationality. This helps us to understand the eventual identification of interest in its original broad sense with love of money.

For in the pursuit of their interests, Locke claimed men are assumed to be *steadfast, single-minded, methodical* in total contrast to the stereotyped behavior of men who are buffered and blinded by their passions. The sociologist Georges Simmel points out that if interests were simply about accumulating *commodities* then there would be fluctuating interests because once the object is consumed, there is disappointment. But in *the process of accumulating capital*, the business of money-making is a different story. It is a steady process which goes beyond the consumption of particular commodities. Though today we know very well that accumulation of capital appears itself insatiable, one of the original justifications of capitalist accumulation was that it implied constancy of mind.

Lastly, Interests is set apart does not just require focus. It requires civility, cheerful behavior consistently from one day to the next with strangers. This sets it apart from passions which are vary from day to day and vary in their attraction and repulsion towards people.

Smith revolutionizes the relationship between passions and interests

In his *The Theory of Moral Sentiments* Adam Smith *collapses* passions such as honor and glory into the drive for the accumulation of fortune. The non-economic drives are all made to feed into the economic ones and do nothing but reinforce them. The passions are deprived of their independent existence because ambition, lust for power and desire for respect can all be satisfied by *economic* improvements. Smith undercut the hope that passion can be pitted against passion as a means of controlling them. He undermined the separation between the passions and the interests. For Smith, passions were dissolved into interests. The two terms 'interests' and 'passions' which had been *antonyms* in the century and a half that had elapsed appear now understood as *synonyms*.

Secondly, pursued in excess, money-making achieves neither public or private good but *when pursued in moderation* achieves them both. Lastly Smith democratized passions and interests. Before Smith, it is only the aristocracy that is animated with numerous noble or ignoble passions which clash with the dictates of moral obligation and reason. Machiavelli thought that the passions of the princes are much greater than those of the people. The ordinary mortal was not thought to be so complicated. The principle concern of the lower classes was thought to be with subsistence and material improvement. The lower classes either had no passions or his passions could be satisfied thought the pursuit of his interests. For Smith *all* classes had self-interest and could be worked into the capitalist economy.

Summarizing the processes from passion to interest we have:

<u>Individual pursuits of glory:</u>

- modified glory of Augustine versus St. Thomas
- expanded glory and honor in the Renaissance
- glory tamed
    - forms of self-preservation—Hobbes

  - self-love—La Rochefoucauld
  - avoidance of self-knowledge—Pascal

State interests:

- improving statecraft within the existing order
  - Machiavelli—the good Republic—interests as reasons of state
  - Vico—interests of the republic
  - Madison—the ambition of one branch of government is expected to counter that of another

Passions and interests in the service of the individual

- Spinoza—applies Machiavelli to the individual
- Mandville—passions and vice lead to material goods and luxury
- Smith—substitutes advantage and interest for passions and vice

Social contract theory and individualism

Hobbes: Leviathan, capitalism and individualism

Hobbes deduced political rights and obligations from the interest and will of dissociated individuals. The *essence of freedom was independence on the wills of others. It is ruthless competition between short-sighted, calculating self-interested individuals, either as capitalists or wage workers that is the foundation of his psychology of the individual. But why such an anti-social, narrow concept of freedom.* This section and the section on Locke are drawn from C.B. Macpherson's great book, *The Political Theory of Possessive Individualism*

In England there were powerful political and economic processes taking place in the seventeenth century: a class struggle in parliament with the king, the civil war (1640), a series of republican experiments, the restoration of the monarch, and a constitutional revolution. Hobbes tried to understand how these forces interacted as well as what kinds of political processes were needed in for restoring public order. Hobbes also offered the most extreme form of individualism and a chillingly pessimistic psychology of human nature. Hobbes was the Sigmund Freud of political science.

There is plenty of evidence that England approximated closely to a commercial, pre-industrial, capitalist society in the seventeenth century. Nearly half the men were full-time wage earners; if the cottagers are counted as part-time wage earners, the proportion is over two-thirds. The tendency for land to be exploited as capital was already well-advanced as far back as the thirteenth century.

The state as a protector of society against capitalism

Macpherson argues that Hobbes' avocation of state centralization was a defensive reaction to keep society from falling apart. Hobbes advocated the extreme intervention of the state in order to reign in what he imagined to be the lawless collision of mindless, self-interested individuals. Neither the markets in capital, land, production, or labor were permitted to be entirely self-regulating. Macpherson argues that It was *because* possessive market relations were penetrating society so decisively that such extensive state regulation was required. Why was this?

- so many men were now *dependent* on employment from a wage
- their employment was dependent on the ups and downs of the commodity markets
- there was recurrent unemployment on a scale endangering pubic order, so states were compelled to interfere
- The incessant state interference with wages, prices, investment, and trade can be seen as protracted attempts to protect England against harsher repercussions of economic fluctuation.

Hobbes' psychology starts from human society

Hobbes begins with a model of market society that is projected back into nature and then into the psychology of individuals. Humans in society engage in a never-ending series of competitive relations between naturally dissociated and independently self-moving individuals. He thought psychological principles could be derived directly by self-observation of men in commercial relations of his day. The behavior of men in Hobbes model of society is anti-social. It is inherent that all men seek ever more power over others. There is an innate desire of all men for more power without limit.

The man who Hobbes presents in the opening chapters of *Leviathan* is very like an automated machine. It is not only self-moving, but self-directing. It has built into it equipment by which it alters its motion in response to differences in the material it uses and to the expected impact of other matter on it. Humans are machines that seeks to continue their own motions, motions driven by appetites. These include fear, courage, anger, confidence, diffidence, covetousness of riches, ambition for office, argumentativeness, magnanimity, love, jealousy, revenge, grief, pity emulation, envy, and aversion.

Since humans are self-moving systems of matter who equally seek to maintain their own motion and are equally fragile, there is no reason why they should not have equal rights. Hobbes sees rights and obligations as entailed in the need of each human mechanism to maintain its motion. Morality is simply what is most conducive to continued motion. The motion of every individual is necessarily opposed to the motion of every other individual. Humans are equally insecure and equally subordinate to the market.

Conditions of inequality

Yet humans are not equal in their expectation of getting their wants satisfied. Some do not strive to acquire more power but simply want to *maintain* what they have. Every person's innate desires are incessant, but not every person wants increased level of satisfactions or power (which includes a desire for riches, honor, glory and knowledge). They do not want to pay the start-up costs of efforts to make this happen. Human beings compete for everything.

Humans have two kinds of power: natural and instrumental. Natural powers include physical power, manual dexterity, ingenuity, flexibility and creativity. We also have instrumental power—the ability to influence others. Every person's power is regarded as a commodity, a thing offered for exchange and offered competitively. Every individual's value translates to prices established in the market. The competing powers of individuals is a zero-sum game. There are only win-lose situations, not win-win nor lose-lose. As Macpherson points out, this state of nature is a deduction from the appetites and other faculties not of humanity in general but of *civilized* men.

State of nature (civilized people run amok)

To convince his audience that the state was essential, Hobbes compared modern society to a hypothesized state of nature. How would men whose desires are already civilized act if there were no authority to enforce the law of contract? This state of nature is clearly the negation of civilized society. Hobbes says there would be no industry, no culture of the earth, no navigation. Famously, Hobbes said life would be 'solitary, poor, nasty, brutish and short.' Because there is natural equality, vanity would lead to the brutish condition of war. Without a state to intervene, fear of others would be pervasive and heightened since there would be no power able to overawe them all. Our lives would necessarily be miserable and insecure. Humans are not absolutely equal in ability, but close enough to being equal that the weakest can easily kill the strongest.

Enter the state as an emulsifier

No society could permit every person's natural powers to

be continually invaded by others through violence. There would be no society. *The state provides peaceful, non-violent ways by which individuals can constantly seek power over others without destroying society.* The causes of quarrel are not a problem for Hobbes, only the pursuit of them without a state as mediator and covenant to restrain the appetites. This is the only hope for the individual to avoid the constant danger of violent death.

The rational market man who possesses substantial property and hopes to hold it can acknowledge obligations to such a sovereign. Market men are adept as calculators to find the net advantage of conventional rules. However, each of them cannot be relied on to keep this long-run advantage steadily in mind without breaking the rules. Only where there is a sovereign to enforce the rules can ruthless competition be kept in manageable proportions. Market humanity confronts each other, but they need a sovereign to keep their invasions within non-destructive bounds.

Evaluation of Hobbes

According to MacPherson, Hobbes penetrated closer to the nature of modern society than any of his contemporaries and many of his successors. Hobbes was the first political thinker to have seen the possibility of deducing obligation directly from the mundane facts of humans actual relations with each other. He was the first to be able to ignore assumptions of morality based on transcendental references.

Most political thinkers before Hobbes had worked under feudal conditions in which hierarchical order appeared to be the only alternative to political and moral anarchy. Market relations had nowhere penetrated all societal relations sufficiently to make it conceivable that values could be established based on objective but not supernatural forces. Market society was creating an equality before the law of the market. The presence of this equality made the deduction of obligation under capitalist conditions plausible.

Assumptions of possessive individualism

Summarizing Hobbes, MacPherson identifies eight assumptions of what he calls possessive individualism:

- what makes a person human is freedom; freedom is *independence f*rom the will of others
- the human relations people do enter are contractual, voluntary, and governed by self-interest
- since freedom from the wills of others is what makes someone human, each individual freedom can rightfully be limited only by such obligations and rules as are necessary to secure the same freedom for others
- the individual is essentially the proprietor of his own person and he
  owes nothing to society
- although the individual cannot alienate his own person (as in being enslaved), *he may alienate his capacity to labor*
- human societies consist primarily of a series of market relations
- political society is a human contrivance for the protection of the individual's property
    - in his person
    - in his goods
- for the maintenance of orderly relations of exchange between individuals regarded as proprietors of themselves, individuals always act in their own self interest

Hobbes had reduced society *completely* to a market and found no room for moral principles not deducible from the market. To Hobbes, not only was labor a commodity, but *life itself* was reduced to a commodity. Hobbes' doctrine was not accepted by any significant group or movement in England in his own century; neither by royalists nor parliamentarians; neither by traditionalists nor radical republicans, nor Whigs nor Tories. Even those like Harrington and Locke—who substantially accepted Hobbes' analysis of human nature and shared his view of society as a market, rejected his full conclusions. Hobbes was addressing a humanity who did not yet think and behave entirely as a market species. However, facing the full consequences of Hobbes' theory is like drinking liquor straight up, no chaser. Even capitalists could not face him. Instead, they preferred the more watered-down brew of the more inconsistent social contract theory of Locke.

Locke: Private property is the foundation for individualism

For Locke, the right to individual private property is central to his theory of civil society. He incorporates no reciprocal social obligations. It is as if when God created humanity, he distributed to each a piece of property. Those who are left with no land are free to alienate, that is, sell their labor. For Locke, the alienation of labor is justified *because those who lack land must be lacking in the virtue of being industrious and fully rational*. We will discuss this later. For now, we will look at how Locke justifies how much more productive it is for society if only the most industrious few own most of the land.

Locke and the creative entrepreneur

It might appear that the selfish act of private appropriation of land by the capitalist *limits* social productivity, but not for Locke (or Adam Smith). The ambitious entrepreneur who appropriates land by his labor does not lessen but *increases* the common stock of mankind. It would yield ten times the land productivity than if it were equally distributed to less ambitious individuals. His enclosure of large-scale farming makes the land more productive than separate plots of land distributed to many individuals ever could be. The greater productivity of the appropriated land more than makes up for the lack of land available for others. Those without land can get a subsistence by their labor for others.

Civil society excludes the working class

While the laboring class is a necessary part of the nation, its members are not full members of the body politic and have no claim to be so. The laboring class was an object of state policy, an object of administration rather than fully a part of the citizen body. Men without estate or goods, without property in the ordinary sense, are rightfully both in and not in civil society. The laboring class, being without estate, are not full members of civil society. Yet they are members for purposes of being ruled, while men of estate are members of civil society for purposes of ruling.

The laborers share of the national income is seldom more than a bare subsistence and never allows enough time or opportunity to raise their thoughts above their work. Therefore, they are not capable of living the fully rational life required to participate in a deliberating civil society. Without the constraints of the Church and State the laboring class is incapable of following a rational ethic. The greatest part of mankind cannot be left to the guidance of the law of nature or the law of reason. They are not capable of drawing rules of conduct from these constructs. Full rationality went with appropriating land while non-rational behavior went with laboring.

As MacPherson points out, the implicit assumptions of Locke's class differential of rationality and rights is derived from a contradiction in his version of individualism. On the one hand the free rational individual is the criteria of the good society, while the requirement for this fulfillment is the *denial of and tearing apart of the individuality of half the nation (the working class)*. By the seventeenth to eighteenth century the sole moral object of the individual's action is his own benefit. The various versions of self-interest ethics from Hobbes onwards maintain that one should seek to secure one's own good, not that of society as a whole or of other individuals. As I hope you can see, most if not all of the foundations for a capitalist version of the individual are rooted in Hobbes and Locke.

The Scientific Revolution and its impact on individualism

Revolution in astronomy

Thanks to the emergence of capitalism, status groups expanded, rose, and fell. But that was not the only force destabilizing individuals in the seventeenth century. The discoveries of modern science rocked the middle class's picture of their place in the Universe.

The cosmos in Medieval science was a hierarchical, static, and closed universe dominated by Aristotelian ideas. With rare exceptions, most people in the Middle Ages believed that the sun revolves around the Earth. Then Copernicus proved not only that the earth orbits around the sun, but that the earth also rotates. In the Aristotelian world, the stars were fixed in number and were the same distance away from the earth. Tycho Brahe showed that stars were not eternal but came into being and died. Gilbert proved that stars were not the same distance from the earth. Some were closer, some were middle range, and some were far away. Imagine what this more asymmetrical and dynamic view of stars and planets would do to the psychology of the individual? It would add considerable instabilities to those classes who learned about these findings.

Medieval science held that the trajectory of the planets was circular, and the planets orbited at uniform speed. Johannes Kepler undermined planetary symmetry by proving that the planets moved in the shape of ellipses and that planets do not orbit at the same speed. Rather, they orbit more quickly or slowly, depending on their distance from the sun. Perhaps even more disturbing was the texture of the planets. Both the ancients and the medievalists held that the moon was smooth. But early modern science had shown that the surface of the moon has craters and that the earth was not the only planet with moons. Jupiter had two moons. We now know from modern astronomers that many of the planets have craters and worse. We now know that other planets, including our own have been hit by comets and/ or asteroids. Given that early modern science did not clearly understand the relationship between comets and planets, it would be unfair to read too much into the presence of craters rather than smooth surfaces. But still, with the planets and stars imaged as fixed, symmetrical, and eternal, it must have caused great discomfort to realize how unlike Plato's and Aristotle's geometrical universe, the early modern universe actually was unstable.

Epistemology and individualism in the hard sciences

In order to understand the world, scientists must reflect on by what means they know things. Prior to the development of science, dream states, trances, possession states, revelations, and visions were just as good as the five senses and the use of reason. However, there were important differences. Trance states and possessed states drew the individual *outside their bodies* to draw knowledge in. In early modern science these altered states began to be seen more skeptically, but it took two centuries for scientists to dismiss them as ways to know the world.

Within science there are two traditions, rationalism and empiricism. The empirical tradition of Locke, Hume and Berkeley claim that the royal road to knowledge starts with the five senses. Rationalists from Descartes to Spinoza consider the senses untrustworthy and rely on the use of mathematical rationality. As different as these two traditions are, *what they both agree on is that the senses and rationality begin and end with the body of individuals*. Individual experience, whether through sensuality or rationality is the source of all knowledge. How could it be otherwise?

A Vygotskian way to examine sources of knowledge is to start with *the socio-historic nature of individuality*. No individual privately assesses the state of the world by themselves. Long before all of our senses are fully formed in ontogenesis they are being socialized by a particular type of society, by a certain class and at a certain period of history. The sensual knowledge of humanity is pooled in concrete social institutions and cultural practices through work and then passed down across generations. These socio-historic institutions socialize the senses of individuals. The senses are mediated by a shared public world and collective language formation.

Because empiricists and rationalists are epistemological

individualists, the social nature of humanity is *not* the starting point of knowledge but the effect of the private experience of individuals. In other words, society is an institution that is logically and practically a derivative after the private individual uses his senses and reason to make sense of his private experience and then comes to engage with social institutions. The source of knowledge for the empiricists and rationalists is *the individual* senses or mind standing alone against nature with no social mediation and no historical conditioning. As different as Locke, Hume, and Berkeley are from each other regarding the trustworthiness of the senses, they all agree that the individual rather than society is the starting point. As different as the rationalists Spinoza, Descartes, and Kant are from each other, they also agreed that the individual not the social is the starting point. With the exception of Marxist and Durkheimian, all sciences in industrial capitalist countries continue to be governed by methodological individualism.

The Enlightenment and individualism

What is the Enlightenment?

Beginning around 1715 and lasting for about a hundred years, there arose an intellectual movement in Europe, centered in France, which aimed to synthesize the fruits of the hard sciences and apply the lessons to the study of human history, human societies, human psychology, and the arts. The eighteenth century had seen the beginnings of a science of history at the same time Europe was learning more about the variety of societies that existed around the world through its own colonial exploitation of these societies. Enlightenment philosophers hoped that these disciplines would find their own Galileos, Keplers, and Newtons.

What the Enlightenment was instrumental in producing was a picture of humans evolving over time: from ignorance to knowledge, from superstition to reason, from instinct to education, and from tyranny to republicanism. The philosophers of the Enlightenment confidently argued that humanity was gradually improving and given enough time, the light of reason would rule the world. We will no longer need heaven in the afterlife, because we will slowly build heaven right here on Earth.

New elements of individualism

As a reminder, three elements of individualism (autonomy, self-control and privacy) had already developed. But the elements that became prominent in the eighteenth century were:

- the individual rights of a citizen
- self-development
- self-reflection

After the French revolution, individuals were told that their rights were not only spiritual but *political*. At the same time, historians were starting to classify and temporalize different types of society in some sort of developmental order. At a micro level they began to think about themselves as in motion, rather than static and subject to development based on social institutions and parental training. Yet instability and anxiety followed when their expectations for themselves became more or less than what their parents were. By the nineteenth century, this began to manifest in psychological disorders. Close on the heels of self-development was self-reflection. The individual became an object of his own scrutiny. While Protestants had been self-reflecting in their diaries for some time, this was a means to a spiritual end, not an end in itself. Eighteenth and nineteenth century fiction writers began to use self-reflection to write their novels. Samuel Richardson's *Pamela* used letters to reveal the protagonist's inner life.

Individuals have political rights

A second major contribution of the Enlightenment was to claim that individuals had political rights from birth. The whole notion of citizen rights—the rights under the Declaration of

Independence in 1776 or the Declaration of the Rights of Man in France in 1789 both gave the individualist self a political identity. Before that, the subject of a king had no rights. Members of elite classes had estate rights, but they were a small section of the population. Locke's *Two Treatises on Governments* and the work of Rousseau and Thomas Paine are all testaments to this new tradition.

Politically, the Enlightenment self is perceived most at home in a liberal constitutional state with constraints on the monarchy. Equality is primarily a legal concept of equality before the law, not economic equality. For this enlightened self, happiness and serenity were the leading emotions. This happiness and serenity were gained through a secular education.

From Natural rights, to utilitarianism

What is the relationship between empiricism and individualism? In the *Politics of Authenticity*, Berman says the impact is mixed. On the one hand, it overturns claims by authorities to rule their subjects through Divine Law while it champions *natural* rights. The utilitarian took a more economic approach. Jeremy Bentham argued that individuals were driven by pain and pleasure and the individual's happiness occurred when more pleasure was accumulated than pain. Later John Stuart Mill created a hierarchy of pleasures to distinguish the deeper from the more superficial pleasures. But how could the calculus of pleasure and pain be organized politically, especially given the fact that people in the eighteenth and nineteenth century live in social classes? Bentham and Mills answered vaguely with the slogan 'the greatest good for the greatest number.' This was later linked to Bentham's ideas about state intervention and to the rise of mass democracy in the late nineteenth century.

Persian letters

Berman believes that an essential part of the Enlightenment self has been captured by Montesquieu's *Persian Letters* written in 1721. Berman points out that it is the first novel of education, self-discovery, and politics in the West. It begins with an exotic encounter, then a Persian sultan's life changes after being exposed to the liberal Enlightenment, which leads to revolution.

Montesquieu roots the uniqueness of personality in the diversity of nature. Just as nature expresses herself through a variety of forms, so identity is expressed in a variety of ways. One of the new qualities of Enlightenment individualism was to perceive nature sensitively, as she really is. When nature is repressed, a revolution follows. When a tyrannical society represses its members, a radical gap emerges between the roles they are assigned to and their real identities. Furthermore, according to Berman, *the Persian Letters* is the first distinctly modern conception of equality, which is not based on scarcity and frugality, but on the growth of society and the abundance it provides.

<u>The Metropolis as the setting for Enlightenment individualism</u>

Drawing from sociologist Georges Simmel's "Metropolis and Mental Life", Berman claims the metropolis is the ideal medium for authentic life during the Enlightenment. City life sizzles with a concentration of energy, intensity, pace, and a variety of activities not crusted with traditional expectations. City dwellers are strangers with no long-term expectations. They are driven by self-interest, yet the growing individualist produces, when they interact, at least ideally, an authentic community. These self-confident selves gladly transverse in and out of different roles without feeling their true identity will be lost in the mix. Montesquieu saw the flexibility that metropolitan life had produced as an advance. By penetrating the life of the social world more deeply, the individual man discovers hidden sources of power in the depths of his social self that go beyond particular roles. In the meantime, people live by their wits and their ingenuity, knowing that living in cities that 'make you free' means you learn to cheerfully improvise and react to the intensity and diversity of city life.

Self-development beyond essences

Just as the Enlightenment began to see human societies as snapshots of a developing movie, what the Enlightenment also did was *to give the individual a developmental direction.* In the Middle Ages, individual identities were understood as temperaments—sanguine, melancholic, choleric, and phlegmatic. While these temperaments were thought to be subject to change, the reasons for the change had to do with the geography or climate. However, thanks to Locke and many others, the human individual began to be understood as determined by social institutions, including parental upbringing. Evolving social institutions might help shape evolving individuals.

Individual uniqueness: from temperament to personality

A vital element of individualism is that each person is unique. While this may seem self-evident today, it was not true throughout human history. In temperament theory, historically, individuals were various combinations of the elements earth, fire, water, and air. When these elements entered the body, they became four liquids: blood, phlegm, black bile, and yellow bile, which in different mixtures, produced four kinds of people: melancholic, choleric, sanguine, and phlegmatic. There was no uniqueness which stood outside these four. To be so, would be to be mad.

Today an individual's temperament is defined by psychologists as individual tendencies to emote or act habitually based on biological predispositions—neurotransmitters, enzymes, hormones, and genes. These tendencies persist despite social expectations, roles, and social situations. Temperament is thought to last a lifetime. If we trace the history of temperament in the West, we find that for most of that history people believed that an individual's identity was determined by their temperament, but the foundation for it was different.

Beginning in the sixteenth century, temperament theory began to slowly lose credibility. By the eighteenth century, temperature was replaced by personality. It was thought that personality was formed by *cultural* influences combined by individual experience in learning. At least in psychology, skepticism about temperament held true throughout the nineteenth century until the 1940s. There were theories such as William Sheldon's three body types—ectomorph, mesomorph, and endomorph—but they were overshadowed by behaviorism and psychoanalysis. Though very different, all psychoanalysis theories agreed that biology had very little to do with personal identity and what was going on with an individual. It wasn't until the 1980s, with the work of Jerome Kagan, that temperament theory returned to respectability.

Greeks and the Romans: Hippocrates and Galen

Strange as it may sound, before the rise of individualism, a person's temperament was thought to arise from the natural world before it become internalized. In her book *Passions and Tempers*, Noga Arikha points out that Empedocles believed that all matter is divided into four mixtures which came from the four elements. These four mixtures produced the seasons:

- Earth and Water mixed to produce Cold and Winter
- Water and Air mixed to produce Moisture and Spring
- Air and Fire mixed to produce Heat and Summer
- Fire and Earth mixed to produce Dryness—Autumn

At the same time Empedocles also argued that these mixtures were imported into human bodies and produced seasonal temperaments (body fluids): black bile (which was dried blood, excrement, and dark vomit), blood, yellow bile (pus), and phlegm.

Ideally, people's temperaments have a balance of warm, cool, dry, and moist. In less ideal types, one of four qualities dominate:

- Cold- and wet—phlegmatic—introversion
- Hot and wet—sanguine—extroversion

- Hot and dry—choleric—mercurial
- Cold and dry—melancholic—nervous

Melancholic had an excess of black bile, which was rooted in being cold and dry. This led to characteristics such as nervousness, refined sensitivity, creativity, madness, and depression.

Sanguine had an excess of blood, which came from being hot and moist and led to sociability, optimism, and warmth.

Choleric had an excess of yellow bile, which came from an elemental mixture of hot and dry. This resulted in someone who was quick tempered and generally argumentative. Those that were phlegmatic were so because of a mixture of cold and moist. Phlegmatic types were slow to act but persevere once they get started. They also hold emotions for a long time.

Both Hippocrates and Galen also thought that there was a direct relationship between the proportion of humors in the body and the body-type of an individual. Body types were muscular, thin, and voluptuous, and they corresponded to the humors. In addition, hair and eye color were thought to be expressions of temperament.

While it is true that neither Hippocrates nor Galen thought that social conditions could change temperament, that did not mean temperament could not be changed. For one thing, both Hippocrates and Galen attempted to improve imbalances in temperament by tinkering with the body fluids of the individuals. This led to bloodletting and purging, among other things. They also believed that temperament could be changed by the food one ate, so they advocated changing diets. Lastly, they believed that a change of climate could impact temperament. If the four seasons were directly connected to body fluids, then the type of temperament would be affected by the seasons and the climate of the geographical region as a whole. For example, an individual who had a choleric temperament (hot and dry) would be made worse in the summertime but also if the climate of the region was hot and dry generally. Hippocrates might recommend moving to a climate that was cold and moist to balance out their temperament.

We can see the vestiges of the temperament theory on climate at work in seasonal affective disorders. Norman Rosenthal has shown that certain types of people will become depressed if they lack a certain amount of sunlight. Rosenthal recommends exposure to a certain amount of artificial light during the winter months to compensate for the lack of exposure to light. He even documents cases where those who are most likely to get seasonal affective disorders are people who have moved from temperate climates with more moderate amounts of light and dark to areas such as Alaska who have some days in the summer where there is next to no darkness at night and almost no light in the winter.

Five differences between Greek and Roman temperament theory and today's temperament theory

These ancient theories differed from contemporary temperament theory in that:

- they attributed temperament to liquids in the body (humors) not neurotransmitters, enzymes, hormones, and genes
- they believed the origins of temperament began *externally* in nature, not within the individual. Today's theories would say people's temperament is completely separate from the natural world. The changing of the seasons has nothing to do with temperament, according to contemporaries
- the ancients believed temperament could be changed by diet. Contemporary theory argues that a person's diet cannot change a person's temperament
- the ancient Greek and Romans did not think social institutions could affect temperament. Modern temperament theories suggest that a person's temperament can be affected by parental treatment, gender socialization and social class
- The ancients claimed that temperament was related to physique including the body, eye and hair color.

Contemporary theory does not make this claim

In the Middle Ages the four temperaments were expanded to include astrological signs and a vast system of correspondences where astrological signs were connected to specific parts of the body. In *Forging Promethean Psychology,* I showed that during the Renaissance High magicians such as Ficino and della Porta believed they could change the composition of humors with sound and song.

Decline of temperament theory

Temperament theory declined in stages with a series of shocks between the sixteenth and nineteenth centuries. Perhaps the first shock was the Black Plague, which decimated roughly a third of the European population between 1348 and 1351. Because temperament theory understood the dynamics of nature as being a configuration of fire, air, earth, and water, it did not have an analysis of why the plague took place. Temperament theorists believed the plague was the result of poisonous, putrid air. The role of micro-organisms was not understood until the nineteenth century. Among their remedies were to overcome the poisonous air with various kinds of incense. Nothing worked—not bleedings, purging, or changes in diet. Both doctors and priests who held to temperament theory were powerless to help others or even to help themselves. The failure of temperament theory to explain or end the plague helped to clear the way for new approaches to health and medicina. According to Arikha, it was partly to repair its damaged reputation that doctors began to look for new causes.

Another shock to the social body was when Copernicus decentered the earth from the heart of the solar system. For medievalists and those in the Renaissance, the relationship between the four elements in nature and its linkage to the four liquids in the body was inseparable from the conception of the earth as the center of the solar system and the human species as the center of creation. Copernicus marginalized the earth and indirectly marginalized the human species. Whatever material elements human beings were composed of, it was no longer so directly connected to a radically changed astronomical order.

As astronomy gradually superseded astrology, the stars were no longer seen as a macro world organically connected to the microworld. They were separated into objectivity (macro-world) and subjectivity (micro-world). Furthermore, the occult slogan 'as above, so below' only applies when the macro-micro link is a *closed system*. Bruno challenged this by arguing that the universe was infinite.

Descartes and the mechanization of the human body

If Copernicus reversed the relationship between the earth and the solar system, Descartes opened up space between the body and the mind. In temperament theory and for St. Thomas, the body consisted of a sensitive soul which animated it. For Descartes, the mind was incorporeal and had nothing to do with body functions. Descartes took life out of the body and treated it as a machine. The body was an automaton and functioned according to the laws of mechanism. While the later findings of Vesalius, Harvey, and Van Helmont would not confirm Descartes mechanistic picture of the body, Descartes insistence that the body had no soulful content cleared the way for physiologists to study the body independently of spiritual or humeral considerations.

Blood, brain localization and nerves

In the same year as Copernicus' discovery,Vesalius demonstrated the falsity of some of Galen's anatomical constructions.

Akikha (2007) says that the vena cava that departed from the heart was not connected to the liver as Galen had supposed. By observing fresh brains Vesalius was able to disparage the ventricular picture of brain functions that had been established for 1500 years.

In the next century, thanks to Boyle's chemical invention, brains could be preserved and studied without decomposition. As a result of this opportunity, ventricles were now understood as empty spaces not filled with the faculties as the scholastics had conjectured.

Harvey's book in 1628 on the circulation of the blood undermined temperament theory in part because he found that the heart, not the liver,was the center of life. Blood was not just one of the four humors. Its circulation was crucial for the entire body.

In the mid-1600s Van Helmont argued that disease was not a *global* condition and subject to manipulation of fluids, but the result of specific irritants on specific organs. In the nineteenth century Boulliard and Broca supported Van Helmont in studying the *specialization* of functions in the brain:

> Bouillard had established over 100 correlations between frontal lobe lesions and speech failure either through memory loss or through motor difficulties impeding word pronunciation. Paul Broca entered on the side of locations. He presented evidence from patients with what he called aphasia in 1864. He showed that the faculty of speech was located within the brain's convolutions in the left frontal lobe and *was not visible* from the cranium surface as phrenologists had believed. (261)

.

In 1874, Carl Wernicke identified that area in the brain's left temporal lobe near the primary auditory cortex as associated with language comprehension.

Albert von Haller and Whytt: nerves replace humors

Albrecht von Haller argued that the body was self-regulating and not dependent on the soul for its movements. Muscles depend on *irritability.* It was their intrinsic sensibility that made them receptive to external stimuli.

> The living body could be thought of in terms of local, mechanically generated actions. All organs and all tissue had an autonomous response to events external to them, and it was their irritability than enabled the body to live. Whytt had identified the sympathetic nervous system as explanation for sensation, motion and perception. (236)

> Nerves replaced humors in determining health and temperament. From the eighteenth century on there was talk of nerves, fiber, tissue, tone irritably, electricity. (230)

Rise of personality: Locke and the blank slate

Up until now we have explained the decline of temperament theory as a result of real changes in our understanding of nature and the stars as well as our understanding of physiology. However, the decline in temperament theory still leaves us with the problem of accounting for the diversity of experience and outlook of human beings. The Enlightenment was the first movement which understood society not as a thing composed of static institutions that only changed due to dynastic intrigue or the stopping and starting of wars. Voltaire described changes in human societies in terms of *cultural* change. So too, individuals began to be seen not as born with a certain temperament uninfluenced by social changes but as products of social institutions. Individuals had personalities, not temperaments. Personalities came from what religious, political, and economic institutions make of us as well as what we do. By the eighteenth century and beyond personality theory acquired the prominence that temperament theory was losing.

Table 2.2 tracks the processes by which temperament evolved to personality.

By the Enlightenment human beings were seen as:

Table 2.2 From Temperament to Personality

Humoral temperament theory	Challenges	Time period
The Earth and human body are the center of an integrated cosmos "as above so below"	Copernicus decanters the earth	1543
Galen says vena cava was connected to the liver	Vesalius challenges this	1543
Ventricular picture of brain function Ventricles were filled with faculties	Vesalius challenges this Ventricles are filled with empty spaces	1543
Body and soul connected	Descartes separates mind from body Body is humorless and mechanical (Discourse on Method)	1637
The liver is the place where the body's life-giving forces were concentrated	Harvey—circulation of the blood Blood was the engine of life not simply one of four fluids in the body.	1628
Disease is **global** and has to do with dyscrasia Black bile is stored by spleen Digestion is due to heat	Van Helmont—disease in local, the outcome of specific irritants affecting specific organs Bile has a positive function connected to the stomach Digestion is due to acidity	Mid-1600's
Four humors come out of matter (fire, air, earth water)	Locke We only experience secondary qualities of matter	1700
Temperament has nothing to do with social life	Parents and social institutions are responsible—blank slate Personality replaces temperament	
	People learn through association and mental errors	
Soul was required for body movements	Von Haller—nerves replace humors. No soul is required Nerves, fiber, tissue tone, irritability, electricity explain the dynamics of the body Galvani discovered that electricity ran through nerves	
Mental illness due to humoral imbalances Treatment used: purging and bloodletting, secretion of yellow and black bile	Pathology of nerves not liquids Straitjackets (Willis) Chains, whips	
	Pinele Benevolent care	1800's
Brain functions distributed throughout the cerebral structure	Brain localization Paul Broca Faculty of speech was located	1864
	Carl Wernicke—language was localized in primary auditory cortex	1874
	Charcot: localization in study of aphasic, epilepsy, hysteria	

- creatures of social institutions and individual experience, not as substantial essences which are the same from birth to death but who are in the process of development
- it is possible that each individual is unique and like no other

Individuals are balanced between reason and emotions

As Huizinga (*Waning of the Middle Ages*) has pointed out, people in the Middle Ages lived shorter, more passionate lives than people in the modern world. By the seventeenth century a stoic view of the emotions prevailed, where emotions were severely constrained (at least for the upper classes) by social roles. But by the eighteenth century emotions were seen as indispensable assets in all operations of the mind. The Enlightenment movement supported the use of reason and included the imagination and emotions, so long as reason was in charge.

Proto-Romantacism and Individualism: Rouseau

> If you have a spark of genesis go spend a year in Paris; you'll soon be everything you can be or else you never be anything at all. (Berman, *Politics of Authenticity* 168)

The machine and the tree

In the high-romantic period of the first half of the nineteenth century, the romantic imagined his struggle against the deadening forces of materialism, capitalism, and mechanistic science as a dualistic opposition between a tree and a machine. The machine was understood as everything that was rigid, externally determined, imposed, and deadening. The tree was the spirit of romanticism, representing freedom, spontaneity, expressiveness, growth, self-development, and authenticity. Standing at the interface between the Enlightenment and

Romanticism, Rousseau would not tolerate this dualism. Modern life had catalyzed discoveries and exposed errors; it had brought to the surface new vices but new virtues as well. The problem of modern life was that the machine was not something externally imposed on the tree but something that *grew out of it*.

In his book *The Politics of Authenticity,* Marshall Berman argues that Rousseau aimed neither to integrate modern men into the machine, nor to destroy the machine. Unlike the full-blown romantics of a century later, Rousseau did not mean for humanity to go back to the woods or return to a savage state. The self of primitive humanity was narrow, undeveloped, and repressed by the community. On the other hand, modern humanity had developed all his faculties and senses but used them to feed alien social institutions.

Another metaphor for modern life Rousseau used was the violent whirlpool, which both creates and destroys life. Just as the highway can crush the self, the whirlpool can tear it apart, scattering it in different directions. Both swoop humanity up to heights we've never seen before. At least in his early writings, Rousseau is terrified at the prospects, but he does not want to run into the woods:

> The paradox of modernity as it was emerging in Rousseau's time was that men were at once unhappier and potentially happier than men had ever been before. The most inauthentic social system in history had generated the ideal of authenticity. (266)
>
> The sensitivity that enabled them to survive by seeing through one another was enabling them to see through themselves. The hand that had made the world of modernity was the hand that could heal it. (265)

Inauthenticity: the commercialized self

In his early years of exploring the relationship between the individual and society, Rousseau thought that Hobbes' 'War of all against all' characteristic of civilization resulted in individuals who were insincere. In his later work, his assessment of individuals was more pessimistic. The foundation for 'false appearances' (insincerity) required having a self that one was *confident* in to begin with. Rousseau thought that individuals did not have a secure self about which to be insincere. He saw modern society as alienating, repressing, and dividing people from each other. To be oneself under these conditions is a problem to be overcome. Having a secure self is not something that can be taken for granted:

> For the first time, wit, beauty, strength, skill, merit, talent could come into their own—yet not for their own sake but as *valuable property*; not for any intrinsic merit, but for their value as weapons against other men. Thus, the unfolding of man's most authentic impulses and powers had been actuated by his least authentic needs. Springing from dubious roots, the process of man's self-development had generated profoundly ambiguous results. (*Discourses on Inequality*, 148)
>
> The modern age was, above all, an age of paradox; an age in which the potentialities for the self-development of men had multiplied to *infinity*, while the range of their authentic self-expression had shrunk to *nothing*. (153)

According to Berman, by the second half of the eighteenth century, the imagination projected less into the sky and came down to earth, but it soon became lost in the marketplace. On the one hand, humanity could do anything if it involved the acquisition of power and money, but it could not do anything outside the acquisition of money and power._

The Enlightenment railed against ascribed statuses, with

the implication that achieved statuses were unproblematic. Rousseau felt that even achieved statuses still kept people from being themselves. Rousseau wanted to undermine all roles and tear down all appearances which undermine people revealing their true identities. Rousseau assessed city life as a diversion. People run from one locale to another to *escape* themselves, not become themselves:

> These contradictions reached their most radical extreme in the modern *metropolis* where in the midst of so much philosophy, humanity, civilization and sublime morality, we have nothing but deceitful and frivolous appearances, honor without virtue, reason without wisdom pleasure without happiness. (152)

Real city life, according to Rousseau, ought to be not an association of self-interested monads but an organic community governed by the general will. Both ascribed and achieved statuses legitimized class inequalities. Eventually, the medium of competition was bound to spread beyond the realm of land and money into every sphere of human activity.

Misplace of education

The Enlightenment movement understood secular education as the key to overcoming ignorance and superstition. Rousseau saw conventional education of any kind, including secular education, as a problem. Rousseau believed than men were born with a unity of self which conventional socialization beat out of them, but which radical education could recover from and reinforce:

> The child's mind was in danger of becoming fixated on its formative experiences, unable to respond to new demands and possibilities. The name of the danger was habit. (175)

Authenticity and the participatory Individualist

Both Montesquieu and Rousseau understood that neither natural rights nor utilitarianism were adequate to express the needs or aspirations of modern men. According to Berman, two forms of inauthenticity were on Rousseau's mind:

- structures of domination of class
- structures enforced by sex

To be authentic means to see critically through the forces that twist and constrict our being. This requires courage to overcome the anxiety that the forces of modernity produce. Authenticity means freedom to be yourself by joining with others to form an individualist community that struggles to dissolve class and gender stratifications.

Humans cannot be themselves within the system or be themselves outside the system. They can only become themselves *against* the system. The politics of authenticity could result in ideal community in which each is for all and all is for each.

It would take years of resocialization to achieve this in education:

> Rousseau would work to keep the child's sensuous reason alive so that the growth of his mind should stem from it. Emile would learn to develop his ideas, *out of his own experience;* thus, he would have few ideas but those few would be thoroughly grasped. (174)
>
> The teacher has to keep the environment as open and fluid as possible. The only habit the child should contract is that of having *no* habits. The child's body and mind, if left to themselves, would follow their own immanent principles of growth. Education should pursue the end of personal growth and self-development. Let there be no comparison with other children, no rivalry, no competition,

> not even running races. Instead the child should be encouraged to "surpass himself." (180)

As an adult, the individual discovers his true identity by writing his autobiography, through which he can rediscover what really matters independent of socialization. In addition, Rousseau wants the individual to come to grips with nature in a very different way than the Enlightenment version. In the Enlightenment part of joy for the individual is in a growing sensitivity to how nature really works independently from the hand of God. Rousseau wants to use nature as a means, not an end. The end is to catalyze fits of revelry.

The classical romantic period goes from about 1750 to 1848. After the defeat of various revolutions in Europe in 1848, beliefs in political authenticity ceased to be linked with individualism. From 1848 on, individualism became inseparable from capitalism. We will have more to say about Enlightenment and Romantic individualism later in this work.

Table 2.3 summarizes the difference between Enlightenment and Romantic individualism. Table 2.4 connected up the seven elements of individualism and links them to the major historical periods and social movements of this book.

Table 2.3 Eighteenth Century Individualisms

Enlightenment individu-alism	Category of com-parison	Proto-Romanticism individualism
Persian letters **Montesquieu 1721**	**Text and author**	**Emile, confessions, essays** **Rousseau 1750 to 1778**
Plays many roles well	**Place of roles**	Challenges all roles Tear humanity's veils, costumes, and masks away to discover the faces, bodies, and souls beneath them.
Metropolis The breathless pace speaks of a great concentration of energy and intensity of life; a dazzling flux of constantly changing forms of life.	**Place of city life**	**City life is a diversion:** gambling, games These men who were in a hurry were compulsively driven out of themselves
Growth and abundance	**Place of material resources**	Scarcity and frugality
Empiricism and utilitari-anism Greatest good for the great-est number	**Sources for the self**	**Inauthenticity or Authenticity?** Self-revelation—through autobi-ographical writing
Associative, and instrumen-tal, liberal constitutional monarchy	**Type of political community**	**Organic**—general will of a participato-ry republic
Happiness, serenity wit and ingenuity	**Emotions**	Spontaneity and expressiveness, revelry
Nature as an end. **Sensibility,** the capacity for richness and depth of per-ception nature as she is	**How is nature seen?**	**Nature as a means** of catalyzing emo-tional irruptions
Legal equality	**What is the rela-tionship between individualist selves?**	**Economic equality courtesy of a material state** that makes no one rich enough to buy someone's labor; no one is poor enough to have to sell their labor
Education is a key to over-coming superstition and ignorance	**Place of education**	Education does not keep up with the times; an educated person must overcome habits; learning more the result of experienc-es (not books); no competition with others, only self-overcoming

Table 2.4 Individualism: Elements, Historical Movements and Major Theoreticians

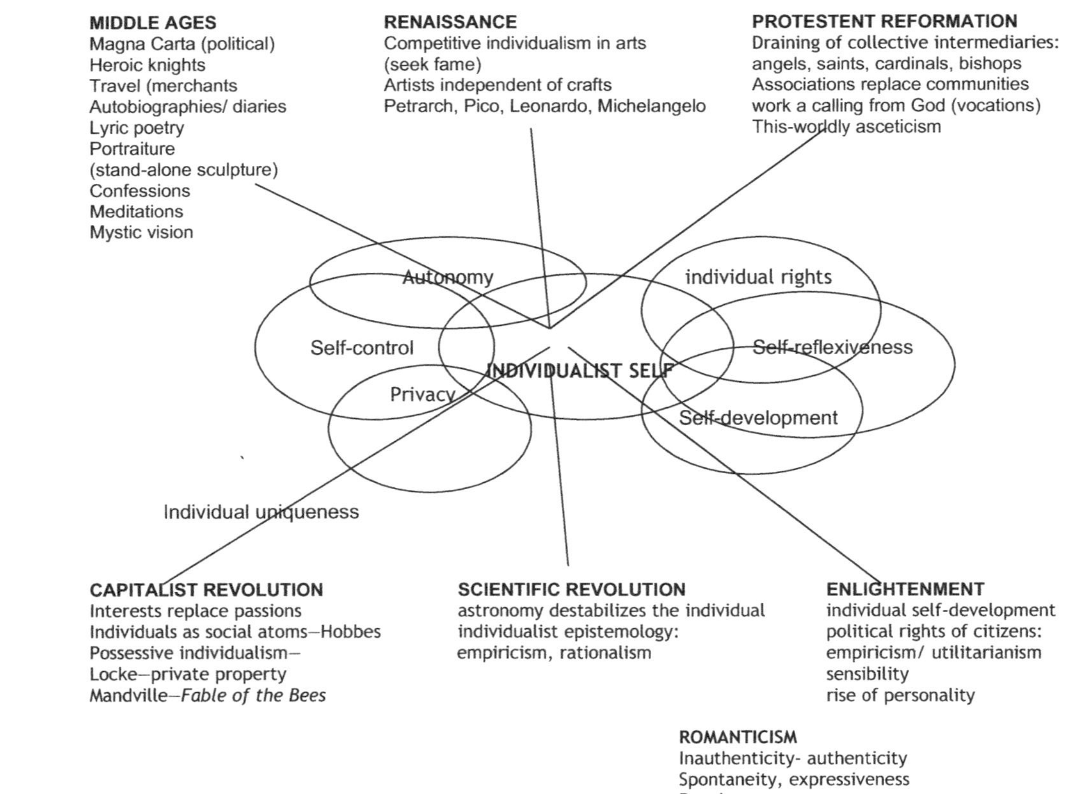
MIDDLE AGES
Magna Carta (political)
Heroic knights
Travel (merchants
Autobiographies/ diaries
Lyric poetry
Portraiture
(stand-alone sculpture)
Confessions
Meditations
Mystic vision
RENAISSANCE
Competitive individualism in arts
(seek fame)
Artists independent of crafts
Petrarch, Pico, Leonardo, Michelangelo
PROTESTENT REFORMATION
Draining of collective intermediaries:
angels, saints, cardinals, bishops
Associations replace communities
work a calling from God (vocations)
This-worldly asceticism
Autonomy
Self-control
Privacy
INDIVIDUALIST SELF
individual rights
Self-reflexiveness
Self-development
Individual uniqueness
CAPITALIST REVOLUTION
Interests replace passions
Individuals as social atoms—Hobbes
Possessive individualism—
Locke—private property
Mandville—*Fable of the Bees*
SCIENTIFIC REVOLUTION
astronomy destabilizes the individual
individualist epistemology:
empiricism, rationalism
ENLIGHTENMENT
individual self-development
political rights of citizens:
empiricism/ utilitarianism
sensibility
rise of personality
ROMANTICISM
Inauthenticity- authenticity
Spontaneity, expressiveness
Revelry

CHAPTER 3

Yankee Individualism: Its Spiritual, Economic and Political Foundations

Orientation: Stereotypes of Yankee individualism

Today, Geert Hofstede in his book *Culture's Consequences* ranks the United States as the most individualist country in the world. Has it always been this way? In order to answer this question, we have to ask the following questions:

- What is individualism to Americans?
- Is individualism seen as a positive or negative aspect of human nature?
- What political, economic or sources does individualism draw from?
- How much or little does Protestantism contribute to individualism?

What does individualism mean to most Americans? Usually it means having one's own business and making as much money as one likes. Americans have unconsciously internalized economic values originated from political economists Bernard Mandeville and Adam Smith. These theorists argued that by everyone pursuing their greedy, immediate self-interest, the result would be prosperity for all. Individualists have little responsibilities to neighbors or obligation to communities. Furthermore, competition between individuals can result in scientific innovation. Lastly, Americans pride themselves on being dissenters against traditional authorities such as kings, aristocrats or popes. On the negative side, collectivist societies and even other individualist societies in the West see

American individualism as materialistic, hedonistic, shallow, and anti-social. They say that these economic characteristics are *separated* from religious life so that every day but Sunday, cutthroat competition is the name of the game.

If you ask most Americans how far back in history this ideal goes, they will probably say all the way back. This country, we are told was founded by Individualists, it goes right back to the first English settlers. This belief however, was far from the reality in eighteenth-century America. In his book *This Sheba Self*, J. E. Crowley shows that individualism, the way we understand it today only began to emerge after the first two decades of the nineteenth century. Until then, the economic action of individuals was constrained by the Protestant religion with obligations to the community and driven by sense of guilt.

But this picture of the history of Yankee individualism has come under increasing criticism from religious historians. According to Barry Alan Shain, American political scientists are almost uniformly committed to Louis Hartz's claim that the United States was founded on liberal principles.

> Scholars Max Lerner (*America as a Civilization)*; Ralph Perry, (*Puritanism and Democracy)*; Yehoshua Arieli (*Individualism and Nationalism in American Ideology)*; and Bushman (*From Puritan to Yankee)* claim that eighteenth century was Individualistic. (12)

What about the sources of individualism? Is individualism primarily an expression of a secular political doctrine of republicanism or liberalism? Two of the most contentious debates are whether liberalism or republicanism best describes the political thinking of the founding fathers. Shain says that the claim for republican origins is *recent*, and that between 1760 and 1790, Americans were not yet dominated by an individualist ideology. Furthermore, *liberalism was for elite nationalists after 1790*. Most historians relate republicanism with the years of the revolution and liberalism to the early national period, between 1790 and 1820.

Is it fair to characterize the Protestant religion as individualistic? For Shain, this is the most important question of all. According to him, before there was either republicanism or liberalism, English Americans were religious. Thus if the Protestant religion was individualistic, it would seem to follow that republican and liberal traditions would be a natural extension. However, Shain's claim is that the Protestant religion in the United States was *not* individualistic in the way it was described by Max Weber.

Shain's thesis

Shain's argument consists of four major points:

- the oldest source from which American identity is formed is neither the liberal nor the republican tradition, but from the Protestant religion.
- the Protestant religion as practiced in America did not see individualism as a source of inspiration, a blessing or a driver of capitalist civilization. At its core it was sinful. What was virtuous was self-denial, the seeming opposite of individualism.

> Most revolutionary era Americans believed it was the legitimate and necessary role of local religious, familial, social and governmental forces to *limit, reform and shape the sinful individual.* These institutions would have to act restrictively and intrusively for in no other way would the recalcitrant and naturally deformed human being take on a godly and publicly useful shape. (13)

- Rather than a fleeting association of individualists focused on their own striving to enter the Kingdom of God in the next life, members of the Protestant religion had a social responsibility that was organically connected to the self. With the exception of Bush, most social historians today agree that most of late colonial American society was communalistic.

- the type of individualism most Americans conjure up in their imagination—'rugged' individualism—was a product of the nineteenth century, beginning with Jacksonian democracy. This democracy produced the 'imperial self' of Emerson and Whitman. In the second half of the nineteenth century, individualism turned politically rightward by advocates of social Darwinism. As we shall see, there were many kinds of liberty, and most of it had little to do with the characteristics of the individualist described in the previous section.

The Protestant identity was communalist, not individualist

The community triumphs over the individual

To say that Americans before the revolutionary era were not individualists does not mean they were collectivists in the style of China, India, or tribal societies. For colonials, public, benevolent religious good was more valued than individual freedom. And the bible was the most important source of meaning for Americans throughout the eighteenth century. According to Shain:

> Puritanism provided the moral and religious background of fully seventy-five percent of the people who declared their independence in 1776. And self-interestedness was the root vice. Until the end of the eighteenth century even the elite shared this view with the commoners. (195)

Puritans believed they were responsible for the behavior of their fellow citizens. Sometimes individuals were prevented from living alone and they were coerced into seeking public acceptance when they moved to a new town or when they left town. Even their clothing was chosen by legislation. In addition, they could be prosecuted for:

- not paying taxes to support a minister they might revile
- being economically unproductive or idling
- gambling or cockfighting
- dancing or putting on a ball

According to Shain, most Americans would never accept Hobbesian or Lockean notions that the rights of individuals were more important than public needs:

> Donald Lutz has shown that the first state constitutions assumed the rights of the community to be generally superior to the rights of the individual. (30) It was the rights of the majority and the common good that mattered. Even the framers of the federal constitution of 1787 were predominately concerned with guarding the public's, not the individual's, welfare and interests. (31)

Public community invades the family

Especially in the past hundred years, the family has been extracted out of the public realm and thought of as a sacred place away from all the wear and tear of public life. Yet this was hardly the case prior to the nineteenth century. Most communities did not recognize the border between local, community, and family as sacrosanct. Even the *parent-child* relationship was subject to communal intervention. The community was not an aggregation of individuals but an organism, functioning for a definite purpose, with all parts subordinate to the whole. Individual sacrifice was for them not a heroic act but a moral obligation. Fulfilling one's obligations comes before consent.

The family triumphs over the individual

The eighteenth-century individual had the following hierarchized set of loyalties:

- God
- his country which included neighbors and villages
- his family

The sinful and selfish individual came last. Contrary to Locke, Lord Bolingbroke said that civil governments were not formed by contracts between individuals but by associations of families. The individual and his family, living in economic independence among reformed Protestant communities with the blessing of Holy Ghost, was the highest form of personal liberty. Property was a means to the end of having economic independence. It wasn't an end in itself.

> Even into early twentieth century, familial independence continued to be the goal of many rural Americans. Owning your own farm, some good stock, being out of debt and having money in the bank. (192)

These were the highest values.

Local decentralization does not mean individualism

According to Shain, ninety-five percent of Americans in the eighteenth century lived in rural, agricultural communities. To persuade them to become loyal to the state and conscious of its problems would have constituted a vast broadening of their horizons that didn't even begin to occur until after the Civil War.

> Even as late as 1870 fewer than one-in four Americans lived in places of 2,500 or more. Not until 1920 would more than fifty percent of Americans live in cities or towns of more than 2500. (65)

Even today, local autonomy in the United States is highly valued, set against the shadow of a federal government. But what has also been smuggled into this local hostility to centralization has been an assumption that local autonomy and individualism are two peas in the same pod. This is not the case. According to Shain, localism in the United States has been confused with the French understanding of centralization, localism and the individual after the French Revolution.

According to Shain, both Tocqueville and Chevalier applied French, Catholic, monarchical, and universalistic standards to the politics and religions of Yankees as they visited. Yankee people who were neither Catholic nor monarchist. For revolutionary France, local organizations were *weak*, before and after their revolution. They were not highly respected, but rather dwarfed by a highly centralized state. For the French, the important relationship was between the centralized state and the atomistic individuals.

According to Shain, Perry Miller thought Tocqueville did not understand Protestantism. What made the United States different from France was the degree to which local communal concerns held their own against a weak state on the one hand and an autonomous individual on the other. On the one hand, each local community looked on each other as a source of competition rather than a unity. On the other hand, even when frontier villages challenged the centralizing tendencies of rural elites, they did not demand individual freedom but *corporate* freedom.

> Rights in the eighteenth century were thought of as restraining *arbitrary government* rather than liberating the individual. They offered scant protection to deviant individuals. (112)

Each local community looks on the other *as foreigners*. Even when frontier villages confronted the centralizing aspirations of rural elites, they demanded *corporate* not individual freedom.

> The central government of the colonies exercises even less control over local institutions than did the mother country over the colonies. (61) Americans did not want either the individualistic, competitive, commercialized social world or the centralized state like in Renaissance England where they fled. (64)

> From the Reformed Protestant perspective, any loss of corporate autonomy to extra-local religious social or governmental power made divine functions difficult to fulfill...American foundations of the good society were English and American local institutions which combined sacred and secular functions: parish, congregation and town meeting. (52)

Skepticism about the autonomous individual and negative liberty

According to Shain, Isaiah Berlin first popularized the difference between positive and negative freedom. Negative freedom meant freedom from state interference and the community. Positive freedom meant freedom to do things (mostly political or economic). For Berlin modern individualism is negative freedom. Yet there is this:

> The negative understanding of personal liberty was foreign to the revolutionary generation. They would have been uncomfortable with the idea that individuals should enjoy freedom from public and even from familial moral interference. The founding generation did not mean negative liberty from authority so much as the positive liberty towards the goals of a dedicated Christian life. To be free in a positive sense meant a good man has conquered himself and declared war against his in-bred unruly inclination. (119) They would have considered negative liberty as license. (120)

<u>Originally, liberty was spiritual, not political or economic</u>

It may come as a surprise to find out that secular, individual autonomy as we know it today would have been seen as a sinful degeneration in colonial days. An individual conscience which is not grounded in either divine law or political sovereignty would run the risk of becoming licentious. The nonconforming individual would be the subject of community conflict. This individual must either be reconciled with the community or driven out.

> According to Shain, the most important value of liberty was neither political nor economic, but *spiritual*. Americans did not believe political activity to be the most efficacious means of achieving the most elevated of human ends. True liberty was accorded with the dictates of God. No amount of individual reason, corporate political effort or republican heroics could remove the stain of original sin (262). The Fall made natural

liberty impossible. (279)

Politically, these Americans were not inspired by John Locke liberalism. Rather, they aimed for communal control and reciprocal dependence—governance which was guided by the Holy Spirit and reason.

> If the colonists had been primarily concerned with securing personal rather than corporate liberty they would have never sought independence from Britain because British subjects *had* these rights. (255)

Spiritual judgment was not given by God to directly to individuals. All Protestant individuals were joined in God through a covenant of grace. Calvin said people will be judged *collectively*, not personally, because of a national public covenant.

The early nineteenth century was not different in this regard. In America, British loyalist hopes for freedom of press, conscience and speech were *ignored* by intolerant majorities. Voltaire's radical skepticism found *few* adherents in America. Local communities did not care about the rights of non-residing individuals. Foreign travelers coming to the United States found the majority of Americans intolerant of individual diversity. In his book *Revolution of the Saints*, Michael Walzer argued that reformed Protestantism rested on voluntarist foundations, but it never led to a respect for *privacy*.

Religious individualism of the Quakers

Surprisingly, religious individualism does not begin among the New England Brahmins or the southern Anglicans but in the Middle colonies, with more of a mixture of Europeans than either the Northeast or the Southeast. Shain says the Quakers were the most individualistic, fighting off loyalty to social both and political corporativism. Unlike that of the Puritans, the Quakers' morality was private, not a matter for public concern. According to Shain, the Quakers were not only the first group in the United States to see the family as an emotional unit and private from public life; they were also the first group in all the Western world to do this.

•

Originally, economic relations were not individualistic

Bernard Mandeville argued that self-denial, while noble in practice,
would never lead to prosperity. This was because, as Nietzsche might say, virtue is just a *disguised form of self-interest*. Mandeville wanted to show that it was impossible to simultaneously enjoy the fruits of prosperity and remain virtuous. Being virtuous meant you were not prosperous; and if you were prosperous, you were not practicing virtue. Mandeville was not advocating being *un*virtuous; he was just saying you can't expect to be virtuous and prosperous at the same time. According to Crowley, Mandeville accepted the contemporary understanding of virtue as the subordination of personal desires to the community. He was not arguing that virtue is a fraud. Rather, there were two possibilities: *either being virtuous without prosperity, or having vices while also being prosperous.*

Mandeville argued way beyond what American historians (let alone the American public) wanted to hear. The public wanted to believe that it was possible to be virtuous and prosperous. Because Mandeville said this was impossible, his readers thought he was advocating committing vices.
According to Crowley, his views were so shocking to his readers that they misinterpreted him as justifying self-interest and recommending that people act according to vices. Instead, people wanted to be virtuous *and* prosperous, which Mandeville said was impossible. According to Mandeville, with the liberation of selfish appetites, luxury would decline and poverty would

increase. Mandeville came to the conclusion that selfishness was both unavoidable and basic to prosperity. In a way, the values of Puritanism were an answer to Mandville's challenge.

Man's active nature and his social responsibilities

According to Crowley, Americans inherited two assumptions about human nature from their English Protestant background which would shape their attitudes towards work. First, humanity is an active species, yet we depended on others for our survival. However, the actions of others needed to be efficient. God created humanity to be *stewards* of the earthly resources, and God was keeping track of what resources were used as well as how effectively or badly they were cultivated. The importance of work to Puritans was so all-pervasive that even in the afterlife God would put people to work.

Industry, frugality, and prosperity as the ideal

If Puritans were committed to working hard then naturally they would produce material goods. So, how could they keep from falling in love with the products they created? According to Crowley, if industry could be harmonized with frugality, that could be rationally harmonized to serve the interests of others rather than wallowing in luxury. Industry and frugality resulted in prosperity, a middle ground between poverty on the one hand and luxury on the other.

For different social classes, prosperity would bring about different motivations to work. The Puritans were essentially middle class. They believed that their formula for prosperity wouldn't work for the poor and working class, because the lower classes were lazy and would work only enough to get by. If they succeeded, instead of working harder they would work less. Cotton Mather made no bones about his disgust with the idle poor. It was better, he said, that they starve to death rather than they waste the time and energy of those who were working. Helping the poor should be limited because poverty was seen as inevitable as long as people insisted on being lazy.

Economic reciprocity

Unlike the current-day stereotypes of American individualism, the American colonists sought an integration of the individual with the community. They saw selfishness as sinful. Today, the total wealth that is produced as a result of capitalism appears to be infinitely expandable, but to the Puritans wealth was fixed. Wealth was a zero-sum game: when someone gained, others lost. Signs of social development were evidenced in economic redistribution. Extension of credit from one member of the community to another was expected. They were horrified at the prospect of treating consumers as complete strangers to whom they had no responsibility. The primary reason for trade was the mutuality reciprocity of goods and services. Profit was a secondary consideration.

Liberty consisted of having economic control of property. To control one's labor meant to own property. To own no property and to have to work for someone else for wages was to be a slave. Enslavement for Americans was *economic dependency.*

It wasn't the market per se that was looked upon suspiciously, but the *commercialization* of markets which would permeate social life and result in the following:

- *impersonality* of relations between buyers and sellers
- the systematization of the range of applicability of exchange values as opposed to use values
- the specialization of rules in buying and selling
- the vertical integration of the economy for market exchange
- the flexibility of prices as a function of competition and the use of money

Luxury and self-indulgence

Industry and frugality were opposed to the vices of luxury and self-indulgence, which were seen by the colonists as 'unmanly.' Luxury resulted from idleness, not work. There were some situations in which too much wealth could lead to a *reduction* of industry. For the Puritans, the history of commerce was inheritably a cyclical one because the development of trade led eventually to luxury, which brought about the decay of commerce as men reduced their exertions. Both the exploitation of others and the accumulation of goods made producers *dependent*; and independence was a core Puritan value. The rational control over the passions was dependent on the intercession of the Holy Spirit. The inability to be independent meant to fall into spiritual slavery to Satan because of original sin.

Here is a summary of American virtues and vices in the early eighteenth century:

Virtues	**Vices**
industry	self-indulgence
frugality	luxury
activity	passivity
independence	dependence
manliness	emasculation
order	disorder (idleness)

Mercantilism as a temporary fix for Puritan anxiety about wealth

In this climate of economic reciprocity, how can we bridge the gap from here to the free market economics of Adam Smith that American capitalism is famous for? To answer this, we start with the English mercantilists. The triumph of laissez-faire capitalism associated with Adam Smith is not part of economic policy of America until well into the nineteenth century. The notion of the economy *as a separate entit*y as was developed in the nineteenth century was an undeveloped idea in the century prior.

It was through another economic philosophy known as mercantilism, a state-centered policy which tried to understand the dynamics of economics *between* states instead of within states. Unlike Adam Smith's free-market philosophers, who viewed the amount of economic wealth in the world as infinite, the mercantilists, like the Puritans believed that the amount of wealth in the world was fixed. States were in mortal competition with each other in a zero-sum game. To them, one country's addition meant another country's loss. Mercantilism helps to explain the fierce competition between states for colonies between 1600 and 1750, and why countries like England forbade its colonies in the United States to trade. In addition, mercantilists did not think that all merchants should be allowed to engage in free trade. The state granted monopoly powers to some companies and denied it to others. The primary reason for foreign trade was to accumulate credits, so that necessities could be imported without weakening the overall wealth of the domestic economy.

Secondly, mercantilists had a very concrete notion of what wealth was: the amount of gold and silver a country had in its state treasury. This meant that mercantilists wanted to have a favorable balance of trade, with exports always being higher than imports. They erected tariffs and subsides to protect their domestic industries. Within the domestic economy they thought that full employment was vital because it would maximize the wealth a country produced.

Unlike Adam Smith, mercantilists had no sense of the labor theory of value. For Smith, as for Ricardo and Marx, wealth wasn't just an object like gold or silver. Behind gold and silver there was a process of work. What was the *cost of labor* to produce gold and silver? How many hours it took workers to go into the mines, extract the gold or silver bring it up from the mines and transport it to state treasuries? Mercantilists believed that wages should be kept at the subsistence level because higher wages would mean workers would lower their work effort. Because mercantilists had little sense of the importance of consumption or the domestic economy, they did not understand that if workers did not make enough to buy the products off the shelves, profits could not be generated for capitalists. The discrepancy between potential and actual wealth was a constant source of anxiety about the soundness of their society.

Furthermore, because mercantilists did not understand currencies as relative to the cost of labor, they tended to be inflexible about the kind of currency used. If currency was not gold and silver it was looked at as suspicious or worthless. They felt that changes in the quantity of currency was directly translatable into how much wealth a country possessed. As we can imagine, without lighter and more easily transportable currency, this would slow down the rate of exchange of goods and services. For mercantilists, the US economy going off the gold standard in 1971 would be proof that it had no wealth. But what does all this have to do with the gradual emergence of competitive individualism between Americans?

The philosophy of mercantilism allowed religious Americans to cultivate their competitive economic impulse and direct them *at other countries* rather than at their fellow Americans within their borders. For Americans *the economic system of mercantilism allowed them to maintain their religious piety and morality in governing their relations within society while they saved whatever competitive, amoral economic exchanging for foreign nations.*

Provincial mercantilism in America

The colonists tried to adopt the economic theory which was dominant in England. but because of their political subordination to the English, they were not allowed to adopt mercantilism as a full national economic policy. Their import and export exchanges were the *reverse* of mercantilists. Rather than produce manufactured goods, they imported them. And rather than import staples, they exported them. However, the colonialists were held to the same policies as mercantilists in seeing the need for full employment, low interest rates and a favorable balance of trade.

Like their British masters, the colonists considered the skilled manual labor of artisan and farmers to be the most valuable of all occupations. Merchants were seen as more trustworthy when they engaged in external trade than in internal commerce. Recognition of the market did not necessarily legitimate *individual* activities in it. Provincial mercantilism made the notion of self-interest tolerable because it postulated the possibility that conflicts in the domestic economy were *avoidable*.

Rather than merchants under mercantilism theory, *landowners* were thought to be the natural guardians of public interests. According to mercantile theory, shopkeepers caught between manual work and the landowners contributed nothing to society. Lastly there was a reason why Americans emphasized the importance of frugality rather than industry with the British:

> Because of the Americans need and propensity to apply foreign credits to the purchase of manufacturing goods and their lack of sufficient economic development to provide manufactured goods for exportation, provincial mercantilism stressed frugality more than industry. For the colonists, useless imports were usually items of conspicuous consumption. (*This Sheba Self*, 89)

Americans weren't fully aware they were not a single system under British rule, but two competing economic systems.

> It seldom occurred to them that two different sorts of economic policy applied to Great Britain and the colonies. Provincial mercantilism was not a critique of the American involvement in the British system. With the development of a nonimportation movement in the 1760's, the latent conflict over the locus of mercantilist interests surfaced

> and became party of the grounds for American alienation from Britain. (*This Sheba Self*, 90)

The value of work

We now turn from the conflict about the nature of economic exchange to conflicting attitudes about work. Does the prosperity that work produces have spiritual value, or is it a distraction from spiritual piety? Is the social order that work produces an expression of God's work or is society a chaotic mess, a reform school for spiritual seekers?

According to Crowley, until about 1730 the God of Calvinism demands not just *occasional* good works as in Catholicism, but a *life* of good works which should be carried out by a specific method. The belief that work was a calling from God, a *vocation*, dominated American ideas about work. Yet Cotton Mather suggested that there should be some personal *autonomy* in determining one's work other than a simple demand from God. This trend continued so that by 1750 colonists talked about work without *any* necessary reference to God's Order.

On the one hand, ethics of the calling condemned the enjoyment of material success partly because it might involve:

- submission to temptations of the flesh
- a distraction from the duties of their vocations
- desire for increased wealth, which might lead to a *denial* on the notion of man's dependence of God

Contrary to extreme individualist interpretation of the calling, there was a *reluctance* to assert self-sufficiency in finding one's vocation. But this did not become a problem until well into the nineteenth century.

Individual identity about the calling went through three phases:

- the calling as described by Calvin—this calling included

community responsibility
- the religious reaction against the calling during the Great Awakening
- the increasing *secularization* of the calling and the justification of its activity based on economic necessity by itself; this represented a major change from an earlier, more social evaluation of work

The Great Awakening and the critique of the calling

According to Phillip Cushman (*Constructing the Self, Constructing America)* the Great Awakening was a way to dampen tension between the Puritanical selves' faithfulness of the community and an expanding entrepreneurial self that emerged in the wake of Andrew Jackson's presidency. The first Great Awakening in the New England colonies were collective emotional experiences led by Jonathan Edwards. These small communities were dedicated to a God who they imagined smothered any individualism. These new charismatic leaders did not advocate self-reflection and a deliberating ledger for self-improvement. The important thing was to be converted instantaneously. Awakening was the unmediated experience of God through use of the senses.

In the Great Awakening, the evangelical clergy attacked what they believed to be the inappropriate spiritual significance attributed to the calling. They felt that spiritual callings could not be reduced to a livelihood and the fulfillment of a social role. The notion that the social order had a divine sanction lost acceptance. Rather, society was a reform school for the afterlife and should not be taken too seriously. These evangelicals lacked confidence that the social order was an expression of God's will. For them, society was a shapeless order, and getting caught up in its social and economic structures would lure people away from spiritual life. According to Crowley, an evangelical's indifference to the place of work in spiritual life goes back to the story of the Garden of Eden. Human beings were most spiritual in a state of innocence *before* work was necessary. For evangelicals, work was a penance for the original sin of eating from the Tree of Knowledge. To glorify an act that was a penance was to miss the forest for the trees. As we saw previously, wealth had been a source of anxiety. Now it was condemned.

An unintended consequence for the evangelical movement was that by driving a wedge between spirituality and work it inadvertently promoted the value of considering work and commerce as *secular* pursuits. Faced with this repudiation of the traditional social ethic, the non-clergy *defended* the demonized secular importance of the calling. Why? Because evangelicals could be dismissed as otherworldly and in revolt against God's material creation. Rather than being preoccupied by the altering states of consciousness in religious revival meetings, work enabled good Christians to achieve a spiritual dignity in daily life. Charles Chauncey criticized the revivalists, claiming that parishioners had social duties to attend to besides revivalist meetings. By the

middle of the eighteenth century, the calling had a more secular relevance to social organization.

Here is a summary of the differences between Non-Evangelicals and Evangelicals.

Non-Evangelicals	**Evangelicals (Great Awakening)**
Charles Chauncey	Jonathan Edwards
Vocation as a calling from God	Any vocation is the result of original sin Spiritual existence does not involve working (Garden of Eden)
Prosperity has religious value	Prosperity has no religious value
Economic activity of redistribution has value	All economic activity is questionable
Conformity and standards are important	Spiritual experience matters more than
Social order is an expression of God's will	Producing social order through work is not important
Fulfilling roles in everyday life is important	everyday life is important

Adam Smith and laissez-faire

Up until now, there was as yet no intellectual framework which legitimately supported the unhindered pursuit of individual interest. There continued to be a persistent resistance to considering humanity as *only* in their economic beings. According to William Appleman Williams (*Contours of American History)* the laissez-faire philosophy emerged around 1820 and lasted to 1896. Crowley points out:

> America, especially from the second to the sixth decade was the scene of an extraordinary economic expansion characterized by the involvement of the mass of the population in commercial life. Few Americans were all self-sufficient, and nearly everyone was involved in the economic ties of the market and credit, a situation marked by the prevalent use and demand for currency from 1720 onward. (*This Sheba Self*, 77)

According to Crowley, the major reasons for this change included the increase in population and the sale of staple exports. With a rise in population combined with a greater demand, there was a motivation to raise the standard of living. As society required greater organization in order compete internationally, the evangelicals' image of society as a weakly organized reform school lost credibility. The meaning of previous vices such as idleness, extravagance and pride shifted from vices that offended God to vices that harmed *society* and the *individual*. Even religious leaders saw these as less as sins and more as personal and social vices.

By the late 1740s, Americans had worked out a scheme of *enlightened* self-interest which could take men's acquisitive inclination into account without a bad conscience. Adam Smith was very cautious about unleashing self-interest as was shown in his ethical writing *A Theory of Moral Sentiment*.

He both championed the social consequences of acquisitiveness for the production of prosperity and was fearful that a psychological reason for acquisitiveness—the drive for approval—might undermine self-respect. For Smith, happiness did not derive from unleashing desires but from restraining them. Such restraint brought about tranquility.

Smith hoped that his picture of market dynamics would not only undermine mercantilist theory between societies, but he wanted that his laisser-faire principles operate within the national level. Within the community, economics could still be governed by rationality in productive work. But people's acquisitive urges could be unleashed *internationally*, in meeting the needs of society as a whole. Humanity had to lose its fear that unrestrained selfishness was inherently anti-social.

Justifications of the free market

More down-to-earth Americans joined Smith in arguing that life would be very difficult without the material benefits made possible by commerce. The problem with barter was it was more disorganized and unpredictable in the availability of goods. It also lacked standardization between commodities as well as being subject to the moods of traders. On the other hand, the rationality of commerce was evident in its ability to overcome physical limitations of space and time through the use of money. After the development of commerce, people were encouraged to *maximize* their production. The increase in the number of towns were also necessary for economic efficiency and diversification. Towns provided places of storage, where the cost of shipping could be reduced. The invention of canals helped to civilize the frontier. Merchants began to be seen in a more favorable light and equally suited to act in the public interest. While being wealthy could not guarantee happiness of each individual, it did seem to create 'the greatest happiness for the greatest number.'

Occasionally, there were hints of understanding that the old social ideal of work relations of the early Puritans was out of step with complexity of work organization by the middle of the eighteenth century. More and more work was considered a means to an end, rather than an end in itself. The old Puritanical framework of reciprocity driven by a belief that this reciprocity was doing God's work, faced competition from a new utilitarianism that was more personal and less community-oriented. Still, it was rare that someone came forward with the nerve to declare that private vices could result in public benefits.

Richard Bushman claimed in *From Puritan to Yankee* that after the Great Awakening rationalists defined public good as no more than the sum of individual goods. They thought self-interest could be given free rein and could be the very basis of society, provided it was *enlightened*. Benjamin Franklin, ever the spokesman for weighting the pros and cons of actions bluntly, said:

> Who is there that can be handsomely supported in affluence, ease and pleasure by another, that will choose rather to earn his bread by the sweat of his own brows? The candor with which he discussed the pursuit of self-interest distinguished him from other men. (122)

Richard Jackson, a correspondent of Franklin's, declared himself a follower of Locke's understanding of social motivation and natural right. The end of every individual was its own private good. The perfection of commerce was not complete until *every good had its price*.

The emergence of individual Self-Interest

The Non-importation movement against the English that had dampened the spirit of acquisitiveness lost its momentum when Parliament repealed the Townsend Duties (except on tea). Furthermore, after the American Revolution there were no longer political constraints in acquisitiveness. Any restraint on trade was associated with British corruption. In addition, the new political and economic independence required a productive urgency that grew more powerful while spiritual considerations took a back seat. Economic expansion made sense in a country that seemed to have unlimited natural resources.

As Crowley says, credit replaced virtuous reciprocity as a principle of public action. Credit meant not a faith in a common spiritual community of individuals but rather a faith in the commercial values of punctuality and consistency in honoring contracts.

Political identity: Republicans and Liberals

Shain says that eighteenth-century Americans had three groups from which to form an American political identity:

- the true elite such as Washington, Jefferson and Franklin (these were Republicans)
- a middle group which includes state and local jurists and the most eminent ministers (these were liberal Protestants)
- the obscure farmer-citizens of the eighteenth century (these were Democrats)

<u>The first Yankee individualists: Republicans of the Enlightenment</u>

According to Shain, it was in the last decades of the eighteenth century that Protestant ideas about liberty being local and communal began to clash with a form of liberty championed by Republicans like Franklin, Jefferson and Washington. Their ideas were politically patriotic and more individualistic.
While Republicans agreed that the public good should be valued over the private good, they did so because of being *virtuous*, rather than for religious reasons. When the common good was sacrificed, it was because people were corrupt. It was a *secular* failure (a vice) rather than a *religious* failure (a sin).

For Protestants, while doing one's duty and being a material success might be signs of being saved, the reward for virtuous behavior for Republicans was public fame. As Alasdair Macintyre points out, without a pubic to serve, the individual would be without an audience for his deeds. He would be blocked from attaining 'pagan salvation'—glory, honor and everlasting memory. The liberty to engage in corrupting vices would only lead to unhappiness. For republicans, political liberty meant actively participating in the crafting of the laws. Equality for republicans, however, did not mean equality between people but among governing bodies that were *constitutional*. Shain points out that a fully worked-out republicanism did not occur until the mid-nineteenth century. Somewhat ironically, it was used to justify slavery. What was missing in revolutionary America were the voices of radical European Republicans who insisted that *all* citizens should actively participate.

Meanwhile, a rural and reformed Protestant American population did not see politics as an end in itself but instead a means to serve a higher spiritual purpose. These Protestant Yankees drew from Biblical sources for their inspirations rather than classical Rome:

> Americans were not dedicated practitioners of classical or Renaissance republicanism. Scant evidence exists that they were. Most Americans' understanding of human fulfillment was *not* intrinsically linked to political life. (320) They were students of Scottish commonsense philosophy and English law and localist agrarian traditions. (321)

Reformed Protestants, unlike Republicans, did not believe political liberty consisted in actively shaping the laws. That was the work of its representatives. Political liberty consisted of the active *consent* of the majority. When laws are broken, people are tried by their peers. It was active consent which was neither passive acquiescence nor direct participation of the republicans which appealed to reformed Protestants.

We saw in chapter two (when we contrasted Enlightenment and proto-Romantic individualism in Europe) that city life was a big part of Enlightenment individualism centered in Paris. But among Yankee Republicans, individualism was less centered in cities. Jefferson and Washington practiced an agricultural form of capitalism. An exception was Franklin, who was rooted in Philadelphia. Franklin's ideas on how to improve personal life was a secularized re-make on some Puritan ideas. Franklin was influenced by Jeremy Bentham's utilitarianism, where virtues simply brought pleasure, while vices brought pain. Franklin's thirteen virtues had much overlap with how Puritans were inspired to act. Franklin was extremely pragmatic in that he did not encourage people to embody all thirteen virtues at once. Rather he encouraged people to work on one per week. In his lists for self-improvement, quantitative calculations of the pros and cons of any decision were not done for religious purposes. Rather it was in the service of a happy life.

Table 3.1 Protestants versus Republicans

Reformed Protestants	Category of comparison	Republicans
Jonathan Edwards	**Theoreticians**	Washington, Jefferson, Hamilton Defenders of slavery
Lower-middle, farmers	**Social class**	Upper-middle, upper
Means to religious ends	**What is politics?**	End in itself
The Bible Scottish common-sense philosophy and English law	**Sources**	Classical Rome
Shaping the laws by direct participation	**What is political participation?**	Active consent to representatives who make the laws
Doing God's will	**Benefits of contributing to the public realm**	Being virtuous
Sin	**Consequences of not contributing to the public realm**	Corruption; production of vices
Private salvation with God in the next life	**Long-term benefits**	'Pagan salvation' of acquiring fame glory, honor in the eyes of posterity

Crisis of working-class whites in the early nineteenth century

The Great Awakening planted the first seeds of an individualist self, at least among the working class. But after the American Revolution of independence from the British, the need to build up its own national economy forced American men to face the reality of an expanding commercial life and the competition that would ensue. As Phillip Cushman says:

> The growing urbanization, industrialism, secularism and immigration combined to produce a disorientation and confusion for people who

> were alienated, uncertain, and frightened of the future. (40)

As is often the case, when a new identity is being searched for, the individual defines itself by what appears to be its opposite. In the United States, two groups played the role of the foil for white American men: African slaves and Native Americans. Cushman tells us:

> It was easier to develop a sense of what the self was *not*: lazy, stupid Negro or heathen savage Indian. This was done through the vehicles of popular theater and political discourse. Minstrel stagings and popular conceptions of the "wild west" served as technologies. (41)

For a summary of these contrasts please see Table 3.2

Table 3.2 Constructing the White Self

Negro self	**White Self**	**Native American Self**
Slave	Yeoman farmer (hard-working)	Hunter-gatherer (perceived as lazy)
Clownish; foolish	Serious; deliberative	Stoic
Dependent	Independent	Communal
Foppish costumes of a pimp or musician	Plainly dressed; prim and proper	Feathers; dressed as animals
Skilled in music, song and dance through ceremonies	Withdraws from the arts, which are seen as satanic temptations of the imagination	Skilled in music, song and dance through ceremonies
Good spirits all the time (child-like)	Glum	
Fickle	Humble; Persevering	
Untrustworthy	Trustworthy	Untrustworthy
Sexual	Sexually repressed (gratification delay)	Sexual (exposure of flesh)
Present-oriented	Future-oriented (delayed gratification)	Present-oriented
	Save money / accumulate capital	Spend money

Liberalism

As we saw in the previous chapters, in mid-seventeenth century Europe the absolutist state had its justifiers in Bodin and Hobbes. In their scenario, competing selfish individuals would be emulsified by the power of the state once the individual was freed from reactionary feudal, intermediate groups such as regional or village loyalties. In France, Benjamin Constant developed an individualist vision of civil liberty which Isaiah Berlin claimed was the foundation of modern liberal individualism.

But neither the right-wing liberalism of Hobbes nor the left-wing liberalism of Constant got any footing in the United States during colonial times, even after the revolution. It was only at the very end of the eighteenth century that this liberal kind of liberty caught on and only then among a small minority. By the end of the eighteenth century, civil liberty had begun to be used to describe two senses of liberty that were distinct from political liberty:

- the old Anglo-American corporate and communal understanding of liberty of the Protestants
- a liberty of individual rights, privileges, and exceptions

The debates over the Constitution included an understanding that civil liberty was designed to protect the right of individuals against intermediate groups.

Shain claims that the greatest American defender of *individual* rights was James Madison. Madison wanted two kinds of protection:

- protection of the rights of private property
- protection of the rights of those individual rights likely to be threatened by democratic majority, probably elites.

Without directly challenging the importance of the

Puritanical public good, he included self-interested behavior as compatible with it.

Growth of national patriotism over localism

Madison also wanted to create a myth of a sovereign *national* people. In this he was not alone. Local cultural differences got caught in the crosshairs of the Enlightenment philosophers. As cosmopolitans, they believed that local attachments led to narrow-mindedness of outlook and superstition. In the States, by the end of the eighteenth century, localism was rejected by national elites who supported nationalism. In the same period, communalism began to lose its ethnical importance for Americans. Hamilton, for one, said that the Federal government is like the solar system that must control the centrifugal tendency of States without which they would continually fly out of their proper orbits. Only in the last decade of the eighteenth century would some Yankees learn to speak the language of patriotism and individualism.

Nineteenth-century individualism and the Constitution

In spite of onslaughts of both Republicanism and Liberalism, most Americans were *opposed* to the French individualism that inspired Liberalism. Yet a modern understanding of the self was slowly chaperoned in under the wings of philosophy, religion, politics, and the arts. Even by the end of the eighteenth century there were still many for whom the human self was still sinful. The term 'individualism' itself was not invented until the nineteenth century. Gordon Wood claims it was not the Declaration of Independence that formed the basis of personal freedom, but it was the *Constitution*, which was neither a Protestant nor a Republican document:

> The purpose of the Constitution is not to serve God or shape or care for souls, but to protect individuals in their absolute rights which were

> invested in them by the immediate laws of nature. It was self-interest, not virtue, that was the most prevalent characteristic of their fellow citizens. (142-3)

With the Constitution's adaptation, the moral, economic and political life of the states became concentrated in the document. The Constitution sucked the life out of public morality, politics, and economics at a local level. The aims of political life were limited to the securing of the rights of minorities while promoting and protecting the rights of property as well as commercial activity.

Conclusion

As Shain argues, Yankees *backed* into modernity in the nineteenth century. The process of forming individualism was neither linear, gradual nor purposeful. Rather Yankees were a confused and reactionary people, trying to manage the titanic forces of economic growth based on an abundance of natural resources, as well as their sudden political independence from England. They tried and eventually failed to integrate these disruptive forces into an unyielding localist communalism and reformed public Protestant philosophy. As we will see in the next chapter, the reign of extreme individualism came about in Jacksonian America in the 1820s. The rise and spread of cities in the nineteenth century and the loss of small-town communal life that had been the foundation of Protestant resistance to individualism was marginalized.

The individualism in the nineteenth century went through four types. First was a kind of frontier individualism associated with the Jacksonian period. Second was a mystical type of individualism, associated with Emerson and Whitman. Third was the 'rugged individualism' of social Darwinism of the 1870s and 1880. The fourth kind was a type of crypto-romanticism that developed in large part as a reaction to the downside of the industrial revolution and the rise of corporations.

Were the chains that bind us invented by society from which we could break away from, as in Rousseau? Or was the community a pale imitation of a higher, spiritual unity in the next life? Was the individual heroic, in the way presented by John Stuart Mill, or was the individual sinful wretch who could only live a rational life with the intervention of the community? Often, Yankee individualism is contrasted with the individualism of the French over the question of whether the individual is primarily communal (Rousseau) or private. But as we have seen, the Protestant individualism of the colonies was not a *political* dream of the prevalence of the general will of Rousseau. It was a *spiritual* dream of a true covenant.

Table 3.3 Competing Political and Spiritual Views of American Individualism

Category of comparison	Rationalism Liberal (Enlightenment)	Republicanism Classical, Renaissance or Whig	Reformed Protestantism
Anthropocentric or theocentric views of the cosmos?	Anthropocentric	Anthropocentric	Theocentric
Was the individual seen as a unitary fashion, or radically divided between elevated and base elements?	Radically divided between base and elevated elements	Natural virtues not very separated from vices; thirst for glory, honor Polity can guide and direct its moral life	Radically divided between base and elevated elements Divine intervention needed
Public good		Yes, but without insisting on stripping away what made the individual unique	Yes, but insisting on stripping away made the individual unique
Theoretical Representatives	Madison Paine	Hamilton (character, reputation) Washington	Jonathan Edwards
Place of pre-social rights	Yes	No	No
Time period	End of eighteenth century (1790-1820)	1790's	Sixteenth century onward
American historians **European historians**	Louis Hartz (Liberal Idea of Richard Bushman— *From Puritan to Yankee)* Ralph Perry Arieli Bodin, Hobbes, Locke	Bayniens Reformists Pangle *(Spirit of Modern Republicanism)* Pocock (applied to the U.S.)	Perry Miller *(Errand into the Wilderness)*
Size of unit	Centralized state	City	Localism
Place of rationalism	Distinguished from license "It is only when reason was freed from ignorance, error, lust, passion and bias that it is made their guide." (44)	Reason used to decide in political participation debates	Works well when guided by the Holy Spirit
Representatives	Madison, Paine	Washington, Jefferson, Hamilton	Jonathan Edwards
Region of the country	Middle colonies (more diverse)	South	North or South (more homogeneous)
Attitudes towards Political minorities	Individuals compete; tolerance of minorities	Intolerance of minorities	Intolerance of minorities
Type of freedom	Negative freedom	Positive freedom	Positive freedom
Religious groups	Quakers—morality is private matter Charity	Deists	Puritans—morality is a public matter No charity

CHAPTER 4

Varieties of Yankee individualism from the early nineteenth century through the Gilded Age

Orientation

In chapter three, we came to understand that the communitarian spirit of the United States goes all the way back to the Puritans. At the end of that chapter, we discussed briefly that the first real form of individualism in the United States was the Republican individualism most typified by Benjamin Franklin. But this individualism was an individualism for elite intellectuals like Washington and Jefferson. It wasn't until the second decade of the nineteenth century that individualism spread to farmers, frontiersman, mechanics, and merchants. But not only did individualism get stronger, it also changed.

In chapter four, we divide the individualist self in the nineteenth and early twentieth century into four types and each type appeals predominantly to one social class more than others:

- early nineteenth century individualist self–farmers, mechanics, frontiersman. and merchants which we will call *utilitarian individualism*
- the mid-nineteenth-century *spiritual individualism* of Emerson, Thoreau and Whitman
- the *entrepreneurial individualism* of the social Darwinists (these were capitalists looking for a justification for their rule in light of the rise of working-class militancy)
- in the late nineteenth century an *expressive, romantic* type of individualism emerged from an anxious middle class caught between the working class on the one hand and the corporations which arose at the end of the

nineteenth century on the other

In his book *Dilemmas of the American Self,* John Hewitt nicely summarizes how different authors have characterized two bookends of individualism, utilitarian and romantic. In the *Lonely Crowd,* David Riesman contrasts the difference between the 'inner-directed' self of the nineteenth century with the 'outer-directed' self of the twentieth century. Psychoanalyst Allen Whellis argues that the in the early nineteenth century, 'character' was largely driven by a superego and that this had declined with the emergence of 'personality' by the mid-twentieth-century. Robert Bellah, in his book *Habits of the Heart,* says that there has been a decline of biblical and Republican traditions in America. A utilitarian individualism based on the accumulation of resources has been replaced by a psychological 'expressive' individualism in the mid-twentieth-century. Ralph Turner's contrast between the 'institutional self' and the 'impulsive self' is similar to Reisman's book. Christopher Lasch characterizes this expressive, impulsive self as 'narcissistic'. For the narcissist, the world is a mirror, whereas the rugged individualist of the nineteenth century farmer or entrepreneur saw the world as an empty wilderness to be shaped by his own design. Narcissists *act out* their conflicts instead of repressing or sublimating them. Phillip Cushman and Richard Sennett argue that 'character' describes individualism of the early nineteenth century and "personality" characterizes individualism in the late nineteenth and early twentieth century. Lastly, cultural studies theorists Chris Rojek and Leo Brandy contrast the desire for 'fame' from the desire to be a 'celebrity'. To be famous means to be remembered in posterity based on reputation for things done. This desire for fame has been common among most of the upper classes throughout history. But by the end of the nineteenth century, notoriety was not based on personality, not achievements. Impulsive selves want to be recognized as celebrities for who they are, not what they've done.

Here is a summary of the way theorists have framed the kinds of individualists:

Early nineteenth century	Theorists	Late nineteenth and twentieth centuries
Inner directed	Reisman	Outer directed
Super-ego	Whellis	Ego
Institutional self	Turner	Impulsive self
Utilitarian individualism	Bellah	Expressive individualism
Character	Sennett, Cushman	Personality
Rugged individualism	Lasch	Narcissism
Fame	Chris Rojek, Leo Brandy	Celebrity

What we must keep in mind, however, are geographical and demographic shifts from a *community* composed of farmers to a *society* that is based on city-life and its industrialized citizens. This change goes a long way to explaining the differences between the two kinds of individualism.

Hewitt's thesis: from community to society

Hewitt suggests that the biggest change that has occurred in the United States is less between the individual and the community, but rather between community and society. What do the rise of cities from towns and villages of the eighteenth century do to communitarian spirit? What does the industrial revolution of the nineteenth century do to communities? According to Hewitt, society is the macro-social institutions which exist at regional and national levels. Communities are small, simple, and enclosing, providing security while producing what Hewitt calls a 'social identity'. In contrast, societies are large, complex, expanding, preoccupied with performing and cultivating a 'personal identity'.

Hewitt's theory of identity

According to Hewitt, a person knows their identity when they know: who they are, where they have been, where they are going, what they are doing, how they are similar to others, and how they are different. However, keeping the answers to these questions stable is not possible because the individual changes through experience over the course of a lifetime. The meaning of a divorce at twenty-two will mean different things to the same person at age thirty-four. So too, a person's work goals at twenty-two will be very different than the same person's work goals at thirty-four. The second reason why all these parts of identity are always changing is that the *socio-historical setting* is changing. An individual's answer to the question of what they are doing at work will change if corporations decide to hire immigrant middle class managers to whom they can pay lower salaries. A large component of who a person's identity is embedded in the place where they live. If the instability of the economy forces a person to move every three years, their sense of who they are will be dislocated in space.

Let's break down more specifically what these components of identity are. 'Who they are' refers to the continuity of self in face of external change. That is, who the person remains in the present. But they are also connected to what has gone before and what will come later. Disruptions to these things, such as finding out your partner has been cheating on you for many years, will rock your identity as a marriage partner. The impact of a stock market crash on your pension may force you to alter your plans for how you expect to live over the next twenty years. Who an individual is then involves where they have been and where they are going.

What a person is doing involves not only work, but the person's life as a partner, parent, and member of a citizen action committee or a religious congregation. These activities form networks and give a person a sense of integrity and wholeness. Disruptions to any of these activities (the death of a child or a grandparent, for instance) temporarily destabilizes this wholeness.

How a person is similar to others involves not family, neighbors, or friends but membership in demographic groups—regions of the country, social class, ethnicity, and religion. All these memberships help the individual to feel they have a place in a larger community. One of the more destabilizing conditions of living a city-life in a modern world is that all these groups do not speak with the same stabilizing message. Religious organizations and families may conflict with one's class, race, or regional membership. How we are different from others within a community doesn't necessarily mean uniqueness in terms of individuality. As we learned the in earlier chapters on European individualism, imagining that we are unique is historically a very late development. However, people in all societies have a sense of being different but it is often based on age, sex, or kinship relations. Unfortunately, this is the basis of segregation and discrimination as well.

Modern life and the tension between community and the metropolis

Modern life makes it difficult to live in one organic community. Most communities possess an organic culture that can't provide the full satisfaction of everyday activities based on religious, ethnic, racial, and neighborhood roles. Hewitt takes issue with linear descriptions of the evolution of modern life which suggest that once a new form of social life emerges the old form disappears. Two examples of this are Durkheim's description of modern life moving from mechanical to organic solidarity and Maine' s description of a social evolutionary movement from status to contract. Rather Hewitt says modernity emerges from a *tension* between community life and larger, social city life that persists throughout the nineteenth century. He says that while modern social forms such as city life have undermined and weakened communities, they have not eliminated them, nor have they eliminated the needs which these communities satisfy. The table below shows some of the tensions between community and society, while indicating the social institutions which are most likely to have created the tension. (Please see Table 4.1.)

Table 4.1 From Organic Communities to Metropolis in Yankeedom

Category of comparison	Organic communities (colonial America)	Rise of modern institutions which create a rift between organic communities and modern metropolis	Modern metropolis (nineteenth century industrialism)
Length of social relations size of communities	Lifetime Deep Few people Stable—one place	**Decline of rural relations and rise of cities**	Short-term Superficial Many people Many places
Type of relations	**Organic (blood),** involuntary		**Contractual, voluntary**
Scope of roles	**Diffused** do many kinds of roles		**Focused** **More specialized**
Stability of roles	Place and a role for everyone Achieved status	**Class struggle**	Greater competition must make your own place Achieved status
Life expectancy	Live to about thirty-five	**Rise of medicine (people live longer)**	Raised about ten years by the end of the century
Public life	More involved Puritans intervene in family affairs	**Rise of the state undermines regional, local loyalties**	Public life declines Privacy more important
Place of work	Within the same community	**Rise of agricultural capitalism**	Working outside the neighborhood
Geography	Stable (one place)	**Expansion of trade**	Mobile, interchangeable membership
Class integration/ class segregation	Different classes live in same neighborhood	**Class-struggle** **Rise of unions and socialism**	Classes segregated in different neighborhoods
Religion/ language	Homogenous religion and language	**Exploration of foreign lands** Immigration of Eastern Europeans	More diversity of religion and languages
Type of social solidarity (Durkheim, Tonnies)	Self-sufficient **Mechanical solidarity** **Community**	**Industrialization and specialization of labor**	Interdependent specialization of labor **Organic solidarity** **Society**
social movements	Religious movements Great Awakening	**Industrial capitalism** **Civil war**	Religious movements: temperance movement, social gospel of progressive movements Secular movements: feminism, unions, socialism Economic instabilities (Panics of 1837, 187, and 1896) Collectivities—fads, fashions
Temporal focus	Past (authority)	**Speed up of the pace of life due to industrialization**	Present (past changes too quickly to revere)
Political life	Elite debates between Federalists and Republicans	**Rise of party system**	Mass democracy for working class whites at end of century Voting
Type of identity	Communal (Puritans)		Utilitarian individualism (first half of nineteenth century)
			Mystical individualism (Middle nineteenth century)
			Entrepreneurial individualism (1870-1890)
			Expressive individualism (1890- to World War I)

Three layers of the self

As a symbolic interactionist, Hewitt has problems with the tradition of how the self is conceived. One problem is that in the interaction between the self and society, the self is one-sidedly focused on the *immediate* situation and the roles that are being played. A situated self plays the roles necessary over the course of a single day: a romantic partner, worker, and a train passenger, for instance. When in these groups, the individual asked himself questions like whether that setting is safe or dangerous? How well are the roles being played in this situation? Will how I play my role be accepted by others? What will be the consequences of playing my role differently?

Hewitt argues that the conception of a self needs to be more overarching than the situated self, what Hewitt calls the social self. The social self arises when there is a problem within a situated identity. This can occur when one's role performance is threatened by another, when the situation itself becomes problematic, when the person moves from one situation to another, when a person wants to stop playing a role in a situation, or when a person wants to play another role and is met by group resistance. A social self also addresses the tension which arises when the individual faces the fact that they play some roles better than others and roles must be prioritized.

Lastly, whereas in a situated self the meaning of what the group is doing is clear, when a person calls on their social identity, meanings are no longer taken for granted. The situation requires a reorganization and legitimation in order to establish a new meaning. Under these circumstances, the social identity of the individual might refer to membership in their regional, ethnic, or religious identity for support. Historically, all cultures throughout history have had both a situated self and a social self. In terms of the work of George Herbert Mead, both the situated self and the social self correspond to Mead's 'Me' side of the self.

Hewitt says that a third layer of the self comes about during modern times, which he calls personal self (in our terms, individualism). This personal self emerges as part of a metropolitan identity where the community relations have weakened. This personal identity is more concerned with his own interests, wants, and needs. It has its own projects and resists to close an association with the group. It has its unique biography, which it takes seriously, and it uses the vast resources of the metropolis to realize them. While a social identity is mostly concerned with the present and past of group life, personal identity is concerned with realizing goals in a personalized future. In Mead's theory, the personal self-corresponds to 'I' part of the self. In answer to a problem with a situational identity the individualist might either withdraw to personal projects or identify with occupational identity rather than with a region, religion, or ethnicity.

According to Hewitt, the social self is rooted in the community and the personal self is located in the metropolis. Hewitt resists the linear version of history which says that once modern cities emerge, previous communities wither and die. He argues that personal self and the social self are conflicted and compete in one's identity construction. There are two possible solutions which arise from a situated self problem. To avoid confusion with terms, I am changing the name of Hewitt's social self to *community self* and his personal self to *metropolitan self* or *individualism*. (Please see Table 4.2.)

Table 4.2 Three Layers of the Self

Category of comparison	Situated self	Community self (social identity)	Metropolitan self (personal identity) individualism
What are the connections?	Tied to situations and roles	Tied to a local community	Tied to the metropolis
Purpose?	Maintenance of defined situation in its usual and routine course	Arises from a problem in a situated identity	Arises from a problem in a situated identity
Roles	Plays a **particular role** in everyday situation	Prioritizes roles across situations Deals with inter and intra-role conflicts, role ambiguity, and role lag	Problematic nature of all roles Searches for meaning in personal projects
Conditions of its arising	Tries to find answers to the following in a group situation: Is the setting safe or dangerous? How well are others playing their roles? What others expect me to do? What others will do if I fail to act in the expected manner? What will be the consequences of me not playing the role they expect?	a) When one role performance is threatened by another b) When the situation itself becomes problematic c) When a person moves from one situation to another d) When individuals want to play new roles	Wants to discover **new** interests wants, needs, goals Seeks a private destiny in biographical projects
Place of meanings	Meanings are self-contained	Meanings are not self-contained: organization and legitimating of various situated meanings	Meanings are not self-contained: conflicts across social groups about meanings.
How is continuity sustained?	Rely on situational integration	Rely on religious, ethnic, and regional identity	Rely on occupational identity
Temporal framework	Present	Past	Present, future
Translation of George Herbert Meads aspects of the self	Me	Me	I

Early nineteenth century utilitarian individualism

Abundance of land and work

Compared to Americans in the early twentieth centuries, colonial farmers did not have to worry about unemployment, as labor was scarce and land was abundant. There was more equal distribution of wealth, at least among farmers. These farmers aspired to own their own land and had the *option* to move elsewhere, at least until the nineteenth century when the industrialization process forced many of them out. The theme of abundance was also common to artisans (mechanics) who had plenty of work and frontiersman who had support from capitalists to take over the land of Native Americans.

Family capitalism

In order to understand the different kinds of individualism during the nineteenth century, we must begin with how capitalism was organized. In this way, we can understand how and why individualism changed. For about the first seventy years of capitalism in the nineteenth century, capitalism can be characterized as *family capitalism* and later forms of capitalism as that of the *robber barons*. In the earlier conditions of capitalism, there were no managers. The owner was usually on the shop floor and could not easily supervise his workers. This gave the workers relative freedom to take breaks.

Labor craftsmanship

In the early days, workers were a very valuable resource and they were not interchangable. They were highly skilled and took pride in their work. In these times, workers employed both their minds and their bodies and controlled the work process from beginning to end. What machinery was used was for rote mechanical work. The creativity of the work was still performed by workers. There was a certain dignity in labor and, when asked, even poor workers defined themselves as weavers or metal workers. As Harry Braverman says:

> The working craftsman was tied to the technical and scientific knowledge of his time in the daily practice of his craft. Apprenticeship included training in mathematics, including algebra, geometry, and trigonometry, the properties .... of the materials common to the craft, in the physical sciences and in mechanical drawing. Well-administered apprenticeship provided subscriptions to the trade and technical journals affecting the craft so that apprentices could follow development. (*Labor and Monopoly Capital*, 133)

Psychology of craftsmanship

Skills were passed on to the next generation. Perseverance and integrity on the job were valuable and were also signs of religious diligence. In part, workers were able to delay gratification because the work process itself was meaningful. Workers worked hard, and membership in a union provided a better chance for the future. Heroes were those of the previous generations of relatives.

In terms of the family, according to Lasch, the parenting was authoritarian and father-centered. Because there was an extended family, the children did not so closely identify with their parents however much they may have respected them. There were no expectations that parents would in any way be emotionally involved with their children.

A sign of development was the ability of a son or daughter to emulate their parents and carry on the tradition. What was important was self-reliance and self-sufficiency. People lived in homogenous communities which meant that in terms of identity, the parents, neighbors, and the church all conveyed the same message to children and adolescents. Average life expectancy was pretty young at approximately thirty-five .

There was less variety in the kind of experiences people had but more opportunity to integrate their experiences among family, neighbors, and church members.

In his book *The Lonely Crowd,* David Reisman uses a metaphor for how children are trained: "Homing pigeons can be taught to fly home, but an inner-directed child must be taught to fly a straight course, when away from home, with destination unknown"(42). The job of the authorities was to equip their sons or daughters with gynroscopes which would keep them on course when away from home, even with the destination unknown. The problem is that gyroscope model will only work if the rate of social change is slow. The rapid social change of the late nineteenth century undermined this model. With increasing doubt about how to bring up children, parents turned to social welfare and schools for help. The upper classes turned to therapy.

A defense mechanisms of these utilitarian individualists was suppression of immediate desires, such as drinking or sex. When they gave in to these things, they felt guilty. Aging and death were treated as inevitable, and those who were old were considered wise. The economic foundations for respect for the elderly rested on the fact that the rate of change in the first half of the nineteenth century was still slow enough for parents to know much more than children. This meant that what knowledge base a parent had to offer a child was not constantly undermined by technological and economic changes that might occur in the child's life.

Another defense mechanism, according to Lasch, was sublimation. This played out in farming and all the work to done around the farm from blacksmithing, to weaving, to tanning leather. Whether on the farm or in the shop, there was respect for craftsmanship. Work was hard, but there was an intrinsic pleasure in the work. At the same time, what people had they saved, and the farmer or mechanic couldn't buy something before they had the money to pay for it. It is not until the end of the nineteenth century with mass production that people began to accumulate debt.

Late nineteenth century expressive individualism

Corporate capitalism

At the end of the century (1890), many family capitalist businesses combined into large corporations. When capitalists combine ownership, it allows them to pool their wealth and produce on a larger scale. Their combined wealth allowed them to invest in complex machines which took over the creative parts of the worker's jobs. Whereas before, workers were specialized within a certain field, under the new organization of capitalism, workers were given *tasks* within the same field. With the added surplus, capitalists added supervisors to watch over the work process to get workers to work faster, harder, and more efficiently. For blue-collar, working-class men and women, the meaning of work began to lose its luster.

As early as 1880, Fredrick Taylor was inventing time studies to get workers to work more 'efficiently' with nose to the grindstone, rather than socializing about their work. As Harry Braverman argues:

> Every detail of the man's job was specified, the size of the shovel, the bite into the pile, the weight of the scoop, the distance to walk, the arc of the swing, and the rest periods. (*Labor and Monopoly Capital*,106)

Later, Frank Gilbreth, one of Taylor followers, added the study of motion to Taylor's time study. Each of the motions of the human body in doing a job was reduced to the operations of a machine. They included "grasp, release load, position, pre-position, assemble, disassemble, use, search, select, transport loaded, transport unloaded, transport empty, unavoidable delay, avoidable delay, hold, rest, plan, inspect, walk, bend, sit, stand up, kneel" (174). The intrinsic joy of working as a craftsman became a *job* which became a means to an end. Satisfaction had to be found somewhere outside of work.

Meanwhile, corporate capitalists could also afford to hire clerics, bookkeepers, and stenographers to take over the work the owner did themselves. But this work was also mechanical and deadening. By the end of the century, there were two kinds of alienation: mindless physical labor and bodyless mind-work.

In the first half of the nineteenth century, advertising was minor and done through local newspapers. The market for advertising was small (as the handicraft goods that were produced were small in number) and relatively expensive. But approaching the end of the nineteenth century, the division of labor at work allowed capitalists to produce goods more cheaply and on a much larger scale. By the end of the nineteenth century, department stores opened and advertising budgets swelled.

Psychology of the deskilled worker: blue and white collar

With the quality of blue collar and white collar in decline, where could identity be found? Because of the mass production of goods, workers could pay less for the same goods. Thus, they began to accumulate commodities. In the same period, advertisers made special appeals to women workers to dress less drably and express their personalities. The rise in the expression of oneself through clothing and objects was sold to them through the newly developing celebrity culture of the movies.

What mattered was not what you produced but what you consumed. How could you stand out from the crowd and be attractive to others? One's heroes were no longer the generations from whom you inherited your skills. This *expressive individualist* had no use for the past. By the end of the nineteenth century, more people were drawn to celebrities and driven by vanity and appearance rather than pride. Rather than training their children to operate as gyroscopes, they were trained as if they were radar devices, set up to be ever alert for changes in the cues of other people.

As the pace of life quickened, the knowledge of the previous generation began to be less relevant to the lives of teenagers and children. What mattered was what was happening *now*, who was making it happen, and how one could be one the happening ones? Personal magnetism replaced craftsmanship in identity.

Allen Whellis argues that around this time the superego and conscience that controlled the utilitarian individualist began to break down, destabilizing the expressive-impulsive self. Anxiety rather than guilt drove the individual.

As women joined the white-collar work force, the status of men in the workforce declined. Also, in the late nineteenth century, religion, hammered by Darwinism, started to decline.

What mattered now was private well-being, not the good of the community or the coming generation. Cushman points out that in the early twentieth century, the concept of personality sounded very similar to the characteristics of narcissism. Anyone who thinks that the disorder of narcissism is about forty years old ought to look at this list of mental hygiene to be overcome at the turn to the twentieth century:

- grandiose self-importance or uniqueness
- preoccupation with fantasies of unlimited success, power, brilliance, beauty
- exhibitionism
- marked feelings of rage, inferiority, shame, humiliation, or emptiness
- entitlement
- interpersonal exploitativeness
- black and white relationships
- lack of empathy (Cushman, 70)

Spiritual individualism of Emerson and Whitman

So far, we have seen two types of spiritualism in America, the Puritan religion (which was mostly middle class) and the fundamentalist tendency (which was expressed in the Great Awakening). The latter trend had some individualist tendencies in that it rejected the importance of contributing to social life as well as insisting on the power of individual mystical experience. Yet, it still required a revivalist community in order to have a mystical experience. What about the *upper-middle classes* and spirituality?

Not all spiritual traditions were sold on the direction American life was taking. Transcendentalism in the United States arose in the 1820s and was a specific reaction against the Calvinist ideas of the innate depravity of humanity and the need for infinite atonement, predestination, and election. Puritanism denied the benevolence of God. On the other hand, it saw religious enthusiasm as dangerous and undignified. Contrary to both Calvinism and Revivalism, nature was seen as a source of religious truth and its beauty was the ultimate aim. By the time of the Unitarians, the miraculous elements of religion were dwindling.

Transcendentalism was both a continuation of Unitarianism and a break from it. Unlike the Unitarians, the Transcendentalists insisted on the importance of personal spiritual experience based on intuition. It was greatly influenced by British Romanticism, especially Coleridge. By identifying himself with the God within, mediated by nature, humanity became a channel for spirits.

Yet as Quentin Anderson points out in *The Imperial Self*, the basis of the transcendental movement typified by Emerson claimed that mystical experience required a rejection of family, society, and even history. The connection with a providential God can only be realized in the individuals immediate experience, not in collective humanity. For Emerson, self-reliance was the key. He says the more exclusively idiosyncratic a man is, the more general and infinite he is.

Entrepreneurial individualism of Herbert Spenser and Social Darwinism

<u>Social Darwinism</u>

> Captains of industry must be paid for their unique organizing talent. Their huge fortunes are the

> legitimate wages of superintendence. In the struggle for existence, money is the token of success. Millionaires are the bloom of a competitive civilization. Millionaires are a product of natural selection. (*Social Darwinism in American Thought*, 58)

As I have argued in my previous book, right wing nationalism developed in Europe after 1871 in part as a result of increased competition between nation-states for colonies. At the same time, capitalist elites faced an increasing militancy among their own working class who were organizing into unions and proclaiming socialism as a solution to capitalist crises. In order to justify their continued competition between states, their subjection of colonized people, and their increasing use of the police to repress the working class, capitalists needed an ideology to justify what it was doing. The ideology of Social Darwinism fit the bill for all three. According to Richard Hofstadter, in the last three decades of the nineteenth century and the beginning of the twentieth century, the United States, even more than Europe, was Darwin country.

Social Darwinists attempted to apply Darwin's theory of natural selection to human social life. This meant that the nation-states that emerged victorious over other nation states did so because nature had favorably selected them. Why did capitalist states subjugate colonized people? Because as members of the white race they were genetically superior. Lastly why was the capitalist class wealthy while the working-class was poor? Because there was something genetically superior in the capitalist class. The British philosopher who justified all this was Herbert Spencer.

According to Hofstadter, no other philosopher was ever the rage as Spencer was between 1870 and 1890 in the United States. The number of books he sold for the subject matter he was addressing was unmatched. Spencer was trained as a civil engineer, and his ideas about the conservation of energy and evolution derived from his work. According to Spencer, evolution of all life moves from an incoherent homogeneity illustrated by the protozoa to a coherent heterogeneity manifest in the higher animals. What drove evolution to take this shape, according to Malthus, was belief that people populate at a rate that outstrips the food supply. The resulting competition leads to extinction of the poorest classes or races. Spencer was stridently opposed to state intervention in helping the poor. He believed such intervention would weaken the race.

William Sumner was the most influential Darwinist in the United States. As a follower of Spencer, Sumner brought together three traditions:

- the Protestant ethic (in his role as a Puritan preacher)
- the doctrine of classical economics (Ricardo and Malthus)
- Darwinian natural selection (as a popularizer of evolution)

For Sumner, the type of human society that evolved was dependent on the human-to-land ratio. Where the human population is small and the soil abundant, the struggle for existence is less intense and society will be organized in a more egalitarian way. When the population is dense, and the land is less fertile, the struggle for existence intensifies. According to Sumner, there are no rights. No one owes anyone else anything. The captains of industry were specimens of the most fit.`

To be fair to both Spencer and Sumner, neither suggested that the *plutocrats* that had inherited their wealth were the most fit. It was the middle classes that rose from the ranks through competition that were the most fit. Sumner thought that plutocrats were responsible for political corruption and their international policy of protectionism was opposed to free trade. According to Sumner, free trade was the economic policy favored because it maximized competition.

A parallel can be drawn between the ingredients of natural selection and that of classical economics. Hofstadter identifies the following:

- both assumed the fundamentally self-interested animal

pursuing the classical economic pattern

- pleasure in economics
- survival in Darwinian instinct
    - both assumed the morality of competition
    - both assumed the fittest survived
- the organism in natural selection
    - the capitalist in the other case

With the closing of the frontier, most immigrants from Eastern Europe in the late nineteenth century never were able to start a new life on a farm. Instead, they got stuck in rapidly overcrowded cities in factories with poor housing. The first generation of immigrants were still following the agricultural pattern of child-bearing, which meant having large families because children were seen as free labor for the family. The consequent growth of slums was interpreted by conservatives as a sign that these immigrants were unfit. This had a great deal to do with the rise of the eugenics movement which included forced sterilization.

Reactions against Social Darwinism

Social Darwinism did not rule America in the late nineteenth century unopposed. Lester Ward, one of the very first sociologists, made a distinction between social and biological evolution. For him, competition often leads to monopolies and these monopolies reduce competition. He argues that Malthus's theory does not apply to the human species. The anarchist and naturalist Peter Kropotkin argues that there is no struggle for existence between animals *belonging to the same species*. Rather, there is cooperation.

Up until now, socio-political struggles were essentially conceived of as Marx and Engels imagined, between capital and labor. But now the middle classes were being drawn in. They were afraid of being crushed between monopolies on the one hand and workers on the other. By the early twentieth century a new progressive movement of populists, radical journalists, social workers, and clergyman were insisting on more state intervention and programs for the poor.

Thorstein Veblen, cultural critic and economist, perhaps more than anyone else, argues against the idea that captains of industry are the most fit. He challenges the connection between fitness and *acquisition* of wealth. Instead, he makes a distinction between the *production* function of industry which was driven by scientists and engineers (the instinct for workmanship) and what was done with those scientific products by capitalists. Veblen argues that competition in the best sense once existed between producers before capitalists became supreme over industry.

From individualist selection to group selection (racism)

As Reginald Horsman (*Race and Manifest Destiny)* has pointed out, expansion into foreign lands by the United States was justified by Manifest Destiny from the early nineteenth century. The United States had embarked in campaigns for internal colonization long before the nineteenth century when it took over the land of Mexicans and Native Americans. But beginning in 1898, it began to expand into the Philippines, Hawaii, and the Samoan Islands. As the United States cautiously entered imperialist competition, its relations with England improved. These friendly relations were used at least partly to justify US imperialism by claiming racial superiority of Anglo-Saxons.

The roots of the major Social Darwinists Spencer and Sumner were in the middle class. But by the turn of century, the middle class was begin drowned out be monopolies and trusts at the top end and by labor unions on the other. The liberal middle class was drawn to the progressive movement as one attempt to get organized. However, the conservative middle class was drawn to racial theories of group selection as opposed to individual selection. What both wings of the middle class agreed on was the individual was no longer the unit by which to understand Darwin. The liberals chose the collectivism of the progressive movement and the conservatives chose race. As Hofstander says:

> While Darwinian individualism declined, Darwinian collective and nationalist or racist variety was beginning to take hold. Darwinism was made to fit the mold of international conflict-ideologies just when its inapplicability to domestic economics was becoming apparent (202).
>
> The survival of the fittest had once been used chiefly to support business completion at home. Now it was used to support expansion abroad. (203)

Hofstadter concludes:

> There is a certain touching irony in the thought that, while *writers* like these preached slow change and urged men to adapting to the environment, the very millionaires whom they took to be the fittest were transforming the environment with incredible rapidity and rendering the values of Spencer and Summer less and less fit for survival. (12)

Differences between the utilitarian vs the entrepreneurial self

The entrepreneurial self began with the same values as the utilitarian self. Through hard work, self-sufficiency, and prudence the individual would adapt. But the entrepreneurial capitalist differs in a number of ways from the utilitarian individualist of the early nineteenth century. First, by 1890, being a capitalist no longer meant owning your own business. Increasingly, capitalists were forced to join with other capitalists in corporations and trusts, hardly a sign of individual risk-taking.

Secondly, more capitalists by the 1880's were not self-made but inherited their wealth.

Thirdly, by the end of the nineteenth century, capitalists were not known for frugality or delaying gratification. In fact, this was the age which Thorstein Veblen called *conspicuous consumption*. Fourth, unlike the utilitarian individualists, these entrepreneurial individualists were not exactly God-fearing men at all. Many used Social Darwinism to justify their activity, because they thought that Darwin was right about how nature worked and that the theological framework of nature was sentimental and out of date. In fact, many agricultural capitalists of the South *contradicted* the bible and argued that races had been created separately (polygenesis). Many of these capitalists supported scientific racist theories about brain size. They looked to nature rather than God to explain their world.

Lastly, utilitarian individualists from the middle class had a better chance of fulfilling their dreams because land was cheap and there were no large corporations. But, by the end of the nineteenth century, conservative middle classes were being crowded out by both capitalist monopolies on the one hand and militant labor unions on the other. In light of this, conservative middle classes caste their fate with US imperialism abroad, and this was justified by an Anglo-Saxon race theory abroad and a eugenics theory at home. (Please see table 4.4.)

Table 4.3 Two Types of Individualism: Character and Personality*

Character (Utilitarian Individualism)	Category of comparison	Personality (Expressive individualism)
Most of nineteenth century Victorian	**Time period**	**Beginning around 1890**
Producing goods through hard work: family businesses Owner on shop floor	**Phase of capitalism**	Corporate capitalism forces an extreme division of labor Owners withdraw and hire managers to watch workers
Body and mind work integrated in creative work Workers control the pace of work Craftsmanship	**Laboring process**	Managers and machines taking over the creative parts of the job Either body work (blue collar) or mind work (white collar) Workers lose control of pace of work—Taylorism Specialized tasks
Handicraft commodities Relatively expensive	**Commodities**	Mass production of commodities which are cheap
Minor, local newspapers	**Advertising**	Major advertising Development of department stores Hiring of celebrities to sell products
Emulate people of higher morality: Heroes of previous generation	**How is notoriety achieved?**	Celebrities Seeking of fortune and chance to be discovered
Hard work, self-sacrifice, and strong religion.	**How is the self-fed?**	Accumulation of objects in the home Fashion—women Emulating celebrities
Frugality	**Consumption**	Spending Beginning of credit
Delaying gratification	**Attitude to the future**	Immediate gratification
Strong	**Place of religion**	Weaker Darwinian threat
Father-centered	**Parenting**	Father loses credibility Progressive movement—shared with social workers, therapists
Character (Utilitarian Individualism)	**Category of comparison**	**Personality (Expressive individualism)**
"Gyroscope"—set by parents and other authorities to keep child on course even when tradition no longer is consistent with mores	**Training**	"Radar"—be sensitive to needs of changing groups
Fame -being remembered by posterity for deeds done	**How is notoriety achieved?**	**Celebrity** being identified with new idols of movies, music that are happening now
Rational—teacher-student Parent-child Pastor-parishioner	**Sources of influence**	Market, Anonymous authority of public opinion
Faithfulness to role models	**What is important?**	Popularity
Obedience to authorities Conformity to small groups	**Obedience and Conformity**	More suspicious of authority Less conforming to small groups Conformity to large anonymous groups
More homogenous groups		Heterogenous groups More immigrants 1880-1890's
Shame in relations to group **Guilt** in relation to moral failings	**Psychological discomfort**	Diffused anxiety—anomie (Durkheim)
Cultivation of superego	**Part of psyche**	Ego—adjustment to changing circumstances
Pleasure of possession and property Anal, hoarding character	**Type of pathology**	Receptive and marketing orientation

- Adapted from Cushman, *Constructing, Self, Constructing America*

Reisman, Lonely Crowd; Whellis, Quest for Identity; Fromm, Sane Society

Table 4.4 Utilitarian vs Entrepreneurial Individualism

Utilitarian individualist	Category of comparison	Entrepreneurial individualist
Early nineteenth century	**Time period**	Late nineteenth century
Owned business alone	**Scale of ownership**	Grouped into corporations and trusts
Self-made man	**Source of wealth**	Higher percentage of inherited wealth
Frugality, delaying gratification	**Virtues**	Frugality, delayed gratification as ideology; in practice, conspicuous consumption
God-fearing	**Sources of Evidence**	Social Darwinism: Spencer and Sumner's "scientific" description of nature.
Monogenism—God creates all races at same time	**Sources of spiritual creation**	Polygenists (especially in the South) Races created separately
Individual genes	**Unit of analysis**	Anglo-Saxon race
		Eugenics—sterilization of the lower races Brain size measurements

CHAPTER 5

Promethean Geography: Households, Theatre and Metropolitan Life

Orientation

Environmental psychology

Environmental psychology is the study of how the natural and constructed physical environments impact human psychology including memories, imagination, emotions, perception, and cognition. But isn't psychology something that goes on *inside* of people? After all, aren't the places we inhabit simply *containers* for dynamics within and between people (social psychology)? Places and spaces are under our control, right? If we reflect on our experiences, I think you'll agree that places and spaces are far from empty containers. The objects we craft, the houses, bridges and schools that we use become inseparable from who we are. The claim in this section and the claim of the whole book is that people's psychology is never something that goes on solely within. As we inhabit the places that we shape, our psychology expands to include them. Like the weaving of an invisible cocoon connecting us to objects and places built, the longer the connection lasts, the thicker the attachments.

Objects affect what a person can do, either by expanding or restricting the scope of our actions and our psychological states. Tools, buildings, tables, and pots have an influence that impacts our identity. Of course, in their natural state, objects and places certainly have inherent physical properties that are separate from human meaning. In a very real sense, people must shape and sustain their societies by adapting to the physical/ecological setting and its constraints. But once objects become socialized through human labor, they become artifacts and hence acquire a certain psychological standing. Our relationship with objects and places is dialectical. We create them, but once created, they co-create us. Taken to the extremes of reification, sometimes we get so caught up in places that we attribute an independent psychology to them, as when we say a house is haunted. At the other extreme, geography is usually presented as being only about maps, aerial photography, or structured field surveys.

In the Middle Ages and throughout most of Western history up until the modern period, people regularly assumed that places had an independent psychic energy, regardless of whether human beings inhabited them. Places were thought to be enchanted. This 'psyche at large' was concentrated in huts, houses and temples. This chapter is largely about how many places lost their psychology-at-large perspective and became either hollowed out or was eliminated altogether. But that does not mean human beings were no longer attached to physical locales. It only means that we became attached to a new kind of physical locale—the 'spaces' which we will discuss shortly.

Eating utensils, furniture and rooms from the Middle Ages to the nineteenth century

In Yi-Fu Tuan's provocative work *Segmented Worlds and Self*, he explores the ways the organization of eating utensils at dinner has changed; the organization of rooms within the house; and how theatre was organized from the Middle Ages through the nineteenth century. More specifically there were movements:

- from the use of benches to chairs at mealtime
- from the general utensils used by everyone to specialized utensils such as knives and forks
- from multiple uses of rooms to specialized use of rooms.

In the Middle Ages, people sat on benches rather than individual chairs when eating. Few utensils were available to the less privileged guests. Guests brought their own knives to dinner and people shared the same utensils, eating soup out of a collective bowl. There were no plates, not even wood ones. A thick slice of stale bread was used to hold the rest of the food.

From the Renaissance forward, guests no longer sat on a common bench, but on separate chairs. The number and kind of instruments used to cut and separate foods multiplied, and they were given out to each individual rather than shared. Another sign of individualism in taste was serving foods on an array of small dishes rather than on a few large platters. The evolution of table manners and utensils was indicative of a growing sensitivity to what it meant to be civilized. A civilized person was someone who consciously sought to put a distance between themselves all that hinted at animalistic, natural functions as well as violence, messiness, and indiscriminate mixing, whether it be different kinds of food or different classes of people. We will have much more to say about what it means to be civilized in a later chapter.

Throughout most of the Medieval period, a large, unpartitioned hall served as an open, almost public area in which all people might meet. Lords conducted their business affairs business and visitors could find temporary hospitality, thanks to the magnanimity of the great lord. According to Tuan, on a festive occasion, as a guest entered the hall he might find a baron with his favorite bird perched on a wrist amidst semi-trained dogs and a few monkeys holding court in of a boisterous crowd. Almost any traveler could make a claim to the hospitality of a manor. Barons took pride in the openness of their house to all comers. Between 1500 CE and 1700 CE, Tuan points out a minor Parisian nobleman might have some twenty-five people living with him—his own family, protégés, clerics, clerks, servants, shopkeepers, and apprentices. People came at all hours, disrupting the routine of the household, but they were rarely asked to leave.

Living in the twenty-first century (in the West, at least) the bedroom is a private place. Yet in the Middle Ages, people of all social classes agreed that sleeping did not require a separate room. The further back we go, the less segregated sleeping quarters. In a twelfth-century manor house, retainers and servants slept in the hall, kitchen or storeroom—anywhere it was warm and dry. During the Renaissance, Michelangelo slept with his workmen, four to a bed!

Until the end of the seventeenth century, interconnecting rooms made privacy difficult if not impossible to establish. Until the introduction of a corridor in the larger eighteenth-century houses, people could not move from one part of the house to another without passing through intervening rooms.

That the poor had no privacy is not a surprise. As late as 1880, forty-nine percent of Berlin's population lived in one-room households. But you might be surprised to know that retreat by the *upper classes* into private rooms was frowned upon. A lord who did this was regarded as a rude and avaricious miser. Even kings had no privacy. *Power and prestige required exposure*. A lord who maintained his privilege and effectiveness needed to be be visible as well.

The great chamber of the lord was no more specialized in its functions than the hall in its heyday. In addition to dining, it could also be used for music, dancing, games of cards, family prayers, and the performance of plays and masques. Multiple use of space discouraged privacy. The late Medieval house was a microcosm of the collectivist society it expressed.

The first room to be abandoned was the hall. In England, from the second half of the fourteenth century onward, a nobleman no longer could be found except on special occasions. By 1500 CE, in both royal palaces and private houses, the hall had become the dining room of the lower servants. Princes and nobles moved upstairs to feast in the great chamber, not in privacy but to ceremonially surround themselves with people closer to their own status.

By the late Tudor period in England, servants (except for valets and personal maids) were pushed farther away out of the sight of the family. In the eighteenth century, servants were summoned from a distance with pull-bells. In the nineteenth century, while the middle class was divided into rooms according to different functions, the working class was forced to herd together within a single apartment, like peasants in medieval times, without any furniture. While middle class members of a family had separate beds, Entire working-class families slept on a single mattress.

Theatre and the privatization of the stage

Resiliency of audience participation

In the Middle Ages, the stage was not understood as a spatial illusion. The boundary separating actors from spectators was porous. From the Middle Ages to about 1600, audiences were invited to participate in the play. Actors and even working-class audiences might find themselves mixing on the stage when the action of the play required the actors to perform at the edge of the stage.

In the absolutist state of the sixteenth century this changed. The stage was controlled by king and the prince, and the actors by patrons. What took place on the stage was an idealized form of a ritual for the king.

In the eighteenth century, the relationship between the theater and the audience again became participatory. For Enlightenment playwrights like Diderot, acting was a *secular* activity, not just a ritual for honoring the King and his court. Because of this, the public got more involved on the stage and felt free to comment on how well or badly the actors and actresses were performing.

Even as late as the eighteenth century, the division between reality and the play is fuzzy. Privileged members of the audience were allowed to sit on the stage, which undermined the illusion of a separate, enclosed world of drama. Spectators still exercised their right to disrupt a scene to express their approval or displeasure. Actors and actresses habitually performed at *the front* of the stage, and at certain high points in the drama they addressed the audience in hopes for applause. It wasn't until later that actors withdrew step-by-step into the world of the play, when they finally could act as though the audience did not exist.

From participants to spectators

After the 1630s, the appearance of sophisticated plays with increasingly secular themes demanded spectators become more detached. Theatergoers came to view dramas as animated pictures. Events on stage were less of a continuation of the world in which the audience sat or stood. The proscenium arch and curtain were installed in public theater to in order to hammer home the separation of the actors from spectators.

Another change that silenced audience participation was the change from theatre in the round to theatre 'up front.' The theatres of Medieval and Elizabethan times offered no single perspective viewpoint. In *perspective* stage scenery, in a hall, the stage could be seen from only one perspective.

This emphasis on perspective illusion signified a growing personal and subjective conception of reality when the way the stage appears was recognized to depend on the position and sightlines of the spectator. Ultimately, the spectator, isolated from others in the darkness, watched reflectively on the meaning of the drama for his own life. Drama, other than music hall comedy, had become a specialized art form, designed for the entertainment of a small social class of Europe's capital cities. Plays and spectators dwelt in different worlds, kept apart in some theaters by the orchestra pit.

The psychology of places and spaces

As discussed in my books *From Earth-Spirits to Sky-gods* and *Power in Eden*, a case has been made by humanistic geographers that after a repeated experience with a location people become attached to it, 'planting' emotions and memories, making it a 'place.' When people form no attachment to an area and they treat it as purely physical, it becomes a 'space.' Upon reflection and experience of applying places and space to geography I found this distinction too simple. I believe that people can become attached to spaces as well as places. The question is, what are the different *psychological needs* people have that they project on to the differences between a place and space? What is it that makes people divide up their world at all into places and spaces to begin with?

Psychologists have long known there is a tension within people from all societies between a desire for order and a desire for change. On the one hand, we need a predictable rhythm of routines in which the danger of the unknown is mostly eliminated. But at the same time, routines can become stultifying. In our work, we need new problems, challenges, and unfamiliar situations to exercise our creativity. Another part of us seeks novelty, the exotic and change. But if taken too far, novelty and change create chaos. Most importantly, the desire for both routine and change is not just an internal psychological need. That need is projected on to the *socio-ecological zones* we inhabit. These zones are what get divided into spaces and places.

Places are zones for repeating the known and predictable—giving rhythm to life. Spaces deal with the unknown or unpredictable, and give novelty to life. Whereas places tend to be cozy, warm and produce continuity, spaces tend to be expansive and cold, invoking both danger and innovation. Places invite a consolidation of tradition based in the past. Places are arenas to plant memories. In some cases they can become nostalgic. Spaces invite a group or individual to consider future possibilities. If places are like tried-and-true paths that people follow, experiencing a space is like blazing a trail. When people are in spaces, they are freer to wonder and dream. For modern society, outer space is probably the most awe-inspiring space we can imagine because it is the most unknown.

Spaces are areas of social life where high adventure is expected. Mountain climbing, parachute jumping, amusement parks, casinos, extreme sports, and the stock exchange are examples. Pick-up bars, masquerade parties, Mardi Gras festivities are all sites in which people might seek thrills. Unlike places, spaces can be created either on a one-time basis or upon repeated visits.

In summary, all societies organize their ecological zones into places and spaces. Each satisfies a need for either continuity and change in society. However, not all societies have an equal proportion of places and spaces. Those societies and time periods which are conservative and slow to change, such as the Middle Ages, will be dominated by places. But the Renaissance, agricultural capitalism, the scientific and industrial revolutions hollowed out and marginalized places, making room (for better

Table 5.1 Psychological Geographical Zones in All Societies

Places	Category of Comparison	Spaces
Supports rhythm, continuity, order, security	**Function**	Supports variation, qualitative change, innovation, opportunity
What is known	**Epistemology**	What is unknown
Bounded, 'cozy'	**Volume**	Expansion 'thrilling' vertigo
The past, nostal-gia	**Relationship to time**	The future, wonder, wandering
Phlegmatic, slow	**Emotions**	Mercurial, fast
Monotony	**At its worst**	Chaos, delirium
Sacred, religious practices	**Social activities**	Profane, secular working, trade, amusement

and worse) for more spaces. Please see Table 5.1 for a summary.

City Life

Characteristics of cities

In their text *Environmental Psychology*, Bell, Fisher, Baum, and Greene list the following unique characteristics of urban life compared to village life:

- more *concentrated*; crowded
- more *intense*, including pace of movement; the rate entering and leaving and exchange of information

- more *diverse* in activities, including culture, recreational activities, food, education, and services
- more *exotic* in population; non-kin, less-rooted people from different cultures
- more *choices* of job opportunities and diversity of goods and services
- more *unpredictability* and *novelty*
- more *danger*
- more individualism and less interdependence
- more *anonymity* (control over what people know about us)
- more *noise*
- more *homelessness*

Given these differences from village life, I hope it is clear that cities build spaces *around* (and in most cases *through*) places. The problem here is that these differences are based on differences of *industrial* cities. What we need to know is:

- how medieval cities compare to industrial cities in terms of places and spaces
- whether cities in the Middle Ages were more like places than spaces
- what political, technological and economic processes did industrial cities emerge from
- what changes occurred to the psychology of individuals

Medieval cities vs industrial cities

Before we systematically compare the two, let's state four differences from the start:

- In Medieval cities there was a larger proportion of places compared to spaces

- In Medieval cities a single space was used for many activities; In industrial cities there was a specialized use of spaces where a single space was used for a single activity; this is the same difference we saw in the evolution of housing areas in the previous section

- In Medieval cities *space is* less monopolized by commerce

- In Medieval cities there are "unconcealed differences between estates in mannerisms, clothing, and dialect" (Lyn Lofland (1973) He calls this "overt heterogeneity of the populace"; In industrial cities, differences within classes are hidden or understated; Lofland calls this a 'masked heterogeneity' in public space.

Medieval cities did not create a system of roads that easily accommodated transport. Only medieval cities which had been founded in Roman times were likely to have a street plan or overall design. The ruling classes of the city—the kings, bishops or merchants—had an image of what the city as a whole should look like, though it was difficult to carry out architecturally. As scholastic activities shifted from rural monasteries to the cathedrals, the principal centers of artistic creativity moved to the heart of the city. Cities were not dominated by trade and transportation as we have come to know them now. Public *places* such as monuments and Churches were more important than public *space*. Public space was the domain for entertainment, festivals, games and socializing.

Within public spaces in Medieval cities there were no zoning laws. Warehouses and workshops were all mixed together. Neither were animals completely separated from public life. Street life with filled with people, horses, pigs, and barnyard animals. As there were neither sewers nor indoor plumbing, street life had a mix of decay, feces and urine. People haggled at flea markets, storytelling was formalized, and parades were a normal part of public life. There were many more holidays celebrated in public than there were in modern cities.

There were no specialized places for children to play or to learn. Children played in the streets, and when tutored, they were taught where teachers could find room outside the shops. There were no specialized places for public entertainment. Public squares and plazas could be used if room could be found. The relatively small use of secular spaces meant activities were going on in the same place at the same time. Medieval cities were a very concentrated juxtaposition of incongruent activities with beggars jostling with aristocrats; children playing games of chance as prostitutes and the mentally ill egged them on. This was in opposition to industrial cities where there were many more singular activities occurring in different places at different times.

As I argued in my previous book *Forging Promethean Psychology*, there were no state agencies or hospitals to house physically or mentally disabled. People with diseases or serious psychological problems wandered the streets and were an integrated part of public life. There were no prisons. Punishment for crimes was carried out publicly, including beatings, branding with scarlet letters and having one's eyes plucked out or limbs cut off. Sacred sacrifices were a normal part of street life.

Unlike industrialized societies, in Medieval cities smaller and more varied social ranks were crowded together in integrated neighborhoods. But as a member of the aristocracy, how would you differentiate yourself from the lower orders if you couldn't live in an exclusive neighborhood? They dramatized their differences in the clothing they wore and how they spoke. The upper classes imposed a strict dress code and type of speech permissible to the lower classes. Lower classes were legally prohibited to wear clothes made of the same materials the upper classes wore. There was no such thing as fashion in medieval cities. One wore the clothing appropriate to one's estate.

As Lyn Lofland argues, the city created a new kind of human being: the cosmopolitan who was able to relate to others in new ways. Those living in cities developed a capacity for surface, fleeting and restricted relationships in which differences could be tolerated. He or she learned to be 'civil,' i.e. civilized.

At this point it might seem that cities were very cold and cruel spaces. But as Richard Sennett tells us, stranger relationships were deepened through membership in the Catholic church:

> In medieval Paris, the almshouses, hospitals, and convents in the city opened their doors more freely to strangers than in the countryside, taking in travelers, homeless people, and abandoned babies. Sanctuary was the point of community, a place where compassion bonded strangers. Medieval economic and religious developments pushed the sense of place in opposite directions. The economy of the city gave people a freedom of individual action they could not have in other places. The religion of the city made places where people cared about each other. (*Flesh and Stone*, 158)

The clock and the imposition of temporal grids

In Medieval cities the rate of exchange for goods and information was far slower than in industrialized cities. But during the Middle Ages, monks were the first group to give a quantitative measurement of time. They broke down the hours of the day into spiritual tasks they had to perform. These times were marked by the ringing of bells. But practical time required reckoning how much time was passing *in between* these rituals. This secular kind of time was tracked by the water clock and the hourglass. In 1674 the watch was invented. At first it was a luxury item but as it became relatively cheaper and more practical, it spread to the merchants. Among the merchants, 'watch time' became an instrument for self-regulation. The invention of the water clock and the hourglass began the process of imposing a temporal grid on the day. Clocks signaled the quantified time for

Table 5.2 Historical Comparison of Medieval vs Nineteenth-century Industrial Cities

Medieval cities	Category of comparison	End of the nineteenth- century industrial cities
Paths, no grid system of streets. Meandering, dead ends	**Type of roads**	Roads, grid system of streets
Cities are smaller Thousands in largest cities	**Population density**	Cities are larger, millions of people
Commerce on the streets, flee-markets, haggling	**Type of commerce undertaken?**	Commercial sector of public space is large; department stores selling at fixed prices
Rich street life Dancing, music, story-telling, parades, many holidays use public squares, plazas	**How prominent is the public realm?**	Public street life begins to be marginalized to make room for trains and department stores
Slow Walking for lower classes, litters or horses; horses for the upper classes	**Speed of transportation?**	Mass transportation Trains
Town criers within a city Not much between cities	**Speed of communication?**	Mass communication—newspapers, magazines
Diffused Many activities going on in the same place at the same time	**Are public activities diffused or focused?**	Focused and specialized; single activities going on in different times and places
Public institutions are less Specialized; no hospitals; maimed, diseased, blind untreated by institutions but part of public life; no places for public education; children are tutored in the streets no prisons—public beatings, physical punishment: branding, loss of eye, limbs, and sacrifice	**How specialized are public institutions?**	**Public institutions are more Specialized>** **Hospitals** **Public education** **Prisons**
Warehouses, workshops, houses all mixed together; farm animals(pigs, horses) part of city street life Rich and poor are integrated within neighborhoods	**Integration of specialization of city space?**	Beginning of retail and wholesale zoning laws; domesticated animals banished from city life except for pets Rich and poor are segregated in different neighborhoods
Since the rich and poor live close to each other, the rich distinguish themselves by their clothing and language	**How are class differences expressed?**	Since classes are segregated into different neighborhoods, elite speech and clothing are more subtle

labor. Please see Table 5.2 for a comparison.

The Rise of the public sphere

The rise of secular geography and secular architecture

With the rise of European science and agricultural capitalism, it wasn't just that the proportion of areas devoted to space and place got reversed, with priority given to space. The very definitions of space and place became transformed. Space came to be clearly marked off as a secular domain by Euclidean geometry, Renaissance perspective, Newtonian physics and capitalist trade networks.

Euclidean geometry provided the theoretical framework for geographers and mapmakers to lay out the natural and social lands as quantitative, infinite open spaces rather than qualitative bounded places. The first modern architects based their designs only on Euclidean geometry, re-making cities in the form of a grid. Cartographers represented space such as longitude and latitude, imagining the globe as a homogeneous surface ruled by a uniform gird, joined by abstract metrical space.

What is the public sphere?

According to Asa Briggs and Peter Burke in *Social History of the Media*, the public sphere was a physical zone in estate or class societies, in which debate about political, scientific, artistic or religious controversies could take place among strangers in public space. The public was larger than the family but smaller than the state or the Church. Discussion could take place through the medium of coffeehouses, taverns, public baths, salons and in royal courts. The arts through which these mediums are utilized included image-making, image-breaking (iconoclasm) plays, street theatre, political oration, scientific lectures, sermons, writing, reading, or painting. Different social classes were predominant in different public spaces. Taverns were places for artisans, coffee houses for merchants and salons were more aristocratic. They latter and were often organized by women.

Briggs and Burke inform us that there were seeds in the public sphere as far back as the Renaissance. In the Italian city-state of Florence in the thirteenth and fourteenth centuries, a high proportion of the population participated in Florentine political life. The squares of the city acted as public spheres in which speeches were given and politics discussed. This was also the case in Dutch and Swiss city-states of Antwerp, Nuremberg and Basel.

The authors also argue that the public sphere had an important religious dimension, beginning with the Reformation. The first religious disputes between Catholics and Protestants appealed to the people of Germany, France, and The Netherlands. In the sixteenth century Calvinists encouraged the destruction of stained-glass windows and statues of the Church. Between the Puritan revolution in 1640 and the Restoration in 1660, the clergy lost control of the public sphere and had to compete with lay preachers, some of them artisans and apprentices involved in politics. During the first period, the public sphere was a *temporary* realm which was a reaction to a religious or political crisis. Beginning in the seventeenth and eighteenth centuries the public sphere became a permanent space for political battles between the king, nobility, and merchants.

Ritualized public space during the Absolutist state

In his book *The Fall of Public Man*, Richard Sennett points out that public spaces in Absolutist states such as France were not treated in the open-ended way that they were in Medieval cities. Rather they were treated as *controlled performances* in which all the estates played their part. People reacted to each other not *as individuals*, but in ways consistent with the etiquette required of one's *membership in an estate*. All gestures and postures should have been consistent with one's estate, much like the plantation culture or the Old South in the United States. All reactions were impersonal, and the idea was to reveal nothing of one's personal life. Emotions were a show and not specific to individual circumstances.

Public space in the Enlightenment

By the eighteenth century things begin to change. For the aristocrats, good taste was synonymous with good manners. European Enlighteners began to equate 'civilized' demeanor with being phony. The public realm was seen by them as the inauthentic creation of snobbery. The aristocracy was attacked for being pretentious, with their elaborate court etiquette, preoccupation with who one is with, and how long to grow one's fingernails.

The Enlightenment opposed this 'civilization' with 'culture,' a unity that could be produced through *discussion in the town square*. For the Enlightenment, culture was not something that a group had or didn't have. Rather it was understood as a *process*, as cultivation, to grow what previously was a wild state into a domesticated state.

Circulation of capital as circulation of the blood

Sennett points out how Harvey's description of the circulation of the blood in the human body was used by capitalist ideologues to describe the circulation of commodities throughout the social body of capitalism. Just as the heart pumps blood through arteries of the body and receives blood to be pumped from the veins; just as health was conceived of by Harvey as the free flow and movement of blood and nerve energies, so too Adam Smith argued that circulation of goods, labor, and money proved more profitable than fixed and stable possessions. City planners aspired to build a city of flowing arteries and veins through which people streamed like healthy blood corpuscles. Just as the heart was the center of the body, the circulation of money, goods and labor was the life of the social body. Just as air was like blood and must circulate through the body, better sanitary conditions in cities were needed for human blood corpuscles.

During the Age of Absolutism, cities were planned for sake of ceremonies and traffic converged on a central monumental destination of the Palace of the king and his court. Once the artery-blood metaphor was made in relation to city planning, Enlightenment planners made *crowd* motion in the city an end in itself. Streets often bypassed connection to the urban heart and were indirectly connected to each other.

Space in the nineteenth century

Impact of the Railroad

How much can changes in our mode of transportation effect how we experience the world? What is the difference in how people perceive the world on horseback, on a stagecoach or on a railroad train? According to Wolfgang Schivelbusch (1986) the railroad profoundly changed not only our sense of space but also our sense perception, our thinking, our emotions, and our expectations.

Unlike traffic on river or seas, land traffic had been the weakest link in a chain of capitalist evolution because of the unevenness of the roads, the relatively slow speed of animal transport and the unpredictability or animal power itself. During the Middle Ages travel was limited to horseback or foot. In the sixteenth century there was improvement in roads and the appearance of carriages. By the seventeenth century the use of stagecoaches began to spread. The high-pressure steam engine maximized work performance and was first concentrated in the train locomotive. The steam engine was first used in Newcastle in the nineteenth century to pump water out of the mines and to transport coal. The land between the mines and the rivers became covered by a dense network of railways up to ten miles. Then steam power began to be an essential part of the manufacturing industry, shipping raw materials instead of using pack horses.

Prior to the railroad, the speed of transportation was relative to shape of the roads, the conditions of the animals as well as how much competition there was between traveling vehicles for space. With the rise of the railroad all this changed. The natural obstacles overcome included

- the friction between wheel surface and road surface
- the irregularity of the terrain

An ideal road should be smooth, level, hard and straight. The steam-engine generated *uniform* mechanical motion. This was achieved by building embankments, tunnels and viaducts. Thanks to viaducts, there was no competitive interaction with other thoroughfares. As a result, travel time between the most important cities was reduced by eighty percent between 1750 and 1830.

Before the joining of the telegraph to the railroad, train operators had to watch for track obstacles. Speed was also not uniform because weather conditions and noise affected how fast the train could go, especially through tunnels. The telegraph relieved the driver of having to focus their perception on the conditions that prevailed around him. Now the engineer just had to follow the signals. He was the operator of a machine. According to Schivelbusch, the telegraph gave the railway system a kind of central nervous system. With the railroads, space was both diminished and expanded. Space was diminished in the shrinking of transport time; yet it expanded transport space by traveling to longer, unknown places embedded in a transport network.

Class and the railroads

In the United States the railroad brought people together socially, forcing all classes to travel together—but not, of course, in the same car. The poor were transported in open boxcars on freight trains until the 1840s and were treated as if they were freight. The upper classes traveled in carriages which looked like stagecoaches mounted on rails. It was as if the more aristocratic bourgeoisie were trying to forget the *industrial* foundations of the train itself. In contrast to European railroads, in American carriages the seats are not arranged in compartments facing each other but in a long car facing one way. This discouraged conversation and promoted an individualist experience of railroad travel.

Railroads and the impact on middle class states of consciousness

Riding in a stagecoach was not a very smooth journey. The ride could be disrupted by a recalcitrant horse, the impatience of drivers, cruelty to animals, or the unevenness of the roads. The animal's irregular movement raised and sunk the human body as they travelled. The passenger experience was directly bound up with the sounds and smell about them. The ride was either exhausting or thrilling, but either way the passenger was involved.

In the case of the railroad, a locomotive had shock absorbers, contributing to smoothness of the ride, even as its speed accelerated. The average traveling speed of early railways in England was 20 to 30 miles per hour, roughly three times the speed of stagecoaches. The speed of the train took the rider beyond everyday five-sense perception. But what exactly does that mean?

In part because the relationship between the wheel and the road was so smooth and relatively quiet the passenger lost a sense of the source of power that had been harnessed. The railroad did not appear *embedded i*n the space of the landscape the way the coach and the highway did. Speeding up travel *experientially flattened* passing towns which now appeared more like pictures on a wall. Railroads transformed landscapes into vistas. The hurtling railroad train and the endless telegraph poles acted as a mediation force with a new perception into a panoramic landscape. Schivelbusch defines panorama as evanescent landscape whose rapid motion made it possible to grasp the whole: impressions, not details. The vistas seen from Europe's windows lost their dimension of depth. The velocity blurred the foreground. Since *the speed of the train prevented the observation of natural objects, it drove consciousness into subjective sources for mental activity.*

Travelers in stagecoaches formed small groups and engaged in intensive discussions. But on the railroad journey, there were much less conversations among strangers. As we said, in the United States, the railroad carriage turned all passengers into face-forward positions, staring at one another's backs. On the railway carriage, people began to treat it as their right *not* to be spoken to by strangers. Before mass transport, people had rarely been obliged to sit together in silence for long periods of time just staring. Now, silence became the norm. Reading became a substitute for talking, at least among the middle classes. The purchase of a train ticket became equivalent to having a theater ticket. The more comfortable the moving body became, the more it encouraged social withdrawal.

Before the railroad, the patchwork of varying local time zones was not a problem as long as traffic between places was so slow that slight temporal differences in standard time between regions really did not add up to much. But as Stephen Kern points out, even as late as 1870 a traveler heading west from the east coast of the United States would have to reset their watch 200 times before reaching the Pacific. But the speed of the train made regional time differences significant. Regular traffic needed standardized time. In 1889 the US was divided into four time zones.

Urban planning and social class

The revolutions throughout Europe—1830, 1848 and the Paris Commune of 1871—were not soon forgotten by the ruling classes, and they set to work to organize the cities of the nineteenth century in such a way as to:

- discourage collective rebellion
- speed up the production, distribution and consumption of products

Haussmann designs, according to Richard Sennett, were the greatest urban development scheme of modern times. Streets were straightened for the purpose of speeding things up. Public space became increasingly commercialized, as roads and public squares were cleared of people in order to circulate raw materials and commodities faster through the city. Social gatherings in the streets were thinned out or in some cases contested. Haussmann's design for cities also separated communities of the working class and poor by *boulevards* flowing with traffic in order to discourage movement of *organized groups* through the city. The street's width permitted two army wagons to travel side by side, enabling the militia to fire into the communities lying beyond the sides of the street wall.

Space compression: the telephone

From the seventeenth century forward, newspapers created an invisible de-sensualized community linked together through print. One liability of the newspaper was that while it widened the community spatially, we found out about events *after* events have occurred. Secondly, communication was asymmetrical. You read about the news; you didn't create news as you read. What the telephone did was to create *in-vivo* discussion about events *as they happened*.

How did the telephone impact the experience of the present? It made it possible to experience many distant events at the same time. It stretched the present beyond face-to-face conversation. According to Kern:

> The telephone allowed people to talk to one another across great distances, to think about what others were feeling and then respond immediately without the time to reflect afforded by written communication. Business and personal exchanges suddenly became instantaneous instead of protracted. (*The Culture of Time and Space*, 69)

> The telephone allowed Wall St. to become a truly national financial center by increasing the liquidity of securities and the speed of fund-raising. J. P. Morgan averted a financial panic in 1907 when over the telephone he extended 25 million in credit to several major banks threatened with excessive withdrawals. (114)

In Europe, the Germans were the first country to understand the value of the long-distance telephone. By 1885, thanks to Bismarck, there were thirty-three cities in Germany linked by phone. This was followed in 1887 by a line between

Paris and Brussels, followed by the first underwater cable connecting France and Paris. In the United States, New York and Chicago were linked in 1892 and twenty-three years later New York was connected to San Francisco.

The timing of the use of the telephone from its use in economic and political contexts to use by the public occurred very quickly. By 1891, seventy thousand phones were in use; by World War I, one million three hundred thousand were operating. By 1912 there were 600,000 phones in Britain and in the United States; by 1914 ten million were in use.

One historian of the telephone, Herbert Casson, identified the following characteristics of the telephone:

- it weakened the preservation of the past through letter writing; the ease and convenience of the phone undermined the linear retracing the past through letters.
- it expanded the spatial range of the present
- It encouraged more self-reflection on the caller's part because they can prepare for a conversation and control it at the outset
- it produced a heightened sense of alertness because of the possibility of a phone call at any time (harder to appreciate in our time because voice machines weaken the urgency of having to pick up the phone); a 'callee' may not prepared and may feel invaded
- it raised expectations of waiting for a call; conversations were a much more intense communication than a letter because a letter might come only once a day, whereas a phone call can come at any time

'Empty' space as an ideology of imperialism

Stephen Kern points out at the very time Western historians and geographers began to *imagine* space as *empty,* in space real time was packed.

> Until 1880 France, England, and Portugal had about one million square miles of coast. In 1884, Bismarck abandoned his opposition to overseas territory expansion and Germany quickly staked

out all four of its African colonies within a year. By 1890, Italy, Germany, Belgium and Spain had taken a total of six million square miles. By 1914 all but Abyssinia and Liberia were under European domination which extended over 11,500,000 square miles.

France	4,238,000
Britain	3,495,000
Germany and Italy	1 million each
Belgium	800,000
Portugal	780,000
Spain	75,000

(Kern 232)

By the end of the century, dominant world powers had finished taking the vast open space of Africa and Asia.

In the United States, as far back as 1845 the doctrine of *Manifest Destiny* was born and then taken up in political circles to justify taking the land of native Americans during the westward expansion. Kern points out that Fredrick Turner's frontier hypothesis was an application of geographical determinism. Turner claimed that it was the wide-open spaces of the American West that created the conditions for the supposed love of Americans for freedom and political democracy. In order for the doctrine of Manifest Destiny to find fertile ground, it needed to imagine the West as wide-open, undiscovered spaces. Whatever Turner's intentions, it certainly worked well to justify the Yankee state's expansion into native lands. By 1898 Hawaii, Puerto Rico, Guam, and the Philippines were annexed and Cuba a protectorate in 1901. The Virgin Islands were bought from Demark in 1917.

Commercialization of places and spaces at the end of the nineteenth century

Decline of public places

Capitalism and place don't mix. Earlier in this chapter we associated place with what is cozy, conservative, slow-moving, qualitative, and sacred. When people make places, they lose track of time and are lost in a kind of magical spell. This spirit must have been present in eighteenth-century coffee houses, and inns of Europe in the seventeenth through the nineteenth centuries. Any owner of an ale house who wanted to cultivate his establishment, had to accept that there was a socializing aspect built into his business. People nursed their drinks and pushed their food around their plates as they conversed and played games.

Why wouldn't commercial places work for capitalists? What sociologist Ray Oldenburg called 'third places' invited people to linger without necessarily spending a great deal of money. These were fine for merchants of small shops with little competition; but capitalists needed to pack people in and move them out. By the late nineteenth century cities were becoming more and more dominated by commercial space. Very slowly, public places were thinned out while space became filled with commodities. Spatial or even sacred places became increasingly subject to commercial pressures. A place that had not changed its appearance was thought to have been bypassed by time. Most any other public human activity which did not immediately serve commercial purposes was suspect, marginalized or driven out.

Invisible spaces: Disorientation through fetishization of commodities

A finished commodity on the shelf is one link in a chain of production, circulation and distribution. One problem with commodities, at least from the consumer's viewpoint is that under capitalism they lack a spatial and temporal context. Commodities appear miraculously on the shelves, while the places where extraction, production, distribution, waste, and pollution are hidden from the consumer. Places of consumption present themselves as a world apart. Only those links directly related to *purchase* become the center of the world rather than links in a chain of production processes. The causes and consequences of the places of how they are produced commodity production are opaque to us.

CHAPTER 6

Temporality From Cyclic To Linear Time (Progress)

Orientation

Discovery of deep time

Before the eighteenth century, geological changes were explained by *catastrophic* processes of either water erosion (the theory of neptunism) or heat (the theory of vulcanism). Not only were both types of changes catastrophic and unpredictable, but they were also connected with religious ideas about divine intervention. Then, in 1785, James Hutton proposed that changes to the earth occurred *gradually* and that the earth was a self-evolving body with its own laws. Hutton argued that these changes occurred over periods of time vastly larger than biblical chronology. Lyell was more empirical and comprehensive than Hutton and he consolidated the theory of uniformitarianism in his *Principles of Geology*. However, while Hutton and Lyell understood *earth's history* as dynamic, they each thought that *species were fixed* and subject to no evolving processes. The discovery of deep time by geology in the eighteenth century and Darwinian evolution in the nineteenth century brought movement into the world and challenged biblical ideas about the age of the earth and the nature of species.

In the last third of the eighteenth century, natural history began to differentiate between organic and inorganic change. This led to a struggle to understand at what point in time organic matter begins. Lamarck posited spontaneous generation from the inorganic to the organic. Pressure in environment modifies the characteristics of species and these modifications directly pass on to subsequent generations. It was left to Darwin and Wallace to deepen, complicate, and correct what Lamarck started. What the theories of the earth (inorganic) and organisms (organic) have in common is that change is gradual and goes on for a long time. As it turns out, not only is space infinite as astronomers (specifically Bruno) argued, but time, if not eternal, operates on a scale way beyond what humanity imagined. If the biological world is dynamic (rather than static) and it changes gradually, then perhaps this is how we can understand change *in human societies*.

This newfound interest in long, gradual change in geology and biology became one of the foundation stones for the theory of progress in societies. Just as the orientation to space changed in households, theater, and city life from the Middle Ages to the end of the nineteenth century, so changes in notions of time were revolutionized. For most of human history, people thought of their societies as static. Whatever existed in societies had always been that way. With the rise of agricultural civilizations, human societies were thought to change, but, basically, they followed the cycles of nature. For most of Western history, human civilization was thought to rise and fall in cycles. But there was a sub-current, a linear perspective in Western history which conceived of social life as having a linear direction. These theories drew the shape of social time as gradually improving. There was 'progress'. The basis for the sections on progress are from Richard Nisbett book *History of the Idea of Progress*.

Then at the end of the nineteenth century, capitalist depressions, nationalism, imperialism, and workers struggles threw a monkey-wrench into the notion that social time could be characterized as gradual and improving. Italian political theorists Pareto and Mosca argued against liberal or conservative pictures of representative politics as motivated by good will and rhetorical debate. Instead, politics was driven by elites who expected to maintain their power by force or fraud. Furthermore, crowd theories argued that masses of people were not interested in democracy at all. Rather, they were subject to gullibility, suggestiveness, and immediate gratification. Trust in reason itself was undermined by the discovery of the unconscious.

In the same time period, skepticism about gradual change was not just coming from political and economic forces. The stability of the material world was challenged by physics both in quantum physics and Einstein's special theory of relativity as we will see at the end of the chapter.

Direction in time: progress

Characteristics of progress

If I were to inquire about how you were proceeding on a work project, you might say 'things are progressing'. What exactly does that mean? For one thing, you probably mean there is gradual rather than sudden change. Secondly, you are implying that it has taken you an extended period of time. Thirdly, you imagine the project is improving with time: it is getting better. The term progress is so much a part of American and European vocabulary that it is tempting to dismiss the term as trite. But the word progress as a way to describe work on a personal project has its roots deep in western religious, political, and economic history. Before going into specific detail about this history, here is a list some commonalities all the traditions of progress share:

- Events or processes are improving. The end will be better than the beginning or the middle
- There is a long temporal span rather than a short one
- The process is accumulating—each step is based on previous steps
- The process is irreversible and linear (rather than reversible or occurring in cycles)
- The end point of the process is inevitable
- There are predicable stages within the movement of progress
- Lovejoy's 'principle of plentitude' is at work: the existence in this world of everything actual or potential that is necessary for perfection (no appeal to external forces)
- the expansion of progress is occurring across the globe
- the future of human societies can be engineered towards

progress through the use of individual and collective reason
- progress is achieved by hard work and sacrifice (not luck or inheritance)

Within this tradition, there are at least four bones of contention. First, in going through whatever stages of progress exist, what is the place of conflict? For some theorists, progress is *gradual and quantitative*. Conflict is dismissed as something that is a product of misunderstandings, lack of insight into long-term self-interest, or some other accidental condition. Proponents of this version of progress include most Enlightenment philosophers in the eighteenth century, capitalists after they had gained power in the nineteenth century, and some evolutionary socialists towards the end of the nineteenth century. The other view of progress understands conflict as a necessary stage in order to proceed to the end in sight. Here the nature of progress includes sudden or protracted qualitative change which revolutionizes the existing order. This tendency has united theorists as different as St. Augustine, the Puritans, Hegel, Marx and Engels.

Another bone of contention is whether the secularization of society is an ingredient in progress or not. Most socialists, a few Enlightenment philosophers, and a handful of scientists think that progress involves the decline and /or the abolition of religion. Religious theorists tend to see progress as a renewal or a cleansing of religious traditions that are mired in superstition, anti-science, hyper-rationalism or idolatry. A renewed religion is an essential in progress.

Closely related to the secularization verses religion polarity is the question of which institutions are the engines of progress. Some say progress is achieved through the use of science, technological advancement, capitalism, and political liberalism. Others look to improvement through spirituality, ethics, or psychological institutions.

Lastly, there are differences over what counts as progress. People like Adam Smith and Marx argue that an increase in material abundance, luxury, and free time is a necessary condition for progress. More spiritually oriented people are concerned that these creature comforts will acquire a life of their own. People will become mired in materialism and the spirit of progress will be lost. To summarize, the controversial issues are:

- Whether change is gradual, quantitative, and conflict free, or is it conflict-driven, sudden. and qualitative (catastrophes, or revolutions?
- Does the secularization of society away from religion count as progress?
- What are the engines of progress? Science, technological advancement, capitalism, political liberalism, religious reform movements, or educational institutions?
- Does increase in material abundance and luxury count as progress or not?

Theories of progress were not just about imagining a better future for all. They were also about *reinterpreting the past*. Theorists on progress interpreted the past as being filled with unpredictability, short-sightedness, technological backwardness, economic scarcity, political chaos, tyranny, parochial clannishness, superstitious rituals, magical beliefs, ignorance, animal instincts, and immorality. In the eyes of these theorists, slowly but surely, human existence has started to get better and better. The possibilities for the future are infinite if only we wake up to our actual condition.

<u>Progress in the ancient world and Christianity</u>

In his book *History of the Idea of Progress*, Robert Nisbet takes issue with historians who claim that the use of the term progress is simply a product of the Enlightenment and the industrial revolutions. While these movements added new elements to the theory, the seeds of the idea of progress go all the way back first to the Greeks, then Christianity, and into the Middle Ages.

Though it is generally true that the Greeks saw change as primarily occurring in cycles, Nisbet argues that reputable historians of the ancient world such as Finley, Guthrie, and E.R. Dodds say that the Greeks had some sense of progression in the arts and sciences.

Furthermore, the Myth of Prometheus (part of the title for my last book) is a *Greek* myth. A myth about stealing fire from the Gods and giving it to humanity would not exist if it was not an existing controversy in that society. The rhetorician Protagoras's claim that 'man is the measure of all things' supports the Promethean myth. Long preceding Max Weber's *Protestant Ethic and the Spirit of Capitalism*, Hesiod, unlike most Greek philosophers and historians, defends the value of work and claims it is *idleness* that is a disgrace. Aristotle's *Politics* describes the story of human societies as evolving from families, to villages, to confederations of villages. Aristotle thinks that more complex societies are responsible for the best inventions and therefore superior. Aristotle says that:

> Civilization is a work of neither gods or heroes, half-human, half-divine but of men cooperating throughout history helping one another and bound to one another like links of a chain. (33)

But the theorist that has the most uncompromising attitude about progress in the ancient world is Lucretius. Like theorists of progress, Lucretius hates superstition and trusts reason. Nisbet argues that Lucretius offers a naturalistic evolutionary picture of the formation of nature and human societies that was not surpassed until the late eighteenth century and into the nineteenth century:

> His work could enter into dozens of works on the progress of mankind in the eighteenth and nineteenth centuries. Everything that is essential is there: naturalness of the process (autonomy from

> divine cause or intervention); stress upon human insight and ingenuity; insistence on gradual, slow and cumulative character of the process (43)
>
> He stressed the hardiness of the human body and mind and aboriginal cunning and ability to invent weapons against larger and more powerful beasts... (39). [The] invention of metallurgy from observation of lightning opening up the earth and producing gold; invention of fine arts of navigation which earliest man could not have dreamed of (42)

Early theories of progress described the spiritual evolution of humanity from animism to polytheism to monotheism. This spiritual evolution can be seen among the Jews, Catholics, and Protestants. In the case of extraordinary holy men or saints, their individual evolution was championed. Beginning in the seventeenth century, the focus of progress began to change from spiritual to secular evolution. The emphasis became *the progress of science and the evolution of societies* from hunter-gatherers to agricultural to industrial capitalist societies.

Progress in the seventeenth and eighteenth centuries

In seventeenth-century France, Fontenelle was the first to formulate the idea of progress in knowledge. He argued that modern knowledge is *superior* to the ancient Greek and Romans in literacy, philosophy, and scientific work. He was also the first to create that fateful analogy between social evolution and individual development from childhood to adolescence.

Perraut in his *Comparison of the Ancients and Moderns* argues that there had been progress over the last thousand years even through the Middle Ages because their knowledge was kept secret in the monasteries.

In the eighteenth century, Vico divided social evolution into three stages:

- Age of gods (religion)—characterized by primitive language, imagination, rhythm, song

- Age of heroes and aristocrats—characterized by the arts and poetry
- Age of prose—culture and philology characterized by rationalism and technique (this age will then degenerate and a new cycle will emerge)

By the mid-eighteenth century to the end of the nineteenth century, the theory of progress had expanded from the realm of philosophers and theologians to become the bedrock epistemology in the hard sciences, as well as in the field of anthropology, history, and sociology. The theory of progress was well received among the lay public. Nisbet points out that for Americans the doctrine of progress was akin to a secular evangelism. Progress also became the epistemological foundation for new ideas about economic and political freedom and united social critics such as Voltaire, Adam Smith, Immanuel Kant.

As we saw in chapter two, the ideas of Adam Smith were crucial to the development of individualism as well as how to justify capitalism. Smith understood capitalism as part of a continuum of progress. He thought that the accumulation of wealth was a necessary part of improving the human condition and he saw the division of labor in society under capitalism as essential in producing that material wealth. The division of labor allows people to produce more goods more efficiently and it assists individuals in developing their skills as experts.

It is hard to imagine anyone who combined political radicalism and science in the service of progress more than the great French hero of the Enlightenment, Condorcet. Condorcet was a mathematician and secretary of the Academy of Sciences. He supported both the American and French revolutions and was imprisoned during the French revolution for criticizing some of the authoritarian ways of the Jacobins. In his *Sketch for an Historical Picture of the Progress of the Human Mind* in 1795, he developed a ten-stage theory of human progress. In his theory, the last stage society was governed by scientists. He argued that through science the egalitarian future will be realized as religious superstition falls be the wayside.

Table 6.1 Nineteenth century theories of progress

Progress as Freedom	**Category of comparison**	**Progress as power**
Freedom from state tyranny; Private right to trade and accumulate property	**What is freedom?**	Freedom to participate in political activity to change society
Individuals as they actually were	**What is human nature?**	Individuals as they ideally were
Spencer, Turget	**Theoretician?**	Saint-Simon—New Christianity
		Hegel and the state
Compact about the past	**Time of contract**	Future, redemptive state
Rights (Locke)	**Place or misplace of rights**	Alienation of all rights to the state (Rousseau)
Liberal	**Political translation**	Republican, radical, socialist

Progress in the nineteenth century

Nisbet differentiates the history of progress in the nineteenth century into two great camps: progress as liberty and progress as power. They can be distinguished as shown in the following table.

In the nineteenth century, the spirit of progress as economic liberty was carried on by Herbert Spencer (whom we met in chapter four). Spencer argues that there is a pattern in social evolution, a predictable long-term process of change which moves from simple homogenous life to a heterogeneous, complex life. Simple societies have no division of labor; they are static, repressive, and authoritarian in religion, caste, race, and political biases. On the other hand, heterogeneous societies possess a diversity of function. They were dynamic, competitive, and have liberal beliefs. Differences between humans are based on merit rather than blood or pomp and circumstance. There was no better ideological system for justifying capitalism in the second half of the nineteenth century than Spencer.

For most of the nineteenth century, theories of progress centered on political and economic reform, either in developing utopian systems such as St. Simon, Comte, and Fourier, or in the revolutionary socialism of Marx and Engels. Nineteenth century theorists both built upon the Enlightenment tradition and criticized it for being too decentralized and not systematic enough. Utopian thinkers like St. Simon and Comte blamed the Enlightenment for the bloodshed of the French Revolution. They thought that progress could not be brought about through open class conflict. In St. Simon's writings on social evolution, there have been two organic periods and two critical periods:

- Organic period 1: Greece and Rome
- Critical period 1: Dark Ages
- Organic period 2: Middle Ages in thirteenth century because it had developed monotheism
- Critical period 2: Enlightenment
- Organic phase 3: New Christianity

August Comte's book *Positive Philosophy* is an in-depth review of the history of all the sciences and places them in a hierarchical and logical relationship. He argues that each of these disciplines went through three phases: theological, metaphysical, and scientific (positive). Between 1851 and 1854, Comte published a four volume *Positive Polity* which is about the organization of the new society. Nisbet reflects that:

> Rarely has any utopia ever been written in the detail that Comte's was. Everything from the rites and ceremonies to the actual dress of scientists and layman; a positivist calendar with each month bearing the name of a great philosopher or scientist (256)

Those theorists on progress who found no place for conflict in their system excluded Marx from their theories because they saw Marx as an enemy of capitalism. For them, capitalism had brought much progress to humanity in the way of science, technology, and material wealth. This interpretation is very unfair to Marx.

It would be one thing to exclude Marx if his revolutionary communism wanted to destroy the modern world and go back either to an earlier age or to build up communism from scratch after destroying capitalism. Marx wanted neither. Though he is merciless in his analysis of capitalism in *Capital*, Marx showed clear admiration of capitalism in his *Communist Manifesto* in describing how important capitalism was as a revolutionary force against feudalism. Throughout his life, Marx thought that communism could only be erected on top of the material wealth built by capitalism. While Marx had always argued that capitalists would stop at nothing to protect their wealth, he hoped the revolution against them by the working class would prevent too much destruction of the material goods, transportation systems, communications systems, and political structures as possible. Communism would be a material paradise with workers working less. He also thought that communism was inevitable.

Freddy Perlman, an anarchist agitator of the 1960s and 1970s, commenting on Marx's three stages of history waxed poetically when he said that:

- humans in tribal society 'were much but had little'
- humans under capitalism 'had much but were little'
- humans under communism would 'have much and be much'

For Marx, progress was not a linear line but a dialectical spiral.

Progress and nationalism

Up until the nineteenth century, the theories of progress had no theory of the place of the state in its social organization. As we saw in chapter one of my last book, it was in the nineteenth century that the state became more centralized. It extended itself into the periphery of society in its impact and more expansive internationally. It was Fichte and Hegel who linked the development of the state through the nation to the development of progress. Hegel argues that society is vastly improved by the emergence and expansion of the state and progress in society is inseparable from the strengthening of the state. Hegel went so far as to say that the state is the divine idea as it exists on earth. As we have seen in chapter one of my last book, by the second half of the nineteenth century, right wing nationalism used a Social Darwinist understanding of competition between nation-states in order to link theories of progress to imperialism.

In this climate, progress become inseparable from the existence of certain racial stocks in history. In his *Essay on the Inequality of the Human Races* written between 1853 and 1855, Joseph Gobineau argues that the mixing of races led to the decline of civilizations. The German Aryans were the chosen race, but they were degenerating because of their mixture of lower races. It is tempting to think Gobineau was referring to non-whites, but we must be careful because he included southern Europeans as one of the degenerate races. Gobineau was just one of many intellectuals in Europe and the United States who identified progress with a certain race whether the superior race was Aryan, Anglo-Saxon, Teutonic (Germans), or Nordic.

Discontinuities in time and space in the nineteenth century

Discontinuities in time in the nineteenth century

In their book The *Discovery of Time*, Stephen Toulmin and June Goodfield call the nineteenth century the 'century of history' because of the interest in geology, archeology, and evolutionary biology. But in the second half of the nineteenth century, the pace of life quickened and respect for the stability and wisdom of the past began to fragment.

Up until the nineteenth century humans were aware of the finiteness of *life forms*. However, the world of inorganic matter was thought of as being eternal or ending only because of divine Intervention. Then, in 1852, Lord Kelvin's essay on entropy predicted the end of the earth due to heat loss. He called this the second law of thermodynamics. For the first time, the world of *inanimate* nature was also seen as time bound. This must have added to the feeling within the middle classes that things were happening too quickly.

Both sociologist George Simmel and historian Karl Lamprecht noticed that in the last decade of the nineteenth century there was a great increase in the number of pocket watches. There was a heightened appreciation for tracking shorter intervals of time—five minutes, one minute—whether on the job or off the job. The best example of on-the-job tracking was Fredrick Taylor and his collaborators on the scientific management of time and motion studies to control workers in factories. When not working, people tracked their time when speaking on a telephone.

In his book *Lived Time*, Eugene Minkowski describes two modes of experiencing time. One is of the future rushing towards us and the other is a sudden burst of interest in human planning to control what comes at us. Stephen Kern suggests that this helps to explain the burst of interest in science fiction. As far back as the 1860s, the books of Jules Verne were promising great futures for humanity. This continued with Edward Bellemy's socialist futurism in *Looking Backward* in 1888 and the work of H.G. Wells beginning in the 1890s. Science fiction was not snooty writing for the upper classes. It was very popular. Kern says that its audience were both horrified and enchanted by the prospect of a future rushing towards them. People began to see themselves less as cogs in a deterministic machine.

Paradoxically, at the same time science fiction captured the hearts of the West, there was a corresponding interest in nostalgia about the past. Kern points out that it is only when the past really seems like it might disappear that people start to cling to it, to romanticize it as a reaction to the pace of events in the present. As village life is gobbled up first by capitalist agriculture and then capitalist industry, people romanticize village life idyllically rather than seeing villages as havens of superstition, plague, conformity, and gossip as men of the

Enlightenment saw them.

Revolution in physics of matter, space and time

Questioning objectivity in science

For many intellectuals the bloom was off the rose of the Enlightenment, as it became implicated with the materialism and positivism of the middle of the nineteenth century. Positivism seemed to attempt to carry on the traditions of the Enlightenment but went too far, reducing the study of human behavior to the methods of natural science. Hughes, in his book *Consciousness and Society* sets the tone of his book by characterizing changes in the development of physics, social science, politics, and psychology as a revolt against positivism.

Philosopher of science and physicist Ernst Mach aspired to dispense with the hope of finding the ultimate material substance on which to ground science. He argues that we all we have is our sensations of the world and we should base our judgments not on trying to understand what the world is independent of our experience but to start and end with our sensations or experiences.

As a physicist, Mach was adamantly opposed to any sort of metaphysical speculation. According to Mach, reification gives birth to conceptual monsters such as terms like force, laws of nature, matter, atoms, energy, absolute space, absolute time, and matter. In religion and metaphysics reification included God and the Devil.

For Mach, the world consists only of our sensations because this is all we have. Physics is a shorthand method of relating and correlating these sense data with the help of mathematics. The scientist stands at one level up from sensations. At its root, the world is no more or less than the sum total of what appears to the senses. Mach sought to avoid both ontological polarities of materialism or idealism by claiming that both are speculative abstractions. For the most part, humans are passive knowers, and knowing consists of describing the world of sensation to ourselves. Max Plank accused Mach of anthropomorphism because Mach's attempt to base physics on the description of sense data assumed that physical states were somehow identical with psychical states. This seemed to imply that there was no objective world independent of our sensations.

Mach died in 1916 and, according to Toulmin, he was disillusioned and disappointed with the contemporary reception of his ideas. However, the influence of Mach's ideas are very clear in the arguments about quantum theory that physicists Bohr and Heisenberg made about the impossibility of looking at the world objectively, independent of observation. In addition, Mach might have been surprised that his ideas had crossed the discipline of physics into law, politics, and social thought. His ideas were embraced with enthusiasm by Austrian revisionist Marxists that penetrated Russian socialism through Bogdanov. Mach's ideas were a direct challenge to their materialist explanation of the laws of nature and society.

Hans Vaihingen defines knowledge not as what is true objectively, but knowledge *as if* it were true. This philosophy of 'as if' does not give us license to believe whatever we want. It is simply an auxiliary construct, a scaffolding which we might later remove when a better hypothesis comes along. If a hypothesis moves the scientific process along, it doesn't matter whether it is a fiction. This outlook could be seen as a precursor to William James' pragmatism which proposes that whatever is true is what *works*. As you might imagine, some scientists worried this could slide into a skepticism about whether we could know anything about the world.

The great process philosopher Henry Bergson believed that the field of science had 'physics envy'. He meant that scientists reduce biological nature to physics in the hopes of mimicking the success of Newton. The problem for Bergson, is that in the movement from inanimate to animate matter, *matter is changed by time*. The implication is that science could never understand the complexity of life and mind while wedded to mechanistic picture of physics which is dominated by mathematical space.

Newtonian time, space, and matter

In this section I am following the description of Stephen

Kern in his book *The Culture of Time and Space: 1880-1918*. Newton's master work, *Principia Mathematica* stood the test of time from its publication in 1687 until the end of the nineteenth century. One of the easiest ways to understand the differences between Newton and Einstein is how radically different their understanding of time, space, and matter is.

For Newton, time and space are independent processes that are simply containers for matter. Newtonian time flows universally and uniformly through events, neither effecting or being affected by then. So too, space is treated as continuous, homogeneous and at rest. Space is understood as an empty container which is filled with matter. Neither Newton nor most nineteenth century physicists could imagine space as performing an active physical function, so they coined the term 'ether,' which they hypothesized permeated space. Whatever change takes place in an object is the result of its motion through the ether. Space can be measured by the distance between the observer and the object. The length between them is absolute. The underlying geometry that grounded Newtonian space was Euclid's axioms and postulates which was the foundation of the properties of space in all classical physics at the beginning of the nineteenth century. As for matter, Newton characterized it matter as hard, solid, massy, impenetrable. This was a tradition that went all the way back to Democritus. Matter was full and outside of matter there was thought to be the void.

Einsteinian time, space, and matter

Einstein did not negate Newton's explanations of the motion of planetary bodies in his law of gravitation. As long as the application of Newton's analysis was of *medium* scale, these properties of time, space, and matter could work. What he did was to show that at a larger, macro reference point, time, space, and matter were integrated and co-created each other.

For Einstein there was no such thing as universal time because time speeds up or slows down based on the relative motion between an observer in relation to a given reference system. For Einstein, time measurements are *modified by motion*:

> With the special theory of relatively of 1905, Einstein calculated how time in one reference system moving away at a constant velocity appears to *slow down*, when viewed from another system at rest, relative to it. (Kern,19)

There is only a *plurality* of local times, each dependent on the relative motion of the clock and observer rather than a universal time. Einstein's picture of space, contrary to Newton was curved, discontinuous and moving:

> Einstein's relativity theory questions the stability of all spatially extended forms—a rigid body that has the form of a sphere when viewed at rest will *begin to assume an ellipsoid shape when viewed in motion*. All three-dimensional objects will shrivel up into plane figures when their relative velocity reaches the speed of light. (Kern, 184)

The difference in Newtonian and Einsteinian space were rooted in two different kinds of geometry:

> The most serious challenge to conventional space came with the development in the early nineteenth century of non-Euclidean geometries. Around 1830, the Russian mathematician Lobatchewsky announced a two-dimensional geometry in which an infinite number of lines could be drawn through any point parallel to another line in the same plane... in 1854 Riemann devised another two-dimensional geometry in which all triangles had angle-sums *greater* than 180 degrees. Riemann's space was elliptical. Both these surface spaces contrasted with the flat, planar surface of Euclid's 2D geometry. (Kern,132-133)

As for matter, the Newtonian conception was challenged

by Ernst Mach and J.J. Thompson. In 1897, J.J. Thompson announced his discovery of more basic corpuscles out of which atoms were built. His model of the atom is composed of corpuscles (which were eventually called electrons) orbiting around the nucleus of the atom. These atoms were largely *empty space* which challenged the classical distinction between the plenum of matter and the void of space. If there is no clear distinction between the plenum of matter and the void of space and if matter may be conceived of as a configurations of energy alignments, then the traditional understanding of matter as made up of discrete bits with sharply defined surfaces was suddenly challengeable. Please see Table 6.2 for a summary.

Neo-Machievellian political theory and crowd psychology

Fin de siècle anxiety

In his book, *Wittgenstein's Vienna,* Stephen Toulmin defines the end of the nineteenth century 'fin de siècle' as a period of 'over-ripeness of perverse and mannered decadence'. In the decorative arts, the epoch exuded a sense of "heaviness, material excess, coupled with a sense of foreboding." According to Stuart Hughes (in *Consciousness and Society*) the generation just before the first World War had an impending sense of doom. On the one hand, it seemed that the old institutions were becoming unhinged from a rapidly changing reality. On the other hand, there grave uncertainty as to what would come in its place.

Dilthey and the cultural sciences

Dilthey, as a cultural scientist and historian, believed that between the world of natural science and the world of human activity was a cultural and historical world which could not be reduced to the natural sciences. Because human beings make history, we are subject to laws that go beyond the natural sciences. For Dilthey, the discipline of history should not be the accumulation of facts which the historian collects as an observer. The historian has to enter sympathetically into *the frame of mind*, the understanding of the historical period *as the participants* experienced it. The social sciences should not search for general laws at all. All historians could do was to describe concrete history or the spirit of the age.

Socialism under fire

In Marx's analysis of capitalism in the first volume of *Capital* in 1867, he proposes that capitalism will fall because of:

- laws of the falling rate of profit
- the increasing misery of the working class
- labor theory of value (which said the value of all goods was based on the socially necessary labor time to produce it)

Ten years later, the German social democratic party formed. The party soon discovered that there is no necessary correlation between the growth in numbers of socialist members and the revolutionary spirit. At the same time, the life of the working classes seemed to be getting better. The middle class was not disappearing and the great day of economic reckoning seemed to have come and gone. Edward Bernstein proposed an evolutionary model of socialism which abandoned the necessity for revolution in favor of a gradual process of winning seats in elections. Within Marxism there was a great rift between this reformism and what later became Marxist-Leninism. At the same time, capitalist economists like Bohm-Bawerk and members of the Austrian school painstakingly challenged Marxism principals systematically.

Political cynics: Neo-Machiavellian elite theory

Unlike much liberal and democratic theory in England and the United States, Italian political theory had none of the smoothness and mystification as to what was going on. Politics topics included force, the struggle for power, and the place of deception.

In his book *Social Systems,* Pareto refutes Marxian economics and sociology thoroughly enough that Hughes claims it caused Lenin more worry than any other anti-Marxist writing. It was a biting and sarcastic book. While he agreed with the materialist conception of history being about a struggle between classes for resources, he found the ultimate goal of socialism to be ridiculously naïve.

For one thing, Pareto cast aspirations on the socialist leadership. Instead of being filled with altruistic good will for the workers, the leaders under socialism were just disgruntled individuals who could not achieve upper class status through the normal channels. The revolution was really a struggle between an old elite and a new elite. The masses below achieved no real power. They were simply the shields in the service of battles between the elites.

Pareto was prescient in predicting that under socialism conflicts would continue to persist between different kinds of workers: between intellectual and non-intellectuals, between different kinds of politicians, between politicians and those administered by them, and between innovators and conservatives. What about the lower orders? Contrary to Marx, Pareto saw them as apathetic and easily duped through war propaganda and religious promises. He called these cognitive errors and stupidities 'residues' and 'derivatives'.

Robert Michaels, who was once a protégé of Max Weber, made even more trouble for socialists because Michaels had firsthand experience in the German Socialist Party with bureaucracy. Michaels thought that Machiavelli's "force and fraud" operated every bit as much in socialist organization as any other kind. In his book *Political Parties, he* applies the concept of elites to socialist parties and trade unions. In his 'Iron law of oligarchy' he argues that political organizations, through internal necessities of discipline and administrative continuity, become closed and self-perpetuating and over time lose any pretensions towards democratic participation of the lower orders. Contrary to both liberal and socialist parliamentarism, Pareto and Michaels sought to pull the veil from the democratic follies and expose it as the machinations of old guard or creative political elites.

Hughes sums of the period beginning in the 1890's this way:

- **The nature of natural knowledge**—Physicists like Mach, Maxwell, Hertz, and quantum mechanics challenged the deterministic and materialistic nature of physics

- **the meaning of time and duration in psychology, philosophy, literature and history**—Bergson, Proust, Thomas Mann—were interested in how to capture the immediacy of past experience in language which the logical memory had already stored away in neat compartments

- **the nature of history**—Dilthey had attempted to establish rules that would separate the study of history from the world of natural science

- **the irrational nature of politics**—Italian political theorists Pareto, Mosca, and Michaels exposed the idealism and vapidity of liberal Enlightenment politics which they claimed was driven by the force and fraud of elites. As for the masses, they were uninterested and incapable of political participation. This was hammered home by crowd theorists like Taine, Lebon, and Tarde

- **the place of the unconscious in human drives**—This could be seen in the work of Bergson's intuitionism and in the drives and residues of Pareto

Table 6.2 Physics of Time and Space and Matter: 1880-1918

Newton **Eighteenth century to end of nineteenth century**	**Category of comparison**	**Einstein** **Early twentieth century**
Uniformly unaffected by real events	**Flow of time**	Uneven—time speeds up or slows down one reference when viewed from another reference system
Universal	**Resulting scale of time**	Plurality of local times
Empty, static, and immutable	**Characteristics of space**	Space is full, dynamic, and has the power of partaking in physical events
Universal, continuous, and uniform (at rest)	**Scale of Space**	Curved, discontinuous, and moving
The distance between the object and the viewer Length is absolute	**How is space measured?**	The relative velocity of the object and the viewer was the crucial factor Length is the relative consequence of the act of measuring
Euclid's axioms and postulates	**Type of Geometry used**	Non-Euclidian geometries Lobatchewsky, Riemann
A force	**What is gravity?**	An intrinsic curvature of a Space-time continuum
Matter was independent of space	**What is the relationship between matter and space?**	In 1876 William Clifford: matter and its motion were manifestations of the varying curvature of space
Atoms: solid and impenetrable against a void of space	**What is the composition of matter?**	Sub-atomic particles were largely composed of empty space
Bodies are rigid and do not change shape regardless of speed	**What is the impact of speed on bodies?**	A rigid body that has the form of a sphere when viewed at rest will begin to assume an ellipsoid shape when viewed in motion; all three-dimensional objects will shrivel up into plane figures, when their relative velocity reaches the speed of light

CHAPTER 7

Ontogenesis in History: The Emergence of Childhoods, Adolescences, and Adulthoods

Orientation

Erikson's stages of psycho-social development

Developmental psychologists often imply that childhood, adolescence, and adulthood are simply universal stages of life. This is typified in psychologist Erik Erikson's eight stages of human development. Here are the stages:

- trust vs mistrust
- autonomy vs shame and doubt
- initiative vs guilt
- industry vs inferiority
- identity vs role confusion
- intimacy vs isolation
- generativity vs stagnation
- Integrity vs despair

According to Erikson, every stage is characterized by a conflict which results in either achieving a virtue as the result of having successfully dealt with a conflict or, if unsuccessful, an unresolved problem. This virtue is carried to the next stage along with unresolved problems of the previous stage. Furthermore, the stages accumulate, meaning they are built on each other. A minimal grappling with one stage is a precondition for dealing with the next stage. There is no stage-jumping. Lastly these are psycho-*social* stages which means they are somewhat affected by social conditions. The individual does not control the *pace* at which the stages emerge, nor the *content* of what is expected of them.

But how applicable are these stages *historically?* In other words, will the stages apply equally to people who lived in the Middle Ages, early modern Europe, the eighteenth century as well as the nineteenth century? Is there a different kind of childhood in the Middle Ages compared to in the nineteenth century? How universal is 'storm-and stress' that was claimed for adolescence during Erikson's time? These are the kind of questions we will take up in this chapter.

Before going into Erikson's stages, we will locate his stages relative to the work of one of the historians of the self, Roy Baumeister. Baumeister's description of development was as a process of negotiating a fundamental polarity between *continuity* on the one hand and *differentiation* on the other. He also argues that development continuity is *harder* to achieve the later we go into history. This lack of continuity results in destabilization or trivialization of individual stages.

Lastly, before touching on Erikson's theory we will examine the work of Philippe Aries (*Centuries of Childhood*) and Lawrence Stone (*The Family, Sex and Marriage in England 1500-1800)* as good checkpoints for how well Erikson's theory applies to the history of childhood.

Theories of development: mechanistic, organicist and dialectical

Any theory of human development must consider the relationship between biological processes (the brain), psychological processes (the mind), and social structures and processes. In this section I have followed the work of Jonas Langer (*Theories of Development*); Klaus Riegel (*Psychology My Love*); Werner's *Comparative Theory of Mental Development*, and lastly Valsiner's book on Werner (2005).

Table 7.1 provides an overview of the four major theories of development. The Freudian psychoanalytic theory is not included here because most of it has been either proven wrong or it has not been subjected to scientific experiment. In this first theory, nativism goes as far back as the turn of the century.

They have argued that heredity and genetic predispositions are primarily, if not exclusively, the drivers of human development.

Later evolutionary psychologists (Cosmides and Tooby) have added a more dynamic approach by specifying the evolutionary reasons why some behaviors are more adaptive than others. All nativists see change as gradual and continuous. Gesell, Bulher, and Hall would emphasize that the individual is passive (genetically determined) and the environment is passive because it takes generations before new adaptive skills are required. Since most nativists don't have specific stage theories, I include them to show that not all psychological theories even contend that stages exist. In Pepper's book, *World Hypothesis*, nativist theories are classified as 'formist' with its philosophical roots in Plato and Leibniz.

In the second theory, radical behavioristic theories of development are mechanistic. Whether Pavlov or Skinner, they see the individual (whether their focus is the brain or the mind) as passive, and an environment as relatively passive. This environment either conditions responses resulting from past associations (Pavlov) or the environment rewards or punishes the individual (Skinner). But the environment for the behaviorist operates at a *micro* level of family, friends, teachers, or classmates. The environment for behaviorists is not macro-social institutions such as capitalism or an authoritarian state. These theories are called mechanical theories of growth because:

- they emphasize what is going on *external* to the individual
- they see change and *gradual*, quantitative adaptations to external conditions
- the individual mind, brain or body is a blank slate which doesn't bring in anything active in the interaction with the environmental slate
- the whole is a product of the build-up of the parts

Langer has called these theories the 'mechanical mirror' theories because the goal is to for the individual to ideally reflect the environment. Its philosophical roots are in Aristotle and Locke's association theory. Like the nativists, behaviorist theories have no stages.

A variant of the second type is Bandura's social learning theory. This theory sees the environment as active and the person as passive. Bandura argues about the power of social models—attractive, powerful experts—to shape the individual. This kind of theory would be a mechanical materialist one in which individuals are seen as victims of social circumstances not of their choosing. In sociology, Durkheim's description of the movement from mechanical to organic society historically might be an example because the individual appears as a passive victim of the social circumstances. In geography, a mechanical materialist attitude would be the environmental determinism of Ratzel, which says that the climate and geography directly impacts how the individual turns out.

The third type of theory emphasizes the active person in a relatively passive environment. Since the work of Piaget on cognition will be considered in depth in a later chapter, there is no point in describing it in detail here. Meaning-making is confined to changes in internal state while the objective world is passive, a prop for a psychobiological drama staged within the body of an individual. Social mediations are secondary.

Heinz Werner is another 'organic' developmental psychologist who saw a child going through predictable stages. In the first stage of child development there is a primitive globalism, a whole without parts. The child in a global primitive state does not make a distinction between the objective and the subjective worlds. Boundaries are fused. Boundaries are porous between:

- dreams and imagery
- percepts and outer reality
- physical body and the objects in the world
- names of things and the things themselves
- motives for doing something and actions

In this primitive globalism, space has no objective properties and is inseparable from the objects or people within the space. In terms of time, children at first cannot tell the difference between objective time passing as measured by clocks and subjective time which speeds up or slows down based on the level of interest. This primitive fusion is also characterized by rigidity and instability in its functions.

As part of the developmental process, these states of fusion are followed by a stage of differentiation in which the objective characteristics of the physical world is clearly separated from the subjective experiences of the individuals. This leads to a stability and flexibility in its functions. After the capacity to tell the difference between the objective and subjective world, a new whole can be created, but this time it is a complex whole with fully differentiated parts.

Werner was very bold in his claims, arguing that the similar patterns can be comprehended not only in the difference between younger and older children, but also in the development of primates; the difference between abnormal and normal adults and even the difference between people in primitive societies and modern societies. If Werner's theories were applied to the subject matter of this book, he would contend that in the Middle Ages there was a primitive unity in outlook. The sense of space, time, cause, and human identity was formally a similar parallel with the fused state of consciousness of a child. Beginning in early modern Europe, societies would be characterized by gradual separation between the objective world and the subjective world. This third theory is organic because:

- development is seen to be an unfolding process of a plan which is *internal* to the organism
- the stages an individual goes through are *qualitatively* different from each other, and go through accumulating levels of complexity
- there is a primitive whole right from the beginning. From there, differentiation takes place, resulting in a new, more complex whole

Werner's theory can be categized by Pepper as 'organicist' with its philosophical roots in Kant and Mach.

The fourth way of thinking of development is the

dialectical approach. Here the *environment is active and the person is active*. This is typified in the work of Vygotsky and Rubinstein. Compared to the dialectical theory, the mechanical and organic theories attitude towards interaction as *weak*. All those theories say either the individual is active or the environment is active. But what they all have in common is that the interaction between the environment and the person is not co-creative. The subjective and objective systems are self-subsisting and only interact through *accidental or pre-determined means, not in a self-organizing way.*

The active-active stage of dialectical development is the only one in which *both the social world and the individual co-create each other*. On the one hand, social forces produce individuals but those individuals, through their work, re-produce social forces. The individual is first the yarn and then becomes the weaver of social life. The individual-social relationship is not static. It evolves into a spiral, either getting better or worse but never staying the same over the course of history.

Where does Erikson fit into this? Erikson started out as a Freudian and was heavily influenced by Anna Freud (at least in his early years). However, like many members of Freud's organization, he was skating on thin ice when he failed to conform to the orthodoxy of Freud's disciplines. While the left wing of the Freudians—Wilhelm Reich, Erich Fromm, and Karen Horney—were all anti-capitalist, and Reich and Fromm embraced some form of socialism, there were centrist forces within Freud's organization that wanted no part of these 'Neo-Freudians.' Instead they wanted to emphasize the ego side of Freud's psychic structure, as opposed to the id and the superego. Along with Heinz Hartman and Anna Freud, Erikson was one of the first wave of 'ego' psychologists. Later versions include the work of Jane Loevinger, as well as the object relations movement. Erich's eight stages of development are eight *ego* stages of development.

For our purposes, Erikson made the following contributions:

- without necessarily embracing Freud's earlier stages, he *expanded* the stages of development to include three

new stages of adulthood
- compared to Freudians, Erikson considered social factors in development, such as the geography and economic circumstances of the individual
- Erikson's work became more *cross-culturally sensitive* by some research among the Sioux and the Yurok for his book *Childhood in Society*
- Erikson added a *historical* dimension to his stage theory with his studies on Luther and Gandhi, and could be classified as the first practitioner of 'psychohistory' (though he disliked what the movement later became)

Erikson is better than most developmental psychologists in proposing that social-cultural factors permeate all stages, and that social change (e.g., the Protestant Reformation) can affect the psychological life of an individual. But the extent to which Erikson either implicitly or explicitly names the social forces, these forces act mostly at the micro level. The economic institution of capitalism is never named, nor the impact of the state control agencies of repression or propaganda. Neither is the impact of technology, such as the printing press, the telescope, nor the microscope seriously considered as having an effect on the developmental changes of the individual. In developmental psychology, to acknowledge that cultural or social factors influence the development of an individual, it does not name:

- which *parts* of culture
- at *what scale* (micro, meso or macro) these changes occur
- what *social mechanisms* are used transmit what is in the social world into the psychological world
- how much in *degree of power* these social forces have over the individual

Of the four theories I've presented, Erikson's theory of psycho-social development doesn't fit into any of them. Erikson was trying to expand and revise Freud's theory while accepting bourgeois liberal ideas of the relationship between the individual, society, and history. Erikson was a cultural relativist who followed the configurational theories of Margaret Mead and Franz Boas. In presenting Erikson's theory in this chapter, I do so in spite of the fact that I don't think he was a good historian, and his ideas of society are relatively shallow. I've selected him because, as far as I know, no theory of human development covers the entire lifespan. Furthermore, his theories are so well-known that it might make this chapter more engaging for the many people who have studied his theories in college.

In this chapter we will see that while Erikson's stages are a good starting point for understanding human development in history, many of his stages require great modification the further back we go in history. A case might even be made that at least a couple of Erikson's stages only emerge in the early twentieth century.

As a Vygotskyan psychologist, I will argue that Erikson's stages of development are not universal processes that happen to a child independently of the social institutions and the historical times the child is living. Rather, social institutions:

- muffle or expand how well the stages are enacted
- suppress stages so that in given historical periods, the stages might not even exist
- create new stages that never existed before

I will argue that throughout these stages, the kind of technology available, the type of economy the individual is living under, and the kind of work men and women perform more or less determines what is likely to happen at each stage. It would be overstating things to say that socio-cultural institutions *create* psychological stages. But more than any other factors, they affect what an individual is likely to become.

Historicizing development: Roy Baumeister

Continuity and differentiation

According to Baumeister (1986), the basic units of

identity are those experiences which give our life meaning beyond the immediate present over the course of time. Our identity consists of two poles, which are interdependent. We are provided with *continuity* when we feel that the things that happen to us are part of a larger orderly framework, and which other people experience similarly. This means the person feels the same whether they are working, interacting in a marriage, with friends, or participating in a ritual.

At the same time, meaning is also derived by what a person does that is unique to them. For example, the craftsmanship is generated when the self differentiates from others and sees itself as having something all its own to contribute. So, throughout Erikson's eight stages, some stages emphasize continuity while others stress differentiation (which we will explain below). Erikson's stage of trust versus mistrust, intimacy versus isolation and generativity versus stagnation are all about continuity and order. The other five stages are all about differentiation. But again, we will ask: does this fundamental polarity between continuity and differentiation *itself* change over from the Middle Ages to the nineteenth century?

How important is it for the individual to differentiate in the Middle Ages and in early modern Europe compared to the end of the nineteenth century? As we have seen in the first two chapters, differentiation is much more important with the emergence of expressive individualism at end of the nineteenth century than earlier.

Furthermore, we will ask what will historically novel *trends* do to this continuity. For example, how will geographical mobility from rural areas to cities that occurs in the eighteenth century affect the continuity and order poles of continuity and differentiation? What will the feminist movement in the early nineteenth century do to the continuity women experienced as mothers?

<u>From simplicity to complexity: Why is stability within the stages are more difficult to achieve in the nineteenth century</u>?

Lastly, differentiation and continuity can be achieved in

different ways, and these ways move from simplicity (the Middle Ages) to complexity (nineteenth century). What this implies is that people's identities in the Middle Ages were fairly easy to achieve and had fewer social demands. However, the increasing instabilities introduced in industrial capitalist systembrought out the best and the worst in people. The increase in social complexity demanded much more in the way of role-playing multiple roles which might have led to inter-personal role conflicts, role ambiguity, role strain and role lag.

In the Middle Ages, continuity was assigned by society. These individuals learned how to navigate through a single role transformation, say from daughter to mother or from son to father. In both these stages, the individual had a passive, stable, and unproblematic identity. In the next couple of stages, due to geographical and class mobility, there was more instability introduced as the individual faced the prospect of living in a new area, doing a new kind of
work. Differentiation was on the rise and continuity is weakened. Differentiation was also brought about by choices in religious affiliation (Catholics versus Protestants).

By the nineteenth century, both continuity and differentiation were difficult to achieve *because the person was obliged to find criteria for choosing among incompatible alternatives* among roles that might conflict. For example, between being a mother and having to work in a factory. This was most common by the end of the nineteenth century. This type of pressure could result in either highly-developed individuals or in various kinds of neurosis which was common among the middle and upper classes in the Victorian times. It also resulted in what Baumeister calls 'destabilization' and 'trivialization.'

Destabilization and trivialization of Identity problems in the nineteenth century

When there is no continuity between past, present and future, destabilization emerges. Prior to the nineteenth century, differentiation was achieved in the crafts or in farming. But when social institutions became as large and bureaucratic as they did at the end of the nineteenth century, then differentiation failed to be achieved. The individualism of the age was trivialized. This means that, on the job, individuals became interchangeable parts, cogs in the industrial machine as we saw in chapter three in the work of Braverman. When important differences between people become superficial and lack meaning, life threatens to become meaningless.

Childhood in history

Phillipe Aries: Children grow up faster in the Middle Ages

Ideas about childhood being a special time; that the home contains only family members; that the early years of life is primary in determining our future, have little to do with childhood or the family in European life prior to the eighteenth century at the earliest. Phillipe Aries (*Centuries of Childhood*) says that children in the Middle Ages, were far from being innocent. They drank in taverns with adults; they gambled with adults; went to war with adults; shared the same bed with adults and played the same games as adults. Children were not differentiated in their dress from adults, and no topics or words were off limits for children. Art in Middle Ages pictured children as little adults. According to Aries, it was only in the sixteenth century that children began to be considered too innocent to fully share in adult information. It was then that etiquette books for children emerged.

Elizabeth Eisenstein and Joshua Meyrowitz: The printing press as an agent in the invention of childhood

How do we explain why things changed? Aries claimed that 'childhood' did not exist until *infant mortality rates declined*. Parents could not afford to become too attached to children or pay much attention to them if they were likely to die. In his very original book, *No Sense of Place*, Joshua Meyrowitz disagrees. He argues that while the decline in infant mortality rates might have been a *contributing* cause, this new-found attachment did not take place until *after* the invention of childhood.

According to Meyrowitz, Elizabeth Eisenstein has linked the printing press and literacy with the invention of childhood. The shift in attitudes toward children beginning among some classes in sixteenth century appeared during the same century in which literacy and printing emerged in the vernacular. There was a shift in learning among the middle classes from learning by doing to learning by reading. Oral cultures make a distinction between childhood and adulthood, but rarely do we see a division of childhood into year-by-years slices until the spread of literacy. This does not mean that schooling was necessarily connected to literacy. However, schools in the Middle Ages were connected to memorization and drill rather than reading and writing.

A group is held together by the information that members have in common with each other, and *do not share with other groups*. For a group to be an 'us' there has to be a 'them.' For most of human history, group identity was narrow, rather than wide; deep rather than shallow; involving few people rather than many. Then, the printing press invited an expansion of the number of roles across greater horizons of space and time.

By end of seventeenth century, some European schools introduced age grading and age-graded curriculum. In the eighteenth century, children's literature began to shift away from moral instruction to books of entertainment. A whole subculture for children developed, including children's fairy tales, toys, and birthday celebrations. Age grading did not become universal until nineteenth century. As the ideal of universal education became a reality in the nineteenth century, 'childhood' spread to the lower classes. People learning to read at different rates led to separating people based on mastery of reading skills.

<u>The printing press slows down the rate of socialization</u>

Childhood innocence, like a rigid gender division of labor, is rooted in *exclusion from adult information* systems that the invention of the printing press brought about. Knowledge becomes sealed through the requirement that a child read and write. This process is institutionalized in schools with specialized age grades. Children must read simple children's books before being given more complex books. If a society is able to divide up what people of different ages know into many small steps, that will translate into many stages or levels of childhood. If societies insist on putting different age groups together, fewer childhood development stages will be found. If a society does not have sharp division between what people of different ages know, there will be fewer stages of socialization into adulthood. From at least the 1850s, childhood was treated as a time of innocence and isolation. Birth, death, sex, and money are now considered taboo topics for children. In the first half of the twentieth century this notion of childhood gained support among psychologists.

In order to play a role in a situation, a more or less slow socialization process must be undertaken. During the eighteenth century, a child being socialized into being an adult was *excluded* from the full information complex as to all of what adult situations constituted. Socialization involved *controlled* access to the information of a group so that they would become another person in maturity, with new qualities. In the early stages of socialization, Goffman's 'backstage' information was kept secret. Socialization involved the regulation of the amount of information given and the speed of exposure. Socialization periods were a means of arbitrating between the need of new members for new social information, while at the same time preserving and knowledge within the socializing agents so it was not squandered on the wrong people at the wrong times and in the wrong places.

New members were a threat—they could not share a full set of beliefs and values of group and they may reveal the groups special information to outsiders prematurely. Rites of passage usually guarded this process to protect the group from exposing its secrets or being infiltrated by outside groups. The more a medium supported the relationship between physical isolation and informational isolation, the more it supported the separation of people *into many distinct socialization positions*. Knowledge founded on print was a gatekeeper in childhood.

Just as childhood was perceived as innocent, adults who could read and write would appear more powerful than they once were. Through books, adults could communicate among themselves without being overheard by children. They could keep information secret from children. Adults could privately discuss how to treat children—what to teach and what to keep from them. It is no surprise that the image of a weak and naive child should have developed alongside the growing impact of printing, giving adults more power.

The printing press deepens gender hierarchies

In Middle Ages, men and women shared many rights and responsibilities. For example, women had the right to participate in municipal affairs, sit in on certain courts and testify before them. Women's words had legal force and they could substitute for their husbands if their husbands were absent. By the seventeenth century all these rights were gone. While family life in the Middle Ages was clearly male-dominated, there were some advantages for women. The family structure was an open lineage family, meaning there was permeability to outside influences. Relationships between husband and wife and between parents and children were not necessarily any more intimate than relationships among neighbors. Marital life was cool and distant. The home was neither a castle nor a womb. The early modern household lacked firm boundaries. Its inhabitants had little sense of privacy or individuality. Advice, problem solving and settling of a husband and wife's disputes were *community* affairs (Stone, 1977). Meyrowitz argues that traditional distinctions in gender roles can be shown to be related to *segregation* in social information's systems, principally through the printing press.

The training of men and women for different roles depends on separate environments of socialization. The separation of male and female domains goes back at least as far as the emergence of agricultural states 5000 years ago. But separate spheres are not equal. Men not only have more access than women to the public world, but they have more access to women's world as well. Traditionally, women are excluded from male rites of passage: workplaces, battles and sports. Yet men have casual access to the kitchens and homes of their mothers, wives, and sisters.

The printing press has been often touted as one of the major technologies that brought about *less* hierarchical social relations. It is true that the printing press allowed subversive ideas more circulation, and allowed readers more privacy instead of having to go to libraries to read manuscripts which couldn't leave the library. Clearly, the printing press supported and broadened the knowledge base of middle-class men. But when it came to women, according to Meyrowitz, the rise of literacy in the sixteenth and seventeenth centuries actually *increased* men's power over women because women were not taught to read. The invention of the printing press and emphasis on reading as a source of wisdom and religious salvation widened the social and cultural gap between men and women.

With the development of centralized states and the Protestant religion, men attained more power over women. On the one hand, the Protestant religion went to war on the mediating institutions, many of which supported women. For example, confession provided an outlet for women in relationship to their husbands. When the Protestants condemned confession, it denied women this outlet. Secondly, Protestant individualism discouraged remaining in extended families. For women, kinship in the home softened and relativized parental fighting. The loss of the kin group intensified the woman's relationship with her husband because there were no diffusing mediators in the home. Middle class families became streamlined and isolated from the extended community and kin. There was more boundary awareness, a greater sense of privacy, and more authoritarian control by the husband over his wife and children. In fact, the father led prayers from one to three times per day. In the nuclear family, women lost these resources and became subservient to a husband who had better occupational opportunities because they learned to read and write. It is in the spirit of these reservations that we turn to Erikson's stages of development. Please see table 7.1 for a summary of the impact of the printing press on childrearing practices.

Table 7.1 Theories of Ontogenetic Development

Category of comparison	Nativist	Behaviorist	Constructivist	Socio-historical
Theorists	Bulher, Gesell, Hall	Pavlov, Skinner, Bandura	Piaget/ Werner	Vygotsky, Luria Leontiev
Philosophical Type (Pepper)	Formism	Mechanism	Organicism	Deep Contextualism Dialectical—place in history, type of society, social class
Philosophical influences	Plato, Leibniz	Aristotle, Locke, Hume, James Mill	Coleridge, Kant, Mach	Spinoza, Hegel, Marx
Is there a qualitative difference between humans and animals?	No	No	No	Yes
What are human beings?	Bio-psychological	Social-psychological	Psychological, biological	Social-historical—psychological
What are environments?	Complex, species- specific	A source of growth but not transformation	An occasion, scene, prop (von Uexkull)	Source of growth to draw from malleable to transformation through collective activity
Relationship between environment and individual	Individual passive Environment passive	Individual passive Environment passive (Skinner, Pavlov) Individual passive Environment active (Models—Bandura)	Individual active Environment passive	Individual active Environment active
Drivers	Genetic predispositions	Pain and pleasure	Adaptation to environment (Piaget) by curiosity	Tool making, tool using
	Instincts	Associations and consequences	Orthogenetic principle—differentiation, hierarchization (Werner)	Activity—motives, goals, strategies
Type of change	Continuous, quantitative	Continuous, quantitative	Discontinuous, qualitative	Discontinuous, qualitative
Does history change stages of cognition?	No Apply everywhere	No Apply everywhere	No Apply everywhere	Yes
How is research done?	Lab	Lab	Interview	Interview

How well does Erikson's eight stages stand up to historical analysis?

Trust versus mistrust

All human beings are born dependent, most especially on their mothers. According to Erikson, the trust versus mistrust stage is testing grounds for all future relations. How the parents treat the child in terms of warmth, consistency, provision of resources, and availability provide a model of how well the infant will learn to trust social institutions later. If parents do their job, the child is moved to the next stage without the baggage of mistrust. If the parents are not trustworthy, the child will grow up suspicious and aloof in regard to larger social institutions. How might a child have experienced this stage differently over the course of history?

Trust was undermined until the eighteenth century, at least in part by the practice of swaddling their children.

> Physical mobility was severely reduced. For the first four months or so after birth, they were tightly bound in bandages so they were unable to move either head or limbs...Swaddling in fact slows down the infant's heartbeat and induces far longer sleep and less crying. Swaddling also allows the infant to be moved about like a parcel and left unattended...or hung on a peg on a wall. (*Family, Sex and Marriage in England 1500-1800*, 161-162)

The result was sensory and motor deprivation. At least among the upper classes, the lack of a consistent mother figure (children were passed on to wet nurses) and the generally ferocious repressive child-rearing practices produced children that were distrustful, cold, hostile, and suspicious.

Generally speaking, families below the middle classes lived poorly. Mistrust might have been sown because, according to Aries, the high infant mortality rate in the Middle Ages translated as mothers being less attached to their children because of the emotional cost becoming too involved and then losing them.

In the Middle Ages, upper class families tended to be extended so that more than one adult was engaging the child. The lower classes could not afford to keep generations within the same house. However, the lower classes lived in villages which provided parents with some support from neighbors. There was geographical stability, since most families lived and died in the same village.

As Allen Wheelis pointed out in *The Quest for Identity*, there must have been less of a transference between children and parents prior to the seventeenth century because the attention of the child was spread between the infant and other adults. This meant that the child focused less on what would become of their identity in the eyes of their parents because their parents are not the sole domestic influence. On the other hand, parents had fewer high expectations of what became of their children *as individuals*. The rise of the Protestant religion in the sixteenth century led to much stricter childrearing practices, as the family now tended to exclude kin groups.

Beginning in the Enlightenment, things begin to change. The rise of both class mobility and geographical mobility along with the rise of cities must have destabilized family life. As some families rose to a different social class than their relatives, it created what Erik Olin Wright called 'contradictory class locations.' The parental values of the newly formed middle class would not sit well with their working-class relatives. Geographical mobility meant that men travelled more to find work, thereby destabilizing the nuclear family.

On the positive side, mortality rates stabilized in the eighteenth century thanks to the advances in medicine. In addition, with less people farming for a living, the need for large families was less urgent. As people began to have less children, they began to pay more attention to them when they did have them. According to Aries, childhood was discovered in the eighteenth century. Up until now, children were treated as little adults, rather than as having distinct needs. This trend continued into the nineteenth century, with the home becoming a haven in a heartless world. Some upper-middle class and middle-class women must have been conflicted between their duty as a mother while also feeling a call to the anti-slavery movements, the temperance movements, and the feminist movements.

Autonomy versus Shame and Doubt

According to Erikson, the body is the first place where the struggle between the child and the parents takes place. When the child learns to say 'no' to demands to control the body though its elimination processes, the issue becomes one of who controls the body. Saying 'no' to parents is a declaration of independence. It doesn't matter what is being refused. It is more the act of *practicing* refusal that matters. If the child learns to say 'no' successfully, he or she is likely to be more assertive in other situations as he grows up. If successful, he or she will be able to say no to dangerous, unhealthy situations in the future. If the child is less successful in this stage, he is likely to be taken advantage of.

It is in this stage and the next that we can see the historical limitations of Erikson's stages. It is difficult to imagine that Catholic peasants and artisans in the Middle Ages, whose life was very difficult, accepting that a two-year old's enacting the terrible twos to be anything other than an act of intolerable insubordination. On the other hand, specifically in relation to toilet training, there literally were no toilets until at least the nineteenth century. In addition, parents in the Middle Ages were less strict and, as Stone says, parents saw their children as pets and looked at their children's elimination process with humor rather than anxiety. While Protestants might be more liberal than Catholics in supporting *adults* finding their own vocational path, this was only *after* they had earned that right. Protestants saw children being little demons who had to have the devil beat out of them. For Protestants, the child saying 'no' would be like channeling the devil.

The eighteenth century was a time in which authority was challenged. This included the authority of kings, popes, and aristocrats. This is also the century in which Locke proposed that how a child turned out was not simply due to temperament, but because of how they were raised by their parents. Towards in the second half of the eighteenth century, Rousseau enshrined children as romantic heroes, untainted by the scourge of civilization. It is hard to imagine, at least among upper-middle class and middle class families, that they might have looked somewhat more favorably on small childhood rebellion against *their* rule. In other words, if politically engaged adults could rebel against institutions, it would be inconsistent for those same parents not to accept their own children's stubbornness.

While the eighteenth century was the 'Age of Revolution' the nineteenth century was more an 'Age of Progress', of gradual change. This gradual change either in slow political reform or in Darwinian natural selection, middle and upper-middle class parents were more cautious in their political outlooks. The Victorian preoccupation with domesticity and propriety makes it a stretch to imagine them tolerating 'the terrible twos' as an acceptable stage. In nineteenth-century Victorian England, Puritanism returned with a vengeance.

Initiative versus Guilt

Autonomy and initiative are not the same thing. According to Erikson, saying 'no' to a range of possibilities given by the parents is a far cry from saying 'yes,' being curious, exploring what is attractive, and acting on those attractions beyond a given set of choices. If this stage is not negotiated well, there is guilt. What children may feel guilty about is taking initiative themselves. If they do, it will be perceived that there is something wrong with pursuing those interests. Erikson says this stage begins at around the ages of three to five. Do children throughout western history all experience this stage?

If adults in the Middle Ages simply inherited the work of their parents, how much will it pay for parents today to support their children in trying new things? Not much. Being curious means approaching the social world as if it is malleable, where work offers many opportunities. The world of the Middle Ages was a very rigid period. Huzinga, borrowing Freud's terminology, says that in the Middle Ages there were only two parts of the psyche: the id and the superego. Neither did people think of their psyche as a self-contained identity. Rather, individuals were seen as the playthings of god or the devil; there was nothing in between. Being curious means making messes, and in the black-and-white world of the Middle ages, mixing black and white either into shades of grey or introducing living color could not be supported.

Furthermore, having negotiated this stage badly would not result in guilt, at least not during the Middle Ages. Guilt is a psychological state which results from a failure to live up to the principle of a holy book or a doctrine. Shame is a social emotion in which an individual is embarrassed because of the real or imagined pressure of others. Guilt is about failure to obey abstract *authorities*. Shame is a failure to conform to *groups*. Thus, in the Middle Ages, a failure to do well in stage three would result in shame, not guilt.

It is only in around the eighteenth century when society was understood as changeable, when more work was created in the towns and in the cities, that individuals felt they actually had options. At the end of the nineteenth century, corporations began to hire stenographers, clerks, bookkeepers, and managers. All this unconsciously must have positively affected parental support for their children taking the initiative.

Four ways of thinking about children

In his book, *The Family Sex and Marriage in England 1500-1800,* Lawrence Stone argues that there were four ways of thinking about children:

- strongly supported by Calvinist theology, children are born with original sin and had to be held in check by repression
- the environmental view of the child being born a blank slate (Locke) and what became of them depended on how the child was raised by the parents along with the forms of social organization the parents lived under; a child raised under an absolute monarchy would be treated differently that a child raised under the constitutional monarchy of the Enlightenment
- the temperamental spiritual view, that children were born with four types of temperament which was connected to astrological signs; this theory goes back to Greek and Roman times
- the Romantic view of Rousseau, the opposite of the Puritanical view; that the child was born good but corrupted by society, which leads to more permissive forms of child-rearing

It was only in ways two and four that children began to be seen as individuals. For this reason, it is crucial to understand that the way parents raised their children was inseparable from what they thought the essence of being a child was. For example, how well or badly a child went though the trust versus mistrust stage depended on whether the parents saw the child as a little devil, a blank slate, a melancholic drain, or a little genius.

Industry versus inferiority

Though Erikson claims that his psychosocial stages are built on each other in a cumulative way, when we look at the stages historically, at least in his fourth stage, it doesn't necessarily seem to follow. 'Industry' for Erikson means being able to find an activity one likes between the ages of six and twelve that one is good at, which is then practiced. Learning to play a musical instrument or learning to cook are examples. From the point of view of twentieth-century development, it makes logical sense that a child would first differentiate themselves from the expectations of the parent by saying no (autonomy), then try out their own activities (initiative) and then choose one activity and get good at it (industry).

However, in the Middle Ages, young children were being trained early to do the work of their parents. It is likely that the autonomy and initiative stages were repressed, if not muffled. If parents raised their child in an authoritarian way, telling them what to do, it is not hard to imagine that training their boy how to farm or craft or smelt iron or training their girl to cook, spin, can and weave should be easy.

It is tempting to think that the child is really 'repressed' because they were denied the ability to be autonomous or take initiative. But is this a projection of twentieth-century psychology onto the past. It is true that most boys (at least in England) were fostered out to do an apprenticeship at the age of seven, and that might have given the boy some independence. But the parent was still in charge of the kind of apprenticeship undertaken. If industry requires sorting (autonomy) and deciding (initiative) before engaging in a practical skill, then either individuals had no industry in Erikson's sense, or their sense of industry was very different from what Erikson proposed. It is important to understand that Erikson's term for industry is highly specific. I do not mean to say that people in the Middle Ages were not industrious in the general sense of being hard-working.

It is more likely that industry in Early Modern Europe might have become *more* authoritarian, at least for the middle-class families whose fathers could read and write. As we saw earlier, fathers had considerably higher knowledge than their children because of access to books, and this certainly gave them more power. At the same time, children were seen as less powerful because fathers controlled the pace at which they learned their skill.

The eighteenth and nineteenth century, industry would emerge as a stage that both boys and girls went through. The opening up of different kinds of work during this period might have translated into a greater variety of materials around the house for the boy or girl to try out. The ability to become industrious became institutionalized in the twentieth century in the school system, especially in organized games, music and art classes.

Identity versus role confusion

For Erikson, this is the stage of being a teenager. From the vantage point of the mid-twentieth century, Erikson sees teenage boys and girls being bombarded by friends, classmates, and mass media (magazines, television, movies) about possible identities they can attain. Having an identity at this stage means being able to sift and weed though these possibilities and sort out what matches with one's skills and what is consistent the character they have crafted in the previous stages.

This is another one of Erikson's stages which seems to be a projection of adolescent life from the 1920s forward. Baumeister cites two historians of adolescence (Demos and Gillis) who argue that adolescence in the West is no older than the last third of the nineteenth century. In the Middle Ages, teenagers were less dependent on adults—and this goes all the way back to being fostered out at age seven. However, they had less choice in the kind of roles they picked. By Victorian times, adolescents were more dependent on parents. They were more likely to conform, be passive and feel awkward. Yet at the same time they had less of a commitment to a specific role (Erikson calls that a 'psychological moratorium').

To begin with, the notion that adolescence is a distinct stage of development is unique to this century. From the Middle Ages to the twentieth century, boys and girls were either tutored (the upper classes) or did an apprenticeship (lower classes). During this time, they were surrounded by adults. The basis for the struggle of identity versus role confusion is the presence of a *teenage culture*, which is distinct. From this culture, a teenager compares to the adult world with its institutions. What happens to the identity versus role confusion stage when the individual does not imagine they have a separate identity as a teenager?

The idea that teenagers are struggling to find an identity with and among their peers presupposes the presence of an institution in which they assemble in a recurring time and place, a site which contains *only teenagers*. There was no such place in European history until the founding of the public-school system in the early twentieth century. Up until that time, there was no place for teenagers to compare notes *as teenagers*, identify common problems or create a common culture.

Neither was there a universal stage of teenage rebelliousness prior to the twentieth century. One seedbed of that rebelliousness may lie in the anxiety and uncertainly early twentieth-century youth face in what Erikson calls a psychological moratorium, when work-life is put on hold. But the association of teenagers with rebellion was a product of the movie era, far outside the historical parameters of this book. Lastly, the type of identities that a teenager might get confused about—aspiring to be a sports star, movie star, or famous musician—were not really options until at least the end of the nineteenth century.

When I was about seventeen years old, I used to dread my relatives coming over for the holidays. One reason was that they would ask me what I wanted to do with myself, meaning how I was going to earn my living. I had no answer for them. That was because I thought I could be whatever I wanted—a major league baseball player, a rhythm and blues musician or the next James Dean. *The choices were killing me* in addition to being ridiculously unrealistic. Erikson describes this stage very well.

But for most of European history, the adults people looked up to were people that they knew, not famous people who they would never know: parents, relatives or perhaps musicians in the village. With the rise of the cities in the eighteenth century, the choice of heroes broadened to include those outside the family. But the hope of believing you could be like celebrities, people you never met and will never know is unique to the twentieth century. There is role confusion here because the choices seem unlimited, while in the case of the United States the individualism here proclaims that you can be anything you want.

Intimacy versus isolation

Erikson's notion of intimacy does not mean sex. Intimacy assumes that you bring to the table your full individual identity, you reveal your inner psychological states while your partner witnesses and supports that state. You, in turn, are able to reciprocate. The result is love. Isolation, of course, does not mean you are unmarried. As many of us know, it is very common to be married and feel isolated.

As Baumeister points out, until the thirteenth century, marriages were mixtures of bigamy and desertions until the Church began to take over the ceremonies and insist on vows of 'until death do us part.' Even in the eighteenth century, marriages did not last very long because one of the spouses died. Speaking for England, Stone says about thirty percent of all marriages were broken up by death of one of the spouses in the first fifteen years. Among the peasantry, marriages were, on average, between twelve and seventeen years. The majority of children in early modern Europe lost one parent before they were fully adult. Marriage lasted the longest in the nineteenth century. People in the middle classes began to live longer lives, and divorces were difficult to obtain.

In England, adultery was highest among the upper classes as men and women saw their marriages primarily as economic alliances. Since the thirteenth century, there were increased pressures coming from both Catholic and Protestant authorities to keep marriages together. At the same time, many working-class people did not get married at all to their partners because they couldn't afford it. When they did get married, the marriages began between twenty-four and twenty-eight years of age. The upper classes married at a young age (around twenty) because the accumulation of resources was not an issue. Surprisingly, before the invention of contraceptives at the end of the seventeenth and into the eighteenth century, the upper classes had the most children in part because they were more likely to survive.

In the dialogue between parents and children about securing a mate, Stone identifies four options:

- arranged marriages, where the choice is made entirely by the parents without the advice of the bride or groom; this type of decision-making lasted longest among the upper classes, since there was political alliances and economic networks to be maintained
- where the choice is made by parents, but the child had the right to veto it
- where the choice of partner is made by the children with the parents having the right to veto if the children pick someone below their social class
- where children make their own choice and parents are informed afterwards

In terms of the motive for choices, the first kind was based on political and economic considerations. The second kind of motivation is called companionate love. This was a product of the eighteenth century, where personal affection and compatibility was combined with an assessment of psychological qualities of the person, along with common interests. The third type of motive for mating was purely sexual, with mutual experimentation before marriage. This applied to young people working as governesses or tutors to upper class families. It also applied to working-class teenagers. The last type of motive was romantic love, also a product of the eighteenth and early nineteenth century. Romantic love had the following characteristics according to Stone:

- a disturbance of mental equilibrium resulting from an obsessive concentration on the virtues of another person
- a blindness to all of his or her possible defects
- there is only one person in the world with whom we can unite at all levels

- a rejection of all other criteria such as money or material comfort as a reason for love
- love is perceived to be like a thunderbolt and strikes at first sight
- love is the most important thing in the world
- giving full range to emotions is admirable

The expectation of intimacy in a marriage is a product of the Romantic movement in the early nineteenth and twentieth centuries. Up until then, marriages were strictly economic arrangements which usually involved intergenerational families in decision-making about a marriage. There was a spirit of romanticism among the troubadours in the Middle Ages and their upper-class lady loves, but these were symbolic or real *affairs*, not part of a marriage. The expectation that romance should be some aspect of *a marriage* is recent. For women, the expectation that marriage should be more than an economic arrangement was championed by the women's movement between 1830 and 1860, and among romantic artists and revolutionaries throughout the nineteenth century. This romanticism was also fed by the explosions of novels in the eighteenth century, led by Goethe's *Sorrows of Young Werther.* It is also in the rise of psychoanalysis and other self-reflective therapies at the end of the nineteenth century.

Generativity versus stagnation

The crisis that produces this stage for Erikson is that by the age of forty or so there are two problems: one is that the children are leaving home; and at the other end, one's own parents are suffering increasing illnesses. From twenty to forty years of age, the marriage has been bookended by children on one side and one's parents on the other. By the age of forty or so, both relationships are changing. A married couple can no longer rely on their parents for support. In fact, the relationship is reversing, as parents must take care of their own parents. On the other end, children are starting their own families and are becoming less dependent. What does this do to adult development of the couple?

One thing it does, according to Erikson, is it invites the adult to examine relationships either within the family in a new way or, more radically, to identify with the human species beyond the family. One way this might play out is by joining political or spiritual movements in which the adult learns to identify with the human species across space (globally) or over time (historically). Stagnation results when the marriage has lost centrality for both children and their parents. There is a crisis centered around their loss of importance. Erikson suggests that this stage occurs between forty and sixty years of age.

Historically this stage is unique to the twentieth century. Before 1875, the average lifespan of person in Europe was between was twenty-eight to thirty-five. Chances were likely that they would not have much time with grandparents at this stage before they died. This stage would be nowhere near the twenty years projected by Erikson. A saving grace was that, unlike today, the elders were treated with great respect. But they were not elders for very long.

In addition, in the Middle Ages there were little, if any, spiritual and political movements. There were certainly spiritual movements from the early modern period forward, which were led by religious heretics or movements like the Levelers. Political and social movements were more a product of the eighteenth and nineteenth centuries. This means that for those who joined these movements, time was of the essence. By the end of the nineteenth century the average person in Europe lived to about forty. There was now more time to go through this stage.

It is doubtful that before the nineteenth century, stagnation would have been a problem for adults. They were scrambling to cope with unpredictable climates, famine, and disease (see below) for stagnation to be an issue. Stagnation is based on an ability to reflect on one's life in relation to surrounding generations, and this requires a stability in climate, food support, and disease control.

Integrity versus despair

Erikson sees the last of these stages as a time when the adult reflects on their lives. What have they accomplished? What have been their strengths and what have been their weaknesses as individuals? In Western history, Catholic confessions and Puritan insistence on journal-keeping helped the individual keep track of their spiritual lives. But confession was a place of a ridding of sins and dumping these infractions on priests. Because it was a verbal exchange rather than written, it was less likely to be remembered. It was the journal-keeping of the Protestants that helped individuals keep track of their lives.

Most people in Western history were religious, and were confident the day of judgment was coming. But in the case of Catholics, they *externalized* the judgement to God. They did not judge *themselves*. There was just the hope that God was keeping track of the ledger, and the individual had more on the positive side. It was the Protestant religion which insisted that middle-class people keep track of their spiritual lives. But again, the huge difference in how long people lived makes a great difference in the experience of this stage.

In Erikson's time, this stage runs from sixty to sixty-five years of age. If the average adult until 1875 died by thirty-five at best, it did not make much sense that there was much reflection by the elderly on their lives, at least during the Middle Ages. As we saw in chapter two, it wasn't until the eighteenth century (thanks to Locke) that individuals saw themselves as developing, and as a product of parental influences. It wasn't until the early twentieth century and beyond that upper-middle class people in the fields of psychology, sociology, and the humanities that had the time and the interest to reflect on their achievements and failures.

Global historical variables that undermine developmental theory

Impact of climate, famine, and disease

Erikson presents his developmental stages as if the Little Ice Age, plagues, famine, smallpox, and tuberculosis had no effect on development. This is because the historical time period in which he was writing (mid-twentieth century) and for the social classes he applied his theory to, plagues, famine, and disease were not issues. But historically, they most assuredly were variables. But Erikson does not comment on how they could have impacted his stages of development.

Brian Fagan, in his book *The Little Ice Age*, says that in 1258 a major volcanic eruption lead to a cold snap that triggered the Little Ice Age which ran from 1300 CE and 1850 CE. In this little Ice Age there was an irregular see-saw of rapid climatic shifts, bringing cycles of very cold winters, erratic rainfall in the late spring, droughts, and heatwaves.

The intense cold period led to crop failure and consequent famine. The great hunger from 1315 to 1319 killed tens of thousands of people. The Black plague decimated twenty-five percent of the European population and it took no less than 100 years to recover from. The seventeenth century had at least six climatically significant volcanic eruptions that would produce more cold and crop failure. In London in 1665 the bubonic plague killed at least 57,000 people. Even as late as 1740, few houses in Europe had decent heating systems. According to Fagan, sudden temperature changes brought increases in pneumonia, bronchitis, heart disease, and stroke. The eruption of Mount Tamorba in eastern Java in 1816 shortened the growing season by fifty-five days. How could Erikson's stages possibly apply to children and adolescence living under these conditions? How could society have a given set of expectations for a child or adolescent when climate and famine were so prevalent?

As for disease, smallpox left many young survivors blinded altogether and their faces were pot-marked for life. How might the impact of smallpox effect a child's development? Would there be *any* development in any meaningful sense? Because of the backward sanitary conditions, there were frequent cases of bacterial stomach infections, including dysentery. Stomach disorders were also the result of either a badly-balanced diet among the rich or the consumption of insufficient or rotten food among the poor. Can anyone imagine how children or adolescents could 'develop' under these conditions?

The unequal treatment of children by parents

Erikson's theory assumes that all children in the household were treated equally by their parents. This was clearly not the case before the eighteenth century. The rule of passing on the land to the eldest son (primogeniture) tended undermine the eldest motives to find work, despite being treated more favorably by parents. At the same time, boys that were *not* firstborn were not treated well. They had to hustle to find work. Sisters were not treated as well as brothers, regardless of when they were born. This explicit ranking of children would impact how well or badly adolescences came to terms with their work prospects. It was only after the eighteenth century that this began to change and that children within the household were treated in a more egalitarian manner.

Instability and trivialization in the nineteenth century: Revisited

We are now in a position to explain why destabilization and trivialization occurred in the nineteenth century. Baumeister has identified ten sociological areas in which differentiation and continuity could be compared as we move from the Middle Ages to the nineteenth century. These include geographical home, ancestral inheritance, marriage patterns, occupation, social rank, gender, age values, body characteristics, religion, and ethics.

Of the ten major components of medieval identity, most were stabilized. On the other hand, by the nineteenth century, continuity had been destabilized and differentiation had been trivialized. (Please see Table 7.4 for a summary.) The result was a difficult individual development because the individual could no longer choose from established social patterns and a stable set of social expectations. The individual had to find criteria for deciding where to take their lives between alternatives that often contradicted each other.

In terms of geographical home, with the exception of travelling minstrels, wandering students or unemployed knights, most people in the Middle Ages lived their lives in the same location. So too, it was clear what one was likely to or not likely to inherit. This was not true of later times. In England, inheritance had shrunk to a one-time transfer of property sold by heirs. There was no longer an expectation of inheritance that spanned generations. On the other hand, by the end of the nineteenth century, serfdom had ended throughout most of Europe and there was more migration of individuals from farms to towns or cities. This produced both hope for a better life as well as fear of downward mobility.

Social rank in the Middle Ages was highly stratified, and moving up ranks was not likely for most people. One knew one's place and rarely asked questions about it. By the eighteenth and nineteenth century, class mobility was far less rigid, and there were greater chances of changing classes within a single lifetime. Conflicts arose because options were many, and there were no established guidelines for deciding.

Work in the Middle Ages was a good example of differentiation. Peasants and artisans were able to express themselves in their work as they oversaw all parts of their work from beginning to end. But in the latter half of the nineteenth century, working-class occupations became 'jobs' with the introduction of the factory. As individuals became cogs in the industrial machine, their identity, at least on the job, became trivialized. Adolescence became destabilized as the adolescent now waited in limbo for years for future work that was indefinite (Erikson's psychological moratorium).

Contrary to what might be expected, motherhood was less important to women in the Middle Ages. The work of spinning, weaving, tanning, and milking cows was far more important.

As we said before, the high infant morality rate in this period would make anyone less attached to the role of mother, for fear of one's heart breaking over the death of one's children. By the eighteenth century, with the mortality rates going down, there was something more in it for women to identify with being a mother. At the same time, this was countered by working class women having to work in factories which was no place for taking care of children. For middle-class women, they could work in clerical jobs in the newly formed corporations, and for upper-class women there were various kinds of social movements to patronize. This situation destabilized their existing identity but allowed for a new differentiated identity.

In terms of age, people in the Middle Ages did not keep track of how old they were. Because of this, there must have been less pressure to do things by a certain age. By the end of the nineteenth century, as the pace of life became hectic, the wisdom of the elders was taken less seriously. Adolescents knew more because they were forced to remain closer to changing times, especially if they moved to the cities. This also produced a growing conflict between adolescents and the elderly that destabilized the identity of both.

Physical identity in the Middle Ages was stable, as it had been for centuries. What mattered for men and women was physical strength for farming, canning, weaving, and childbearing. Physical beauty was far less important. On the other hand, by the nineteenth century the harnessing of inanimate sources of energy made physical strength *less* important. Together with the rise of advertising, beauty was much more highly valued. This caused developmental confusion.

When we turn to religion, it is tempting to believe the accounts of religious authorities that in the Middle Ages people were pious Catholics. In fact, in the rural areas, the Catholic church had little impact as people held on to their magical practices, as Keith Thomas points our in his *Religion and the Decline of Magic*. It was in the sixteenth and seventeenth centuries that religion became more important to people because of the religious wars being fought. But by the eighteenth and nineteenth century, religion was actively challenged by Enlighteners, materialists and atheists. Throughout most of European history, people were less committed to religion as a source of stability than one might first imagine.

Table 7.2 Impact of the Printing Press in Childrearing

Middle Ages	Category of comparison	Sixteenth century print revolution
General knowledge	Kind of knowledge	More specialized knowledge through books
Less gap between men, women and children	Distribution of knowledge	Middle class men know more than women and children because they can read and write
Oral, storytelling town crier	Technology	Print
Fast—children become adults quickly	Speed of socialization	Slower—it takes time for children to decode the roles and rules in books
Parents, children knew what each other knew	Knowledge access	Children know less about about what their fathers knew

Table 7.3 Stages of Family Evolution In England 1500-1800

Types of families	Open lineage family	Restricted patriarchal nuclear family	Closed domesticated nuclear family
Time period	Sixteenth century	1530-1640	After 1640
How religion impacted family	Catholicism: family not accountable for religious education	Protestantism: family (father) responsible for religious education	Protestantism
How state impacted the family	State is weak	State assumes more power—Inquisition	
Kingship impact on family	Weak	Divine right of kings and political expression of father's role in household	Constitutional monarchy supports more community within the family
Place of kinship and neighbors	Loyalty to ancestors and to living kin (among upper classes) Loyalty to neighbors (lower classes)	Decline of loyalty to kin and local community	Decline of loyalty to kin and community (rise of salons and clubs)
Place of romantic love	Outside court circles, romantic love regarded by moralists and theologians as a kind of mental illness	Romantic love among the governesses, music tutors of the upper classes	Romantic love possible inside marriages
Relations within the family	Relations between husband and wife, parents and children not much closer than with neighbors	Relations within the family much closer, but authoritarian	Relations within the family much closer and less authoritarian; children and women have more power
Are children seen as individuals?	Not distinguishable from other children; they would give children two names, anticipating one will die	Not distinguishable from other children	Children start to be seen as individuals
How are children characterized?	Configuration of different types of temperament	As little devils who need to be repressed (flogging)	Blank slates (Locke) Or Inherently good (Rousseau)
Childrearing practices		Swaddling. Leads to children being cold, suspicious, hostile and withdrawn	Swaddling ends. Children freer to move. Show more affection
Place of pleasure	Sinful for the religious, acceptable for aristocracy		Pleasure less sinful for all classes
Mate selection	Arranged marriages (upper classes)		Companionate marriages among the middle classes; romantic marriages
Boundaries with the outside world	Permeability by outside influences	Nuclear	Home sealed from outsiders
		Geographical and class mobility; material world more threatening; devil and its agents everywhere	Improvements in disease control
		Traitors were hanged; religious radicals and gypsies exterminated	

7.4 Erikson's Stages Historically Grounded

Erikson's stage	Middle Ages	Eighteenth to nineteenth century
Trust vs mistrust; testing of the social world through the parents	Mistrust—lack of food supply	Mistrust—geographical and class mobility; destabilization of family
	Mistrust—high infant mortality rate; parents not attached	Trust—lower infant mortality rate; parents more attached
	Trust—support of extended family and village	
Autonomy vs shame and doubt; learning to say "no" to a given range of choices	Doubt—authoritarian parenting would repress autonomy; children seen as little demons	Anti-authoritarianism of enlightenment autonomy—child seen as a product of parental influences (Locke); childhood romanticized by Rousseau
Initiative vs guilt; learning to say "yes" but trying new activities which cultivate curiosity	Shame before groups, not guilt (violation of an internalized authority)	Importance of groups conformity recede; if stage doesn't go well, it is guilt at violation of a religious principle
	Intergenerational work patterns discourage initiation. No need to experiment; superego and id create black-and-white thinking	Initiative—the variety of occupations available might encourage parents support of curiosity
Industry vs inferiority; developing a skill through perseverance (tool manipulation)	Authoritarian industry	Industry based on experiment first; greater variety of materials
Identity vs role confusion; preserving one's identity in the face of pressure from friends, school, or mass media	Teenagers have more independence; work for other families, but constricted in the work	Teenagers more dependent on parents, but more choices of work without choosing (psychological moratorium)
	No time or space available to consolidate a youth culture	Schools provide time and place to develop a youth culture
	Role models are parents and relatives	With development of national baseball teams, movies and music clubs, adolescents begin to value famous people (celebrities)
Intimacy vs isolations (intimacy meaning mutual revelation of psychological states and secrets)	No intimacy expected between spouses; intimacy between troubadours and upper-class women	Intimacy expected among women (rise of feminism 1830-1860) and between artists and revolutionaries; rise of therapy at end of nineteenth century; women expect intimacy
Generativity vs stagnation Feeling part of the future of the human species beyond the family	Time period for generation stage much less (five years); less spiritual and political movements to be identified with	Generativity phase longer (twenty years); more spiritual and political movements to be identified with
	No stagnation—tight intergenerational interdependence	Stagnation possible, as couple is left when children start own household and parents die
Integrity vs despair Being able to evaluate the strengths and weaknesses of how one lived	People do not track their individual lives as having milestones; God keeps track in Day of Judgment; sense of being an elder gives integrity	Puritan journal keeping of sins cultivates individual reflection; people start to live longer; more time to reflect; end of the nineteenth century; a loss of respect for elders

Table 7.5 Continuity and Differentiation Historically

Middle Ages	Category of comparison	Nineteenth century
Stabilized—continuity; most people live their entire lives in the same locale	Geographical home	Destabilized; the end of serfdom and urban migration; shift from agricultural to industrial jobs
Stabilized—continuity; one inherited not only land, but passed it on across generations	Ancestral inheritance	Trivialized; inheritance has shrunk to a one-time transfer of transient property and sold by the heirs
Stabilized—continuity; when the Church took over in thirteenth century; marriage was indissoluble until death	Marriage	Stabilized—continuity; marriage lasted longest during the Victorian era; people lived long lives and divorce was difficult
Stabilized; guildsmen, serfs and peasants set on their occupational paths early in life	Occupation	Trivialized; people given jobs involving tasks and labor specialization; loss of a sense of carrying through all parts of the craft process from beginning to end
Stabilized; society highly and rigidly stratified and difficult to change	Social rank	Destabilized; increase in social mobility could change rank in a single lifetime; conflict between monetary accumulation and blood loyalty for the upper classes
Differentiation; motherhood less important; identity through spinning, canning, weaving	Gender	Differentiation for middle classes; get an education, work as clerks; working class women's work is trivialized working in a factory; motherhood more important
Stablilized—continuity; age meant little (except some added experience); elders seen as wise	Age	Destabilized; people are more aware of their specific age, which creates new developmental pressures, thanks to the budding developmental psychology of Freud and Baldwin at the end of the nineteenth century; elders not seen as wise because of rapidly-changing times
Stable—continuity; strength and child-bearing ability matters on more on farms, where the expenditure of human energy was essential; physical beauty less important	Physical characteristics	Destabilized; thanks to motors, strength and size are less important; new emphasis placed on physical beauty
Destabilize; in the villages, paganism practiced; Catholicism tolerated	Religion	Destabilized; impact of Darwinian evolution, materialism, atheism
Types I and II: simple, passive, well-defined	Baumeister's five ways of handling differentiation and continuity	Type V: complex, active, uncertain, no clear guidelines

CHAPTER 8

Becoming Civilized In Europe: How the Upper Class Got “Class”

Orientation

As seen from previous chapters, there was a qualitative change in the psychology of people as we moved from the Middle Ages towards the modern world. We saw it in the movement from collectivism to individualism, from loyalty to the village to loyalty to the state. In chapter five, we examined how places turned into spaces, and in chapter six, how cyclic time was transformed into linear time which philosophers called *progress*. In chapter seven,
we saw how little Erikson’s psycho-social stages of development of childhood, adolescence, and adulthood applied to Medieval or early modern life until at least the eighteenth century.

In this chapter we will make the following inquiries:

- how are the social-psychological and psychological processes of becoming civilized *internalized* by individuals from the early modern world to the end of the nineteenth century?
- by what process do these internalized processes of becoming civilized seem to become natural, seemingly operating below the level of consciousness?
- what socio-political institutions initiate this process of becoming civilized?

We will begin our discussion of what it means to become civilized in terms of manners, attention to body functions, control over emotions, and aesthetic taste. Then we will study three periods: the feudal states of the Middle Ages, the absolutist states of the seventeenth century, and the bureaucratic states in the eighteenth and nineteenth centuries. In each period I will describe the sociogenic conditions followed by a psychogenetic section which shows how the sociogenetic conditions led to changes in psychology. This chapter follows the work of historical psychologist Norbert Elias.

In chapter twelve of my book *Foraging Promethean Psychology*, I made a distinction between becoming civilized and becoming disciplined:

> Each involves control over actions, emotions, the senses and behaviors so as to suppress or delay gratification. This control involves foresight, hindsight, and insight. (335)

However, there are class differences. Becoming disciplined is the coercive-forceful process by which *working class* people are hammered into being obedient in factories, warzones, churches, asylums, prisons, and schools. *The working class never became civilized.* It is the *upper classes* who become civilized and this first occurred in the kingly courts of France. This is what I strive to show in this chapter.

Becoming Civilized

What does it mean to be accused of being uncivilized? Whether someone is civilized or uncivilized has something to do with manners, the arts, literacy, speaking skills, clothing, personal hygiene, emotional life, and sensual gratification. The process of developing a what I call Promethean psychology is inseparable from the process of becoming civilized.

Social psychology of politeness and manners

As we will see, a big part of being civilized means knowing how to navigate in public among different social classes. To be civilized is to be polite. But polite is a lot more than being nice. Being polite means being courteous *in spite* of social differences.

This requires hard work because it means managing conflict, confusion, and insults between classes without breaking stride or losing one's composure. Being polite means maintaining poise under pressure. Being impolite means calling attention to social differences rather than making believe they don't exist. To be impolite means breaking stride and expressing oneself emotionally and sensually. In other words, being uncivilized means losing control.

Having manners has something to do with understanding the expectations of an occasion and a command of the roles required for that occasion. Being uncivilized means either having the wrong clothing for the occasion or wearing coarse fabrics. It also means being incompetent in understanding in two ways:

- what the limit of your own roles are
- misinterpreting what to expect from others

At a dinner party, being uncivilized might entail eating with your hands, or (heaven forbid) using the wrong forks and knives.

Being civilized also has a great deal to do with writing, speaking, and reading skills. A civilized person is articulate, has command over their vocabulary, uses impeccable grammar, and has perfect diction. An uncivilized person is at a loss for words, fumbles and bumbles their words, and has bad grammar and inconsistent pronunciation. Civilized people are at home with both reading and writing; uncivilized people are not. Being civilized involves not only good form but presenting superficial content. Why superficial content? Because civilized discussions already have built into them an awareness of class differences. Being superficial means unconsciously agreeing not to bring up controversial topics, and there are few topics more controversial than social class. An uncivilized person will talk about subjects that are taboo and not realize it.

When a civilized person cannot avoid a disagreement, they hope to settle it non-violently, with the use of rhetorical techniques and a quick wit. An uncivilized person will use violence to settle disagreements, and they will openly enjoy cruel actions such as taunting, torture, and public spectacles of humiliation. A civilized person will not admit to being interested in cruelty. They avoid finding out what is done in prisons.

Bodily functions

In personal appearance, being civilized means being neat rather than messy. But even more important than being neat is being *clean*. What is uncivilized is not just being messy but being *dirty* and ungroomed. This includes being smelly with sweat, sex, or feces. Being uncivilized means not hiding or marginalizing body functions. This includes farting, burping, spitting, or not using a handkerchief in public. A sure sign of a barbarian is loss of social control over biological functions. A civilized person would much rather have no bodily functions at all. The least one can do is take care of them privately and never talk about them. An uncivilized person will discuss them and even joke about them. These type of discussions about body functions is unsettling for the upper classes because it has a leveling affect. Above all, a civilized person has self-control over their body functions.

Emotional life and sensual gratification

A civilized person strives to have an even temperament and not be volatile. Everything is taken in stride. They will accuse someone of being uncivilized if they are too emotionally expressive or if they have explosive reactions to events. As might be expected, a civilized person will deny or delay sensual gratification and when they are sensually gratified, they will remain self-controlled rather than abandoning themselves. An uncivilized person in the eyes of a civilized one is enslaved to their senses, loses their composure, and behaves in an unpredictable way.

Class nature of being civilized

The demand to become civilized is an attack by the middle and upper classes in cities on the working classes (artisans and peasants). These veiled attacks keep working-class people from dining in middle-class or upper-class settings or showing up at art museums or opera houses. Being accused of being an inarticulate mob is what keeps working class people from claiming that they could run the places they work without the upper classes leading them. The threat of being accused of being uncivilized today keeps working-class people from speaking up in high schools and college and from reading books and believing that their lives are interesting enough to be written about.

Putting a spatial and temporal frame around what is civilized

What is civilized and what is uncivilized is not just about class divisions within a society but also *across cultures*. Early anthropologists classified all non-industrial, non-white societies as being uncivilized: more sensual, lazy, immoral, dirty, illiterate and sexual. Even within European societies, people who lived in the Dark Ages and Middle Ages prior to the Enlightenment were classified as barbaric. In the nineteenth century, developing a capitalist society was a sign of being civilized. By these standards, any societies, even the great agricultural civilizations of Egypt, Mesopotamia, China, and India were understood as less civilized because they failed to develop capitalism. In the earlier part of the twentieth century, European racism broke through on its own continent, with the Greeks, Italians, Spanish, and French being seen as less civilized than the Germans, Dutch, Yankees, and most of all, the English. Politically, any society without representative democracy was backward and unenlightened. Here is a summary:

Uncivilized	**Civilized**
working-class, poor	middle-class, upper classes
southern Europe	northern Europe
non-whites	whites
tribal redistributive, feudal	capitalist
authoritarian	representative political institutions
Paganism, Hinduism Confucianism,Taoism, Buddhism	Judeo-Christian
Dark Ages, Middle Ages	Modern Age from seventeenth century

Manners in the Middle Ages as uncivilized

Manners in the Middle Ages correspond closely to what we would today call uncivilized. Let's examine some of these differences in more detail. Suppose you were at a dinner table in contemporary times and served a bowl of soup from a large serving bowl. What you would expect is for each individual to pass the bowl around, with each person using a ladle to pour as much soup as they wanted into their individual bowl. If someone from the Middle Ages were transported via a time machine to your dinner, what would you find? When you passed the soup in a large serving bowl, the transplant would drink directly out of the serving dish, slurping the soup, smacking their lips, and then passing the bowl on. In the Middle Ages if there were spoons at all there would simply be one spoon which everyone used. Back to present time, the middle-ager would not understand what the smaller bowls were for, and they would not know how to use individual folks, knives or, spoons. It wasn't until the sixteenth century that individualized forks, spoons, and dishes made their appearance. The very notion of having formal courses for a meal was foreign in the Middle Ages. As I've shown in *Forging Promethean Psychology*, people in the Middle Ages ate a great deal of food, but the sequencing of courses into salad, soup, meat and desert would be foreign to them.

After dinner, your friends take the middle-ager out for a walk. It is wintertime and a number of guests have caught a cold. These guests have the standard runny nose and watery eyes. For you and your guests, handkerchiefs are on full display. To your disgust, the middle-ager simply blows his nose with his fingers out into the open air. When his throat needs to be cleared, he hacks and spits with no apology. Not only does he spit unabashedly, but he does not limit his spitting to the streets. He makes no distinction between spitting in public and spitting on the floor of your home! It takes a good couple of hundred years before spitting is limited to spitting in public. In the Middle Ages, it was not only *not* bad taste to fart or burp in public, but discussions about body functions were a normal part of conversation. People in the Middle Ages relieved themselves in public as a matter of course. There was neither shame nor repugnance in the behavior.

It is now time to go to bed. You lay out a pair of pajamas for your guest in the guest room. You go in to check in on your guest, but find he is no where to be found. When you return to you own bedroom, you find him in your bed, with no pajamas and are amazed that he has invited the rest of your guests into your bed and is holding court about how life was in the Middle Ages. This is not an invitation to an orgy. He expects the guests to spend the night and for everyone to sleep in the same bed. What etiquette books existed would have specified that common courtesy dictated that everyone slept in the same bed. As for pajamas, the existence of specific bed clothes did not begin before the Renaissance.

In some cases today, if one person is nude and the other has their clothes on, we would think that the person with their clothes on had more power because they are not exposed. This is certainly true in the relationship between courtly aristocrats and their servants. However, in the Middle Ages it was the reverse. It was not acceptable for the lower classes to be nude in front of the upper classes but is was acceptable for the upper classes to be nude before lower classes. It was a sign of the lord's benevolence to do so. It wasn't until the nineteenth century that there was a prohibition against appearing nude for any social classes.

People in all societies feel ashamed about some things. However, cultures are different about what they feel ashamed about. What is new about the shaming process is that in the Middle Ages, you needed the presence of other people to feel ashamed. In the high bourgeois Era of the nineteenth century, people can feel a sense of shame even when they are alone.

Sociogenesis and psychogenesis in the Middle Ages

Sociogenetic conditions of the uncivilized mentality of the Middle Ages

To begin with, according to Medieval historian Johan Huizinga, life in Middle Age manors and villages was largely self-sufficient and low in interdependency. The population density was low and any interdependent aspirations were muted by muddy roads that were difficult and dangerous to travel and posed a great risk of being robbed, attacked, or even killed. The feudal state was weak and unable to control local feuds, and medieval populations were armed. There was no centralized currency, so all exchange happened through bartering. Periodic famines and plagues created conditions where becoming civilized would not pay off.

According to Spierenburg (*The Broken Spell*), marriage patterns in Western Europe were different compared to other pre-industrial societies in four ways:

- It avoided households containing more than two generations. Neither grandparents nor married brothers or sisters lived under the same roof.
- Whoever could not achieve economic independence had to give up the thought of marrying. Many men remained

bachelors all their lives. Most women entered their first marriage in their mid-twentieth, while the men approached thirty years of age.

- As we saw in the first chapter, adolescents from other households lived with a family and were taught a trade. Households could be large, but they did not contain more than one couple.
- Unlike Non-Western societies, there was no age where children took care of their parents.

In cities, grandparents were regularly committed to hospitals or boarding houses. Even in villages, after the transfer of property occurred, grandparents lived in a smaller, separate house on the farm.

In his book *Popular Culture in Early Modern Europe*, Peter Burke makes a distinction between two traditions: the greater and lesser traditions. High culture consisted of the art and music of the Church and the elites, and these activities were conducted in palaces, universities, court buildings, and patrician homes. The lesser culture was the culture of peasants and artisans who performed in the street, in taverns, in fields, and in barnyards. These traditions included Carnival, mystery plays, farces, and fairytales. What is important here is that while popular culture did not mix with elite culture, elites did participate in popular culture. According to Michael Bakhtin, in *Rabelais and His World*, popular culture was looked on as a game by the upper classes, but they participated, nonetheless. In the case of Carnival, elites participated in role reversals and allowed themselves to be mocked. This was not the case later on.

Psychogenesis in the Middle Ages

From these sociogenetic conditions, it makes sense that for people in the Middle Ages, self-observation, careful observation of others, self-control, and a steady temperament were not high on their agenda. While there was extreme deference from a peasant to his lord, peasants did not treat those in their own social class politely. People in the Middle Ages lived hard, played hard, and died young.

For example, during Carnival there would be singing, dancing, and feasting for a week while roles were reversed between classes. Feasts of the Middle Ages went beyond anything we can imagine, perhaps as a reaction to the threat famine, which could come at any time. Games were organized. This included the organization of fights between animals, as well as the burning alive of stray cats. While there was no incarceration in the Middle Ages, lawbreakers were whipped in the streets. Public events included the burning of heretics and public torture.

Surprisingly, people in the Middle Ages were tolerant of homosexuality. Spierenburg points out the contrast with early modern states.

> In the later Middle Ages, repression is said to have increased. With the Reformation and Counter Reformation, this ambivalence gave way to unequivocal intolerance. For England and the Netherlands, the appearance of a gay identity can be dated around 1700. A distinct subculture emerged in both countries at the end of the seventeenth century. This subculture arose in the context of increased persecution, which caused a sense of identity to strengthen. (The Broken Spell, 271-272)

How were mental disorders explained and treated? One possibility was that the person was possessed by the devil and exorcism was required. Another possibility was that they had an excess of one of the four fluids in the body which caused temperamental deficiencies. If problems got too severe, they were put in madhouses. The first madhouses were not sequestered institutions. Spierenburg points out that windows facing the public street made it possible for onlookers to tease inmates mercilessly.

Death was an accepted fact of life. Phillip Aries characterizes the Middle Ages as a time of 'tamed death', meaning one of resignation and not knowing fear. Aries tells us that people accepted death more readily than moderns and openly talked about it. Even during funerals, middle-agers played hard. According to Spierenburg, adolescents not only played cards, but danced, performed pantomime, and performed mock-fights in which one of them died. Exhibitions of skulls and bones were regularly placed in the galleries of the Church.

These social conditions led to a volatility of temperament, a sudden switch from mood to mood, from intense merriment to violent brawling. In the Middle Ages, there was less psychological internality. Conflicts were externalized as taking place between God and the Devil or between saints and sorcerers. Because it was neither necessary nor possible to anticipate the effects of one's actions on anyone, it was difficult to plan many moves ahead. Shame and embarrassment were more unpredictable, less uniform, and less comprehensive. Because people were not living in dense, interdependent networks, they could act more directly from their drives and be less careful. Using Freud's terminology, people in the Middle Ages had an underdeveloped ego, being driven between the super-ego (the Catholic church) and the id (the Devil). Further, Elias was convinced from his research that people in the Middle Ages had a much greater tolerance for pain than in the modern period.

The Socio-historical grounds of psychogenesis: the work of Norbert Elias

As a historical sociologist, Norbert Elias wanted to understand the process by which people in Europe became civilized by drawing from historical documents, literature, and painting. Since many of the characteristics of what it meant to be civilized were *psychological* processes, he wanted to show how *historical* processes changed even seemingly private psychological states. In his book on Elias, Stephen Mennell tells us Elias intentionally focused on the most natural and animalistic human functions---eating, drinking defecating, sleeping, and blowing one's nose, because these things humans cannot avoid doing, no matter what society, culture or age people live in. Elias compared three countries: France, Germany, and Britain.

Elias takes issue with social-psychological theories who talk about social impact as beginning and ending with face-to-face encounters. The implication being that if you don't *sensually experience* your social relations, then you cannot be interdependent. Elias argues that people are already interdependent with people with whom they *never interact* through a division of labor that crosses regions and even states. Furthermore, the greater the division of labor, the greater the interdependence. The greater the interdependence, the more alert the individual becomes of time, timing, place, and circumstance. The individual becomes more aware of his appearance, words, and actions. Here are the long-term trends that were necessary, but not sufficient conditions for cultivating civilized behavior:

- Urbanization
- The growth of trade

These first two were common during the first commercial revolution in the twelfth century, so this by itself does not create civilized behavior. Further trends include:

- A vast division of labor which included an expansion of interdependence *within a given society*
- Long-term growth of complexity in spreading web of social interdependence *across societies*
- A movement from private to public monopolies. The administrative functions became too large to be handled by a king, so bureaucracies of increasing public character replaced patrimonies

- The formation of absolutist states. The state formation process was Janus-faced. On the one hand, larger territories underwent *internal pacification* with a monopolization by the state of the means of violence. At the same time, the state disarmed the population, and expanded the scale of its warfare

All these forces dialectically interact, mutually reproduce each other, conflict with each other, and sometimes amplify each other. For example, internal pacification of territory facilitates trade, which facilitates the growth of towns and the division of labor. This, in turn, generates taxes and support for larger administrative and military organizations which, in turn, facilitates internal pacification of larger territories.

- A widening circle of *mutual identification* despite class differences
- A shift from violent crime to property crime (with markets)
- A shift from violent blood sports (cockfighting) to spectator sports

More specifically, for Elias the origin of becoming civilized lay in what he called the royal mechanism. This meant the socio-political process by which the king played off the nobility of the robe against the newly arising merchant class while siding with the merchant class. The competition in early modern Europe between aristocrats in the courts of absolutist France and merchants required the ability of aristocrats their cool, cultivate appearances, and control their emotions, all while acutely observing their social circle and their image. The court was the key conduit through which civility was first imposed and then diffused. The imposition of external norms and controls on behavior gradually became internalized as having manners.

The growth of non-sensual networks of communication and transportation combined with increasing interdependence in growing cities was the sociological foundation for becoming civilized. Being civilized meant more habitual self-constraints, foresight, hindsight, insight, and increased sensitivity to shame and embarrassment. It also meant the development a negotiating technique so that violence was rarely an outcome in encounters. These included voicing expectations while anticipating the interests of others, being friendly but firm, and coming up with creative solutions while maintaining self-interest. After these processes are learned they become unconscious, seem innate, as if we never learned them. This second nature, Elias called habitas. This habitas led to changes in sexuality, sleeping patterns, appetite, aggressiveness, the ability to delay gratification, and tolerance for pain.

Sociogenesis and psychogenesis in absolutist states

Sociogenetic conditions promoting a civilized mentality

Turning to society in the seventeenth century, we find that aristocrats land had been bought by the bourgeoisie in increasing amounts. In defeating the aristocrats, the merchants had helped to build up built up a stronger centralized state. The state had made roads easier to travel and patrol with less danger of physical attack, especially for merchants. The European population had grown back from the Black Plague of 1340 to 1350 and they were as packed into growing towns and cities as before, with longer chains of interdependence because of the increase in trade. The state had minimized feuding and the population was more pacified. The religious tendency for ritualized behavior of the Middle Ages remained, but it was joined by secularized rituals of pomp and ceremony in the courts. The power of the state was demonstrated by public hangings, flogging, and branding. The public was encouraged to throw rotten fruit and stones at the offenders. Children were encouraged to attend these public humiliations even through the first half of the nineteenth century. The occupation of a single public space with gallows and a wheel must have been a chilling reminder of what happens to those who oppose the state. Puritans attacked blood sports, claiming that to enjoy the spectacle was sinful. But this didn't stop the general population from continuing blood sports. All of this, of course, was uncivilized.

In the courts it was a different story. Socio-political and socio-economic conditions under which western civility emerged was rooted in class struggles within the European court between old and new aristocrats. The warrior class of the Middle Ages had their land sold from under them by the merchants and the king excluded these aristocrats from the standing army. This was because he rightfully felt they were not trustworthy. In France between 1515 and 1517, with nowhere else to go, the aristocrats flocked to the courts of the king, beginning the reconstruction of the upper class.

As old social ties were breaking up, aristocrats of different social origins were increasingly thrown together as upward and downward class mobility increased. Forced to live with one another in a new way, along with rich merchants, these classes were at once acutely confronted with the problem of what constituted a uniform standard of good behavior. Very gradually in accordance with new power struggles and new interdependencies, a sub-culture developed with more subtle ground rules as to how to act. This was the foundation of becoming civilized.

In the Middle Ages, knights sought adventure in wars, whether religious or secular. By the seventeenth century, the court aristocracy *read* about the chivalry of knights in novels. Because the court aristocracy lived so close to those above and below them, they were far more sensitive to any behavior that would mistake them for a class other than what they were. Instead of feeling contempt for other classes, they are embarrassed by them. Contempt comes more from a position of dismissal of someone who was clearly inferior. Embarrassment is an emotion that comes out of a closer experience and a common fate.

One of the criteria Elias used to mark the civilization process was the distance between children and adults. Because life in court society required much impulse control and observation, it took longer for children to be socialized. At least in manners, there is less distance between children and adults in the Middle Ages, as Phillip Aries confirms in his *Centuries of Childhood*.

Psychogenesis in the courts

Any class of people living in a society with a dense interdependent population is going to have a more mediated psychological life. Those aristocrats living in the court could not afford to have emotional outbursts. Membership in court circles meant that extreme caution was required to avoid permanent interpersonal damage. Therefore, people of the court developed an extraordinary sensitivity to the status and importance that should be attributed to a person on the basis of fine distinctions of bearing, speech, manners, and appearance. Observing and engaging the right people became an art in itself. At the same time, these aristocrats had to become more self-reflexive in how they appeared to others. They became specialists in the elaboration and molding of social conduct. What becoming civilized taught them was to:

- develop foresight in strategizing and calculating their next move
- hindsight in recollecting the time, place, and circumstance of previous deeds.
- insight into their own psychological states

For these aristocrats, drives were seldom immediately acted upon and were more mediated by social consideration. The French court was a hot-bed of faction and intrigue within an aristocracy that was declassed, humiliated, and dependent on the king. The development of a culture of being civilized could be looked at as a kind of class reaction-formation. Shame and embarrassment were more comprehensive emotional reactions than they had in their lives as warriors in the Middle Ages. Here are some contrasts between these types of aristocrats:

Warrior aristocrat	**Courtly aristocrat**
Courageous	Prudent
Impetuous	Restrained, self-controlled
Wild	Tame, refined
Cruel	Humane, gossipy
Living with joys of the present	Foresight into thefuture
	Hindsight into the past
	Insight and self-reflection

Again, using Freud's terms, it is not so much that the court aristocracy developed an individual ego as much as a social-ego in dealing with those in close quarters. Delaying gratification was central. Perception of others was not based on individual characteristics, but in terms of how well they were playing their social roles. Elias suggests that the greater the number of contacts that people have with different classes, ages, and genders, the greater the number, length, density, and strength of the chains of interdependence. As a result, individuals become more observant and self-reflective. Over the long haul, the civilizing process involves:

- the concentration of power centers (the state) which *increases* with the growing differentiation of functions of society
- power between classes *decreases* relative to resources
- the degree of control the human species increases over
    - biophysical nature
    - people over each other
    - each individual over him or herself

Please see table 8.1 for a summary contrast of sociogenesis in the Middle Ages and sociogenesis in the Absolutist state, and Table 8.2 for the psychogenesis in the Middle Ages and the Absolutist state.

Table 8.1 Socio-genetic Conditions for Psychogenesis: From the Feudal Middle Ages to the Absolutist State

Medieval aristocrats	**Time period and social class**	**Early modern court aristocrats**
Muddy roads	**Transportation**	Roads are easier to travel on
Traveling is dangerous and there is little of it Main risk is being robbed, attacked, killed	**Danger level**	Roads are safe and patrolled Low danger of physical attack
Sparse population	**Population distribution**	Dense population
More self-sufficiency between villages	**Self-sufficiency—interdependency**	**More interdependency** between aristocrats
Barter economy Short-chains of interdependence	**Economic exchange**	Agricultural capitalist economy Long chains of interdependence
War is a permanent state Population armed	**Political Violence**	War a less permanent state. Less people armed; state has monopoly on means of violence
Battlefield outside: Wilder; knights search for adventure—Crusades	**Where are aggressive outlets?**	**Battlefield within:** Tamer. Aristocrats look for outlets such novels of chivalry
Decentralized public spectacles—hanging burning heretics, pubic torture Vendettas	**Public Punishment**	**Centralized public spectacles** Permanent public signs of repression—gallows, breaking at the wheel Vendettas repressed; state repression
Extreme ritualization Hard play—carnival	**Ritualization/ play**	Extreme ritualization in courts. Decline of carnival (impact of Protestants)
Upper class feels contempt for lower orders	**Relationship between classes**	Behavior of lower orders is embarrassing for those above
Position of warrior aristocrats is secure	**Security of class position**	Position of the "nobility of the robe" is insecure. Threats from above with the king; threats from below with the merchants
Customs limited to social class	**Spread of manners across classes**	Customs spread across more social classes Aristocratic reaction is to polish their manners
High contrast of classes, less variety	**Social composition of classes**	Diminishing contrasts and increasing variety of social classes

Table 8.2 Psychogenesis in Feudalism and Absolutist States

Psychology in the feudal Middle Ages	Category of comparison	Psychology in absolutist states
Neither necessary nor possible to anticipate effects on anyone else's actions many moves ahead	**Place of foresight and calculation**	Can anticipate effects and makes foresight and calculation more possible
Shame and embarrassment are less stable, less uniform, and less comprehensive	**Shame and embarrassment**	Shame and embarrassment are more stable, more uniform, and more comprehensive
Drives permeate consciousness more, and little is left in unconscious	**Relationship between consciousness and unconsciousness**	Consciousness less permeable by drives and more is left to the unconscious
Superego vs id Tossed between religious mortification and sensual binges	**Delaying gratification**	Superego had less great contrasts; easier to delay gratification but not self-denial
Simple roles of deference to higher classes	**Simplicity or complexity of role taking**	Learning complicated roles within the same social class
Volatile temperament Free play of emotions Impetuosity, swift wrath, uninhibited violence	**Volatility of temperament**	Self-regulation of behavior Monitoring others behavior More even-tempered
Greater toleration of pain and freewheeling in inflicting pain on others	**Toleration of pain**	Less toleration of pain or inflicting pain on others
Warriors derive pleasure from cruelty; Mutilation of prisoners; cruelty to animals	**Cruelty-kindness**	State intervention and social control over cruelty
Control less automatic, must be conscious, and experienced as unnatural	**Degree of Control**	Control more automatic, unconscious, and experienced as natural
Command is direct do's and don'ts	**Obedience**	Obedience is not an issue in becoming civilized
Less important because there is less interdependence	**Conformity**	Because of interdependencies, conformity is more important
Less distance between children and adults in exposure and in manners	**Developmental difference between childhood and adults**	Greater distance between children and adults (children have to spend more time learning self-control)

Sociogenesis and psychogenesis in the nation-state

Socio-genesis from the absolutist state to the nation-state

We already discussed in previous chapters many of the institutions responsible for socio-genesis, covering the one-hundred-year period from the end of the eighteenth century to the end of the nineteenth century. Throughout the early modern period, merchants controlled the agricultural economy of absolutist states. However, political power rested with the king and the aristocrats. With the possible exception of Puritan merchants, whenever merchants acquired great wealth, they only wished to be accepted by the aristocracy and to copy their ways of life.

However, unlike the aristocrats, merchants saw their future connected to the expansion of new markets with the help of better navigation technology, shipbuilding and improvements in travel. Therefore, merchants were often the patrons of scientists. In order to be a successful merchant, it was crucial to be astute at counting, weighing, measuring, and calculating. These were all skills that were directly opposed to aristocratic concern with quality of relationships. Keeping track of exchanges was considered the bad in the eyes of aristocrats.

This led merchants to criticisms of aristocratic tastes. The Enlightenment movement saw courtly values as superficially concerned with form. For them, to be civilized was to have scientific knowledge that spanned from the natural sciences to the social sciences. The Enlightenment movement was cynical of all ritual, seeing it as being synonymous with superstitious religion. The process of being civilized for them meant doing away with mindless formal roles and hollow rituals in the name of progress (see Chapter 6).

Probably in part because of the lower-class rebellions in early modern Europe, by the eighteenth century elites began to withdraw from participation in popular culture. Allowing themselves to be mocked in Carnival role- reversals was a little too close to real rebellions happening in actuality.

As we saw in chapter two of my *Forging Promethean Psychology,* the rise of nation-states required the suppression of local competition for its loyalty, as nation-states attempt a superimposition of a single national culture and language. As the industrial factories were only developed in certain cities, many artisans and farmers left their local towns and farms to do wage work in larger cities. This left less people to carry on local traditions. These land enclosures and capitalist farming undermined peasant life and limited the physical possibilities to celebrate local ritual. In Protestant countries, the abolition of Saint's days shrank the opportunities for days off for rituals. Spierenburg points out the capitalists and Protestants had a common interest opposing fairs and sporting events because they encouraged diffused attention spans which undermined being sober, productive wage workers. Fairs and sporting events also drew vagabonds.

After the French revolution, the bourgeoisie swept into political power. It began to industrialize the cities, further undermining popular traditions. It is important to note that the rise of a new kind of national loyalty was first driven by the lower middle classes—teachers, journalists and state workers. This shifted loyalties of the middle classes from dynasties to nations. Merchants supported attempts by states to centralize administration by doing away with the tolls and local tributary procedures that slowed the rate of travel and shipping.

Please see Table 8.3 for a contrast of sociogenetic conditions from the Absolutist state to the Nation-State.

Table 8.3 Socio-genesis Conditions for Psychogenesis from the Absolutist State to the Nation-State

Absolutist state	Category of comparison	Nation-state
Seventeenth—late eighteenth century	**Historical time period**	Late eighteenth —Late nineteenth century
Animal transport, horses	**Transportation**	Railroads
Rural agricultural land dominates small cities	**Urban-rural relation**	Larger cities dominate shirking rural agricultural zones
Harnessing energy through animals, wind, water	**Technology**	Industrial revolution Harnessing inanimate sources of energy—coal electricity
Moderate division of labor—interdependency	**Division of labor**	Extreme division of labor—most interdependency
English civil wars English revolution (1688) Aristocrats gain control over parliament	**Political revolutionary situations**	French Revolution Aristocrats overthrown by bourgeoisie
High politics of dynasties	**Structure of Politics**	Rise of political parties and representative politics
Aristocrats vs bourgeoisie	**Class struggle**	Bourgeoisie vs the working-class
Centralized public spectacles	**State Power and Control**	Disappearance of public spectacles: Sequestered institutions—asylums
Village, city	**Group loyalties**	State—nationalism
Baroque vs puritanism	**Culture conflicts**	Enlightenment criticizes baroque culture Bourgeois materialism vs Romantics
Anti-science	**Attitude towards science**	Pro-science
Past, old ways, cyclical	**Relationship to time**	Future—ideology of progress Linear
Anti-commerce Commerce is contemptable activity	**Attitude towards commerce**	Pro-commerce and trade as a source of wealth: Adam Smith
Catholic	**Religion**	Protestant or deists
Vitally important	**Importance of manners and roles**	Respectful but also find them stuffy and slow
Very important	**Important of ritual**	Obstacles to commercial exchange
Quality, distinction. Measuring and weighing is beneath their dignity	**Quality—Quantity**	Importance of quantity and measuring

Psychogenesis in the Enlightenment and the industrial revolution

The rise of the private sphere

Emotional life

Both aristocrats and merchants agree that emotions should be controlled, but their reasons were different. Aristocrats saw emotions as sentiments that are feminine and unmanly, therefore they should be suppressed. Their emotions were competitive emulation resulting in either smug superiority or jealousy. The Enlightenment movement believed that humans had suffered badly at the hands of the Catholic Church, which cultivated fear of hell in the next life and guilt for sins in this one. As part of their project, Enlightenment thinkers wanted humanity to be happy. However, this happiness was grounded in reason. Other emotional states were not to have a life of their own and were subjected to the control by the mind.

In absolutist states, there continued to be explicit deference between classes, as was the case in the Middle Ages. By the eighteenth century, the Enlightenment sought to find the characteristics of humanity *in general*. This meant there was a growing sympathy developed for *all* social classes. Yet at the same time, the class struggle intensified with industrialization and the working classes became less deferential to capitalists, possibly because of their perceived common humanity.

This emotional sensitivity also affected a change in people's attitude towards animals. Before the eighteenth century, the European population saw no problem being cruel to animals, pitting them against each other in games. But as Keith Thomas points out, by the eighteenth century this began to change. Studies of the natural world in the seventeenth century showed people more sensitive to the emotional life of animals.

In addition, as the industrialization process made it impractical to continue to work with animals, people began to keep animals as pets.

Sensual life

Aristocrats were great sensualists and it is tempting to interpret this as meaning they were uncivilized. They were *connoisseurs* of the senses, not blind hedonists. Further, they competed with each other in contests to evaluate who could last the longest in *denying* the senses despite great temptations. During the Enlightenment the senses were always treated with respect. However, Enlighteners were aware that the senses were subject to error and must be controlled by reason.

Avoidance of physical pain

Aggression and the infliction of pain was accepted up until the nineteenth century. The majority of the population of seventeenth century Amsterdam carried a knife as a matter of course. Peasants in eighteenth century France who were robbed risked their lives going after their assailants. Bystanders in serious fights were eager spectators and were indifferent when servants, children, or thieves were punished. With the rise of the police force in the nineteenth century, the ritual violence of the young gangs, formerly tolerated, was increasingly criminalized. As the nation-state emerged, and populations were increasingly disarmed by the state, physical violence was less of an everyday event in large cities, at least compared to life before the industrial revolution. Furthermore, between the fourteenth and eighteenth centuries, plagues and epidemics were common. During the eighteenth century, disease and pain were brought under control by the field of medicine. With this, people's tolerance level for physical pain declined.

Sleeping patterns

Before capitalists were able to control the pace at which people worked in the nineteenth century, sleeping patterns were more dispersed throughout the day. A craftsman or a peasant would take naps in the middle of the day. Furthermore, in towns and cities, sleeping in public was acceptable. It was only after the industrial revolution with its emphasis on working at an *even pace and working throughout the day* that sleeping patterns became more regulated. Naps in the middle of the day became impossible, and sleeping in public became suspicious activity. Sleeping was a private affair done inside of houses preferably within a uniform period of time.

Death and funerals

In the early modern period, death was openly talked about. As the desire to be buried near a saint became common, some churches were built *in town* near the grave of the martyr (becoming churchyards). In the case of the king or the upper classes, funerals were theatrical productions consistent with a baroque life on earth. In Catholic countries, the authorities donated gifts to monasteries for the poor in the hopes the poor would pray for them. The poor were even invited to the funerals attended by thousands of people. Since the Enlightenment, death was less and less discussed and cemeteries were relocated outside of the hustle and bustle of life, as if not to be reminded of one's own coming death. After 1720, funerals became privatized and the poor were no longer included.

Table 8.4 Psychogenesis from the Absolutist State to the Nation-State

Absolutist state Baroque aristocracy	State, time period, and leading class	Nation-state Enlightenment bourgeoise
Superiority, emulation, coolness—emotions controlled by will	**Emotional ideal**	Happiness, serenity—emotions controlled by reason
Emotional life more deferential to the upper classes	**Emotional life between stratified groups**	Emotional life less deferential across stratified groups More appreciative of common humanity
Sensual indulgence, but also controlling the senses through warrior denial	**Attitude towards senses**	Keys to understand nature, but fallible
More tolerance of physical pain through everyday violence Tolerance of physical wounds due to lack of anesthetics	**Attitude towards pain**	Emergence of police-force in the nineteenth century pacifies violence among population Development of anesthetics by doctors dull pain
Seen as good for work Cruelty to animals in games	**Attitude towards animals**	Animals taken as pets Sympathy to animals
Recurrent plague epidemics from the fourteenth to eighteenth century	**Disease**	Diseases less lethal
Looser in relation to public Body relief in public	**Bodily conduct**	Stricter in relation to public Body relief in specialized places Sewer systems developed
Sleeping and waking cycle of individuals undisciplined Sleeping the daytime anywhere Sleeping in public acceptable	**Sleeping patterns**	More disciplined to nighttime with the industrial revolution Sleeping done away from work and in private
Havens from external physical threats	**Protective functions of houses**	Havens from psychological damage for working class under industrialization
Discussed openly	**Attitude towards dying**	Not discussed openly
Cemeteries lie within town limits	**Place of cemeteries**	Cemeteries outside immediate city or towns

Please see Tables 8.3 and 8.4 for the sociogenic and psychogenetic conditions which existed from the absolutist state to the nation-state.

European noble savages: early romantic revolts against becoming civilized

In Chapter two, in Table 2.3, we contrasted the differences between the Enlightenment and romantic individualism. In this section, I want to return to that table for the purpose of showing how the values of romanticism were *against* the project of becoming civilized that both the aristocrats and the merchants embraced. Though the Enlightenment wanted to replace being civilized with having culture, it still embraced some of the characteristics of being civilized. On the other hand, *most, if not all, of the characteristics of romantic individualism on the right side are a revolt against becoming civilized.*

In general, the romantics were against any structure that seemed to constrain individual emotions, will, or spontaneity. Romantics think that becoming civilized is to become compromised, imprisoned, and corrupt. For example, whereas merchants look at taming the wilderness by agricultural methods as *improving* nature by making her more productive, the romantics see cultivated fields as indicators of nature chained and bound. This can be seen in the romantic appreciation of artistic landscapes which are sublime: unpredictable, exotic, new, and dangerous.

With the growing knowledge of tribal societies in the eighteenth and nineteenth centuries, the romantics were drawn to the ways of life that civilized aristocrats and merchants dismissed as primitive. Because tribal societies had avoided becoming civilized, romantics thought they were freer in how they lived, loved, and experienced the world. This carried over into romantic spirituality which was pantheistic, possibly based on what they knew about tribal sacred beliefs.

Though many aristocrats did not know how to read and

write, they certainly cultivated their tastes in art and music. While the Enlightenment movement criticized the tastes of aristocrats, they still thought that cultivated good taste was important. In addition, the Enlightenment championed the value of education in helping individuals shed religious superstitions to become more enlightened. The romantics, on the other hand, were precursors of Pink Floyd's lyrical message about not needing education and leaving kids alone. In other words, civilizing children ruins their natural spontaneity and skills by burying it in old books, rules, and memorization.

While the Enlighteners criticized the stuffiness and pretentiousness of the roles the aristocrats took, they still believed in the importance of playing roles, with the understanding that individuals can change roles. For the romantics, playing roles was simply a mask to placate conventions. Roles repressed how people were naturally. The romantics wanted to unleash the primitive self whose true identity breaks through all social bounds and flies free as a bird.

Unlike their civilized aristocratic brothers, the Enlighteners championed change over stability. However, whether at the level of the individual or society, Enlighteners saw change happening *gradually,* becoming better and better. The romantics were having none of this. They believed when change occurs it only happens through personal or social crisis. It was the revolutions that come out of crisis that were the only processes that could break the bonds of civilized existence. Social evolution was seen as *degeneration* from a pristine ideal of primitive societies.

One of the signs of being civilized for both aristocrats and merchants was that one's emotions were in check. The aristocrat depended on will and the Enlightener on reason, but both agree that emotions are uncivilized embarrassments. For the romantic, emotions were not embarrassments; rather, they were what made people most noble. All forms of deliberation and thinking hid what was really going on and what needed to be expressed. It was the expression of 'storm and stress' that are fueled personal fires or social revolutions. Manic elation and depression were signs of real living.

In the high Middle Ages and to a lesser extent during the baroque period, insults between aristocrats were settled by dueling. By the nineteenth century, dueling had been outlawed by the state. How did romantics handle attacks on their honor? They threatened to commit suicide. Whereas in the early modern period suicide was criminally prosecuted, by the nineteenth century suicide was reclassified as a psychological problem. While most of the readers of Goethe's *Sorrow's of Young Werther* and the work of Rousseau might not commit suicide themselves, they became more sympathetic to those who threatened or actually committed it.

Lastly, for both aristocrats and Enlighteners, self-revelation was bad taste. For them, prudence dictated care because competition within aristocratic circles or between merchants required it. The romantic wanted to throw all caution to the wind. If only people knew and then shared what they were feeling inside, an authentic human community could be built. Mutual self-revelations are the key to human happiness.

Summing up, romantics are against being civilized in:

- refusing to play roles and the calculation that goes with it (violation of sincere self)
- refusal to act in a courteous and civil way (being phony)
- championing of primitive states of origin (children, tribal societies or feudal times)
- valuing what is wild, unpredictable, and dangerous in nature or society (sympathy for outcasts, criminals)
- denial of the value of formal education
- championing the spontaneity as opposed to deliberation and planning
- championing emotions as opposed to reason
- valuing self-revelations as opposed to keeping internal life private
- satisfying the senses as opposed to the denying their satisfaction.

Crypto-romantics in the second half of the nineteenth century

Romanticism old and new

In first half of the nineteenth century, romantics opposed both aristocratic pretension and the materialism of capitalists. But by the middle of the nineteenth century, industrial capitalists had driven aristocrats from power and the romantic criticisms of aristocratic pretension, extravagance, stoicism, and lack of depth were becoming increasingly irrelevant. Instead, romantics newly attacked those who were hardworking small merchants within their own lower middle-class origins. Once aristocrats were safely defeated, there developed within romanticism a *nostalgia* for the aristocratic life. We will call this crypto-romanticism.

Romanticism was up against a capitalist system that was rapidly penetrating all facets of life. Before the nineteenth century, most European states were still dominated by the countryside. Large cities such as London, Paris, and Amsterdam were the exceptions. By the middle of the nineteenth century, capitalists were expanding cities, building railroads through the countryside, and buying the land from peasants and forcing them to migrate to the cities to work in factories. The countryside had long been a refuge for romantics as sources of inspiration. As capitalists increasingly controlled the countryside, it was difficult for romantic painters to paint or write poetry about bucolic landscapes. In the times of early romanticism, villages were championed as sources of community life as opposed to the growing power of the state and capitalists. But as village life became increasingly marginalized, romantics in cities began to lose their ideal template for community life.

From 1750 to 1850, romantics rebelled against the mechanistic- materialist view of nature depicted by seventeenth century science, instead arguing for an organic view of nature. For romantics, nature and culture were in the process of growth and decay just like the lives of animals. By the latter half of the nineteenth century, with the rise of imperialism and nationalism, civilization itself seemed to be in a process of decay. While early romantics were eager and curious to study the origins of culture (Herder) or through folktales (Grimms), for late romantics this was becoming less possible because their own peasantry was in decline. Instead the subject matter of romantics became cityscapes typified in the work of the Impressionists, Post-Impressionist Van Gogh, and the Futurists in 1909.

Early romantics were interested in the *origin* of processes, including cultures. Crypto-romantic historians, filled with pessimism about the prospects for civilization, became interested in how other civilizations *declined or ended.* They also became intrigued by those populations rejected by capitalists: criminals and the mentally ill.

Romantics have always been interested in altered states of consciousness wherever they could find it. They have been drawn to secret societies which promised spiritual experience as in the eighteenth century Rosicrucian Order. Crypto-romantics were also very interested in altered states of consciousness. In 1882, William James founded the *Society for Psychic research.* By the end of the nineteenth century, there was also a great deal of interest in Eastern mysticism as evidenced in Madame Blavatsky's Theosophical Society. They were also interested in esoteric Western traditions like The Golden Dawn.

Early romantics proudly fought against the trappings of civilization, determined they would never succumb. Late romantics became increasingly pessimistic. They saw themselves as corrupt, sophisticated, civilized men, weakened amidst the luxuries of the great city. It is no accident that terms for sadism, masochism, and fetishism were all coined during this period. Women were seen as sources that sapped men's strength. Interest in prostitution (as the paintings of Toulouse-Lautrec) and in female vampires are examples.

Lastly, early romantics supported a sublime theory of art rooted in realistic representation in its paintings. But beginning with the Impressionists in painting and symbolism in poetry, artists began to move away from the representational work and they became more psychological.

Please see Table 8.5 for a contrast between the old and new forms of romanticism.

Figure 8.5 Romanticism Old and New

Old Romanticism (1750-1848) Germany	**Category of comparison**	**New Romanticism (End of nineteenth century) Paris, Vienna**
Predominantly small cities while championing rural life	**Relationship between urban and rural**	Large-scale industrialization, urbanization
Disgust with aristocracy	**Attitude towards the aristocracy**	Mimic the aristocracy (dandyism) (aesthetes) Disgust with aristocracy (bohemianism)
Rebellion vs mechanistic view of nature; nature like an organic body Emphasis on *origin* of processes	**Metaphors of nature**	Rebellion vs mechanistic view of nature. Nature like an organic body; emphasis on *end* of processes: decay
Idyllic scenes in the countryside	**How is nature painted?**	Cityscapes—Impressionism Van Gogh
Interested in the origins of culture *within its own peasantry and in tribal societies* through philology and folklore	**Attitude to history**	Interested in origins of culture in tribal *societies in other places than Europe;* loss of its own peasant population as a source because its own peasant population was dwindling Interested in destiny and decay of civilizations
Villages as vestiges of authentic community	**Community**	Loss of ideal community Artist groups in cities as a partial substitute
Poetic genius; how one is inspired	**Sources of inspiration**	Interested in mental illness and the criminal mind Creative genius (bohemian)
Yes (Rosicrucian's) Robert Fludd	**Interest in the occult**	Yes. *Society for Psychic Research;* theosophy
Confident he can hold out against the decadence of civilization	**Confidence level**	Loss of confidence; sees self a corrupt, civilized man weakened by the luxury of cities
Sensibility	**Sexuality**	Cult of eroticism—Anatole France—sadism, masochism, fetishism coined
Gothic novels of male vampires	**Novels/ Painting**	Gothic novels of female vampires Interest in prostitution Toulouse-Lautrec
Art as sublime	**Theory of art**	Art for art's sake Cult of aestheticism—refined elegance, search for the rare aesthetes

Crypto-romantic individualists: dandies, bohemians, aesthetes

Dandyism

The term dandy originated in England and then spread to France, dating from the late eighteenth and early nineteenth century. The word commonly refers to a man who shows fastidious concern with his dress and has wit and cynicism about life. *Dandyism can be seen as a reworking of courtly aristocratic values to meet the challenge of the actual decline of that class.* Dandies were men who had little real claim to aristocratic lineage or land. They owned no serfs yet they experienced a privileged education. Unlike the cavalier aristocrat whose values rested upon physical heroism and loyalty to the king, dandies had little connection to the halls of power. For the dandy, the only thing that mattered was having good taste.

Bohemianism

Bohemianism first appeared in Paris in the 1840s, and from there spread to all the major cities of Europe and North America. In *The Protestant Ethic and the Spirit of Consumerism,* Colin Campbell defines bohemians as self-consciously in rebellion against what they see as the corruption of bourgeois society, namely its poverty in creativity and imagination. They saw the cause of this to be the practicality, prudence, and work ethic of merchants. In reaction to this, the bohemian pursued his art. Fearful that having to sell his product would corrupt him and his work, he worked unskilled jobs, generally beneath his middle-class formal training. Bohemians chose this work life done for the love of art.

The bohemian is forever in search of authentic experience, whether induced by alcohol or drugs. The resulting dissipated health condition is worn as a badge of honor. Clustering together in whichever sections of a large city offers the cheapest rents, bohemians create their own social circles, usually around a café or restaurant. They often produce a literary magazine, publishing it on a shoestring as it moves in and out of circulation.

Rather than the *material* indulgence of the commercially minded bourgeoisie, the bohemian is *sensually* indulgent. Whereas the bourgeoisie restrict their pleasures while forever adding to their comfort, the bohemian embraces deprivation of material comfort in order to pursue sensual pleasures. For the bohemian, pleasure matters more than utility, as he values voluptuousness above opulence. Rather than being ambitious and delaying gratification, the bohemian lives his passions in the present and forsakes the future. Rather than possessing things, he pursuits his desires. The bohemian is a reversed Calvinist.

Bohemians and dandies contrasted

Like their cavalier and dandy predecessors, bohemians had adopted some upper-class values such as the desire to live a leisured life and a special aversion to work. They borrowed money extensively and rarely paid their debts. Like dandies, they congregated in cliques, but unlike dandies they were not ashamed to be poor. Their sense of honor and reputation did not depend on impeccable social conduct or the mastery of good form, but on the display of commitment to romantic ideals, essentially art-for-art's sake. For the dandy existence was cultivated based on managing the impressions of what others thought, while the bohemian answered to a spirit or genius within himself.

Aestheticism

As artistic expression began to slowly move away from realism, so too the purpose of art changed from its previous association with having utilitarian, spiritual, or moral value. First associated in the late nineteenth century with Whistler and Oscar Wilde, aestheticism developed out of romanticism which understood art as having a life of its own, that is, 'art-for-art's-sake.' The original classical conception of art was that art should please and instruct. The art-for-art's-sake movement proclaimed that art should *please* the spectator not instruct them. Oscar Wilde rejected the romantic identification of the *natural with the aesthetic*. Instead, the artificial can be redeeming if it follows aesthetic principles. In fact, art is *superior* to life. Life is *bad* art, says Wilde.

The treatment of life as a bad approximation of art led to an attitude of detachment, one in which events were appraised not from their *content* but simply something to be judged with the eye of a critic and connoisseur. But by attempting to dissolve art into proper form, the aesthetes lost the power to challenge conventional artistic *content* which the Bohemians possessed. Although they could condemn society for being ugly, the aesthete could not condemn it as corrupt, degenerate or vapid. While the aesthete was likely to be indifferent to society’s conventions, they lacked good reasons for challenging them. Since he was probably dependent on society for his reputation and livelihood as perhaps an art critic, the aesthete would not defy society too openly. The Bohemian by contrast, needed to flout convention and only romanticism could supplied a philosophy to justify it.

The claim that art imposed a higher morality on those few souls who could appreciate it led aesthetic individuals to cultivate special, highly refined tastes, separating themselves from the public. This isolation can be seen as an ultimate extension of the romantic’s claim of belonging to a special group of misunderstood souls which goes all the way back to Rousseau. Unlike the early Romantics, Campbell points out there is a form of emotional stoicism in aestheticism resembling dandyism. Baudelaire disliked the romantic for their storminess and high-flung spontaneity.

Aestheticism *did not* represent a powerful impulse to reject the world as bohemians did. Aesthetes repudiated utilitarianism, but not materialism. Luxury, in the form of exquisite, rare and beautiful objects of little use symbolized the aesthetic attitude. Aestheticism helped to promote the phenomenon of fashion by making individuals aware of themselves as objects of beauty.

Table 8.6 is a comparison of aesthetics to dandies, bohemians and pre-industrial romantics. Notice how far aesthesis has come from its pre-industrial romantic roots. In short, aestheticism is romanticism gone sour.

Conclusion

In this chapter we studied the psychogenesis of the upper classes as they become civilized through two phases: among aristocrats in absolutist states in the seventeenth century and among the merchants in the late eighteenth and nineteenth centuries. We also examined the romantic revolt against becoming civilized, also in the eighteenth and nineteenth centuries. These included early romantics and three forms of crypto-romantics: dandies, bohemians, and aesthetes. The early romantics were in rebellion against both the aristocracy and the bourgeoisie. The late romantics were mobilized against capitalism and in the case of dandies and aesthetes, turned nostalgically to elements of aristocratic taste against the bourgeoisie. A current look at the world of modern art today along with the glorification of anti-heroes in movies shows that both aesthetes art for art's sake and the stereotype of the starving bohemian artist show that crypto-romanticism has survived very well into and beyond the twentieth century.

Table 8.6 Spectrum of Romanticism

Category of comparison	Early romantics	Late romantic dandies	Late romantic bohemians	Late romantic aestheticists
Time and place	Late eighteenth century Germany	Late eighteenth century England	1840's France	Late nineteenth century, England
Class origins	Lower middle class	Middle class	Middle class	Upper middle class
Attitude towards convention	Defy convention	Support convention	Defy convention	Neutral towards convention
Message of renewal?	Yes	No	Yes	No
Relationship between life and art	Art should Attempt to capture life			Art is superior to life; life is a bad imitation of art.
Value of appearances		Appearances Matter	Contemptuous of appearances	Appearances should be a work of art
Attitude towards money	Reject	Reject	Reject	Reject
Attitude towards emotion	Emotional expressiveness	Emotional stoicism		Emotional stoicism: Cool judge of a critic
Attitude towards materialism	Reject	Accept (clothing)	Reject	Accept Precious art, object accumulation
What is poverty?	Sign of sincerity	A source of embarrassment	Sign of sincerity	A source of embarrassment
Social approval	Proud to be Outcast; loyalty to genius	Craves social approval	Proud to be an outcast. Loyalty to genius	Proud to be an outcast; loyalty to community of art collectors
Attitude towards work	Creative work	Aversion to work	Creative work	Creative consumption
What is tasteful?	Art is one expression of taste			What is tasteful is necessarily art
Place of morality	Art should instruct as well as please			Art should please independent of instruction or morality

CHAPTER 9

Becoming Civilized in Yankeedom: How the Upper Classes Got 'Class'

Orientation

<u>What is an American is not so easy to tell</u>

Whether we think about the French, English, or Germans, we would agree that there are vast differences. But *within* each country there is usually a clear image that comes to mind. But when it comes to the United States, is there a clear image? Will it be a Puritan preacher, a slaveholding planter, an oil barren like Rockefeller, a mountain man of Appalachia, a Kentucky frontiersman like Daniel Boone, or a prospector for gold in San Francisco? I think it is a fruitless prospect to try melding these types together, and I will explain why below. But to accept that 'America' as simply too large a political territory to cover with a cultural generalization, what can we do? We can section off the regional cultures and identify those regions where American culture principally took root. We can also name those regions that 'went along for the ride' along with those regions that were completely rejected.

<u>Was the royal mechanism in place?</u>

Norbert Elias's concept of becoming civilized was greatly dependent on the conditions of Europe, specifically the 'royal mechanism.' But there was no king in colonial America, nor were there courts. Does this mean that whatever the civilization process that took place, it didn't conform to Elias's model?
While in France the royal mechanism played off aristocrats against merchants in the closed settings of the courts, in Yankeedom there were no kings within the states. However, the English king played off the colonies against each other, especially the East against the Southeast. In New England, the ruling classes there

emulated the English, while at the same time hating them.

Differences in state pacification processes and diplomacy

In Europe, there was pacification of the former medieval warriors into the courts. Was there a corresponding pacification of aristocrats America? No, the European state has done a far better job than the Yankee state in pacifying its population as a whole. Does the violent way of life that the United States is known for signify that Americans are less civilized? In Europe there is great commitment to international diplomacy, which goes all the way back to the Treaty of Westphalia in 1648. American diplomacy developed much later. What does that say about the differences in the civilizational processes?

Did the state emerge before or after political representation?

In Europe the state mechanism was in place *before* there was any political representation. In America, political representation occurred first. What did this have to do with how territorially far and wide the civilization process spread within social classes?

Borders versus borderlands

In Europe, competition between states was roughly equal and in terms of the struggle for land, the borders in Europe were clear and distinct. But in the US, the federal state did not have to compete with other states. It successfully subdued the natives, who never developed statehood. How did that impact the civilizational process here? In the United States, there were borderlands which were fluid, across which French, British, and Indians traded and fought. How did this impact the civilizational process?

The presence or absence of frontiers

In Europe in the seventeenth century there were no frontiers. This meant that Europeans had no wilderness to tame. What does it do to American civilizational process to have frontiersman and cowboys who, over generations, 'tame' the land and the animals?

<u>The presence or absence of migration patterns</u>

The European process of civilization took place with relatively few immigrants, refugees, or slaves. In America, there was a constant flux of immigrants from Europe and slaves from Africa. What did this do to the Yankee civilizational process? Did it help it to spread across the land or did it inhibit it? Did it help or hinder the spread of Yankee civilizational process within its social classes?

<u>What does capitalism do to people's manners</u>?

In Europe, the courts were developed *before* full-fledged capitalism, which meant that manners were formed before capitalism. In the United States, if there were no courts, then capitalism was a great civilizing force in America. With the exception of Italy and Holland, banking and credit systems in Europe developed much later than in the United States. How did the cultivation of a banking and credit mindset advance or detract from the civilizational process?

<u>Literacy and hygiene</u>

There was more literacy in America in than in the seventeenth-century courts of Europe. It would seem that this would make Yankees more civilized. But is this true? There was a lack of respect for hygiene in Europe throughout the seventeenth century, despite aristocratic claims to be civilized. In the US, Mennell reports that European visitors claimed that Yankees were obsessed with cleanliness. Does this mean American habits of being civilized were fundamentally different from Europeans?

<u>Deference versus bragging</u>

Hierarchies along estate lines went deep into the Middle Ages and required deference between estates. In America there were no estates. So how did this effect use of surnames, clothing, music, ceremony and dance? Did this make the civilizational process easier or harder for Yankees? Contrary to what we might think, Mennell found that Yankees were *more* boastful than Europeans despite their lack of deference. How do we explain that?

The place of individualism in the civilizational processes

As we saw in the first and second chapters, the individualism that developed in Europe beginning with the Renaissance has been a staple in Europe ever since. Across the Atlantic, it was only in the early nineteenth century that individualism emerged. How did individualism amplify or dampen the civilizational process in Europe? Did the late development of individualism in the United States enhance or constrict the civilizational process in the US?

Does language variation make a country more or less civilized?

As it turns out, it makes a great deal of difference that throughout Europe many languages are spoken and very different political traditions exist on the same continent. In the United States, while migrants enter and leave much more fluidly, there is less language variation across regions. While the different regions across the country have their own cultures, those cultures are not as different as the differences between countries such as France and Bulgaria, or Iceland and Spain. For all the fuss about Yankees claiming hostility to the centralized state, that state successfully propagandized Americans to give up their most of their regional loyalties to the state by the late nineteenth century. Because of this, Yankee nationalism has made Americans less different than Europeans according to the great American historian, Lord Bryce.

Was there a romantic reaction to becoming civilized in America the way there was in Europe?

In the last chapter we saw that romanticism was the enemy of the civilizational process. The basis for that romanticism was an aristocratic poetry and literature about bygone days when aristocrats controlled the land. But what about romanticism of Americans? Were the paintings of Thomas Moran, Remington, and Church, of the great Yankee western frontier in the second half of the nineteenth century, a similar rebellion against civilization? If so, what was it a reaction against? The industrialization processes? The closing of the frontier? Both Europeans and Americans had evangelical religious movements in the eighteenth and nineteenth centuries. Are they also part of an anti-civilization reaction?

Where are we going?

It turns out that if we treat Yankeedom as a whole, it will be difficult to find comparison categories between Europeans and Americans. But if we put aside the American west, the southwest and central United States and focus on New England and New York area on the one hand and the plantation south on the other, we will find that:

- the southern plantation owners had a great similarity to the aristocrats of France
- it was in the Eastern and Midlands regions of the United States where 'what it meant to be an American' was formed
- there are two civilizational process in the United States: one in the south-central United States and one in the Eastern and Midlands

The power of regional loyalties in the United States

In the previous chapter, we discussed the process of becoming civilized in three countries. The problem of comparing these civilizational processes to the United States is that the US so much larger than either France, Germany, or Britain, taken separately or even combined. Yet the federal government of the United States began to try to unify the country from the Atlantic to the Pacific only after the Civil War; and it is questionable how successful they have been. To talk about a common civilizational process over such a large territory is beset with many problems.

David Hackett Fischer, in his book *Albion's Seed*, identified four major regions in the United States with significant differences in their means of subsistence, their religion, the conditions of settlement and the parts of England these first settlers were from. In his book *American Nations*, Colin Woodard has expanded these settlements from four to eleven regions. (Please see Table 9.1.)

Table 9.1 Regional Diversity in the United States

Name of region	Who settled it	Time of settlement	Geography of the United States
El Norte	Spanish	1595	Southwest
New France	French	1604	Louisiana (New Orleans) Nova Scotia, Quebec
Tidewater	South English	1607	Virginia, North Carolina
Yankeedom	East Anglia, England	1620	New England
New Netherlands	Dutch	1624	New York
First Nations	Native Americans	Already present	Reservations
Deep South	Barbados, West Indian slave trade	1670	South Carolina, Georgia, Alabama, Mississippi, Florida
Midlands	North Midland, England, Germany	1680's	Southeastern Pennsylvania, Ohio, Illinois, northern Missouri, most of Iowa
Greater Appalachia	Borders of Northern Ireland, Scottish Lowlands	1717	Tennessee, Oklahoma, Arkansas
Far West	Yankee Brigham Young	1847	Washington, Oregon, Idaho, Montana, Colorado, Utah, Nevada
Left Coast	Merchants, fur traders, missionaries, woodsmen from New England	1830	San Francisco, Portland, Seattle, Vancouver

For this section of the chapter, I will be following Woodard's description. According to him, Americans have been divided since the days of Jamestown and Plymouth. Colonists saw each other as competitors for people to settle their land, for the land itself, as well as for their ability to draw capital to their settlement. Here are some of issues that divided the colonies:

- loyalty to England: royalist Virginia (Tidewater) vs Yankee Massachusetts
- individualism: Yankees and New Netherlands were for individualism as to the more social orientation of the French colonies of New France
- religion: Puritanism (Yankees, New England) versus Quakers' freedom of conscience (Midlanders); in addition, there was tension between liberal and evangelical spectrum about how to practice their religion
- politics: the importance of politics for the deep South and the Yankees as opposed to apathy to politics of the Quakers (Midlanders)
- use of force: active use of force by Tidewater, the Deep South and Appalachia versus Midlanders, Quakers
- secession: not just Tidewater and the deep South but Appalachia and New England also considered secession

These regions had differences in religion between Catholics, Puritans, Anglicans, Quakers, and Mormons. Each region differed in the kind of work people did from cattle rearing, hunting, fishing, fur-trapping, agricultural capitalism (producing tobacco, sugar and cotton), subsistence farming, herding, and industrial production (mining, railroad work, and smelting). These regions were formed with different intentions including for religious purposes, commercial purposes, political independence, or as a home for refugees. The politics of the regions differed drastically, from authoritarian (deep South) to egalitarian (New France) to liberal (New England townhall and the Left coast) to classical republican (Tidewater) to libertarian

(Far West).

Regionalists in the US respected neither state boundaries nor international boundaries. It was only when England began to treat these colonies as a *single unit* and implemented policies that threatened them all that they formed a united force. It is important to realize that uniting against an enemy does not create unification *after* the confrontation is over. The greatest sectional battle in US history occurred almost a hundred years *after* Independence Day.

Woodard points out that Americans are one of the only countries in the world that does not make a distinction between a statehood and nationhood. A state is a sovereign political body that monopolizes the means of violence. A nation is a group that shares a common culture, ethnic origin, language, historical experience, artifacts, and symbols. Some nations are stateless like the Kurdish, Palestinians and Quebecers. Most agricultural states such as Egypt, China, Mesopotamian India had states without having been a single nation. (Anthony D. Smith's work is great for these distinctions.) Using these criteria, the regions of the country are like the 'nations' of America. Americans may have a federal state, but not a single nation.

The Conflict Between the South and the East

With all these regional differences, does this mean that we cannot speak of an American civilizational process? If there were no courts in which aristocrats forced aristocrats to develop a highly sensitized social psychology of manners, does that mean the civilizational process did not take place? If there was no warrior aristocracy to fight the merchants within the court, does this mean that another kind of civilizational process took place? To begin with, there *was* an aristocracy in America, but this aristocracy did not rule over peasants, who did subsistence farming. The plantation owners of the South ruled over slaves who produced commercial goods of sugar, tobacco, and cotton for a world market. In the East, there were university-educated professionals of lawyers and clergy ('Brahmins') who joined with merchants attempting to develop home industry (rather than trade with England, as the plantation owners did.)

While all eleven regions had their conflicts with each other, some regions were settled longer, and they concentrated more economic wealth at their disposal. For example, the mountain men of Appalachia herded sheep, pigs, and goats. They were in no position to compete for cultural dominance with the planters of Tidewater or the deep South. The settlers of what became known as New France made their home in Canada and in Louisiana. They were fisherman, fur-trappers, and hunters. They could not compete with the Yankees of the Northeast or the fur traders of New York. Even those with capital who settled late (as in the Far West) did not have centuries to build up a culture the way those in Tidewater, the deep South, Yankeedom and New Netherlands did. These regions had over a 200-year head start.

When we compare the civilization processes of the United States to Europe, we are really talking about the differences between the New England, New Netherlands, Midlands, and (to a lesser extent) Appalachia as compared to Europe. In the case of the other regions, El Norte was long abandoned by the Spanish, and New France by the French. Both these regions were inhabited by people who never accumulated capital. Native American tribes were decimated. Tidewater and the deep South are not from what is usually termed 'American.' While the far West and the Left Coast certainly had wealth, they were settled too late to have civilizational impact. This is Zelinsky's argument in his book called *The First Effective Settlement Law*:

> Whenever an empty territory undergoes settlement, or an earlier population is dislodged by invaders, the specific characteristics of the first group able to affect a viable self-perpetuating society are of crucial significance for the later social and cultural geography of the area, no matter how tiny the initial band of settler may have been. (*American Nations*, 16)

The fundamental arena in which American civilization played itself out lies between Tidewater and the deep South on the one hand, and the Yankeedom and New Netherlands on the other. Civil War historians might call this the battle between the 'North and the South' but this crudely lumps the eleven regions we discussed into two. The people of Appalachia might technically be in the South but they always had animosity to the planters. The Midlanders of the North might have sided with Yankees and New Netherlanders against the slave traders, but they were not industrial capitalists who had a material interest in luring poor farmers into their factories. Therefore, there are *two* process of being civilized in the United States, one southern and the other from the eastern and central parts of the United States.

Culture of honor in colonial America

Roger Lane, in his book *History of Murder in America*, traced the major differences between the North and the South to a southern 'culture of honor' that did not exist in the north. But where does this culture of honor come from? Lane argues that the process begins when we examine the differences in the kinds of work people did in the regions of England that they came from before settling in America. The inhabitants of Tidewater came from the Scotch-Irish borderlands of Britain where they engaged in herding. With moveable property, herders always had to be on guard, lest their animals were stolen. Because herding was a difficult life, herders were not competing with many other herders for grazing ground. The sparseness of the settlement pattern made it difficult for herders to rely on others to protect their land. Lastly, in both the borderlands of Britain and the areas of Virginia they settled in, there was no centralized state to act as law enforcement. Under these conditions, herders developed a very rigid protective mechanism, being suspicious, while reading body language for potential thievery. The culture of honor was where a people cultivated a trust among equals.

A culture of violence was the result of what happens when the culture of honor was violated. Someone who did not stand up for themselves had a sense of deep shame among herders. He had a reputation to defend. If insulted, the insult was addressed publicly in a duel or family feud.

On the other hand, the New England farmers came from East Anglia in England where farming was practiced. Farming lent itself to living in close quarters thus providing a social protection against theft. In addition, once they settled in New England they lived near large cities under the rule of law. This meant there was some *legal* ground for recovering stolen property. These conditions meant that farmers did not cultivate suspicion and a code of honor. Consequently, they were less likely to kill as a result of stolen property. Rather, the farmer cultivated a sense of 'dignity' based on universal rights. These farmers were more likely to be self-constrained and feel guilty over imagined violations over God's law. Violations were less likely to be settled publicly. Farmers did not engage in duels. Though farmers had been known to engage in family feuds, they were just as likely bring their case to the law, depending on the region of the country and their social class.

South and the East After Independence

By the nineteenth century, the capitalist interests in New England and New York area had crystalized into an investment in industry, building factories for textiles and railroads for transport. This form of capitalism was irreconcilable with the plantation economy of the South. As mass commodity production spread and geographical mobility of workers increased, it became more and more important that consumers were able to get along with strangers as they bought and sold goods. What became 'civilized' in the East was to treat strangers with an even-handed polite indifference or 'tolerance.' What was also civilized was for industrial capitalists to have same values as the Puritans: hard work, punctuality, planning, and investing. In the East, the industrial capitalists were politically liberal. To be conservative in the North in the nineteenth century was more about holding on to rural, Puritan traditions that were discussed in chapter four.

The plantation system in the South had a very different notions of what was civilized. In plantation life most everyone knew one another, and among other plantation owners there was a culture of honor which carried over from their south English heritage. Between plantation owners and slaves there was a deep expectation of deference. Encounters with strangers were much more loaded. While the Eastern cities cultivated a cool indifference to strangers, in the South what was civilized was 'southern hospitality' which meant bringing hospitality to a stranger. This meant being generous with time, food, and culture. But strangers who, for whatever reason, were not candidates for southern hospitality were not ignored. They were driven out or killed. Southern gentleman planters, like their aristocratic brothers in Europe, had a contempt for hard work and Puritanical values. What was civilized to them was the cultivation of taste in the arts, manners, and clothing. For them, being civilized meant to enjoy life and display wealth. Politically, the Southern planters justified their existence as classical republicans who believed that liberty was for the upper classes. They were contemptuous of the Enlightenment value of science and technology and saw themselves as the inheritors of Roman values.

Manners in the East, the Midlands, and Appalachia versus Europeans

Tocqueville famously commented that on the one hand Jacksonian America was far more egalitarian than anywhere in Europe, and less deferential. On the other hand, there was more bragging. His reason was because of a lack of clear class boundaries. According to Mennell, both Hegel and De Masistre commented on the lack of manners in America. Baudelaire described America in the 1850s as 'a great hunk of barbarism illuminated by gas...a construction of hardened chewing gum and idiotic folklore.' Complaints about Americans chewing tobacco were common by Europeans. By the mid-nineteenth century, Europeans also commented on what they saw as a general American obsession with cleanliness. But Yankees weren't always like this:

> Those who washed daily did so at the kitchen sink. Soap was mainly used for laundering clothes. By the 1830's the bathtub and daily bath were beginning to spread beyond the very rich. Immigrants new to cities were taught by social workers, educators and employers how, where and how often to bathe with soap and warm water (66). In 1840, only a tiny minority of the wealthy city-dwellers had running water and flushing water closets in their homes (65). *(The American Civilizational Process)*

According to Mennell, American manners books penetrated deeper into the class structure in part because of the lack of English social elite in the colonies to draw inspiration from and because a higher number of lower-class people could read.

The impact of the frontier on Eastern and Midlands civilization

Mennell says that the following stereotypes are common among frontiersman about people in Eastern cities. The East was seen as decadent, whereas the frontier was pristine. The East was mired in interdependent social ties such as proletarians being linked to wage labor and factories in cities. The frontier, on the other hand, was the home of independent hunters, fur-trappers, ranchers, or miners, who called their own shots. While the East was the home of elite bankers and industrialists, there was rough social equality on the frontier.

But what does living in a country with a frontier do to the civilizational process? Turner, in his book *The Frontier in American History*, traced the steady penetration of the frontier westward from the eastern seaboard in the seventeenth century all the way to the Rocky Mountains in the nineteenth. He distinguishes three phases:

- the trader's frontier—characteristic of French colonization and fur trade
- the miner's and rancher's frontier of the West
- farmer's frontier—which left the trademark of the English in the Midlands

Turner argued that the constant availability of free land meant that Americans would be less in danger of creating elite hierarchies, because these hierarchies would be broken up due to a constant return to more primitive conditions.

The uncivilized nature of the frontier

According to Mennell, when people who have been socialized in more settled conditions are cast out into the margins of society, their behavior will change. It will become more blatant self-interest if they can get away with things that they couldn't under more settled conditions. This behavior will become even more confrontative if, because of the rough balance of power, calculations of what will happen are less predictable. These higher levels of danger will produce emotions that are more impulsive and more violent, just as Huizinga claimed occurred during the European Middle Ages. Their extremes of violence and cruelty in combat is reminiscent of Elias's account of the joy in attacking among early medieval warriors.

For example, among fur-trappers:

> Billington produces some vivid evidence of their lowered thresholds of repugnance in relation to eating, drinking, sex, violence and cruelty (201)... For the mountain trapper (more like the medieval warrior), a capacity for unrestrained venting of

> impulses was essential. (202)

According to historian Patricia Limerick, the image of the self-reliant and individually responsible pioneer did not work with her research account that outside of every farm in the 1880s stood a great mound of empty food cans. She further pointed put these 'self-reliant' pioneers often blamed the federal government for their problems along with everyone else.

Meanwhile in Europe, there was no equivalent to the frontier process with the exception of Russia. As Mennell points out:

> Europe had not experienced anything closely comparable with American's western frontier. The nearest comparison in the nineteenth century was with the expansion of Russia eastward across the Siberian vastness of Asia...but the numbers were not large and they settled almost entirely in regions in which the Tsarist government already had some presence. (196)

The consequences of the frontier process, according to Turner, were that:

- the westward move diluted the predominantly *English* character of the eastern seaboard
- he advance of the frontier *decreased* America's dependence on England for supplies
- it helped to develop the central government; the very fact that the unsettled lands had been vested in the federal government was vital to the federal government's battle to control recalcitrant regions of the country

The Western frontier as Yankee romanticism

Towards the end of the last chapter, we discussed ways in which European romantics rebelled against the prospect of becoming civilized. Let's see how much this overlaps with the romanticism of the western frontier in the United States. As Richard Slotkin warns us, we must distinguish between the people who actually lived on the frontier—hunters, trappers, miners, gold prospectors—versus how the frontier was portrayed in *American literature*, as in dime store novels and the work of Cooper's Leatherstocking tales. We are interested in how the frontier romance in literature was a way for readers to:

- escape the dark side of the industrialization process
- escape the increasingly militant class struggle taking place between New England, Yankeedom on the one hand and the southern plantation owners on the other
- muffle the class struggle in industrialized cities, in hopes that the frontier stories that could provide an outlet

The romantics in Europe were disgusted by the foppishness of the nobility of the robe. Some of these romantics were aristocrats themselves, pining for the day in which they would own the land again. Hence these early romantics were drawn to idyllic scenes of the countryside. But other romantics were civic servants and teachers. These folks felt secure that their landed nobility was *defeated*. Because of this, their focus was against the crass mechanistic view of nature brought about by *capitalism*. In their attacks against capitalism, they tended to romanticize aristocratic life as a time prior to money grubbing, and the buying and selling of everything. In addition, in rebellion against what they perceived as the cold mechanism of science, European romantics were drawn to an organic view of nature that had been the basis of high magical traditions and alchemy from the Renaissance to the present time.

In America, the rebellion against civilization was directed not at an aristocratic class but at lawyers, merchants, industrialists, and bankers of the East. Whatever their dissatisfactions were with relentlessness of the industrialization of the cities, it did not result in an organic view of nature or in an exploration of magic. As Puritans, both of these were practiced by the heathen Native Americans, and so were out of bounds. To use magic to return to the pristine way of life was to adapt the way of the savages, which for them would be 'hell on earth.' Puritans bitterly condemned those who 'went native' and lost their souls.

While aristocratic romantics of Europe used tame country scenes to trigger collective memories of bygone days, in the New World, what was romantic was pristine, depicted in the wild and subtle paintings of the West from Remington and Thomas Moran. While romantics in Europe took the occasion to delve into the premodern world of the peasantry through the study of language and folklore, writers on American romanticism did not do this. In America, there was a deep anti-historical sense. What appealed to romantics was the exotic world of mountains, rivers and forests that had *not been seen before*. In addition, the frontier was about trappers, hunters, miners who were half-way between Eastern decadent civilization and the savagery of the Native Americans. Stories about the frontier were about Puritans' 'errand into the wilderness.' Puritans were terrified of the savagery of Native Americans. Their roots were *in Puritanism*, not in knowing more about native culture which represented a non-Christian world.

The source of inspiration for European romanticism was the poetic genius buried within every individual. In the New World, the sources of romanticism were men of action, who fought Indians, gambled, and blazed trails. Different frontiersman represented different regions of the country utilizing different means of subsistence. For example, stories about Daniel Boone were located in Kentucky, Tennessee, and Missouri. The stories of Kit Carson were that of a fur trapper from the mountains. Stories about Davey Crockett were more about the frontier in the Southwest.

What romantics on both sides of the Atlantic had in common was a refusal to play roles. This was certainly true of the frontiersman attitude towards the ways of the East. Second, both kinds of romantics refused to act in ways that showed they were civilized. While in Yankeedom there was a championing of what was wild, unpredictable, and dangerous, this did not lead to *identification* with mental illness, as the romantic did in Europe. However, the *romanticism of outcasts* in the wild west, such as gunfighters like Billy the Kid, Jesse James, Wild Bill Hickock, Calamity Jane, and Buffalo Bill was taken much further than in Europe. The glorification of the frontier, the West and the cowboy hasn't let up even in the twentieth century!

European versus American processes of becoming civilized

We are now in a position to better answer the questions posed in the introductory section. What must be kept in mind is that the 'America' being compared is the Yankeedom (New England), New Netherlands (New York), and the Midlands (from Pennsylvania to Indiana). Tidewater and the Deep South were never part of another American civilizational process.

In terms of social class, how wide did the penetration of being civilized go? In France, the civilizational process did not penetrate beyond the 'nobility of the robe.' In part this was due to the constricted nature of the courts, and because a higher percentage of the lower classes were illiterate. In addition, the absence of a frontier in Europe insulated the aristocrats from having to integrate civilized waves of frontiersman. Its civilizational 'crust' was narrow and thick.

In the end, Mennell says there was a greater variety between individuals in Europe than in America. In Europe the difference between the French, German and English was greater than the difference between Yankeedom, New Netherlands, and Midlands. Partly this is because there were greater language differences in Europe compared to America, at least until the late nineteenth-century waves of immigration. Secondly, all three countries in Europe have well over a thousand years of cultural build-up. In the United States, cultural build-up is less than 300 years if we end our survey at the end of the nineteenth century. Lastly, with the exception of a sprinkling of deism among the Founding Fathers, most of the United States consists of Protestants with the same wide-spreading civilizational mission (whether they were evangelicals or not). In Europe, we have not only a rivalry between Protestants and Catholics, but also the presence of Jews and Muslims (especially in Medieval and Early modern Europe). This would keep civilization bottled up to thicken in three separate countries.

In the United States the social areas in which the upper classes ruled were in law courts and in universities. While this is not exactly a 'public square,' the American 'mechanics' and farmers were more literate than in Europe and they were able to participate in reading manners texts and intellectual culture. In addition, the presence of frontiersman, whether they be farmers, herders, or trappers insured that whatever 'culture' was developed in the East had to deal with its frontier barbarians which led to a thinner civilizational 'crust.'

As mentioned earlier, in Europe, the state was much more successful in disarming the warriors and getting most of the middle and lower classes to give up their weapons. In Yankeedom, its colonial status and its lack of a centralized political force made an armed population the norm. While the right to bear arms was initially meant to form militias, it was later interpreted to mean individuals owning guns. This 'gunfighter nation,' as Richard Slotkin called it, is what Europeans consider the crudity of the American. The Japanese once said 'Americans still think they are living in the wild west.'

In America, political representation in the face of imperial England had a long colonial history, and colonists were very wary of being pushed around by another centralized power. Mennell points out the resistance of Andrew Jackson against the federal civil service set the tone:

> The federal civil service started in the first quarter of the nineteenth century. The election of Andrew Jackson, with his contempt for educated expertise and his distrust of large-scale organizations, curtailed the development of efficient administrative practices and trained civil service. (225)

As Mennell points out, seven of the original thirteen colonies printed their own money and passed tariff laws *against their neighboring states*. Nine states had their own navies which seized the ships of other states. Whatever we may think about the corruption and lack of interest in politics of most Yankees today, the importance of politics to the civilizational process was very vital to Yankees earlier.

In Europe, the absolutist state was built centuries before the French Revolution introduced bourgeois democracy. This, combined with the strong presence of the Catholic church, made French politics much more theatrical and formal. The state administration and the Catholic Church made France ooze feudalism long after feudalism as a system was formally defeated. In terms of the civilization process, it was tight and rigid. This translated into formal clothing, frock coats and breeches. Addresses were more ceremonial such as 'sir,' 'madam,' 'lord,' and 'lady.'

While this formality was certainly present in the Southeast of the United States, in the eastern and central parts of the country (especially on the frontiers or among the Appalachian mountain men) this was all pomp and circumstance. In New England, and most of all New Netherlands, with its great cross-fertilization of cultures started by the Dutch, short coats replaced frocks and trousers replaced breeches. People were more likely to call one another 'mister' and 'missus,' or even be called by their first name. In ceremonies, music and dance, Americans were less formal than in Europe with their baroque music and ballet.

In Europe, intense competition between states, and the lack of migration of people entering France, Germany, and Britain allowed the civilization process to cook and thicken within separate countries. In the colonies, whatever civilizational process was happening between the Eastern United States and British was happening *at long distances*. At the same time, the constant presence of immigrants in the United states looking for land allowed the British colonists to civilize them on their own terms. As Mennell reports, by the middle of the eighteenth century there were borderlands, rather than borders. On the borderlands the French and the English traded, mingled and fought each other. These included claims to fishing rights of the Gulf of Saint Lawrence and the control of fur trading in the interior.

If the *courts* civilized the French in how to behave, it was *markets* that civilized the East and the Midlands, as we saw in chapter four. Whereas banking and credit systems were weakly developed in France and Germany, these constituted an early part of the civilizational processes in Yankeedom, with colonies issuing their own currencies. The growing banking capitalist class sought to minimize formalities to maximize the toleration of strangers in order to buy and sell commodities.

Lastly, Yankees were not up against native people with their own state that Yankees had to contend with. The subjugation of Mexicans and Native Americans was brutal but not at the level of a war between equal states. Once they were subjugated, Yankee civilizational process spread far and wide. So, in Europe we can characterize the civilizational process as narrow and thick. In the Eastern and Midlands of the U.S. it was thin and wide. This thin and wide civilizational process was called 'Manifest Destiny,' which spread to Hawaii, the Philippines and Cuba, with missionaries spreading Yankee civilization beyond the Pacific.

Table 9.2 East, Midlands, and South

East Yankeedom, New Netherlands, Midlands	**Region of the country**	**South** **Tidewater** **Deep South**
East Anglia Britain Farmers	**Original settlement**	Came from Scots-Irish borderlands of Britain; herders; movable property
Better land allows for larger communities to act in self-defense	**Quality of land (lush, barren)**	Marginal areas which can't support large populations to watch out for each other
Stronger—more internal pacification with state and judicial authority that claimed a monopoly of legitimate use of violence	**Role of the state**	Weak—population armed in Appalachia, West and South, where there was no effective central authority
Dignity Middle class respectability and religious training	**Code for individual**	Honor; importance of cultivating a reputation
Individual conscience, or God Guilt	**Who judges**	Community; shame at failure to live up to reputation
Ignore Take them to court (some feuds)	**Method of dealing with insults**	Addressed publicly in duels, feuds
Industrial Capitalism (Gilded Age) Robber Barons—Vanderbilts, Fricks, Stanfords, Morgans, Rockefellers in the areas of railways, steel, coal, oil, and banking	**Type of nineteenth-century capitalism**	Agricultural capitalism (plantation slavery); production of cotton, tobacco, sugar
Protestant work ethic, even for the upper classes	**Attitude towards work**	Leisured upper-class ostentatious display
A person who is threatened is to retreat; only when cornered is one allowed to kill in self-defense	**Legal protocol**	Person could legally stand fast and, without retreating, kill in self-defense
More strangers, more diversity of standards; superficial tolerance	**Place of strangers or outsiders?**	Less strangers; smaller community; less tolerance of diversity; hospitality or hostility
Liberals—Enlightenment Ben Franklin, Tom Paine	**Political tradition**	Classical republicanism, to justify slavery in the mid-nineteenth century; inheritor of Roman values

Table 9.3 Cultural Differences in the Civilizational Processes

European civilization (French, German British)	Category of comparison	East, Midlands America (Yankeedom, New Netherlands)
Already settled; closest comparison is expansion of Russia eastward	**Place of the frontier**	The necessity of taming a wilderness before cultivating the graces of living was constantly renewed (frontier theses) Manifest destiny—westward, ho!
Less literacy across classes	**Literacy**	More literacy across classes
Hygiene not very important	**Hygiene**	Obsession with cleanliness; late nineteenth-century standards of cleanliness as a badge of social respectability
More deference and superiority	**Degree of deference**	Less deference and superiority
More formality; formal attire—frock coats, breeches; superiors called sir, madam, lord, lady	**Degree of formality**	More informalization; short-coats, trousers, in forenames, ceremony, clothing, music, dance, tobacco chewing
Less boastful; social status assured	**Boastfulness**	Americans are more boastful than Europeans because their social status is more uncertain
Aristocrats maintain emotional control	**Emotions, volatility, and impulsiveness**	American frontier; more emotions, impulsivity in drinking, sex, violence, and cruelty
Bubonic poetry for aristocrats being alienated at the court; past, rural idyll, tales of wandering knights and shepherds appeals to their estrangement from the land and longing for a vanished world	**Romantic rebellion against being civilized**	Wild, pristine west; paintings of landscape painters in second half of nineteenth century—Thomas Moran, Remington, Church; against industrialization, bankers
More variety in Britain, France, Germany, Italy, or Spain	**Variety between individuals**	Less variety among all American regions (Lloyd Bryce)
Narrow to the aristocracy and thick in cultivation and not much being civilized outside the courts	**Breadth and depth of penetration of becoming civilized**	Widely penetrated to farmers and artisans class-wise and across wide regions of the country
No frontier to have to reintegrate to civilizational processes which make the 'crust' of civilization thicker	**What the frontier does to the civilizational process**	The presence of the frontier forced civilized socialization over and over again, keeping the 'crust' of civilization thinner
Protestant sects, Catholics, Jews, Muslims (unity in early modern Europe)	**Religion**	A handful of deists (founding fathers), minority of Catholics, predominantly Protestant sects

Table 9.4 Causes of the Difference in Civilization Processes

European civilization (French, German, British)	Category of comparison	East, Midlands America (Yankeedom, New Netherlands
In place, with kings who played aristocrats off against merchants	**Was the royal mechanism in place?**	No royal mechanism; no kings in US; British king played colonists off against each other
Former warriors who owned land, outmaneuvered by merchants who bought up their land; forced to enter the court of kings	**Who were the upper classes?**	No warrior upper class who owned land; in the East, University-educated professionals—clergy and lawyers together with a growing proportion of merchants
Absolutist state pacified the aristocrats and rest of the population, as standing army replaces them	**State pacification and violence**	No centralized State before the late nineteenth century; population kept arms; America more violent; greater absolute level of violence at any given time *Myth of Frontier: Regeneration Through Violence* (Slokin)
Courts civilized before capitalism emerged; lack of banking and credit, strengthened civilizing pressures	**Major social arenas for becoming civilized**	Capitalism civilizes upper classes, rather than courts; seven of the thirteen states printed their own money; development of banking and more impersonal and institutional arrangements for credit
Political representation came after state centralization; strong, centralized, absolutist state	**The relationship between political representation and state centralization**	Political representation came before state centralization; fighting against England; House of Burgesses; Articles of Confederation; hostility to state centralization; many passed tariff laws against neighboring states; nine of the thirteen states had their own navies which often seized ships of other states; federal State emerges only after the Civil War, later nineteenth century
Competition between roughly equal states, without competition from the New World	**Power dynamics for territory**	North America was driven as much by rivalries between the various established states back in Europe as it was by local regions
Borders more clearly established between states	**Competition for land**	In the mid-eighteenth century there were borderlands in which French, British and indigenous groups mingled, traded and fought
Few immigrants, refugees, or slaves	**Migrant peoples**	Slaves and immigrants in colonial days, as well as later in nineteenth century

CHAPTER 10

From Reason to Rationality: How Rationality Lost Its Way

Orientation

Are rationality and reason the same thing?

Normally when we hear these words, we probably think reason and rationality are more or less the same. What they have in common is:

- they have something to do with thinking processes
- emotional states are unwelcomed

The opposite of reason and rationality is when someone is being unreasonable or irrational. In these states, the emotions appear to be out of control and have the upper hand. But after a careful delineation between reason and rationality, I will argue that there are important differences between the two and that emotions are involved in both, whether we like it or not.

One of the purposes of this chapter is to argue that reason and rationality are not the same thing. More importantly, there is a history to how these two forms of cognition have been used and abused. After clarifying the differences between reason and rationality, we will compare how the Greeks understood reason and rationality and how it compared to the seventeenth century baroque era. We will also study how these two terms were understood during the Renaissance, the Enlightenment, and the nineteenth century.

One difference is that rationality is based on the quest for absolute truth, while reason is satisfied with what is probably true. In this chapter we will follow John Dewey's analysis of the reasons why there was a mania for certainty in the seventeenth century. We will see how rationality was used by the state in both domestic and international contexts as a mechanism for social control. We will also examine how the same obsession with rationality during the baroque period was combined with the use of black rhetoric and gray propaganda in religion, the arts, and theatre. Lastly, we will see how rationality was challenged by LaMattrie's conception of matter as active rather than inert, how quantum theory in physics challenged Newton's deterministic claims about matter, and, lastly, how Marx and Veblen's challenged bourgeois contentions that capitalism is a rational system.

By way of qualification, I am following the work of argumentation theorists Stephen Toulmin and Chaim Perelman's distinctions between reason and rationality along with that of the pragmatic philosopher John Dewey. This chapter is not based on contemporary theories of rationality.

What is reason? Judgment made under uncertain conditions

We live in a world of perils and we are compelled to seek security. Yet beliefs, assessments, and judgments regarding which actions should be performed to achieve and maintain security can never attain more than *temporary* results. Planning and choosing, no matter how thoroughly executed, individual or social action, no matter how prudently conducted, are never the sole determinants of any outcome. Beyond what we do as individuals, there are all the conflicting interests of other individuals, social classes, and larger social forces that determine the extent to which our plan will succeed or fail.

If human conditions were only the result of necessity, we would be completely determined by outside forces and there would be no need for problem-solving. On the other hand, if existence were completely contingent or lawlessness, there would be no point in problem-solving because anything could happen. It is a *combination* of the settled and the unsettled, the necessary and the hazardous, that makes experimentation and planning a good strategy. Reasoning is the process of problem-solving and planning under circumstances of uncertainty.

Conductive reasoning: weighing the pros and cons

Reason seeks knowledge about practical, complex problems whose ultimate conclusions are uncertain because more than one conclusion could be right. These are problems for which the facts needed for a solution have to be found *outside t*he problem. An example is trying to decide what college you want to attend. In order to figure this out, you would you need to:

- Brainstorm a list of criteria for deciding which is the best school
- Prioritize the criteria according to your values
- Compile a list of the best schools
- *Collect data* on each of the schools and put them in a table so you can compare and contrast them
- Develop a quantitative and qualitative system for comparing the schools.

All these steps may sound elaborate and perhaps more work than you think it is worth. But what's worse is that even if you follow this procedure, you never know for sure if you picked the right school, short of starting to attend one. When you undertake projects like problem solving and decision- making, we use our reason. The kind of reasoning we use when we are weighing the pros and cons of making a decision is called Trudy Govier calls conductive reasoning.

Inductive reasoning in science: experience vs experiments

Dewey argues that the natural tendency of humanity when

faced with a problem is to do something *at once*. There is impatience with suspense and waiting long enough to collect data accurately, analyze data, compare and contract data before evaluating, let alone the time it takes to act. The volitional state is notoriously connected with emotional reactions. Nevertheless, despite our tendency to rush into things, experiences are acquired and accumulated through the exercise of common sense in everyday life.

But the scientific use of reason takes things to a deeper level. Instead of rushing to do something about a problem, science engages in something deeper and broader than action: *practice*. Conducting experiments requires formal training of the mind in how to:

- formulate specific questions for the experiment
- state a hypothetical answer to the question
- design a research plan to test the hypothesis
- note the conditions and problems which might get in the way of the experiment
- carry out an experiment
- analyze the results publicly
- discard or tinker with the hypothesis
- ask a deeper set of questions which anticipates a new experiment

Future experiments are conducted based on sharper inquiries founded upon the feedback from the last experiment. *The learning process that occurs between experiments is called scientific practice*.

In experience, we use our senses and reason for short-term ends. Once the results of these ends have materialized, there is less care in distinguishing what is true from what is effective. If something is effective and working, that usually suffices. Experience in everyday life does not require *replication* by anyone else as it does in science. The evidence works or doesn't work and from there we move on to the next problem. In an experiment, it is hoped that the hypothesis and the research design are so articulate that someone else can recreate the same conditions to test our evaluation.

Experiences are not happenstances that have no relation to the past. One's experiences are mostly built either on past experiences or what the authorities or valued groups have suggested about how to solve a problem. On the other hand, experiments are based on previous scientific data which may *contradict:*

- personal experience
- what some authorities may say
- what your peers might argue for

Regarding experience we mostly use a trial-and-error approach. You tinker with things to see what happens, and you keep tinkering until something clicks. There is little systematic attempt to consider *all* theoretical possibilities before beginning. Most of the time, people are only aware of *some* of the possibilities for a solution. In an experiment, the parameters for alternatives are framed by different research programs of different schools within a field. The results of an experiment are systematically applied so as many alternatives as possible are given a chance. As much as possible, results are grouped into successes and failures. Those cases that are vague or ambiguous are clarified as to why they are vague or ambiguous. Dewey argues that the scientific attitude may almost be defined as that which can *enjoy the doubtful*, not in the service of philosophical skepticism but with respect to the specified problematic situations.

More times than not, the tools used in experiences are the five senses and they will operate in the wide field of everyday life. In experiments, various devices such as lens, instrument, appliance, and apparatus are used. For our purposes, instead of the five senses and reason being used in experiments, mathematical calculations might be used to disclose relations that are not a normal part of everyday life, say, for example,

Table 10.1 Experience vs Experiment

Routine arts Experience	**Category of comparison**	**Specialized arts** Experiment
Acquired by exercise and practice in everyday life; common sense knowledge	**Knowledge bases**	Formal training in research questioning, designing and evaluating experiments
No attempt to replicate	**Is replication necessary?**	Replication is required
Past personal experiences; conventional authorities; peer group	**Sources**	Past empirical research that may contradict personal experience, the authorities or peer group
Trial and error Tinkering with things just to see what would happen	**Methods**	Systematic testing: Process of elimination Inductive reasoning Abductive reasoning
Use of five senses	**Tools utilized**	Various devices like lens or instruments, appliances and apparatus Mathematical calculations for disclosing relations not otherwise apparent
Uncontrolled change	**Controlled or uncontrolled change?**	Directed and regulated change (part of a research program)
Solve problems Whatever works	**Purpose**	What is true
Individual actions	**Conduct**	Group practice

in astronomical dynamics. Please see Table 10.1 for a summary.

What is rationality? Judgment under certain conditions

Besides reasoning, there is another kind of thinking, a rational thinking process that operates with knowledge systems that are *closed*. For these kinds of systems, it is possible for solutions to problems to have one right answer which you can be certain about. For example, in solving visual puzzles or word problems, all the facts needed to solve the problem are contained within it. You don't do research outside the problem to find a solution. You work within the problem that is given. When an accountant performs simple arithmetic—adding, subtracting, multiplying, and dividing—they are using rationality. They are calculating as they enter these numbers into a budget sheet. In philosophy, these are formal logical syllogisms in such as:

> All men are mortal.
> Socrates is a man.
> Therefore, Socrates is mortal.

Whether any of these statements are objectively true is irrelevant. So, we could say:

> All men are immortal.
> Socrates is a man.
> Socrates is immortal.

The *form* of the argument is still valid even though the first and third statements are objectively false. Rationality uses what is called deductive logic. This means that if the form of the premise are set up correctly, one and only one conclusion is possible. The syllogism above is called a categorical syllogism because it is about the relationships of inclusion or exclusion. There are also if/then conditional syllogisms and either/or disjunctive syllogisms. These forms are taught in courses on formal logic.

The term rationality derives from the term ratio which means to compare. Our thinking processes are rational when we can compare proportions to keep things in perspective. So, for example, an artist is using their rationality when they shrink or expand the size of objects on the picture plane, so the size of the objects is proportional to other objects on the picture plane rather than their absolute real-life size. In the field of geometry and trigonometry, when we build proofs from axioms or compare the measurement of angles, we are using rationality. All higher mathematics is the science of comparing numbers.

In the practical world of human problems, we use our rationality when we see our problems in proportion to the problems of other people. For example, if I live in the Bay Area and I complain because this winter it is forty eight degrees and raining, this is irrational (i.e. out of proportion) compared to the weather conditions people face in New York.

What is the relationship between reason and rationality?

Reason is more complicated than rationality for several additional reasons. For one thing, reason includes emotions. When you are deciding about college, you must pay attention to whether or not you are fearful or excited when you consider your prospects. Secondly, practical problems require you to be sensitive to *where* something is taking place and *when* it is taking place. If you have decided you want to propose to someone, where you propose and when you propose have some impact on the reception. Lastly, in using our reasoning, we must consider *who is* listening and we must tone down or amplify our claims based on the needs and desires of who we are trying to convince. The science and art of rhetoric was developed by the Sophists and Aristotle to deal with the dynamics of persuading audiences.

Conversely, in solving rational problems, it is irrelevant to ask how Socrates feels about whether or not he is immortal to find out if he is a man. Nor do you need to inquire whether Socrates is at the gymnasium, at the polis, or in his home in order to determine if he is a man. Neither does it matter whether you inquire about Socrates's immortality in the morning, afternoon, or evening.

Of the two forms of thinking, reason is the more complex and older form. All the problems tribal societies had to face, such as deciding on a means of subsistence or planning the hunt or the harvest involved reason. Reason was also involved in developing social intelligence, including interpreting body language, as well as considering the time and place for rituals. Craftsmen in agricultural states had to use their reason in coming to understand the most suitable material for making, firing, and glazing pots. Women had to be sensitive in comparing the differences between edible and poisonous plants as well as learning to spin and weave. Of course, there are elements of rationality involved in reason, because seeing things proportionately was also involved. However, a full-blown science of rationality required the invention of literacy and numeracy.

As we will touch on in chapter twelve, committing one's thinking process to paper invites you to deliberate *about* your thinking process. As Jack Goody has pointed out, putting thoughts on paper freezes them for future analysis and these "frozen" thoughts can be preserved independently of:

- the needs of social diplomacy in conversation
- as tools for problem solving

The use of clay tablets, papyrus, or parchment also made people more aware of the *contradictions* in their thoughts. As people became more sensitive to the formal elements of thinking on parchment, they also become more sensitive the *formal processes of thinking independent of the content* of what the argument or problem was. Especially in the case of mathematics, placing numbers and geometrical forms on paper made it possible to decouple the numerical and geometrical systems originally designed to solve architectural problems to study and develop these systems *on their own*. This involved cultivating geometrical theorems and solving quadratic equations. Rationality, at least its full-blown version, only emerged when it was possible to first see our thinking processes externalized in some form.

It is most important to consider that as mathematicians discovered mathematical solutions to architectural problems such as surveying and designing and constructing buildings, they also began making value judgments about the superiority

Table 10.2 What is rational? What is reasonable?

Reasonable	**Type of cognition**	**Rational**
Open Must go outside the presenting problem to gather resources for solving the problem	**What type of problem?**	**Closed** All the information to solve the problem is embedded within it
Many conclusions	**How many conclusions are Possible?**	**One conclusion**
Probability is enough	**Confidence criteria in solving the problem?**	**Certainty is required**
Premise must be factual for the argument to be **sound** (content matters)	**How true does the premises have to be?**	Premises can be counterfactual yet the argument could be **valid** (form matters, independent of content)
Conductive-weighing pros and cons Abductive Inductive	**Type of Logic Used?**	Deductive
Solving practical problems	**Purpose**	**Seeking proportion, ratios**
Emotions are inseparable from thinking; emotions can be reasonable or unreasonable	**Place of emotion in thinking processes**	Separation of emotions from Thinking; emotions are seen as irrational
Important: dependent on time, place and circumstance	**How important is context?**	Unimportant; universally true regardless of time, place, or circumstance
Rhetoric is important: who is speaking to whom? In what format? What is the occasion?	**Place of rhetoric in thinking processes**	**Anti-Rhetoric** Universal—speaker, listener. Form or occasion is irrelevant
Aristotle, Sophists	**Ancient philosophical representative**	Plato, Aristotle
Deciding what school to attend Deciding where you want to live (conductive)	**Example of a problem**	Visual puzzle, word problems, geometric proofs mathematical calculations
More complex	**Complexity of the problem**	Less complex

of mathematical knowledge based on rationality as compared to the solving of practical problems using reason. Table 10.2 is a summary of the differences between reason and rationality.

The Dark Side of Rationality: The Pathology of the Quest for Certainty

Longing for security

We now need to return to the discussion in the beginning of this chapter about the difficulty of living in an uncertain world. Dewey argued that under optimal circumstances of practical life, the best we can do is know that specific events are *probably* true. In other words, in practical life, reason, not rationality should be the way we think. Through the scientific method, we learn things about nature and society and through technologies (which are the fruits of science), we make social life more predictable, more secure but never *completely* secure. But what of those who are not satisfied with this? What about those who want to apply *rationality* to practical life in hopes of giving humanity a *guarantee* of security?

In his book, *The Quest for Certainty*, Dewey throws down the gauntlet and argues that the quest for certainty in a world of probability is a compensatory perversion. In what way? Dewey points out that when human action lacks a means for control of *external* conditions, it takes the form of ritualistic *religious* acts and beliefs.

> The commonest fallacy is to suppose that since the state of doubt is accompanied by a feeling of uncertainty, knowledge arises when this feeling gives way to one of assurance. The tendency towards premature judgment, jumping at conclusions, excessive love of simplicity, making over evidence to suit desire, taking the familiar for the clear all spring from confusing the *feeling* of certitude with a certified situation. Uncertainty

> is got rid of by fair means of foul. Long exposure to danger breeds a overpowering love of security. *Love for security, translated into a desire not to be disturbed and unsettled, leads to dogmatism,* to acceptance of beliefs based on authority. Intolerance and fanaticism...(227)

Anxiety about uncertainty leads to invention of spiritual worlds

For many, because to act often involves peril, the risk of wrong turns, frustration and failure, the search for security within the material world is not an optimal project. Abother, older solution than science emerged with the rise of Western religion. As long as humanity was unable by scientific means to direct the course of human events in this world, it was natural for us to seek an emotional substitute, a flight to another world in which there would be no uncertainty. According to Dewey, in the absence of actual certainly amid the precarious and hazardous material world, religion gives us hope for the existence of a better, spiritual world that *feels* secure.

For the perpetually insecure, the problem with the material world—including matter and the senses—is that they always change and there always have unintended consequences. This means we cannot build a completely secure world based on this foundation. If change is the root of insecurity, then stillness and permanence must be the foundations for a secure world. Where can we find a world in which matter and the senses don't exist and there are no unintended consequences?

One place to find certainty is in another spiritual world which contains all the properties that make us secure: it lies beyond the natural world, before the natural world, beyond the senses; it lasts forever; it has no unintended consequences because the whole operation is part of God's plan.

Who inhabits this world? Only good, predictable loving beings who can only produce good results. What part of the known world might have links to this world? What part of human psychology can tap into this world? If the senses are always changing and human body decays, what do we possess that seems less likely to change? What do we have that seems still, silent, and less chaotic? Human thought. Human ideas about the good are then projected on to beings in the more perfect world.

Religious rationalism puts its money on ideas. Who is the first to have ideas? God. God's thought is imagined to be the creator of the world and rational ideas constitute its building blocks, such as Plato's eternal forms. Cosmic evolution is achieved once and for all by thought in a transcendental aboriginal work of God. Human thought can participate in the thoughts of God not by reason but by rationality the way we've defined these terms in this chapter.

Furthermore, a foundational commitment to this superior spiritual world requires us to imagine *another world which is demonized.* This demonized world can be a spiritual inferno like hell, which has the opposite characteristics of heaven. *Another alternative is to disparage the material world.* Someone like Plato would say that what is real is the world of eternal forms, of divine reason existing in the stars. The material world is an inferior world of change, governed by the senses and filled with imperfect appearances. From world of the deceptive senses, the world of puppet shadows arises filled with shallow beliefs and opinions.

Geometry and the spectator theory of knowledge

Those theologians who followed Plato and Aristotle saw the human mind and the ability to think *rationally as the key link* between the degraded material world of nature, the senses, and the body and the superior, divine world that never changes. Dewey points out that:

> The Eulogistic flavor which hangs about the word "idealism" is a tribute to the respect men pay to thought and its power. The obnoxious quality of "materialism" is due to its depreciation of thought, which is treated as an illusion or at most an accidental by product. (108)

Do we have any human disciplines that seem to be based on rational thinking that seem independent of the material world, change, and the senses? Dewey thinks so:

> Geometry seemed to reveal the possibility of a science which owed nothing to the observation and sense beyond mere exemplification in figures and diagrams. It seems to disclose a world of ideal forms which were connected to with one another by eternal and necessary relations which reason alone could trace. The discovery was generalized by philosophy into the doctrine of the realm of fixed Being which when grasped by thought formed a complete system of immutable and necessary truths. (16)

Geometry and mathematics generally were the key to knowledge which was necessary and subject to demonstration rather that knowledge based on argument or probability. By comparison, even scientific beliefs about verifiable facts, beliefs backed up by evidence of the senses and that might yield modest fruits of human knowledge had little glamour and prestige by comparison.

But what is this image of rational knowing? It is a *spectator* rather than an interactional theory of knowledge. The spectator stands transfixed before an unchanging light.

> The theory of knowing is modeled after what was supposed to take place in the act of vision. The object refracts light to the eye and is seen; it makes a difference to the eye and to the person having an optical apparatus, but none to the thing seen. The real object is the object so fixed in its regal aloofness that it is a king to any beholding mind that may gaze upon it. A spectator theory of knowledge is the inevitable result (23)

The quest for certainty is a quest for a peace, which is assured by an object of knowledge which is unqualified by change, ambiguity, or risk. One must possess a passionless rationality to find perfect reality and complete certitude.
For over 2000 years the weight of the most influential and authoritatively orthodox traditions has been devoted to the

problem of purely cognitive certification by revelation, intuition, and rational contemplation.

How do we know? Contemplation trumps action

'Safety first' has played a large role in creating a preference for knowing through contemplation as opposed to knowing by doing and making. Contemplating does not allow itself to get entangled in the risks which tentative, half-baked, or even well thought out action cannot escape. The exaltation of pure intellect and its activity in mathematical or philosophical contemplation above practical affairs is fundamentally connected with the quest for a certainty that seeks absolutes and unshakable foundations. The depreciation of action, of doing and making has been cultivated by philosophers who glorified their own profession by placing theory above practice. A depreciated meaning has come to be attached to the very meaning of the practical. Instead of being extended to cover all forms of action including the fine arts and the cultivation of taste (in the sciences and technology) the meaning of practical is limited to matters of ease, comfort, riches, bodily security, and political order.

The class basis for the quest for certainty and rationality

In tracing the roots of our quest for certainty, Dewey identified the origins of the superiority of rationality over reason in Greece, specifically to aristocratic disdain for the professional Sophists who taught reason and rhetoric to the middle classes. The Sophists were dismissed as money grubbers. The idea that hostility toward philosophers had a class basis was first popularized by Benjamin Farrington in his books on Greek science. However, aristocratic attitudes cast long historical shadows, right into the seventeenth century, as we will see.

After a distinctively *intellectual* class had arisen, a class having leisure and, to a large degree, protected from the more serious perils which afflict the mass of humanity, its members proceeded to glorify their own collective mental work as separated from practice. *Rationalism is the manipulation of mental operations independently of practice*. The split between a superior spiritual world and an inferior material world is only possible when there exists in society a division between mental and manual labor. This invites mental workers (like religious authorities or mathematicians) to imagine that their work in the real world—planning, supervision inventing systems of knowledge— becomes unhinged from their social function and spins worlds of its own. These intellectuals then fall in love with their own collective creations.

On the other hand, these same mental workers look at the necessity of using their minds to carry out social planning as an inferior activity because the results of their work are filled with conflict, mistakes, and unintended consequences. They depreciate the notion that the true test of ideas is to put them into practice in the world. The unpleasantness of practical activity is as much as possible fobbed off on the middle or lower classes (artisans or merchants) or is neglected completely. Just as the spirit world they have invented is uncontaminated with matter, so their minds don't want to be contaminated by their hands or the practical social consequences of their responsibilities as social planners. Work done with the body by means of mechanical appliances and directed upon material things is beneath their dignity. We can ascend to knowledge only by isolating knowledge from practical doing and making.

The creation of spiritual dualities

Because the quest for certainty excludes scientific practice from its understanding of the world, it separates into mutually exclusive dualities what are simply *polarities*. The quest for certainty separates a spiritually clean theory from a gritty, unclean practice; it pines after a spiritual world of love and light while it disparages the grossness of matter; it champions the mind as it degrades the body; it finds it wings in philosophy, literature, and education and finds the sciences for the middle class and apprenticeships for the unwashed. The other-worldly mystic can only imagine trusting the senses as leading to hedonism. This is the spastic dance of the wraith and the beast, or as Koester says the ghost and the machine or the yogi and the commissar.

Please see Table 10.3 for a summary.

Table 10.3 The Hollow Quest for Certainty: The Ghost in the Machine

Thinking (the ghost)	Category of comparison	Doing (the machine)
Disembodied theory	**Relationship between theory and practice?**	Crass, mindless action
Otherworldly spirit	**Ontology**	Inert matter
Antecedent reality	**Time**	Current reality
What stays the same	**Synchronic-diachronic**	What changes
Essences (Reality)	**Reality vs appearances**	Appearances
Ascetic mind contemplation	**Within a human being**	Mechanical body
Upper classes	**Social class location**	Lower classes
Philosophy Religion Geometry	**Discipline**	The natural physical and biological world
True knowledge	**Epistemology**	Belief, opinion
Necessary, implicit—formal logic	**Causes**	Contingent, inferences
Mystical experience	**Ecstatic states**	Hedonism

Rationality and Reason Among the Greeks and Romans in the Middle Ages

Plato and Greek Rationalism

Many of you know Plato's likely answer to the question: 'Which is better, rationality or reason?' Plato was so impressed with mathematically certain, non-contradictory answers to questions that he saw mathematics as divine. He believed that all the objects in the material world were inferior copies of perfect, mathematical eternal forms that created the Universe in the first place. Plato was especially critical of the sophists because they taught that all knowledge was relative to time, place, and circumstance. The sophists taught people how to increase their chances of winning cases in court by considering the rhetorical situation: who the audience was, when and where the argument was taking place. Even today, the pejorative use of the term sophist is embedded in our definition of the word sophisticated, which means someone who is worldly, but shallow. It is clear that the sophists were using reason in the way I've defined it to defend arguments. Plato thought very little of the type of thinking that went into practical affairs, because the result was not certain truth.

Despite Plato, Greek thought as a whole never made a sharp separation between the rational, perfect realm on the one hand and the natural world on the other. Though the natural world was thought to be inferior and infected with non-being, it did not stand in any sharp dualism. According to Dewey, in his *Quest For Certainty*, the Greeks thought they could take the material supplied by ordinary perception and:

- eliminate varying and contingent qualities
- find the fixed and immutable form
- define the form as an essence—which included harmony, proportion, and symmetry
- gather together a group of perceived objects into a species which is thought to be eternal, though its particular examples are perishable.

The Greeks discovered by trial and error many interrelated properties of figures and proceeded to correlate these with one another. At a certain point, operations made possible by symbols *were performed on other symbols* (instead of solving architectural, real world problems). The symbol world took on a life of its own, resulting in trigonometry and calculus. Specialists who engaged in perfecting symbolic systems lost interest in the *application* of the results of their operations. This played a part in the generation of a priori rationalism, as we will see when we come to the seventeenth century.

Rationality and Reason in the Ancient World and in the Middle Ages

Unlike Plato, Aristotle argued that logical non-contradictory syllogisms like those stated about Socrates earlier do not show us anything about the *substance* of our reasoning. They are simply a warning against claims that are internally inconsistent in *form*. According to Toulmin (*Return to Reason*), Aristotle's books Ethics, *Politics, and Rhetoric* shows that the circumstantial nature of practical issues means that certainty is not possible and probability is the best we can do. That does not mean that reasoning is an inferior thinking process to rationality (or as Aristotle might say, a demonstration). Rather, reasoning is a more creative form of thinking because it deals with a more complex and unpredictable world.

In addition, for Aristotle, a reasoning criterion for thinking must be sensitive to the ways in which fields of argument differ from one another. The criteria for determining quality of arguments in science, art, politics or law are different and the *standards* of reasoning for them must vary. For Aristotle it is the *occasion* and the *content* of an argument more than the form that determines the quality of thinking. Lastly, Aristotle, while acknowledging that Plato's fears about rhetoric becoming nothing but smoke and mirrors, still thought it was impractical to abandon rhetoric.

At its best, rhetoric considers the time, place, and circumstance along with the specific ethos, pathos, and logos required to persuade an audience. However, this "white rhetoric" invites dialectical *cooperation* between speaker and audience to solve a problem and appeals to the *long-range* interest of humanity. White rhetoric appeals to the best in humanity—kindness, generosity and foresight—and it *welcomes* audiences that are hostile. In white rhetoric, the audience is treated as active and sturdy enough to accept challenges. The source of the message (the speaker) has *character*—they are trustworthy, likeable, have a sense of humor and perspective, and possess good will toward the audience. The power of the source is used in the service of telling the truth; being effective is secondary.

In white rhetoric, you what to convince (changing someone's mind) before persuading them to act. Turning to pathos, white rhetoric will appeal to emotions, but these emotions have depth, so that people are moved and shaken to their foundations. Emotional appeal is done not in order to bypass critical thinking but to take critical thinking to a deeper level. The imaginary side of pathos appeals to alternative futures which are practical and down to earth.

Toulmin summarizes as follows:

> Rhetoric is not a rival to logic. It puts logical analysis of arguments into a larger framework of argumentation. If you present a train of reasoning forcibly and vividly, you do not seek to convince your hearers by arousing their passion. Instead you try to give them a fuller and easier grasp of your substantive claims. However, rhetorical tricks are, on occasion, used to evade or conceal a substantive point. (*Cosmopolis. 165)*

The Romans were very sympathetic to rhetoric, as Cicero and Quintilian developed Aristotle's system. Quintilian developed the five canons of rhetoric which included the invention of the argument itself: the arrangement—i.e. the ordering of the parts of the argument, the style (word choice), the delivery (voice control, gestures and body movement), as well as the memory-tracking system. In the Middle Ages, St. Augustine developed rhetoric essentially for preaching.

Reason and rhetoric in the Renaissance

Moderate skepticism of the humanists

As we've seen in earlier chapters, the Renaissance way of thinking was more open and skeptical towards the intellectual dogmatism of the Catholic schoolmen. Humanists found sources of material in ethnography, geography, and history. As they did, they became more sensitive to the importance of knowing the differences between places and times (ancient vs modern) and because of this, recognized the relativity of human knowledge. In politics, Machiavelli and Guicciardini based their account of Italian politics on a reflective analysis of historical experience as it operated in actual historical fact, rather than conforming to religious doctrines about human history.

Montaigne was skeptical that reason or the senses were very reliable sources of knowledge. Though not as skeptical of science, Francis Bacon warned against spinning cobwebs of rationalism that were unconnected to sense data. Bacon's methods of observation remained close to everyday experience and fell short of authorizing rationalist mathematical constructions of seventeenth century physics which were to follow. In literature, Erasmus exposed human folly, Rabelais celebrated the sensuous, bawdy side of human nature, and Shakespeare showed that complexity and conflict were built into human nature without reducing humanity to 'sinfulness'. Up until 1620 mathematical rigor was a sub-category of human reason.

Rhetoric in the Renaissance

According to James Herrick, rhetoric reached its highest point of respect in the Renaissance. It flourished in these four areas: as a method of instruction in writing, as an avenue for personal refinement, as a means of navigating through civic and economic intrigue (the orator was a prototype of the Renaissance Man), and as critical tool for studying a variety of literary texts, both ancient and modern:

> Humanists wanted to place the text in its historical context in order to establish the correct value of words and phrases. They contributed to studies such as hermeneutics, the discipline of textural interpretation. (*History and Theory of Rhetoric*, 158)

George of Trebizond sought to reunify the various genres and methods of rhetoric which had been dismantled in the Middle Ages back into a synthetic whole. His *Five books on Rhetoric* brought together both Greek and Latin rhetorical theories. Women such as Christine de Pisan were important in moving the practice of rhetoric into a more *conservational dialogue* direction (as opposed to a monological speech). According to de Pisan, conversation rather than public speaking is the mortar that holds society together. Petrarch, one of the most creative writers in the Renaissance, hoped to revive Cicero's ideal of uniting wisdom with eloquence. Eloquence in speaking, rather than ratification of already completed thoughts (as in logic), *civilized* the human mind and domesticated its unreasonable flights.

Yet despite its success in Italy, the shadow of Plato haunted rhetoric in the cultures of northern Europe. Rhetoric there was seen as a body of cheap tricks which appealed to the worst in people. Peter Ramus claimed that disputation in argument belonged to dialectic and logic rather than rhetoric. Rhetoric was marginalized into the study of style with words and delivery:

The invention of the printing press had something to do losing our appreciation for rhetoric. Once the printed page supplemented the spoken word, it was easier to slow down and deliberate about the thoughts that were written. Questions about the soundness of an argument no longer addressed how well or badly they were received by particular audiences at particular forums. The quality of arguments was based how well-written *chains of logical statements were organized.* Of course, there are *readers* of arguments that are considered audiences. However, it is easier to dismiss a readership that is invisible than it is to dismiss the visible reaction of people at a live public forum. The prestige of mathematical proofs led philosophers to disown informal kinds of argumentation. All informal logic or reasoning was tarred with the brush of rhetoric and dismissed as irrationality.

Seventeenth-century science and the continued quest for certainty

Times of turmoil

Stephen Toulmin points out that the conventional view of the origin of modern life credits seventeenth century philosophers with a concern for human welfare and an appreciation of diversity that really belonged to the Renaissance. The seventeenth century rationalists would actually have little of the more careful, tolerant, and skeptical attitude of sixteenth century humanists such as Erasmus, Rabelais, Shakespeare, Montaigne, and Francis Bacon. After 1600, the focus of intellectual attention turned *away* from human preoccupations of late sixteenth century. As Theodore Rabb points out in *The Struggle for Stability in Early Modern Europe*, the rise of rationalism was a reaction to political, social and theological chaos. Here are just some of the conflicts.

What made the seventeenth century crisis different from crises in previous historical periods was the threat to an existing way of life. These threats included demographic over and under population, food shortages, a rise in food costs, mass migrations, and the spreading of pandemics that were common in the Middle Ages. In the seventeenth century, these were combined with events that were unique in their intensity, both for better and for worse:

- The coldest climate of the Little Ice Age between 1670 and 1710
- The rise of a centralized state which slowly controlled the means of violence
- A revolution in military technology
- The largest armies since the Roman Empire was established
- Virtually constant warfare between states. According to Geoffrey Parker, during the seventeenth century only four complete calendar years saw peace over the whole

continent. Spain spent most of the century engaged in war

- By the end of the century, most states had standing armies in peacetime
- 1648: The Peace of Westphalia attempted to organize a system of states and set up international rules
- Peasant rebellions against increased state taxation to fund wars between 1625 and 1675:
    - Insurrection in Catalonia and Portugal in 1640
    - Insurrections in Naples and Palermo in 1647
    - Fronde in France between 1648 and 1653
    - The revolt of Ukraine from 1648 to 1653
    - Provence saw 108 popular rebellions between 1596 and 1635
    - 156 popular rebellions between 1635 and 1660;
    - Local peasant revolts in Austria, Poland, Sweden, and Switzerland
- The Thirty Years War in Germany exceeded all other early modern European conflicts in violence, duration, and the extent to which outside powers became involved
- The Puritan Revolution in England, which involved Scotland and Ireland
- A red-hot class struggle between the traditional wielders of power—Crown, courtiers, higher clergy, and aristocracy against the middle classes: the gentry, lawyers, merchants, yeomen and small tradesmen
- A continental shift from commerce centered around the Mediterranean, featuring Italy and Spain as leading players, to the Atlantic coast with France, England, and the Netherlands as the leading state actors
- The capitalist revolution which drove peasants off the land while at the same time raising hopes
- The Catholic Counterreformation
- The witch craze in England, France, and Italy
- In art, a conflict between the High Renaissance of Raphael and the distortions of the Mannerists
- In literature, through the characters of Marlow and *Faust*,

there were men of knowledge who sold their souls to the Devil. In Cervantes' *Don Quixote*, there is a contradiction between his hopes and material realities

- The rise of a literate and educated laity which weakened church credibility
- The expansion of 'masterless' men—printers and artisans whose ways of life did not easily square with a deferential attitude towards nobility
- The scientific revolution in astronomy
    - 1660 British Royal Society founded (scientific community)
    - 1666 Robert Hook discovers cells using the microscope
    - Newton publishes *Principia Mathematica*
- 1689 Locke publishes his first *Letter Concerning Toleration*

In his book *The Culture of the Baroque*, Jose Antonio Maravall characterized the seventeenth century in the following way:

> Its tensions affected the relation between nobles and commoners, rich and poor, believers and nonbelievers, foreigner and subjects, central governments and peripheral townships. Everywhere there were mutinies, riots, rebellions of great violence. (45)
>
> There were calls in the court for the banishment of the "noveleros" the nonconforming and alarmist commentators of political events. (43)

These crises described could be framed dualistically between:

- traditionalism versus individualism
- deference to authority versus challenging authority
- miracles and witchcraft versus science
- geometry versus sense experience
- asceticism versus hedonism

- religious order versus love of trade and self-gain

Living in a society with these dualities all coexisting made people sick. Maravall claims that melancholy and hypochondria were held to be the dominant claims of mental disturbance at the time. These conflicts also manifested in the introduction of exotic and ephemeral vogues in men's and women's clothes and in their personal appearance—beards and long hair for men and high shoes for women. Because of very religious, political, economic, and geographic instabilities in the seventeenth and eighteenth centuries, scientists were not satisfied to know what was *probably* true. Like religious authorities, they needed the hard stuff. They wanted *certain* knowledge. This led them to emphasize rationality over reason.

Why did science in the seventeenth century continue the quest for certainty?

Despite all these crises, seventieth century science did not give up the quest for certainty. Dewey says the reasons for not abandoning the quest for certainty were:

- science could shed its inferior status to religion if it could prove certainty
- while not aristocrats, scientists were in the middle-class or upper-middle class. They retained a class hostility to recalcitrant matter and an uncertain reality
- scientists would have more credibility with the lower classes if they could prove certainty

> To a constant succession of philosophers, the role of mathematics in physical analysis...has seemed to be a proof of the presence of an invariant rational element within physical existence. Mathematical conceptions as expressions of pure thought have also seemed to provide the open gateway to the realm of essence, independent of existence.

> Mathematics is based on first truths or axioms, needing only that eye of reason should fall upon them to be recognized for what they are. (*Quest for Certainty*,140)

Dewey argues that the nature of essences—universality, invariance, immutability, formality, and deduction were too attractive aspirations to give up easily, for they exercised a hypnotic influence on the mind. As it turns out, seventieth century science inherited the *framework* of Greek ideas about the nature of knowledge, although it rejected its empirical conclusions about natural objects.

The religious wars weren't just ontological battles about the divinity of Christ or the saints. Catholics and Protestants were also fighting an epistemological war over certainty. Each side was committed firmly to their doctrines being proved correct.

In the face of these crises, European hunger for certainty began to pervade the secular world of science. With the power of religion temporarily weakened, philosophers and scientists tried to develop a rational approach to science while hoping to minimize the interference of Catholics and Protestants. In a sense, it is understandable that they got caught up in the quest for certainty and tried to out-rationalize the theologians. Stephen Toulmin tells us:

> Facing dogmatic claims by rival theologians, it was hard for onlookers [scientists] of good will to restrict themselves to the cool modesty of Erasmus or Montaigne. Living in a time of high theological passion—[they looked] for a new way of establishing central truths and ideas, one that was independent and neutral between particular religious loyalties. (*Cosmopolis*, 70)

To repeat, though the scientific revolution dealt a blow to religious ideas about *how* the natural world worked, seventeenth century scientists did not give up the ontological framework of the theologians: the quest for certainty. They simply transposed it from the spiritual to the material world. The scientific revolution of the seventeenth century effected a great modification: science, through the aid of mathematics carried the scheme of Aristotle's demonstrative knowledge over to natural objects. While the specific *content* of Platonic and Aristotelian knowledge about the natural world was challenged and superseded, its insistence that security be measured by the certainty of knowledge carried on.

The great compromise

Among religious authorities in the seventeenth century all sciences which were matters of inductive inference from observation were imagined to be inferior. Scientific arts of practice were stamped as matters of *belief* rather than of knowledge. The rivalry between religious philosophy and the new science resulted from the claim to know reality. The rivalry erupted between spiritual values guaranteed by older philosophic traditions and the conclusions about knowledge acquired from nature. Out of this there arose what Toulmin called 'The Great Compromise'. Reality was parceled out into a great dualistic division. The world of inanimate matter governed by physical and mechanical laws. This was the domain of scientists. The world of life and mind was thought to be the domain of theologians. Most scientists accepted the terms of this great compromise. (See Chapter 8 of *Forging Promethean Psychology* for more.)

Epistemological dualities: rationalism (the ghost) versus empiricism (the machine)

How do we know things? One of the major fruits of the quest for certainty was the dualistic epistemology that resulted in science. The rationalists were the ghosts and the empiricists were the machine. For seventeenth century scientists in search of certainty, there were two choices: rationalism (trust in the mind) or empiricism (trust in the senses). On the side of mind, one school emphasized the *synthetic* deliberate movement of thinking and its higher processes such as analysis, compare-and-contrast, and evaluation. The other school (empiricism) argued that all knowledge is based on the senses. Empiricists see the mind is a relatively passive calculator of the results of what is heard, seen or smelled. In fact, Locke's *Essay on Human Understanding* is one continued effort to test all beliefs and ideas by reducing them to original simple ideas which are drawn from the senses.

The sensationalistic theory of knowledge is a reaction to rationalism, but it is merely the flip side of it. Sensational empiricists hold that thought does not initiate our relationship to the world; it merely organizes the data of the senses. It proclaims the necessity of direct, first-hand contact with objects. Ideas are pale ghosts of flesh and blood impressions, dying echoes of firsthand intercourse with reality which takes place in sensation alone.

Traditional empiricism has also misread the significance of *conceptions* or general ideas. According to empiricists, objects are formed by comparing particular objects *already* perceived with one another, eliminating the elements which don't fit and retaining that which they have in common. Concepts are thus simply memoranda of identical features in objects *already* perceived. The value and function of ideas is essentially *retrospective*. For pragmatists such as Dewey, sensory qualities are important, but they are intellectually significant only as *consequences* of acts intentionally performed in experiments, as we will see shortly.

The basic error of traditional theories of knowledge, both rationalism and empiricism, resides in the *isolation and fixation* of some phase of the whole process of scientific inquiry. In scientific practice they are both used, not as competing epistemologies but as a means for conducting an experiment. It is the fruits of the experiment and what it reveals that tells the truth. Both rationalism and empiricism fetishize the tools used (the mind or the senses) and lose sight of the overall picture which is the quality of the experiment. In the quest for certainty, rationalism is tried, then empiricism, in the desperate hope that one will turn into a magic bullet.

The quest for antecedent reality

Earlier, we saw that Dewey proposed that the religious quest for certainty assumes that the spiritual ideal and static world exists prior in time to the material, changing world. In addition, this prior changeless world has a structure, as in Plato's eternal forms. While seventeenth century rationalists and empiricists may challenge teleological purpose, depictions of nature, or religion, they maintain that whatever they may discover should be measured against an antecedent reality. This antecedent reality may not exist in the form of God's plan, but it exists in the form of invariant scientific laws. These natural laws substitute for Plato's eternal forms.

As different as they are, both rationalists and empiricists agree that the conclusions reached must be reduced to things *already known*. The foundation of the quest for certainty is that knowledge is concerned with the disclosure of the characteristics of *antecedent* existences and essences, rather than the standards and tests of validity found in the *consequences* of overt *collective scientific activity addressing future social problems*.

The controversy between the schools is simply as to which organ *is* best in judging the nature of previous knowledge. Epistemological disputes exist, but they are over whether sensuality or rationality constitutes the basis for certainty. One the one hand, logical processes belonging to the *operations* of effective inquiry are unhinged by rationalists from an experimental situation and then measured against an antecedent existence; on the other, the empiricists know through a pulverized multiplicity of atomically isolated elements.

Dewey's pragmatism as a quest for consequent reality

For pragmatists like Dewey the object of knowledge is *eventual*. It is an *outcome* of directed experimental operations instead of something which existed *before* the act of knowing. In Dewey's pragmatic approach to science, what is true is not measured against an antecedent static reality. It is measured against *what works in the future* in humanity's collective attempt to tame a dynamic reality through experiments. Pragmatists do not bow down to an antecedent state of nature to test the fruits of experiment. Instead they refer to whether the results of the experiment in the future will make us more secure or happy. The true test is not how well it reproduces a previous state through verification, but how well it can be applied to improve human conditions.

For Dewey, sensible and rational factors cease to be in competitors for primary rank. They are allies, cooperating to make knowledge possible. Their Isolation in the hands of rationalists or empiricists severs each from its organic connection to practice based on experiments. Pragmatists do not quarrel over whether sensations or thinking are the road to truth. Both are organized not as ends in themselves but are incorporated into various stages of the experimental practice in the service of making life more secure and better for humanity.

Rationality in the natural sciences in the seventeenth century

Greek science vs seventeenth-century mechanistic rationalism

In order to understand what was unique about the seventeenth century rationalist attitude towards nature, it is helpful to compare it to the Greeks. For Greek science, the starting point of observation was *the senses* used in everyday life which was then corrected by reason. Dewey gives an example of water having qualities that are sensed by the eye, the ear, through smell, taste, and touch. The results of the observation of water was either than one enjoyed water or feared it in the case of being threatened by drowning. For the Greeks, water was an end in itself, perhaps to be refreshed, cleaned, or healed by ice or steam. The truth of nature is perceived by the senses. The results are either using it to bring comfort or being overwhelmed by it, in the case of floods.

In the case of the first chemists in the seventeenth century, they ignored the sensuous qualities of water. Rather it was framed water at a micro-level below the senses: the chemical compound H2O. These chemical properties were mixed with other chemical properties to create combinations not only unknown to the Greeks but also used for different purposes. The mixing of chemicals, including H2O, could be used to improve the human condition, including the sanitation problems in European cities. Using the elements of a chemical combination had larger social implications.

According to Dewey, for seventeenth century science, the properties of H2O were not ends in themselves, but rather *indicators*, means to further knowledge. H2O is simply data, subject matter for further investigation. Data are indicators of evidence, signs and clues, a means, not an end. They are a set of problems to investigate in the service of later application. Here sensuous objects are neither enjoyed nor suffered as ends but *controlled* as part of the larger project of humans mastering nature by modification and invention. Seventieth century *scientists' reduction of sensuous objects to the form of relation in which qualitative properties are neutralized and dissolved into mathematical quantities* was a prerequisite for the ability to impose social regulation on nature.

For the Greeks, movement was a term covering all sorts of qualitative alternations: warm things becoming cold, moist things becoming dry, or organisms that grow from an embryo to an adult form. For the Greeks, movement was never considered merely motion (a change in position in a homogeneous space). For them, movement occurred in heterogenous space. Aristotle treated quantity as an *accident* indifferent to the essence of matter.

For seventieth century scientists, matter was merely a change of position in a homogeneous space. Galileo traded off the sensuous qualities of objects for quantitative relations between objects understood mathematically. In addition, he showed how mechanical laws applied *regardless* of the regions of space they were located ignored sensuous qualities of matter, treated *quantity* as the essence of matter.

Descartes

As Toulmin tells the story, when the Thirty Years War broke out in 1618, Descartes was in his early twenties. When it ended, he had two years to live. He lived his is whole life under the shadow of these wars. For him the most important thing was to find a way out of the doctrinal contradictions that had fueled the religious wars. He hoped the time had come for discovering some rational method for demonstrating certainty in order to end religious conflicts.

At the foundation of Descartes epistemology is a dualistic separation between two substances: mind and matter. For Descartes, human thought and action are governed by rationality. To understand the actions of the human mind, we have to inquire about why we undertake projects. At the other pole stands matter, passive and governed by mechanical causality and repetitive like clock-work. Descartes persuaded his fellow philosophers to renounce the concrete, complex, and uncertain fields of study like ethnography, history, and poetry for fields that were more abstract, geometrical, and epistemological. For example, the subject of history for Descartes is like foreign travel: it broadens the mind, but it does not deepen it. He had confidence that mathematical exactitude and logical rigor would provide the intellectual certainty he was looking for.

The use of reason in the science of the Renaissance was based on a knowledge of crafts and was grounded in manual labor rather than a theoretical foundation. The craft "how to" tradition is a product of the artisan acting holistically all the way through the creative process, from beginning to end. In the case of sculpting, this means being well-rounded, understanding of the material being used, its composition as well as firing and glazing techniques.

Beginning in the seventeenth century with Descartes use of geometry, the crafts suffered a demotion as a new, more theoretical base of knowledge developed: academic disciplines. A theoretical design procedure was organized, using the physical sciences as a model. Specialized theoretical disciplines develop which:

- lose their practical base
- become increasingly specialized in particular fields with less and less capacity to know (or care) what is going on in other fields. This specialization continued to get worse in the eighteenth and nineteenth centuries. Three of the chief dreams of rationalism were crafting an exact language, discovering a rational method for science, and a single science which could turn any field of inquiry into a hard science. These form a single project designed to purify the operations of human mind by separating them from time, place, circumstance and practice

Descartes hoped that starting from clear and distinct ideas would keep knowledge from falling into complete skepticism. He wanted to find a starting point to test the validity of the truth of rational arguments independent of who presents them, who listens to them, and what the situation they are in. Using Euclid as his model, Descartes wanted to know how clear and distinct ideas of matter in motion could extend the geometrical method of finding empirically adequate theories of physics and optics.

Descartes, of course, was not the first to contrast reason to rationality. The rational tradition goes all the way back to the Greeks with Plato, Aristotle, and Parmenides to St. Augustine, Abelard, and St. Thomas, plus the rest of the Medieval schoolmen. But the work of the new rationalists—Galileo, Kepler, and Newton—was even more revolutionary. Instead of *renouncing* the use of sense data in the service of spinning rational spiritual webs *alongside* empirical reality, the new rationalists proceeded by starting with the senses, exposing their unreliability, and proceeding mathematically to discover the true properties of matter in motion. Rationality was applied to planets and their motion. If problems *larger* than human scale could be solved with mathematics (rationality), rationality might help Europeans think their way out of political and theological chaos.

Galileo

It is easier to understand Galileo's place in rationalism if we compare his work to Greek science. First, Galileo did away with the Aristotelian notion that scientific objects were qualitative polarities such as wet-dry or hot-cold. Neither were the senses to be trusted in explaining physics. Rather, Galileo wished to measure quantities of motion—size, velocity, and number—using mathematical formulas. Dewey tells us that in the results of his experiment with falling bodies at the tower:

> He destroyed the old distinction of intrinsic *qualitative* differences of gravity and levity. It showed that the immanent motion of bodies was connected with a common homogeneous property, one measured by their resistance to being set in motion. This inertia was finally identified by Newton as mass...
>
> His experiment of balls rolling down a smooth inclined plane is the nearest approximation he could make to observation of freely falling bodies. The result was that space traversed is proportional to the square of the elapsed time. The heavenly bodies were subject to the same mechanical laws of mass and acceleration as mundane bodies. (*Cosmopolis*, 95-96)

The idea that different physical locations in space—

heavenly or earthly—effected physical laws was proven wrong. Physical science disregarded the qualitative heterogeneity of color, sound, heat, light, friction, and electricity of experienced objects to make them all members in one comprehensive homogeneous scheme.

Seventeenth-century rationalism applied to the state

Hobbes: Leviathan: the state as an emulsifier

Was it possible to organize *political* ideas about state politics along the same lines as scientific ideas about Nature? Hobbes thought so. His political theory treated the individual as an atom or particle in a mechanical political system. Hobbes' program for centralized state intervention into society was the application of rationalism to politics. According to Hobbes, without a state to intervene, the fear of others would be always present and heightened, since there was no power able to overawe them all. Individual lives would necessarily be miserable and insecure. Human beings are not absolutely equal in ability but close enough to being equal that the weakest can easily kill the strongest.

No society could permit an individual's natural powers from being continually invaded by others through individual acts of violence. There would be no society. The state provides a peaceful, non-violent way by which individuals can constantly seek power over others without destroying society. The causes of individuals quarrel are not a problem for Hobbes, only the pursuit of quarrels *without a state as a mediator*, a covenant to restrain their appetites. This was the only hope to avoid the constant danger of violent death.The rational marketman who possesses substantial property and hopes to hold it can acknowledge obligations to such a sovereign. Marketmen calculate well enough to see the net advantage of conventional rules, but each of them cannot be relied on to keep this long-run advantage over everyone steadily in mind. Only where there is a sovereign to enforce the rules can ruthless competition be kept in manageable proportions. Marketmen invade each other, but they need a sovereign to keep their invasions within non-destructive bounds.

But why is Hobbes advocating state intervention *now?* Because of the crisis of the seventeenth century. Macpherson points out that at the time of Hobbes's writing, England was going through a protected struggle between the king and parliament. Macpherson argues that Hobbes's advocacy of *state centralization was a defensive reaction to keep society from falling apart.* The incessant state interference with wages, prices, investment, and trade were protracted attempts to protect England against harsher repercussions of economic fluctuation. As Macpherson points out, Hobbes's 'state of nature' is a deduction from the appetites *not* of humanity in general, but of anxious Englishmen of the seventeenth century.

Mercantilism

The rising and soaring of markets also led to state intervention in capitalist markets and a discouragement of full free trade. This mercantile policy put protective tariffs around its home industry to control price fluctuation. Mercantilist policy defined wealth not as the cost of producing a good but the amount of gold or silver bullion in the state treasury. The mercantile state also developed state policies for dealing with migrations and vagabonds as a method of imposed order.

Rationalism in the service of kings

Politically, conservatives used rationalism to justify the monarchy. We can see their use of the work of Newton, Galileo, and Kepler to justify the existence of the monarchy:

> God would never set up the order of nature less rationally and prudently than a wise King would organize the state: nor would God care for nature with any less concern than a Husband and Father

> has for his Wife and Family... Everything in the natural order testifies to God's dominion over nature. *What God is to nature, the King is to the State*. It is fitting that a Modern Nation should model its State organization on the structures God displays in the world of astronomy. (Toulmin, *Cosmopolis* 127)

This analogy also allied to the subordination of the masses. Just as in Newtonian physics matter was conceived as inert and moved only by an external force, so the masses or the lower order was inert unless guided wisely by a king:

> ...any attempt to deprive physical mass (i.e. matter) of a spontaneous capacity for action or motion [go] hand in hand with proposals to deprive the human mass (ie the lower orders) of the population of an autonomous capacity for action. (*Cosmopolis*, 121)
>
> Behind the inertness of matter, they saw in Nature as in Society the actions of lower things depended on... oversight and command by higher creatures. The more confident one was about subordination and authority in Nature, the less anxious one need be accordingly about social inequalities. (*Cosmopolis*, 128)

Rationality applied to international relations

Leibniz and Grotius

Europe also faced difficult regional political reconstruction because religious wars had undermined diplomacy between societies. After 1600, all countries of Europe faced the problem of devising ways in which a single state could accommodate citizens with *several* religious beliefs. Leibniz's *Characteristica*

Universalis sprang from the ideological deadlock of the Religious wars. Leibniz dreamed of creating the intellectual and practical conditions for renewed dialogue among theologians. He believed many problems between societies and between religions stemmed from the variety of language differences between cultures which undermined fruitful communication.

In this spirit, Leibniz hoped to construct a universal language that could be as precise as mathematics. Just as arithmetic expresses numbers, and geometry expresses points, lines, and planes, he hoped to devise mathematic symbols to express human thought. He wanted to categorize all forms of argument so that people could rationalize together without confusions, errors or misunderstandings. Leibniz believed that with this language everything in the world would be intelligible.

In 1629 Hugo Grotius argued in his book, *The Laws of War and Peace* that laws must be crafted which would govern international relations. In his treatise, he reorganized the general rules of practical law into a system whose principles were the *counterparts of Euclid's axioms*. One application of Grotius's dream was the Treaty of Westphalia of1648. Seven years in the making, this treaty set up a system of sovereign states with agreed upon boundaries, prerogatives, and sanctions. It helped to restore diplomatic relations between countries that had been divided religiously. In the field of law, after 1650, Henry More and the Cambridge Platonists made ethics a field for general abstract theory.

Table 10.4 Reason vs Rationality: Fourteenth—Seventeenth Centuries

Reasonable (open practical problems; probability is enough)	Type of cognition	Rational (closed problems, certainty required)
Fourteenth and fifteenth century Renaissance	Historical period	Seventeenth century Scientific revolution
City states, kingdoms Decentralization	Political organization	Absolutist states Centralization
Theism, divine intervention	Type of deity	Deism; god a watchmaker Application of Newton to religion
Rhetoric most important during the Renaissance	Place of rhetoric in thinking processes	Anti-rhetoric form or occasion is irrelevant: Descartes, Peter Ramus, Bacon (Idols of the cave)
Ethnography, history, poetry	Interdisciplinary entry points	Math—algebra, geometry, (Descartes) Trigonometry, calculus (Newton, Leibniz)
Craftsmanship, amateurship	Work: cross-disciplinary or specialized?	Professional disciplines Amateurs marginalized
Oral—persuasion must work in interaction with audience attitudes	Medium of communication in thinking	**Written**—read written questions and then answered in **uninterrupted** chains of statements
Limitations of definition;vagueness and ambiguity built into language	Definition of terms	Search for clear, distinct and certain ideas (Descartes)
Skepticism based on limits of human experience (Montaigne)	Attitude towards skepticism	"Mitigated skepticism" Descartes, Gassendi
Local— differences between particular places (humanist study of texts)	Attitude towards space	Universal—absolute space (Newton)
Sensitivity to what is unique, exceptional, accidental (humanists)	Focus on the particular or universal?	Cut away the inessentials and identify what situations have in common (Enlightenment)

CHAPTER 11

From Rationality to Reason: How Reason Lost and Regained Its Balance

Orientation

In our last chapter, we discussed the differences between reason and rationality and a substantial part of the chapter was about how the quest for certainty turned rationality from a tool to be used under very specific conditions to an being an end in itself. This occurred not only in religious settings, but in the natural sciences as well as in domestic and international politics. In other words, *rationality was applied to complex situations where only reason should have been used*. We discussed the psychological motivations for the quest for certainty both in the ancient world as well as in the seventeenth century.

In this chapter we complete our survey of rationality, covering the Enlightenment and then the late nineteenth and early twentieth century as it applied to Schoenberg's music as well as the mathematical logic of Frege, Russell and Wittgenstein. We then discuss the challenges to rationality that came from many different disciplines, including Lamettrie's subversive challenge to mechanical materialism's claim that matter is inert. Up until the nineteenth century, mental life seemed to be solely based on thinking. But fiction writers like Richardson, Stendhal, Balzac and Dostoevsky had other ideas, as we will see. The work of Bohr in quantum theory challenged the conviction that objectivity meant *detachment* and Darwin challenged the belief that human motives were driven by reasons as opposed to natural selection. In economics, Marx and Veblen gave countless examples of how capitalism is an irrational rather than a rational system. Finally, in the realm of ethics, Tolstoy and Wittgenstein claimed that it was impossible to construct a rational system of ethics independent of facts.

In the last section we will study how rhetoric and propaganda were used during the baroque period by the Catholic Church to control the lower classes by amplifying sensory saturation. Techniques in art, architecture and theatre were used in order to produce astonishment and awe.

Rationality in the Enlightenment

Newton

Unlike Descartes, Newton insisted that the objects to which he applied his mathematical calculations *were not the products of thought* but *sensory data*. But Dewey says otherwise:

> Newton with respect to the doctrine of space, time and motion frankly *deserted* the empirical method. He assumed in addition to atoms having mass, inertia and extension, the existence of empty, immaterial space and time in which these substances lived. (*The Quest for Certainty*, 142)

Newton had the senses on a short leash. He asked how the unity of anything could be secure, unless there was something persistent and static behind all change. Without such fixed indissoluble unities, no final certainty was possible. There needed to be some guarantee that nature would not be dissipated or revert to chaos. These were *metaphysical* fears, rather than any experimental evidence that determined the nature of the fundamental assumptions of Newton regarding atoms. 'God in the beginning formed matter in solid, massy, hard, impenetrable particles.'

Dewey argues that this statement is a scientific restatement of the spiritual desire for something fixed as a warrant for absolute certainty. These principles were *not necessary* for Newton's application of his mathematical method. For Newton, all changes that did occur in nature were only the *separations and new associations of permanent particles* and these were the sole ground of assurance that ultimate hard and massy particles persisted without internal change. There was *no direct human experience* of the ultimate massy, hard, impenetrable and individual unchanging particles.

It wasn't only atoms that Newton thought were fundamentally unchanging. Absolute space, time and motion were the immutable frames within which all atoms interacted.

> Invariant time, space and motion furnished phenomenon those properties to which mathematical reasoning could be attached as a disclosure of inherent properties. The positions of bodies could be treated as an assemblage of geometrical points. (Dewey, *Quest of Certainty*, 144)

Contrary to this, in the early twentieth century, Einstein's theory of relativity assumes that mass, time and motion were no longer regarded as fixed independent substances. But as Dewey says, Newton could have assumed that none of these were fixed in, and still got the same mathematical results for his argument. They were unnecessary assumptions born out of the quest for certainty.

Kant

Other examples of western non-theological commitments to the quest for certainty include the writings of Kant. In *Critique of Pure Reason*, he attempts to secure on a priori grounds, the foundations of natural knowledge:

> Upon the scientific side [Kant] was concerned to provide a final philosophical justification, beyond the range of skepticism, for Newtonian science. His conception of space and time as necessary forms of the possibility of perception was the justification of the application of mathematics to natural phenomena. Categories of thought, necessary to understand perceived objects—an understanding necessary to science—supplied the foundation of permanent substances and uniform relations of sequence—or causation—demanded by the Newtonian theories of atoms and uniform laws. (Dewey, *Quest for Certainty*, 59)

In his *Critique of Practical Reason*, Kant tries to do same thing for religion and morality. Ethics up to this time was based on *common case law*, following *Nicomachean Ethics* and casuistry. Common case law applied ethics for pastoral care. Contrary to this, Kant's emphasis on *universal* moral axioms extends into ethics an ideal of rationality that had been formulated by Descartes in logic. When rationalism got hold of ethics, ethics lost its practicality in helping people, and focused on an ethical criticism separated from practice.

The moderate rationalism to eighteenth-century Enlightenment

Stephen Toulmin has long contended that reason ruled in Europe during the humanist Renaissance period, and then rationalism took command of the sciences in the seventeenth century. Extreme rationalists such as Descartes and Spinoza started from the deduction of certain principles and axioms and then tried to apply them to the world. In Descartes, physics was reduced to geometry; investigation started with definition. Rationalism separated philosophy as a category from the sciences. But where did the Enlightenment fit with this controversy? Was it a continuation of rationalism of Descartes and Galileo or was it a return to the reason of the humanists? The Enlightenment movement was convinced that the ultimate destination of philosophy was to *generalize* what was learned in the sciences. In the process of doing that, did philosophy have to become less rationalistic or more rationalistic? Does that mean the Enlightenment became more 'reasonable?' Yes and no.

Newton is a great case-in-point of a transition figure. It is easy to associate Newton with Descartes and Spinoza. But Newton was not an extreme rationalist. Just because he *used* mathematics to understand physics doesn't mean he *began* with mathematics. Newton started with an *analysis* of relationships between gravity and tides in different locations in the real world. The concepts and axioms formed came *after* his investigation.

There is no question that the philosophers of the Enlightenment idolized Newton. Voltaire devoted a significant part of his life to popularizing Newton. The Deist conception of God which was prevalent for most Enlightenment philosophers likened God to a watchmaker who created the world and then walked away, rather than intervening in his creation. The work of scientists and philosophers was to discover how the watch worked or to solve the mystery of a cosmic jigsaw puzzle.

In engaging that process, the Enlightenment started with observation and facts. Lamettrie indicated that 'the senses are my philosophers.' Reason was the process of monitoring and correcting sense data. Extreme rationalists were deductive; Enlightenment approaches were inductive. In this more moderate rationalism, rationalism was a process used only *after* observation.

Enlightenment social philosophers saw mathematics as a necessary condition of understanding, but it was not sufficient. This is not the otherworldly rationalism which detached from the world and found its home, into a few Platonic eternal forms. Rather, *rationalism operated as a socio-political policy for determining the future of humanity.* This determining social policy was provisional, and subject to mistakes and temporary backsliding. It required tinkering. Though the future of humanity was uncertain, it could become a little more certain and probably better if scientific research and scientific method were used for social ends.

Rationality in the late nineteenth century

Schonberg: Music as sound in motion

Toulmin tells us that In the latter half of the nineteenth century, the music-loving public had been sharply divided between those who were enthusiastic for Richard Wagner's music and those who supported the more traditional approach of Brahms. The central question was whether music was sufficient *unto itself* or whether it was essential to express feelings that were part of a larger human condition.

In the latter half of the nineteenth century, romanticism had made composition a matter of *inspiration* and as a result, according to Schonberg, composers had neglected discipline. This resulted in cumbersome works which required simplification. For example, Mahler's pieces required a large orchestra, chorus and solo vocalists. Another example was the complex harmonies of Richard Strauss.

Schonberg argues that how a composition *sounded* was

not important. He criticizes modern music lovers who do not understand anything about music but 'know what they like.' Only the authenticity of the musical idea and its articulation according to *musical logic* mattered. For Schonberg, music is not a language of feelings as the romantics assert, but a logic of sound in motion. It was the logic of composition than needed to be revised. Here is another attempt at the creative *separation* of all dramatic or poetical ornament from the musical idea itself and its presentation according to the laws of musical logic. This is what qualified Schonberg for partnership in the enterprise that Kraus was carrying on in letters and Loos in architectural design. Toulmin points out that one can draw a close analogy between Schoenberg's music theory and Whitehead and Russell's *Principia Mathametica,* which attempted to mathematize logic.

Mathematical logic of Frege, Russell, Moore, and Wittgenstein

Before 1914, scientifically-minded intellectuals in Germany and Austria were disgusted with the entire state of official European philosophy. They followed with sympathy and interest the mathematical innovations of Frege. In Cambridge at the turn of the century, there was an alliance between formal logic and philosophical analysis in the early work of Bertrand Russell and his closest ally, G.E. Moore. They saw their task as sharpening and mathematizing philosophical logic and insisting on clear definitions of those terms that could be defined. The purpose was to reveal the true logical forms and articulations underlying the often-deceptive nature of grammar and syntax. Russell and Moore wanted to reform philosophy by making an analysis of philosophy.

Wittgenstein had very mixed feelings about the value of philosophy. He was not the first person to suggest that a more rigorous understanding of language was necessary. Mauthner, Frege and Russell all understood this. Wittgenstein hoped to develop a language which could cut across the disciplines of the physics of Mach to the ethics of Tolstoy. His first attempt was the *Tractatus.* He sought to transcend the limits of representative language to achieve this.

Wittgenstein thought that, despite the philosophical skepticism of Mauthner, a representational language was not impossible. The same principles which physicists spoke of theoretically were also applied practically in the construction of machines.

The most fundamental branch of physics was a consequence of the *mathematical structure* which the physicist imposed on mechanical phenomena in the process of constructing his models. So there existed *one area* of language, the language of mechanics, which was sufficiently univocal and well-structured to convey facts about the world. If one could only establish a corresponding all-embracing mathematics of natural language! If Wittgenstein was to establish a comprehensive 'model' theory of language he needed a similar mathematical of language. (Toulmin, *Wittgenstein's Vienna* 180-181)

Just as Schonberg had sought the essence of music in the logic of composition, the propositional calculus becomes for him the a priori scaffolding of language. (Toulmin, *Wittgenstein's Vienna* 188)

But propositional calculus gave him only the scaffolding. Frege and Russell were only interested in developing symbolic logic to apply mathematics to philosophical problems. Wittgenstein wanted to develop a symbolic logic using natural language.

The return to reason: dismantling the scaffolding of rationality, 1750-1914

Stephen Toulmin points out that there are at least seven assumptions about rationality:

- nature is stable
- matter is inert
- mental activities must be entirely *conscious*
- mental activities are entirely *rational*
- objectivity means *noninvolvement* in processes being studied
- explanations about human actions are *reasons* which are based on choice
- explanations about nature are *causes*, or mechanism

because in nature there is only determinism

In the coming sections we will see that all seven assumptions were challenged.

Nature is older and more unpredictable than rationalists had imagined

Between the middle of the eighteenth century and the beginning of the twentieth century, all these foundation stones were shaken. Among other things, the Lisbon Earthquake of 1755 reminded eightieth century European intellectuals that nature was not always a benign predictable Newtonian universe.

In the same year as the Lisbon earthquake, Immanuel Kant published *Natural History and Theory of the Heavens*. In this book, he used Newtonian ideas of motion and gravitation to show how the whole astronomical universe might have developed from a first *random* distribution of material particles. In the same century, as we've seen in chapter five, geologists like Hutton and Lyell showed that nature had a history far older than the Biblical creation, a dating that most scientific rationalists still believed in. At the turn of the twentieth century, Poincare showed that even objects under gravitational attraction do not move uniformly. Unpredictable collisions take place. In his book *Science and Hypothesis,* he argued that we can learn very little when we run our knowledge bases through on a quasi-geometrical foundation.

Lamettrie challenges the idea that matter is inert

As early as 1726, Lamettrie denied the rational mechanist contention that matter was inert. He argued, like Diderot, that matter was *self-organizing*, citing the power of regeneration possessed by the hydra (or polyp). He rejected the notion that matter could be reduced to Cartesian extension. The vital and mental activities of organisms were natural outcomes of their material structures.

Quantum physics challenges the idea that objectivity meant detachment

In the late nineteenth and early twentieth centuries, even at the level of physics itself, quantum physics showed that even the most elementary form of matter was unpredictable. In the eighteenth and nineteenth century, objectivity was associated with detachment. However, at the turn of the twentieth century, we find that it was not possible to study matter completely from the outside. Quantum physics made human participation an inevitable part any examination of subatomic particles. As Dewey says:

> The fundamental principle of the mechanical philosophy of nature is that it is possible to determine exactly both the position and the velocity of a body. They assumed that these positions and velocities are there in nature independent of our knowing. Observations merely register a fixed set of changes according to laws of objects whose essential properties are fixed. (*Quest for Certainty*, 201)

A mechanical science is completely understandable because, until recently, physics dealt with bodies of *middle level volume and low velocity*. However, the characteristics of these bodies were mistakenly assumed to be still in operation when engaging *minute particles of high speed*. These were treated as mathematical points, located at fixed unchanging instants of time. Humanity is an outside spectator of a rational world already complete in itself. The function of the rational mind was simply to copy or represent that world symbolically. However:

> Heisenberg's principle has upset this. He says that interaction prevents an accurate measurement of velocity and position for any body. When one is fixed, the other is defined only within a specified limit of probability. The element of indeterminacy is not connected with defect in the method of observation but is *intrinsic*. The particle observed does not have a fixed position or velocity (*The*

Quest for Certainty, 202)

Novelists argue that emotions drove motives

For novelists of the eighteenth and nineteenth century—Richardson, Stendhal, Balzac and Dostoevsky—as different as they were from each other, they could all probably agree that human *emotions* drove mental activity. In addition, as I've shown in chapters two and eight, that the romantics of the eighteenth century argued that much mental activity was *unconscious*.

Human behavior is driven by unconscious bio-evolutionary processes

Darwin argues that human behavior is not driven by reason. As he shows in his great book *The Origin of Species*, the actions of human beings were driven by selective pressures of adaptation and sexual selection that were formed tens of thousands of years ago. The choices of one partner over another had little to do with conscious choices and more to do with fertility prospects or upper body strength.

Marx and Veblen challenge the rationality of capitalism

Unlike other disciplines, rationality did not develop in economics until the last third of the nineteenth century. Before then, what counted as economics was called 'political economy.' Its earliest proponents were Adam Smith and Ricardo. Among other things, the political economy school argued that:

- economics could not be separated from politics, but rather was connected to decisions made by politicians at a state level
- economics could not be separated from history; there is a history to how people thought about how to exchange goods and services that was not capitalist
- the field of economics was described using natural language
- the results of economic transactions could not be rationally understood but was a matter of probability

In short, political economy was *reasonable* about economics in the way that I have defined reason in this chapter.

Though coming out of the political economy tradition himself, Adam Smith wanted to understand the economy as a self-subsisting system that was subject to its own laws despite influences of politics and history. His description of the laws of the economy as an 'invisible hand' was a rational interpretation of economic processes. Even though individuals buying and selling their goods may have seemed like a chaotic way to manage an economy at a macro level, the underlying laws of supply and demand were accessible to human rationality. Later theories of economic analysis (equilibrium analysis) used an analogy of planetary stability, even though the hope of finding guarantees of the stability of planetary systems had faded among mathematical astronomers.

Rational choice theorists also took human needs as biologically given and not subject to cultural influences. They saw people as greedy hedonists and they congratulated capitalists for being able to harness this potentially dangerous force. Of all the human sciences, it is economists who are most confident that mathematical modeling contains the secrets of how capitalism works.

This rationalist analysis was challenged by another political economist, Karl Marx, in the second half of the nineteenth century. Marx insisted that capitalism was a *historical* system that had a definite beginning point and traced its history in the early modern world. Secondly, he mocked the idea that there are no politics in economics. Capitalists have influenced European politics from the beginning and have been instrumental in having state laws passed to hinder working-class organization which might diminish their profits. In much of his work from the fetishization of commodities to the tendency of the rate of profit to fall, Marx believed that capitalism was an irrational system rather than a rational one and eventually it would destroy itself.

Lastly, at the turn of the twentieth century, Thorstein Veblen challenged rational-choice theorists by arguing that human needs are irrational. In his book *Theory of the Leisure Class*, he showed how all social classes were driven by emulation, copying the classes above them. More importantly, he pointed to the power of advertising to effect and change human needs and desires. Needs were a product of changing social institutions, not biological givens. The return to reason in economics was driven by Marx and Veblen.

Against Rational Ethics: Tolstoy and Wittgenstein

Tolstoy believed that morality bypassed rationality and was based on the relationship between emotions and actions. As morality was based on feeling, Tolstoy saw art as the language of feeling. In his short parables written over thirty years beginning in 1872, and in his book *What is Art?,* Tolstoy criticized the aestheticism and esoteric nature of the art of his day. He thought aestheticism had become a palliative for the upper classes. When it became a servant of the class interests, art became simply a matter of amusement. It was art that had forgotten its social obligations. Ethically, Tolstoy seemed to have exerted the deepest and most direct moral influence upon Wittgenstein. Specifically, it was in Tolstoy's belief that the ultimate answers to questions about ethics could not be found in rational systems. Speech was a medium of rational thought which was good for everyday life or for science but would be no help in giving meaning to life.

What Wittgenstein later recognized was the limitations of language. He came to hold that the other side of language is not a silent wasteland. The silence is not an absence but a presence. He believed that all that really mattered in human life was precisely what we must be silent about. Wittgenstein thought that what could *not* be said had general moral value. We could recognize the higher only in that which the propositions of our language were *unfit* to capture. Wittgenstein's silence in the face of the unutterable was not a mocking silence but rather a respectful one. For Wittgenstein 'there can be no ethical propositions not because they are meaningless because they are higher order.' (193) The *Tractatus* was primarily an attack on all forms of rational systems of ethics. Before moving to the next section please have a look at Table 11.1, which is a summary of the application of reason and rationality across the disciplines.

Table 11.1 Application of Reason and Rationality Across the Disciplines

Reasonable	Type of cognition	Rational
Francis Bacon—certainty a mere idol; we should explore strengths and weaknesses of particular beliefs using experiential instead of mathematical methods Copernicus Gassendi—non-mathematical trust in senses	**Application to philosophy and science**	Descartes—applied algebraic methods to Euclid's geometry Galileo Leibniz—universal language through mathematics, codifying all modes of argument Newton—mathematical calculation of planetary and gravitation
Machiavelli—based on historical experiences; strategizing and disguising the self in relation to others	**Application to domestic politics**	Hobbes Application of Newtonian physics to human societies; the individual atom is the particle of politics Bodin's theory of Absolutism
Anglo-American jurisprudence—cases and precedents Common case law Nicomachian ethics Aristotle	**Application to international law**	Grotius— reorganized rules of practical law; counterpart of Euclidian theory 1648 Treaty of Westphalia—separation of state from religion
Renaissance humanism	**Application to artistic movements**	High Renaissance—principles of perspective Baroque (monumental, universal scale) Glorification of absolutism
Erasmus, exposure of human folly Rabelais—sensuous, bawdy side of human nature Shakespeare—plausible presentations of all to human reality	**Application to literature**	Moliere, Racine—formality in plays
Montaigne Ethics based on practical pastoral care	**Application to ethics**	Kant Universal ethics
Political Economy (Adam Smith, Ricardo)	**Application to economics**	Mercantilism Rational Choice Theory (last third of nineteenth century—Jervons, Menger, Walras, Bohm-Bawerk)

The baroque of black rhetoric and white propaganda

Social class and political control

Up until now, we have identified the differences between two forms of thinking: reason and rationality. According to Toulmin, reason was prevalent during the Renaissance while scientific rationalism arose in the seventeenth century. Furthermore, I have argued, following Toulmin and John Dewey, that the rationalistic quest for certainty was a reaction to turbulent times in the seventeenth century. In addition, in this section I want to suggest that the rationalism of science as a system of security did not penetrate all social classes. The rationalist vision might have comforted scientists, merchants, state civil servants and teachers living in the seventeenth century, but it left the lowest classes untouched. What could be offered to the lower classes?

I want to suggest, following Jose Antonio Maravall, that the cultural movement of the baroque was used by secular Absolutist monarchies and the Catholic Counter-reformation to try to control the lower classes. The use of baroque art, theatre, architecture and processions were attempts to awe and distract the lower classes. Earlier we saw that that becoming civilized was a process aimed at upper class aristocrats. In my book *Foraging Promethean Psychology*, I argue that becoming disciplined targeted the poor and working class. Now I want to argue that the seventeenth-century elites pitched scientific rationalism at the middle classes and *black rhetoric and gray propaganda* to the lower classes. We will discuss what gray propaganda black rhetoric are shortly.

What is baroque?

The baroque is an artistic period in Europe whose appeal rested on the saturation of the senses of the audience through exaggerated motion of figures to produce drama, tension, exuberance, and grandeur in sculpture, painting,

architecture, literature, music, and dance. The etymology of the word includes 'elaborate with many details; excessive ornamentation, exaggerated lighting in painting and in theater with a multiplicity of plot turns and opera.' This is contrasted to the logical, restrained realistic, clear, and serene depiction of the Renaissance. Baroque arts have been characterized by Maravall as
"irrational, irreal, fantastic, complicated, obscure, gesticulating, unrestrained, exuberant frenetic, transitive, wondrous and marvelous"(207). There is antithesis in baroque rhetoric between its fire and ice and shining and darkening. Landscapes are darkened by stormy violence, as human figures stand in fierce postures among ruins that convey the uncontainable destructive force of time. The baroque can be divided into three phases:

- Early baroque, 1590 to 1625
- High baroque, 1625 to 1660
- Late baroque, 1660 to 1725

In part, the baroque was funded by the Catholic Church as a campaign tool to regain ground lost to the Reformation. The Counter-Reformation was launched between 1545 and 1563, beginning with the Council of Trent. One of its many purposes was to lessen the gap between the clergy and the laity. The Church wanted to communicate religious themes by direct, emotional involvement pitched to the illiterate rather than to the literate. Monumental baroque could give the Papacy as well as secular absolute monarchies an imposing command of the arts that might restore its prestige. From a political view, it was important that *centralization* replaced balance in pictures, just as centralization was crucial to the building of absolutist states in the seventeenth century. The work of Jose Antonio Maravall seeks to connect the baroque with the political circumstances of absolutist monarchy.

Epistemological insecurity and fortune

During the baroque, there was a lack of confidence that

what one sensed empirically had much to do with the truth that was real. This insecurity cut across ascetic religious teachings, the rigors of scientific knowledge, the belief in apparitions and the artistic discovery of perspective. Montaigne wrote 'our life is nothing but movement.' To show how movement was thought to be at least as important as stillness, Maravall reports that Bernini asked the king to *move around* to do his portrait (177). In the baroque, substances were constantly changing—but it is not pure change. The natural movement of things has a rising phase and another of decline while substance remains immutable. Maravall has drawn attention to the baroque's obsession with the contradictory character of experience:

> All reality possessed this condition of not being done—unfinished paintings; architecture that eludes its precise outlines; emblematic literature that requires the reader to bring the development of thought to an end on his or her own account. (169)

These insecurities of the time can be seen in the changing concept of fortune over the course of history. For the ancients, fortune was a decision of the gods, resulting in someone's fate. In the Middle Ages Fortune was God's hatchet man (or in this case, a woman). God as Providence was in charge but the problem was how to account for the disorder of the Middle Ages? Fortune, blind in her choices, helped to explain European humanity's difficulties in the seventeenth-century situation without daring to blame God for it.

By the fifteenth century, reflecting on the confidence of the Renaissance, fortune is now part of the *human* condition (rather than the doings of the gods), but now it is possible to manipulate fortune with human will and create a new result. This might be called 'destiny.' For Machiavelli, informed human beings could confront fortune with a strategy and come to achieve favorable verifiable results. By the seventeenth century, fortune can be transformed by human will by *seizing the right occasion*. The occasion is the time, place and opportunity.

Machiavellian self

The seventeenth-century self was a suspicious sort. Maravall points out that a lexicographical study on the baroque would show a high degree of frequency of use in the use of words: waylaying, caution, and distrust. This was individualist self-thought where one discovered himself through disguise, because truth itself is disguised. "Man is nothing but a masking, lying hypocrisy" (Maravell, 62). To face this type of environment, the play of tactics or the wager was necessary. The full pragmatic formulation is found La Rochefoucauld: "Vices enter into the makeup of virtues just as poisons are in the makeup of medicines. Prudence unites them, tempers them and make use of them in the ills of life" (Maravell, 62). *Prudence* was the most important of the virtues. The baroque version of the hero was a person of *discretion* and very different from the hero as a knight in the High Middle Ages.

This can be seen in the art of Shakespeare. All Shakespeare's great protagonists were beings that were most themselves in solitude, only *tactically* related with others in their approaches and retreats. These were revealed in the internal battles displayed in the soliloquies from the tragedies of Shakespeare, Racine and Calderon. Politically, among the Tacitists, secrecy went hand-in-hand with suspense. Maravall tells us there was a total lack of intimacy in the baroque's literary creations. Yet all this plotting and scheming came to nothing for Hobbes, since Individualist interactions could be compared to simple collisions between billiard balls.

The instability of both society and the individual could be seen when Shakespeare asked us to imagine the world as a *stage*. Maravall points out that this involves:

- the *transitory* character of the role that is assigned to each person
- the *rotation of role distribution*, so that what role one person plays today is played by someone else tomorrow
- a contradiction between the role and a deeper, real self

The condition of the role was as *appearance,* not as substance. What *appeared* did not affect the ultimate foundation of the person. Their temperament remained underneath the surface of the apparent.

Strategic choices for the monarchy

According to Maravall, the absolute monarchy saw itself faced with two choices:

- strengthen the physical means of repression by building and strengthening military system of citadels and artillery in case of uprisings in the cities
- find a means to penetrate *the consciousness* of the lower classes *and achieve psychological control,* which was the material basis for the baroque

According to Maravall, the political program of the baroque was a propagandistic answer of a monarchical-aristocratic ruling class to the threats (real or imagined) that were launched against their traditional political structures. It was an attempt at restoration of the socioeconomic powers of old and new aristocrats through the ostentation and externalization of abundance in order to persuade the lower classes to accept their authority.

The baroque was an artistic tool of social control, organized in the shadow of the absolute monarchy. The purpose was to awe the lower orders by dazzling them with the pomp and circumstance of its art, theatre, architecture and processions. The purpose was to stem the tide of doubt or asking too many questions by persuading the lower classes that the traditional privileges assumed by the king, nobles and Church were justified after all.

The baroque did not attempt to suppress the passions of the lower classes. Rather, they wanted to make use of their power. The agencies of authority not only tolerated sentiments but frequently they fomented them. The baroque did not want to manifest a satisfied calm existence but instead a state of excitation and turbulence. The key was to channel it in a harmless direction.

The ways to penetrate the consciousness of the lower order had at least two possibilities. One was to make use of the power of novelty to consolidate an established system by:

- *diverting* the impetus for the new towards spheres of collective life where innovations will not be dangerous; for example "kitsch, a popular culture characterized by the establishment of types with a standardized repetition of genres representing a tendency toward social conservatism"(83)
- sanctioning the presentation of the *inherited* tradition under *new* names or processes

Strategies of the baroque

The baroque accepted the skepticism that we live in a world in which nothing real resembles what we perceive. The goal was not to make the disillusioned individual abandon the world, but to teach him to adapt to it. Human beings were confronted with things that look as they appear, but not as they are.

Exaggeration and incompleteness

Because appearances can be deceiving, it can invite a feeling of instability; and this was amplified by the baroque. Mannerists like Rubens and Michelangelo understood that what was unrestrained, taken to the extreme, possessed an ability to impress by exploding proportions, resulting in astonishment. They arrested attention by creating a state of anxious instability, such as a horse rearing up at a crowd and indirectly at the spectator. Copying real world experience, the subject matter of painting was often a crowded and moving world of superiors and inferiors swarming before the spectator.

Anamorphosis

This technology of perspective painting helps to put the world of appearances in order. Spectacles and mirrors made distant objects seem near and close objects far away. Beautiful things could be made to appear unseemly, while what once seemed ugly could be seen as passable. Velasquez was a master at accentuating the incertitude where the play of images passed over into the real. The technique of anamorphosis was applied to representation of every sort—biblical, political, and natural phenomena.

Appearances were not falsehoods, but something that in some way belonged to things. Perspective was truth *under certain conditions*. Beyond this, truth disappeared because it was a mask. We had to accommodate ourselves to the game of appearances surrounding us. Maravall says:

> The boundaries between actor and spectator, between the daily world and the world of illusion come to be very fluid (199). In art, the modes of striving used produce a certain degree of indetermination concerning where the real ends and the illusion begins. (198)

Exploitation of biblical themes: kings and aristocrats become saints

One powerful propaganda technique was to picture the saints and other sacred presences not wearing the clothes of the actual biblical time period but instead wearing aristocratic apparel. The intention here was to:

- present the nobility and monarchy as having been present in other historical periods
- link the rulers of society indirectly to sacred history of Christianity, legitimizing them

Biblical characters became inseparable from the genesis

of kings.

In theatre, the baroque was the first culture to make extensive use of stage engineering to produce large effects. This is attested to by the character of the theater. Theatrical works organized painters (of sets), musicians, set designers, costume makers, actresses, and actors in the production of a grand pageantry, designed to assault all the senses simultaneously. The use of pulleys allowed for mechanical apparitions, strange illuminations, rocks that opened up, meteors that rained down, as ships, horses, and wild animals moved on and off the stage. They all showed the complex development of theatrical techniques. Even Shakespeare had statues coming to life.

More importantly for propaganda purposes, these techniques were utilized to control vertical space. Not only was a sense of awe created whenever the authorities appeared in vertical space, but the upper classes seated themselves in positions in the theatre that were invisible and above everyone else. As kings and persons of high status attended theatre, it was difficult to imagine they did not merge themselves into the heavenly vertical space during and/or after the performance. It was no accident that tickets to the theatre were very inexpensive, allowing the lower classes full participation in the spectacle.

Maravall informs us that the cities of the baroque were teeming with arches, tombs, and artificial fountains to enhance the pomp and circumstance of processions. Fiestas were organized along with dazzling fireworks and adorned altars, in the hopes of cultivating amazement:

> Comedies, contests, public taunting, games, light shows, dances, mock war games on horseback, the bulls and masquerades were diversions and necessities to be able to withstand so many adversities. (242)

Why is the baroque gray propaganda and black rhetoric?

What is propaganda?

According to Jowett and O'Donnell (*Propaganda and Persuasion*), the use of propaganda goes all the way back to the first ancient civilizations. Propaganda is the deliberate, systematic, and often covert attempt by institutional elites to control the perceptions, cognition, emotions, and behavior of masses of people while hiding, restricting, distorting, or exaggerating the claims and evidence of alternative views. Why would propaganda be necessary in any society? In class societies, with the few who were wealthy and most who were not, systems of information control became very important in explaining and legitimizing why the wealthy and the poor are in the places they are in. Up until the rise of the printing press, the means of propaganda was essentially the same throughout the world—in the use of monumental architecture, larger than life art, royal processions, and the use of coins with the emperor or king's face on it. What was new about propaganda in the sixteenth century was the use of printed material.

Gray vs black propaganda

The type of propaganda used to attempt to stabilize the baroque population is gray propaganda. This meant that the sources of propaganda and the accuracy of information were usually unknown. Secondly, messages were distorted. Some information was played up while other information was played down. Lies of omission rather than lies of commission were perpetuated. The purpose of communicating with the audience was to distract and divert them from focusing on real social problems. White propaganda was perpetuated in that the opposition was treated as invisible, in order to create the illusion that there was consensus.

In wartime, propaganda was black. Falsehoods were perpetuated; the opposition was demonized and accused of perpetuating atrocities; hatreds were inflamed and thinking was narrowed into categories of black and white. What was new about black propaganda in seventeenth-century Europe was the use of *print* media, first between Catholics and Protestants and then later by secular authorities in times of war.

Earlier in this chapter we discussed the importance of ‘white’ rhetoric in the process of reasoning. But in the baroque period, in addition to perpetuating gray propaganda, the machinations of Church leaders and the Crown could also be classified as black rhetoric. It was classified as black rhetoric because what the church, the aristocrats and the crown did was to use rhetoric as a means to questionable ends, which was exactly what Plato was afraid of.

Black rhetoric appealed to the myopic short-team interests in humanity—self-interest, entertainment, hedonism, and demagogy. Black rhetoric ‘played to the house’ and ignored skepticism and critical thinking. Black rhetoric appealed to the *charisma* of its source not the character of the source. This meant using form as a *substitute* for content. Black rhetoric used the pathos part of the Aristotlean rhetorical triangle by bombarding the audience with images to minimize the time spent thinking. Images of the future were unrealistic fantasies that simply comforted the lower classes instead of inviting them to face the actual social circumstances that exist. Furthermore, it appealed to the superficial side of emotions—titillation, awe, envy and the desire to be taken care of. Have a look at Table 11.2, which summarizes the use of gray and black propaganda.

Table 11.2 Use of Gray and Black Rhetoric During the Baroque

Gray propaganda	**Seventeenth-century example**
Sources and accuracy of information was unknown	There was no independent news service in the seventeenth century to verify information or its sources
Messages are distorted; lies of commission	Economic crisis and political crisis were not shared with the population
Purpose of communication with the audience was to distract and divert	Awe-inspiring art, theatre, processions
White Propaganda	
Opposition is treated as non-existent	Amplification of sensory saturation techniques in hope of drowning out oppositional voices
Black rhetoric	
Appeals to the short-term myopic self-interest, entertainment, hedonism, demagogy	Bullfighting, kitsch in art, masquerades
Plays to the house and ignores opposition	
Ethos—appeals to charisma	Kings are depicted as saints in paintings, becoming magical characters in vertical space in theatre
Pathos Infantile emotions	Exploding proportions in art produces awe, astonishment Theatrical stage management: pulleys Promise that the Crown is looking out for the interests of the people
Infantile imagination	Church promises to take care of the population in the next life

CHAPTER 12

Quantitative Rationality Theories of Probability and Chance from the Middle Ages to the Eighteenth Century

Orientation

When, where, and why did theories of randomness begin?

How far back in history do notions of randomness go? In her book *Games, Gods and Gambling*, F. N. David points out that the talus was the most common randomizer of ancient times and it is the predecessor of dice:

> The talus is the knucklebone or heel bone of a running animal in creatures such as deer, horse, oxen, [and] sheep. This bone is so formed that when it is thrown to land on a level surface, it can come to rest in only four ways. Well-polished and often-engraved examples are regularly found on the sites of ancient Egypt. Tomb illustrations and scoring boards make it virtually certain that these were used for gaming. (2)

Even in historical periods such as the Middle Ages where the Catholic Church was very powerful, people maintained their interest in games of chance. But *playing* games of chance is not the same thing as having *theories* of chance based on mathematical calculations of randomness.

According to Ian Hacking, in his book *The Emergence of Probability*, there was no mathematics of randomness until about 1660 and hardly any history about the subject in Europe before Pascal. How could it be that such fundamental concepts as probability and chance emerge so late in European history? Why hasn't any theory emerged earlier?

One theory suggests that necessity is the mother of invention, because people won't innovate unless they are driven by external circumstances. For example, the first European calculations on chance by Pacioli in 1494 were developed to help merchants perform double-entry bookkeeping to keep track of accounts payable and accounts receivable. Furthermore, in the seventeenth century, long-distance traders needed to develop insurance and annuity policies in order to recover some of their potential losses on the high seas due to bad weather, bad navigation, or competing traders. Annuity mathematics was invented by students of Descartes in the Netherlands. In the eighteenth century, a theory of measurement was needed for astronomical purposes to improve navigation on the high seas. In the nineteenth century, an analysis of new biological data demanded a new kind of mathematics.

All these necessities emerged as part of the European modernization process. Before then, according to the necessity theory, there was no need for a theory of probability. Only recently has probability theory had application in enough areas to create its own problems and generate its own programs of research.

Hacking argues that this theory is good for explaining why probability theory *expanded* once it emerged, but it does not explain its origin. For one thing, double-entry bookkeeping was *unsuccessful* in solving probability problems. Secondly, while annuities were used to finance Dutch trade, the Dutch calculated their annuities very badly, and Dutch towns lost money on them regularly. Thirdly, there is no causal relationship between the need for annuities and probability theory. Calculating annuities was done fifteen centuries ago with some skill, yet there was no probability theory.

Probability mathematics is Arabic in origin, but what other sources besides the Arabs did Europe draw from? As it turns out, two thousand years ago, India had an advanced merchant system and its theory of causation was like that of Europeans.

Is it a coincidence? Randomness is in the air in the mid-seventeenth century

In 1657, Huygens wrote the first probability textbook to be published. At around the same time, Pascal made the first application of probabilistic reasoning to problems other than games. His famous wager about the existence of God was the first attempt to invent a decision theory. This was about the same time Leibniz thought of applying metrical probabilities to legal problems looking for degrees of proof in law. In the late 1660's, annuities were first being put on a solid footing by John Huddle and John de Witt. Within ten years, several scholars had stumbled upon ideas about the nature of randomness *without knowing anything about each other's existence*. What made the time ripe for this? We will soon see.

Plan of the chapter

In the first third of this chapter I discuss the more theoretical and historical aspects of our subject. We begin with the difference between probability and chance as well as the historical and dialectical relationship between these twin forms of randomness over the course of history. In the field of the philosophy of science, I make a distinction between qualitative and quantitative empiricists. The next two sections discuss the differences in how early modern science developed a criteria for how we know things which was very different from epistemology in the Middle Ages, including the birth of inductive logic. In the next chapter, I will discuss how probability theory was *applied* to law, gambling, annuities, political control by the state as well as mental illness.

The two faces of randomness: probability vs chance

Historically, some of the problems in developing a theory of randomness is in the use of the terms chance and probability to mean the same thing. If we save each of these terms to describe the two different processes, we will have a clearer comprehension of what exactly we are trying to understand.

There are two aspects of randomness:

- One is the *degree of belief* which is warranted by evidence. This is like saying, what is the likelihood that a particular belief is true? This will be called probability
- Chance has to do with the likelihood that real events in the world are likely to occur. The results are generated by devices of *events* that produce *stable relative frequencies such* as rolling dice or drawing lots

When we are assessing reasonable degrees of belief, we are dealing with probability and the disciplinary field of probability is *epistemology*. Other terms for probability are propensity and proclivity. Epistemological probabilities concern our *confidence level* about our knowledge. When we are trying to discover the laws which regulate real events, we are dealing with chance, stochastic laws, and aleatory processes. The proper disciplinary field of chance is statistics. Leibniz distinguished between two types of *possibilities* which are roughly equivalent to probability and chance.

Ian Hacking makes a nice distinction between *possible for* which is equivalent to chance and *possible that* which is about probability or likelihood. For instance, to pose the question "Is it possible for me to drive from San Francisco to New York in one day?" we need to consider objective factors such as how fast it is possible to drive a car, what are the speed limits are, and what is level of physical stamina the driver has. The chances here are impossible. Chance has to do with what is physically possible independent of our confidence level about something. But if I say to my friend "I wonder: is it possible that she will ask me on a date again?" we are dealing with the state of our knowledge. When I ask what the chances are of my winning the lottery, I am asking what are the possibilities or the relative frequencies that when I place a bet, the lottery will turn up my number. In the case of games that are not rigged, we need to use a physical device so that all numbers have the same opportunity of coming up. When I achieve this state, it is called equi-possibility. This definition of chance as a ratio among possible cases originated with Leibniz.

Let's do some more examples. When I ask myself if it is possible for me to build a bookcase that is level, that depends on the state of my knowledge of carpentry. The answer to this question does not depend on the relative frequency distributions of the atomic or molecular structure of the wood. Rather, it depends on my psychological confidence level of how feasible building a bookcase is based of my physical skills. I am dealing with confidence levels of belief, that is, epistemology. This is the doctrine of chance that *possibilities that* are a matter of *physical* propensities.

These distinctions between probability and chance are not new. Poisson distinguished more clearly than any predecessor between *relative frequency* (which were objective events) *and degree of belief (*which were about confidence levels or epistemology) approaches to probability. When we examine the objective world, we are examining the frequency of an objective event, that is, what are the chances of something occurring? When we estimate probability, we are weighing our degree of reasonable or unreasonable belief. When we are measuring frequency distribution in the objective world, we are measuring whether an event will have a greater or little chance of occurring. In the case of probability, we are measuring our degree of confidence in whether future events will happen, relative to our knowledge base of education or ignorance.

What kind of knowledge do we need to measure probability? A knowledge of epistemology so that we make reasonable inferences. What kind of knowledge do we need to measure chance events in nature? What are the laws of large numbers is one angle on this, as we will see?

Table 12.1 is a summary of the differences between probability and chance. The second half of the table is a summary of four theorists who have come to similar conclusions about these terms.

In her book *Classical Probability in the Enlightenment,*

Table 12.1 Two Faces of Randomness and their Theorists

Probability **"Possible that"**	**Category of comparison**	**Chance** **"Possible for"**
Assessing reasonable degrees of belief which is warranted by evidence	**What is being measured?**	Discovering the frequency of physical events
Epistemology Our state of knowledge	**What Discipline does it draw on?**	**Statistics**
Law, philosophy	**What areas was it applied to?**	Games, state census, Annuity policies of merchants
Mind: propositions	**Where is the source of operation?**	The world: physically possible independent of our knowledge of them
"I wonder if she will ask me out on a date again?"	**Example 1**	"Is it possible for me to drive from San Francisco to New York in one day?"
"Is it possible for me to build a book case that is level?"	**Example 2**	"What are the possibilities I will win the lottery?"
Feasibility **Confidence level** Degree of certainty in the mind	**What is being weighed?**	**Relative frequency** with which different outcomes occur—what events happens more or less often
Propensity, proclivity	**Other terms for randomness**	Stochastic laws
Induction	**Forms of reasoning**	Induction
Epistemological journals	**Tools used?**	**Equi-possibility:** physical devices which generate stable frequencies of events so that all chances are equally possible to turn up
Psychological and qualitative	**Hume**	Objective, mathematical, and quantitative
Relative probability derived from the assumption of equi-probability from ignorance—relative to the state of knowledge	**Laplace**	**Absolute probability** derived from the nature of events themselves—the true shape of the coin or the relative skills of the players
Probability will be the reason to believe that an event will occur	**Poisson**	Chance Events in themselves, independent of our knowledge
Subjective probability—our manner of judging and feeling, varying from one individual to the next	**Cournot and Ellis**	**Objective possibility**—the existence of a relation which subsists between things themselves

Loraine Daston points out that by the end of the eighteenth century mathematicians had come to think about probability in four different ways:

Objective

- physical construction of certain objects (symmetry or uniform density of a fair coin or die)
- the frequency with which certain events happened (how many people of a given age died annually)

Subjective

- As the measure of the strength of an argument (how evidence is weighted for or against judicial verdict)
- The intensity of belief (the firmness of the judge's conviction of the guilt or innocence of the accused)

The historical relationship between chance and probability

The distinctions introduced between chance and probability are relatively new. In the Middle Ages, chance was thought of as exceptional circumstances of real-world events, whereas probability was merely subjective opinion. Real knowledge was achieved by demonstration which was *certain*. So, in the Middle Ages chance was understood as something objective, whereas probability was a subjective, cognitive appraisal. The tradition of rational demonstration based on certainty began to be challenged with the coming of the Renaissance.

To counter this erosion of belief, a group of seventeenth century thinkers (Mersenne, Gassendi, Grotius, and Boyle) advanced a new philosophy of rational belief called constructive skepticism that we encountered in chapter five of *Forging Promethean Psychology.* They wanted to bridge the gap between the dogmatic certainty of the scholastics and the absolute doubt of what could be called *destructive skepticism*. Their pragmatic rationality was a partial certainty which acknowledged *degrees* of certainty.

As a result of the scientific revolution, this changed world was thought to be *determined* by universal laws. Chance was no longer thought to be exceptional events in the real world, for the real world was thought to be determined. Chance became rolled into probability which was seen as a sign of *temporary* subjective ignorance about the laws that actually determined what was going on. Chance was merely apparent, a figment of human ignorance. For example:

> Bernouli insists that the throw of the die is no less necessary than an eclipse. The only difference between the gambler and the astronomer lies in the relative completeness of their respective knowledge of dice and eclipses. Contingent events only exist relative to our ignorance. A perfected science would no longer need probability theory. The new metaphysics had banished luck and chance as figments of human ignorance. Determinism, old fashioned necessitarian or new-fangled mechanism lay at the very heart of the classical creed. (*Classical Probability in the Enlightenment*, 35)

Nevertheless, these classical probabilists were confident that the mind would ultimately comprehend what was going on in the world because the mind was a passive mirror of nature. Minds were reasonable, and the foundation for this was Lockean association psychology, as we will see. Philosophers as different as Hobbes, Spinoza, Holbach, and Laplace also held to this view.

In the third phase, chance and probability returned to being understood as two distinct processes. It wasn't until Questscet's work in the 1840s that chance was again understood as part of the objective world. Chance continued to not be seen as an exception to the rule, but this time it was not because there was subjective ignorance. Rather it was because the *real objective world had chance built in (law of large numbers.)* In the meantime, critics of the mind as *reasonable* pointed out the shortcomings of the mind such as prejudice, habit, and slavishness towards convention. Because of this the only way to understand statistics was to develop the *rational* side of the mind which was able to calculate statistics. Please see Table 12.2 for a summary.

Table 12.2 History of the Relationship Between Chance and Probability

Category of comparison	Middle Ages	Seventeenth century	Eighteenth century
Is chance objective?	Yes Accidents, exceptional circumstances	No Nature operates by deterministic laws	Yes Nature operates by laws of large numbers, statistical regularities
What is subjective Epistemology?	Probability	**Expectation:** odds of equi-probable cases **Equal contracts** **Equity**	**Mathematical probability, risks combinations:** the ratio of the number of combinations favorable to the event to the total number of combinations Algebra **Equal outcomes** **Chances**
Type of likelihood		**Qualitative likelihood**	**Quantitative likelihood**
Criteria for judgment	Demonstration		Likelihood
Form of cognition	Mere opinion vs real knowledge	Reason	Rationality
How trustworthy is the mind?	Trustworthy	Trustworthy Association psychology: Passive theory of mind as a mirror of nature	Untrustworthy due to conventions, prejudice, superstitions

Qualitative vs quanitative empiricism

Within seventeenth and eighteenth century science, there were those who claimed that the senses, checked by reason, could tell us the truth about nature. Daston called these constructive skeptics or qualitative empiricists, and they included Bacon, Gassendi, Boyle, and Locke. Others such as Galileo, Bernoulli, and Laplace argued that the senses could *not* be corrected by reasoning but by mathematical rationality. These thinkers are called quantitative empiricists because of their association with mathematics.

Qualitative empiricism

Qualitative empiricists believed that ultimately nature was governed by natural law, not by chance. This meant that the combinations and permutations of the various sizes and shapes of atoms only *appeared* to produce their observed effects by chance. In reality, natural laws instituted by providence overrode chaos. The Epicurean atomism of Gassendi made frequent appeals to combinations of *concepts* in order to explain how homogeneous matter took such diverse forms. Combinations of atoms produced distinctive observable *qualities*.

For qualitative empiricists, empirical inference applied only to events that were virtually *identical* and that occurred *repeatedly*. They debated whether such expectations were rational, but not over the summing process itself. Induction progressed horizontally by collecting instances of the same type and eventually turning this into a generalization. They wanted to know to what extent experience must confirm a claim before it may be legitimately extended to cases beyond the scope of observation. They trusted common sense to figure this out.

Quantitative empiricism

Over the course of the eighteenth century, empiricist philosophers shifted their emphasis from qualitative to *quantitative* aspects of experience. For these probablists, combinations and permutations of the various sizes and shapes of atoms produced effects by chance, not by natural laws. Combinations of atoms produced no qualitative change, just quantity.

Quantitative probablilists endorsed the common sense of mankind. They reasoned from past to future *about causes* in cases where the number of trials was *large*. Here common sense needed little aid from mathematics to accept the ratio of events as a good approximation to the ratio of causes. But quantitative empiricists did not trust common sense when the number of trials was too *small* to:

- judge accurately the *rate* at which the probability of a conjecture increased or decreased with the number of

confirming instances
- to single out the *soundest* conjecture from the variety of contenders; Only quantitative arguments could help the empiricist

As we will see later, Bernoulli and Bayes' theorems specify the relationship between the observed frequency of an event and its underlying probability. The probability of causes was to be a mathematical description of rationalizing from effects to causes.
See Table 12.3 for a contrast between qualitative and quantitative empiricists.

Table 12.3 Qualitative vs Quantitative Empiricists

Qualitative empiricists expectations	Category of comparison	Quantitative empiricists probablists
Combination of atoms produced distinctive observable **qualities**	**Is matter qualitative or quantitative?**	Combination of atoms produced distinctive **quantities**
Fixed	**Are the proportions of one shape of atoms to another fixed or mutable?**	**Mutable**
Yes The combinations and permutations of the various sizes and shapes of atoms only appeared to produce their observed effects by chance. In reality, natural laws instituted by providence dispelled chaos	**Is natural law operating in the world or chance?**	**No** Combinations and permutations of the various sizes and shapes of atoms produce effects by chance, not by natural laws
Sought fundamental causes and principles beneath the level of appearance	**The value of appearances?**	Worked with appearances
Sensory observation: collection of facts mediated through reason	**Methods**	Sense observations translated into mathematical calculations
Bacon, Locke, Gassendi Boyle: mitigated skeptics	**Theoreticians**	**Bertolli Laplace**
Endorses common sense They debated whether such expectations were reasonable, but not over the summing process itself	**How trustworthy is common sense?**	**More skeptical about common sense** Endorsed the "common sense" of mankind that reasoned from past to future **about causes when the number of trials was large** They **did not trust common sense** when the number of trials was **small**

Qualitative expectation theory vs quantitative probability

How does expectation differ from probability?

The type of probability that qualitative empiricists used has been called expectancy by Lorraine Daston. Expectations are conventional quantified estimates for assessing the odds of equiprobable cases in legal practice. This is opposed to probabilities in which a ratio of the number of combinations favorable to an event is compared to the total number of combinations. *In expectations you are weighing likelihoods of comparable cases without knowing the total number of cases available*. In probability, you can figure out mathematically what the precise likelihoods will be because there is a finite number of cases. With expectations, you never know the number of all possible cases. Until the development of state censors and state record-keeping, no probability reckoning can exist. *Expectations are about judgment. Probability is about calculation.*

Cardano was the first to find the tendency or disposition of the dice to display certain stable frequencies on repeated trials. Galileo explored how some combinations of numbers more easily appear more frequently than others. This depends on being made up of a greater variety of numbers. Cardano was a visionary who saw beyond classical theory but he didn't have the statistics to back it up.

> He explained the discrepancy between calculation and actual outcome as luck. Only in the case of *many* trials do the calculations come close to the fact of the matter. Luck was a reality. Cardano was no determinist and he was not greatly troubled by the interventions of chance (small temporary fluctuations) or luck (systematic trends or streaks). Inscrutable but real forces like luck would, from time to time, throw off the match between calculated and actual outcomes. (*Classical*

Probability Theory in the Englishtenment, 36)

By 1711, with the publication of de Moivre's *Doctrine of Chances*, the mathematics of chance was recognized as a discipline in its own right. In order to understand this, we have to make distinctions between partitions and permutations. How many equal alternatives can arise from rolling three dice of three? We can have just the permutaton 1-1-1. If we have the partition of four, we have one partition 1-1-2. But unlike the outcome of three, the partition of four can have three permutations 1-1-2, 1-2-1, and 2-1-1. *Before Galileo, it was not obvious that permutations rather than partitions were equally subject to chance. Now, it was understood that permutations not partitions are equally probable.* In the case of the criteria for a fair game in expectancy, a game is considered fair because the *conditions of the players* are indistinguishable. In probability theory, the conditions of the players are equal for all players because of *the way the game is structured.*

Expectation theory is based on an passive theory of the human mind as a mirror

In the seventeenth century, there was no separation between what was really going on in the world and our cognition of degrees of confidence in understanding what was going on. In this period, experience, belief, and probability were three aspects of a single psychological operation. This confluence of subjective and objective worlds was rooted in a qualitative, empiricist theory of mind. For Locke, the mind is a passive calculator of objective events. The more constant and frequent the observation, the stronger the mental association, which intensifies the probability and belief. Deeply engraved impressions in the brain create involuntary associations between ideas frequently paired in sensation. The objective probabilities of experience and the subjective probabilities of belief are, in a well-ordered mind, *mirror images of one another.* The healthy mind is *intrinsically* probabilistic.

Locke's association theory affirmed the bond between probability theory and reasonableness by linking subjective and objective aspects of probability. Probability assessed the accuracy and sufficiency of observations at the same time as the justification of the reasoning that applied to them. Daston points out that despite Locke's suggestive reference to frequencies, he still understood probability as an *inferior* form of knowledge, or a make-do substitute for genuine knowledge-based intuition and demonstration.

Skepticism of the mind as a mirror

Hume incorporated some mathematical probabilities and divided Locke's empiricist associational framework in two directions:

- one psychological and qualitative (which Hume distrusted)
- objective mathematical and quantitative

No Enlightenment thinker drew a sharper distinction between how we come to believe and the rational grounds for that belief than Hume. Unlike Locke, Hume thought there was a third category of proofs between demonstrative knowledge on the one hand and uncertain probabilities on the other. These were those arguments which derived from the relation of cause and effect.

Locke was very aware that many minds were not reasonable. For example: when we go along with conventions, when we are prejudiced against other groups, when we are slavish to authorities, when we let our passions rule, when we make judgments based on self-interests, when we make judgments based on habit, and when we allow circumstances of time and place that are linked associationally rather than causally to affect our judgment. These are all cognitive impediments to seeing the world as it really is.

Impact of the French Revolution

After the French Revolution and Napoleonic era, the conduct of reasonable men no longer seemed an obvious standard.

> Distinguishing prudent from rash behavior in post-Revolutionary France was no easy matter. With the demise of the reasonable man, probability lost both their subject matter and criterion of validity. (*Classical Probability Theory in the Enlightenment*, 107)

Concordat also argued that the natural reckoning of probabilities could be easily disrupted by self-interest, imagination, and prejudice. After the French Revolution, he added demagogy to his list of forces corrupting the mind. His social mathematics was to supply the antidote to the corrosive effects of what he called mob politics. To remedy the situation, he recommended a public course on mathematics and an elementary text on probabilities:

> Just as sailors could determine longitudes from lunar tables without any technical knowledge of celestial mechanics, the use of calculus of probabilities could be taught to everyone regardless of mathematical preparation. (*Classical Probability Theory in the Enlightenment*, 218)

Condillac proposed a radical form of sensationalist psychology. Whereas Locke had acknowledged two sources of ideas—experience and reflection—Condillac attempted to reduce epistemology to a monistic system based on experience alone. More than Locke, Condillac was preoccupied with *pathological* associations instilled by prejudice, overly vivid imaginations, and chains of association which grew stronger depending on the degree of pleasure or pain attached to the associations. Condilliac argued that the presence of needs and interests was as natural as balancing frequencies of past events and the illusions perpetrated by imagination were almost as common. This emphasis on personal needs and interests and on the widespread pathologies of uncritical habit and unbridled imagination, undermined the more optimistic psychologies of Locke, Hartley, and even Hume. Laplace also wanted to expose the psychological roots of one class of probabilistic illusions: superstition, astrology, and divination.

When it comes to making bets on annuities or life insurance, Buffon says we must consider the psychology that people are more sensitive to losses than to gains. Probabilities must be gauged *psychologically* according to the fear or the hope they arouse in reasonable men. Even Buffon's notion of value stemmed from the psychology of habituation: we need what we are accustomed to having.

Daston sums up, saying Condillac's reservations about the reliability of the link between the probabilities of experience and belief were the beginning of the end for the classical interpretation of probability. Once wishful thinking became the rule rather than the exception in the psychology of hopes and fears, subjective and objective probabilities could no longer be so automatically equated. Please see Table 12.4 for a summary of the changing theories of the mind.

Table 12.4 Battles in Epistemology: Expectation vs Probabilities

Category of comparison	1660	Late eighteenth century
Epistemological confidence level	Expectation	Probability
What is the mind?	Passive calculator of associations	Prone to error due to habit prejudice
Theorists	Locke, Hume, Hartley	Condorcet Condilliac, Laplace, Bayes
Epistemological consequences for probability	Merger of subjective and objective probability	Subjective probability differentiated from objective probability
Commonality	Nature is objectivity determined	Nature is objectively determined

Knowledge as deduction in the Middle Ages

Probability not certainty as good grounds for evidence

As we also saw in chapters ten and eleven, rationalists fought hard striving to make the criteria for knowledge certainty. It wasn't until the second half of the nineteenth century in the West that we have come to realize there are very few times when the quality of evidence can render a conclusion certain. Evidence is too fragile to be captured in deductive syllogisms. We must settle for what is likely or probably the case.

Probability in the Middle Ages

In the Medieval world, knowledge was based on certainty, or it wasn't knowledge at all! Understanding a problem by referring to probability was considered mere opinion and not serious knowledge. For Medievalists, knowledge (in contrast to opinion) was based on universal truths which are true by necessity, not probability.

Furthermore, the basis of evidence was one which was approved by some authority, or by the testimony of respected judges. In the Middle Ages, *there was no empirical evidence independent of either witnesses or observers, or the claims from the authorities in books*. People provided evidence for both testimony and authority. The only way one showed a claim to be wrong was by *demonstration*. In order to have knowledge, evidence had to be one hundred percent true. All you had to do to demonstrate something was untrue was to cite one exception to the rule. Another way of proving something wrong was through verisimilitude. Here evidence is compared to what something is supposed to be under normal circumstances. In contrast to both demonstration and verisimilitude, inductive evidence must point *beyond itself* and its definition.

Cracks in the cosmic egg: Jansenists vs casuists

One place we can see cracks in the medieval cosmic egg of certainty is in the field of religion. In the sixteenth century, the Jesuits debated what was to be done when the authorities disagreed about Christian doctrine. One option was the Jansenists solution: to *cut down* on the authorities whom they recognized and stick only to scripture and reason. The bolder, casuist side wanted to consider a wide range of authorities and use the *anticipated social and moral effects on people* to decide among several doctrines. Though the principle of casuistry was defeated in the seventeenth century, it showed that even the most conservative institutions like the church could no longer hold out for deductive reasoning without at least a fight.

Pascal bets on the probability of God

Do you believe in the afterlife? Do you want to make a bet on the existence of the afterlife? The great philosopher Pascal wanted to show *statistically* why it was a good bet to believe in God and the afterlife. In his book *Penses,* he showed how aleatory arithmetic could be part of a general art of conjecturing. Aleatory arithmetic made it possible to understand how the structure of rationality about games of chance could be transferred to spiritual inferences.

In deciding whether to believe in God and an afterlife, he says we are in the same position as someone who is gambling on a coin toss whose aleationary properties are unknown. Pascal takes as his starting point two extreme positions: either there is no God or else there is a God whose characteristics are correctly reported by the Church. Now even though there are problems with this formulation (for instance the exclusion of other possibilities than these two) the approach to the problem is based on quantitative rationality rather than faith. Pascal's hypothetical wager for acting as if one believed in God was the first well-understood contribution to decision theory.

Decision theory addresses the question of what to do when it is uncertain what will happen, given:

- an exhaustive list of possible hypotheses about the way the world is
- the observations or experimental data relevant to these hypotheses
- inventory of possible decisions
- the various pros and cons of making these decisions

Here is what Pascal comes up with. He argues that God exists based on weighing the *potential consequences* of believing in God as opposed to not believing in God. If God doesn't exist, the actions of a libertine will be validated and the actions of the pious will be taken as that of a fool. However, if God does exist, then wagering that there is no God brings damnation. Wagering that God exists can bring salvation. Since salvation is far better than damnation and since both are much longer than life on earth, it is a better decision to believe in God and the existence of an infinite afterlife. Pascal dared to make God an object of decision, not belief.

Roots of scientific experiment

Induction as evidence of things and relationships between things

Was there no room for observation based on the five senses in gaining knowledge in the Middle Ages? Yes and no. As we said earlier, the five senses could be used as evidence if it is attached to people—to the testimony of witnesses or to the authorities. If not, sense data was just opinion. Any facts independent of people and witnesses had no place as evidence. What was lacking in this formulation was evidence provided by things derived from sense data which existed and *recorded as public information*. Furthermore, there is a difference between evidence and mere sense impression.

> The situation in which I would properly be said to have evidence for the statement that some animal is a pig is that...in which the beast itself is not actually on view, but I can see plenty of pig-like marks, on the ground...If I find a few buckets of pig food, that is a bit more evidence, and the noises and smell may provide better evidence still. But if the animal then emerges and stands there plainly in view, there is no longer any question of collecting evidence. (*Emergence of Probability*, 32)

While I can report to others that I saw a pig and smelled a pig, the time in which I did this has come and gone and can no longer be verified. But what remains—pig prints, buckets of food, pig sties—can be verified without my presence. Furthermore, I can now make a claim based on evidence *between* things, independent of either testimony or authority. This is inductive reasoning.

Until the end of the Renaissance, there was no inductive evidence by which one thing can indicate, contingently, the state of something else. There was no concept of evidence with which to pose the problem of induction. In what fields did induction first develop? Surprisingly, it was not in the high sciences such as astronomy, mechanics, or optics. Hacking claims these fields were still holding out for demonstrations. It was in the 'low' sciences like alchemy, geology, astrology and medicine where inductive evidence first took hold in the lowly opinions of probability theory.

Even at late as the eighteenth century, probability was not considered good evidence. In the first half of the eighteenth century, there had been controversy in Britain over the relation between miracles and testimony. It wasn't until 1748 that Hume made an attack on the credibility of miracles based on his view of probability rather than authority or testimony.

<u>Different types of inquiry: hypothesis testing, dabbling,</u>

diagnosis, dissection

Hacking argues that different types of experimental methods converged in the seventeenth century. He distinguishes between four different types of experiments:

- the test is a matter of deduction or hypothesis testing.
- The individual tests a hypothesis when the hypothesis implies that if an event occurs, then they predict that a certain result will follow. If the result fails to follow, then the hypothesis is disconfirmed
- the adventure or dabbling—this is not guided by a theory. We only make guesses as to what might happen. Any theory that develops happens *after* the adventure with reality. Hacking says that much of early alchemy had this spirit
- the diagnosis consists of specifying the character of an illness. The experimenter infers what is wrong by reading signs
- the dissection is a matter of taking something apart to see what is inside. A surgeon cuts people when they are alive, or an anatomist dissects them when they are dead

Tests, adventures, dissection and diagnosis all provide evidence and this evidence, in turn, leads to different consequences. The test either refutes or confirms a hypothesis. Dabbling at its best suggests a theory. A dissection reveals the inner working of an animal and a diagnosis leads to a prognosis about what to do about a physical or mental problem.

Please see Table 12.5, which summarizes these.

No chance in the Middle Ages: physical signs as signatures

12.5 Types of Experiments in the Seventeenth Century

Types of evidence	Example	What does it do?
1) **Test**—inner seeing that is deduction	**Hypothesis testing**	**Demonstratively** refutes a hypothesis or else corroborates it **Proof—passing the test**
2)**Adventure, dabbling** —not guided by a theory and we may only guess what happens	**Much early alchemy.** You heated, mixed materials to see what would happen	**Suggests a theory**
3)**Diagnosis**—formed from the character of the problem by reading signs	**Physical or mental illness**	**Prognosis** What to do to relieve the illness
4)**Dissection**—taking something apart to see what is inside Visual motivation	A surgeon operates on the brain or an artist dissects the anatomy of a cadaver	**Inner workings of man or another animal**

Hacking argues that the Middle Ages had a concept of each kind of evidence, but there was a difference between the use of signs for making diagnosis in the Middle Ages as opposed to looking for signs in diagnosis in the Renaissance.

Paracelsus stands in the twilight zone between Medieval magic and seventeenth century science. Even though his alchemical ideas were later proven wrong, he helped us to understand medicine with his alchemical theory of the relationships between mercury, salt, and sulphur. For Paracelsus *all signs were signatures*. In chapter eight of my previous book, *Forging Promethean Psychology*, I pointed out that each object in the world has a signature and is connected to a set of correspondences both at the macrocosmic and microcosmic levels. Paracelsus thought that a bountiful God had left his signature in the stars, in nature, and in humanity for those who can decipher it.

He distinguishes between two operations in signs:

- one produced by *nature herself*, where nature works and transmits her influence for good or evil through a magician

- one which works *through other things*, as in pictures, stones, herbs, words, or when nature makes comets or halos in the heavens

For Paracelsus, *nothing of significance could be due to chance*. Everything is linked in a vast correspondence system of the very large (macrocosm) to the very small (microcosm). The foundations of these correspondences are the four elements—fire, earth, air, and water. From these, colors, musical tones, herbs, rocks, and gems are all grouped into one of these four elements. Not only are physical signs signatures, but human language is also a signature. Language was created by God and written on every leaf and stone. They are signs written by God into nature. Since Paracelsus mixed together processes going on in nature with the language people used to describe it, this meant that words had power over material objects. This was one of the foundations of sympathetic magic.

Secularization of the physical and the linguistic in early modern science

One of the major achievements of the new science was to secularize both the physical world and human language, separating them from both from their magical beginnings. Language was no longer used for understanding sacred origins. Rather language was understood as a conventional and arbitrary sign which had no inherent magical influence on the objective world. Further, conventional signs of language were separated from the secular signs in nature. It was now necessary to make distinctions between natural signs and conventional ones.

According to Hacking, in medical textbooks of the Renaissance, there was a characteristic distinction made between causes and signs. Causes were basically *efficient* causes or symptoms based on diagnosis or dissection. Signs were simply *circumstantial evidence* which were present when something happened, for example when planets were in conjunction, or a comet appeared. What this meant was that *signs were free from sacred signatures and could be either circumstantial evidence for causes or they could be chance events.*

Hacking then distinguishes the old Aristotelian concept of science that the Middle Ages had taken up from the new science of the seventeenth century:

> In the old Aristotelian tradition *scientia* was to proceed by the demonstration of effects from first causes. In the new science, one was to infer the causes from experiment. The old causes got at the *essence* of things. The new causes were *efficient* causes, explaining how things were made to work. You inferred efficient causes from experiment. You inferred something small, inner, atomic and precise from something larger, outer, gross and inaccurate. (*Emergence of Probability*, 37)

The basis of scientific reductionism is that complex, visible, phenomenon in nature is nothing but what is simple, elementary and small. There are no levels in nature. The further we break things down, the truer they are.

Within the low sciences of the Middle Ages, observation of signs was conceived of as reading testimony from God or the authorities. With the new science, evidence from testimony now included not only influential judges, but testimony *from nature*.

In the Middle Ages, the distinction between signs and efficient causes was not made because there was no inductive science. *It was the transformation of signs into possible efficient causes or chance events that was a landmark for induction.* For the new science, looking for signs was not looking for formal, final causes as it was for Aristotle. Signs were only indicators, circumstantial evidence that must be analyzed, dissected, and organized as an experiment with a hypothesis which was verifiable. Searching for causes was no longer primarily looking for signs or dabbling to discover a theory. Neither was it testing by demonstration. Now the result of passing a test was to get *new inductive evidence* for the hypothesis. It was evidence of one thing that pointed to evidence somewhere else.

A new conceptualization of the diagnosis of signs emerged from the Renaissance forward. It used one thing as evidence for another. By the end of the Renaissance, the sign was transformed into the concept of evidence described in the previous section. A new kind of evidence conferred probability on propositions, making them worthy of approval. At the same time, it did so in virtue of the *frequency* with which it made *correct predictions*. Signs could be assessed by the *frequency* with which they spoke truthfully. If they spoke truly, epistemological probability were increased. If they did not appear frequently, they were chance events.

For us today, some signs are to be trusted and others not. The signs that are to be trusted depend on the frequency with which they occur in relation to other events. It was here that stable and law-like regularities become more observable and worthy of observation. A new kind of testimony was accepted, the testimony of *nature*. *Nature* could now confer evidence by law-like regularities and frequencies.

This transformation from sign into evidence is the key to the emergence of a concept of randomness of either probability or chance. Induction is the method by which we appraise both probability and chance. Both are based on evidence which is contingent and not implied on our claim.

Please see table 12.6 for a summary of the differences between Medieval and seventeenth-century epistemologies.

<u>What is inductive logic</u>?

Table 12.6 Comparing Medieval and Seventeenth Century Epistemologies

Medievalists	Category of comparison	Seventeenth century
Demonstration Reductio absurdum Looking for exception to the rule; Demonstration of effects from first causes.	**Criteria for evidence**	Chance, statistics
Verisimilude—comparing something to how it operates under normal conditions		Likelihood, frequency
Authority or Testimony of respected judges	**Sources for evidence**	Empirical facts Or testimony of nature
Useful only when attached to witnesses and authority	**Place of the five senses**	Sense data can be facts independent of witnesses and authorities
Not taken seriously	**Place of the objective world independent of people**	World of objects and the relationship between objects is the basis of science
Certainty, necessity	**Standard for evaluating evidence**	Probability
Did not exist	**Place of induction**	Primarily tool of empirical investigation
Religious doctrine	**Fields of operation**	**Low sciences** of alchemy, geology, astrology, medicine, and mining **High sciences** of astronomy, optics, and mechanics still held out for demonstration

According to Hacking, the *Port Royal Logic* written in the second half of the seventeenth century by Antonine Arnauld was a landmark book on probability:

> The first three books of the Logic cover Conception, Judgment and Reasoning. The Fourth book is about Order...Reasoning deals with the syllogism, order with deductive, non-syllogistic reasoning such as characterizes most mathematics. In particular, the first ten chapters of Book IV are an elaborate discussion of the notions of "analysis and synthesis"

> which, since classical times, had been supposed to constitute the two kinds of geometrical inference. (*Emergence of Probability*, 74)

The last few chapters have to do with chance based on induction. For example, in book four of *Port Royal Logic* Arnauld has chapters on:

- when to use rationality in determining when to accept human authority
- rules about conditions for considering miracles
- a chapter applying to historical events
- a chapter on contingent events

In the case of miracles, we can see how different this is from the approach of casuistry of the Jesuits we discussed earlier:

> For Arnauld, in order to judge the truth of some event, the event need *not* be considered in isolation, such as a proposition of geometry. Rather, all the circumstances of the events, both internal and external, should be considered. The goal is a calculus for combining evidence to discover which proposition has an acceptable level of probability. It is opposed to casuist arguments where, after settling that a proposition is possible and compatible with some source of doctrine, we consider whether belief in the proposition is approvable—probable—in terms of its consequences. (*Emergence of Probability*, 79)

What do we mean by internal and external circumstances?

- internal circumstances of an event are those that bear on *the time, place, and circumstances* of the event, and whether it is the sort of thing that tends to happen
- external circumstances are those that pertain to the

persons by whose testimony we are led to believe in the occurrence of an event

In other words, internal circumstances are the evidence; external circumstances are the source(s) of the evidence. *Probability became possible only when internal circumstances (signs) were turned into sufficient or at least necessary evidence.* For inductive logic, there are criteria for measuring the quality of evidence, from cogent to weak. These criteria are standards that are *independent of the opinions of authority or the testimony of others.* Inductive probabilities are relative to the evidence.

Why couldn't there be inductive methods sooner?

Inductive methods of reasoning could not have arisen much before 1660 because there were only *indicative* not *associative* signs. Indicative signs only led back to theoretical entities that were not in themselves observable, so these signs were unfalsifiable. For example, the alchemists believed that matter was organized into primary qualities of earth, fire, air, and water. It was thought that these primary qualities were organized according to principles rooted in astrology. They experimented using the secondary qualities of sight, sound, touch, and taste, but whatever they discovered was rooted directly back to primary qualities and, ultimately, to astrology. Neither primary qualities nor astrology lent themselves to being falsifiable.

In the Middle Ages, knowledge and opinion were differences *in kind.* Low sciences such as traditional medicine or the crafts were matters of opinion; high sciences such as religion or law (and for the alchemists, alchemy) were matters of knowledge. On the other hand, an associative sign points to an object or event which is hidden from view, but which in principle could be discovered later, making it falsifiable. Any natural sign becomes *internal evidence.* With internal evidence, it is possible to order different degrees to which hypothesis are supported. In inductive logic *the distinction between knowledge and opinion were matters of degree, not differences in kind*. Now both the high and low sciences collapsed into one another and knowledge became empirical and found through induction. Please examine the table which compares how signs were understood in the Middle Ages as opposed to the seventeenth century.

In the next chapter we will examine how chance and probability were *applied* to law, annuities for merchants, and in games. Further, we will discuss what became of probability theory and chance in the nineteenth century as well as how they were used by the state for crowd control and in accessing mental health.

Table 12.7
Transformation of Signs to Either Circumstantial Evidence or Chance Events

Medieval Science	Category of comparison	Seventeenth century science
Resemblances of macro-micro magical links Paracelsus	**How are signs interpreted?**	Conventional and arbitrary signs invented by humanity
Signs and causes are inseparable	**Relationship between signs and causes**	Signs and causes are distinguished
There are no coincidences Every sign has a meaning	**Place of chance**	Signs are **circumstantial evidence** for causes or **chance events** that may have nothing to do with real causes
Formal or final causes An answer to the essence of something	**Type of cause signs are part of**	**Efficient causes**—how things are made to work
Verisimilitude—evidence is compared to with the object it is supposed to be in essence	**How knowledge is gained?**	**Experiment**—you infer something small, inner, atomic from something larger, outer
Comfort by confirmation of what one already believes	**Why are signs valuable?**	Judged by the **frequency** with which signs **help make predictions** Gaining new inductive evidence for a hypothesis or disconfirming evidence that allows for other exploration

CHAPTER 13

Quantitative Rationality: Application to Law, Economics, State Politics, and Mental Illness in the Eighteenth and Nineteenth Centuries

Orientation

Up until now, I have limited the discussion of probability and chance to the realm of philosophy and science. In this chapter I will apply expectation theory to three areas: law, gambling, and annuities as they were understood in the eighteenth century. I then apply statistical probability theory as it developed in the nineteenth century to the same three areas, with very different results. In addition, I discuss how probability was used by the state to control its population through taxation, recruitment for wars as well as tracking births, marriages and deaths. Lastly, what constituted mental illness in the nineteenth century went from being defined by priests to being the domain of psychiatrists. In the nineteenth century, what was considered mentally ill was weighed against *a statistical norm of the average person*, rather than the judgment of a priest or moralist.

In the last section, I discuss how chance morphed from a wild, accidental exceptional and circumstantial phenomenon to becoming, in Ian Hacking's words, 'domesticated' in the nineteenth century. Domestication meant that chance became built into the structure of *all* phenomenon. Statistical irregularities were a *normal* course of affairs, and it was *determinism* which became the exception rather than the rule.

Qualitative expectation applied to law, annuities, games, and state census

In the previous chapter, I made distinctions in science between qualitative and quantitative empiricists. I also made distinctions between primitive probability of expectation and mature probability, using statistics. I will first apply the methods of qualitative empiricists using expectation theory to four areas: law, annuities, games, and the state. I will then apply quantitative empiricism and statistical rationality to the same four areas. I will begin with qualitative empiricists' use of Roman law.

Reasonable expectations in the seventeenth-century law

The Roman canon theory of proof was intended as a set of mechanical rules to assign arithmetic values of evidence. These included confessions, oaths, written documents, and witnesses which were weighed with varying degrees of conviction by the judge. The hierarchy of proofs within Roman and canon law led theorists to conceive of degrees of probability along a graduated spectrum of belief, ranging from total ignorance or uncertainty to firm conviction or moral certainty. They assigned fractional measures to each type of evidence. Judges were advised to consider the reputation of the witness; age; sex; social standing; relationship to the accused; and any private interest in the case, as well as body language under interrogation. These were matters of *judgment*, not calculation.

In the seventeenth century, legalists aspired to understand what was objectively true by striving to overcome their subjective ignorance. They imagined they did this by being 'reasonable.' In the law, reasonable-ness was a choice made among alternatives by:

- developing a criterion for weighing alternatives
- prioritizing the criteria and converting criteria to a homogenous medium that made comparisons of degree possible

Reason was abstract, deliberate, and analytical. Legalists made a distinction between *intrinsic* probability of the nature of the object or process, as opposed to the *extrinsic* probability that the witnesses are telling the truth.

Between the seventeenth and nineteenth century, the following criteria were further developed by Boyle, Locke, Concordant and John Stuart Mill:

- the number of witnesses
- witnesses' integrity and skill
- the witnesses' social standing
- witnesses' comportment
- internal consistency of statements of witnesses
- eyewitness versus hearsay about the event in question
- ulterior motives of witnesses
- circumstances of the narrative
- corroborative testimony versus contradictory testimony

Condorcet argued that the probability of the account of a witness varied with the difficulty of the observation. He made a distinction between simple and complex facts. A simple fact was one of which a man of ordinary capacity can grasp both the whole and the details in a single glance without a great effort of attention. At a deeper level, complex facts were extraordinary facts and were beyond a person of ordinary capacity. Though they made efforts to specify what the criteria were, they were against quantifying the qualitative.

> Jurists would not have counted the *number of times* someone had seen someone flee a murder scene. Rather they make *causal* inferences between guilt and observed circumstances, not the frequency with which the correlation held. (*Classical Probability in the Enlightenment*, 192)

Probability had been connected to the hierarchy of proofs based on *types* rather than with the *amount* of evidence. The later practice of counting
instances inaugurated by the political arithmeticians was thus a

novel, extra-legal approach to evidence.

Reasonable expectation in annuities

Qualitative legal models were joined to economic ones when applied to merchant ventures, such as what to invest and what insurance premium to charge. In insurance policies on sea-going practices, annuities were adjusted according to the cargo, season, distance, latest reports on pirates, and the reputation of the captain. All of this required prudence. Although these are different qualities from what we just applied to law, they share the same spirit, in that they:

- take apart the individual case
- develop a criterion for weighing
- prioritize the criteria
- weigh the pros and cons

This was not a law of averages, as would develop in the nineteenth century. Expectations were weighed on a case-by-case basis. In the Port Royal version of expectation theory, no general means of reckoning probability were offered beyond the conventional estimations of odds for equiprobable cases. There was no mention of combinations. Like other early expositions of early probability, the Port Royal logic made *expectation* (rather than probability) the central concept, in order to ascertain the conditions that made risk equitable.

Just as law did not spark a quantitative analysis of guilt or innocence, so too, the sale of maritime annuities also failed to spark a quantitative analysis or even a compilation of statistics. The first attempt to apply expectations to annuities made no direct use of mortality statistics. Annuities were framed in legal terms, drawn from contract law.

This order made sense in the context of legal theories that assumed *expectations* rather than *risks*. They aimed at equalizing these expectations in partnerships and other contracts. *Except in extremely simple cases, such as coin tossing and dice throwing, combinational arguments were not feasible, and the data required for statistical evaluations were generally unavailable.* The more complicated situations that involved unequal risks, such as the problems of judging probabilities, were not possible to be solved without more extensive statistical information. Even in games of chance, the enumeration of combinations of equiprobable outcomes quickly became unmanageable. Even Pascal complained about it, according to Daston.

Primitive expectations in games

In dealing with any problems involving chance, we cannot entirely exclude astrology, magic, and signs, because the first known enumeration of combinations of outcomes from three dice was part of a oracular device for *interpreting the future*. For the alchemists of early modern Europe, combinational problems of chance remain thoroughly in league with the alchemical magic of indicative signs.

On the other hand, in everyday world of gaming, the ranking and values of various tosses of dice or combinations of cards were known in considerable detail. Long before anyone could prove mathematically that in poker a straight has a better chance of coming up than a royal flush, it was a standard part of the game to value the flush more highly.

Bringing reason to games of chance

If we were invited to gamble for a given set of prizes, depending on various outcomes, how do we figure out what is a fair price to play in a game? Christian Huygens thought that the lottery was fair if it passed three tests. Three parameters are that:

- the lots must be perfectly symmetric so each can be drawn as easily as any other
- they establish that each drawn lot has an equal chance of turning up

- only one ticket can be distributed per person, and one cannot sell tickets more cheaply if they are purchased in large amount

How do we determine what the fair price is for any gambler who has to pay to enter the game? Partly, the price must factor in the risk of taking the gamble in the first place. Huygens first needed to know the value of any particular gamble when gambling *only once*. Then how do you calculate the expected *average* pay-off in the *long run* of similar gambles? Finally, there is the question of how to justify your answer. To be able to calculate the answer is to develop an expectation theory.

The crudeness of early chance theory can be seen in the following example. Three players, Sandy, Bill and Tony take twelve chips of which four are white and eight are black. The winner is whoever first draws the first white chip. Given that Sandy draws first, Bill draws second and Tony third, what is the ratio of their chances? One of Huygens' parameters was drawing a lot *with replacement*. Each time a black chip was drawn it would be put back into the hat before the next person would draw. But that is only one of at least four parameters that he failed to consider.

Jacques Bernoulli pointed out that there are at least three different interpretations (I've added a fourth):

- drawing a lot with replacement; each time a black chip is drawn it may be put back into the hat
- drawing a lot without replacement; chips are eliminated with every draw out of the hat
- the supposition that each of the three players begins with his own hat of twelve chips and draws without replacement
- each of the three players beginning with their own hat of twelve chips and drawing with replacement

In other words, the chances of drawing for each gambler will vary with these two different parameters: first, whether gamblers are playing with or without replacement of draws from the hat; second, whether they are using a common hat or three separate hats. The possibility of such basic misunderstanding shows how naïve the first expectation's calculus was. Huygens wanted to justify expectation, and did so by the device of equivalent gambles. But he took for granted the simple case of a fair lottery.

In the Middle Ages, an expectation theory was not possible because the very concept of averaging was new. Before 1650, most people could not observe an average because they did not take averages. Huygens wrote the first printed textbook on probability using expectations as the central concept.

Throughout the eighteenth century, the governments in England, Holland, France, Italy, and Germany held lotteries to replenish the treasury and to finance special projects like bridge construction. These lotteries were a state bureaucrat's dream because they could raise revenues without raising taxes. There was little motive for governments to consult mathematicians, since the traditional lottery methods returned good profits (15 to 20 percent).

Pre-statistical chance: fortune

In his book *Man, Play and Games* Roger Caillois argues that there was a relationship between people's willingness to gamble and the degree of despair they felt about their social prospects. Whoever despaired of their own resources to change their situation relied on fate or destiny for a windfall. By studying and utilizing heavenly powers, they could gain a reward they doubted could be won by their own efforts. Where there was uncertainty there was hope, and fortune's wheel, or the wheel of the lottery, became the emblem of hope, especially for those whose lives were crushed by grim predictability. While this tendency was strongest among the lower classes, wealth alone provided no immunity to the passion for playing these games.

It is tempting to think that calculations of mathematical probability such as those of Huygens or Bernouli entered the minds of those who gambled. But the average players of lotteries paid even less attention to the records of the cities and states that ran them. The only 'mathematicians' most lottery players read were *numerologists.* In France, the broadsides and almanacs poured from the presses about magic numbers, prophetic dreams, and lottery stories with happy endings. Apparently, the average player understood chance to mean equal proportions of gains and losses in the short as well as the long run. As Daston says, these players were not the reckoning sort. The extent to which this gambling had a hold on people can be seen in that, even the *storming of the Bastille* could not interrupt the regularly scheduled drawing two days later!

Medieval and Renaissance thinkers wanted to make a place for fortune somewhere between divine providence and willed human agency. Fortune could be saddled with the responsibility for inequality in that it would be too dangerous to charge directly to God. Fortune could be charged with doling out the external goods of wealth, power, beauty, and health.

In the seventeenth and eighteenth centuries, fortune was the ally of all those who sought a crack in either the tightened determinism of the natural order of science, or in the rigidity of the social order. Fortune, after all, was blindfolded, and was impartial and unfair, the champion of equality or the spoiler of just deserts. Fortune was the opposite of prudence, rationality, and calculation.

The message of the lottery was implicitly one of social subversion, and was not lost on conservatives. Anti-gambling legislation drove wealthier players indoors, and the free-for-all cockfights gradually gave way to horse racing and hunting. The professional middle classes gradually withdrew from gambling scene completely in the second half of the century and became its sharpest critics.

Annuities and gambling as seen as interchangeable in the eighteenth century

Generally, we tend to characterize annuities and life insurance as conservative, long term protection against disasters. This, however, is close the opposite of the way we might think of when we gamble using slot machines. Gambling appears to be impulsive and extravagant. But in the eighteenth century, annuities were perceived to be just as reckless as gambling.

Daston informs us that gamblers and insurers (particularly life insurers) were often the *same people*, and insurance offices doubled as betting centers. Like gamblers, insurance office clients were for the most part *betting on the future*, not planning for it. Short-term, immediate buyers and sellers of annuities were reluctant to substitute *general* rules for judgments about the individual case where that option existed. For them, what actually occurred was arbitrary unforeseeable circumstances which could be predicted by using ritual, by claiming to have a lucky charm. If one lost, it was due to being on a streak of bad luck. Daston asks:

> Why was the practice of eighteenth-century insurance and annuities so resistant to the influence of mathematical theory? The case of life insurance is particularly baffling because *the availability* of mortality statistics drawn from several locales and the growing belief that they did revealed long-term regularities. (*Classical Probability in the Enlightenment*, (171-172)

According to Daston, intellectuals in the eighteenth century couldn't make up their minds whether reasonable men were even-handed judges or prudent merchants. Either way, the history of the concept of expectation during the eighteenth century is the history of unsuccessful attempts to get reasonable men to do mathematical calculations. Whether in law or in annuities, classical probabilists probed the psychology of the rational *individual*, seldom turning to large-scale social organization for their answers.

Classical probability theorists did not understand that insurance claims would inevitably increase as the population of members *aged*. Their fixed premiums were constructed more by guesswork than by tables. When De Witt and Halley wanted to price annuities with respect to the *age* of the buyer, they were ignored. It was only when gambling was *severed from insurance* that insurance came to be understood by buyers and sellers as a suitable subject of mathematics. One way to do this was to show the difference in the kind of risks. Gamblers took *unnecessary* risks and were seen as irrational and immoral. On the other hand, buyers of insurance paid to avoid the consequences of *necessary* risk. That made buyers of insurance rational, moral, and prudent.

Transition from qualitative expectation to quantitative probability

Yet all these attempts at measurement were qualitative and prosaic rather than *numerical*. Mathematical calculation of probability was to be the codification of a *new brand of rationality that provided a method to reduce this prosaic good sense to a calculus*. To understand the laws of chance, it is necessary to understand *numerical ratios*. Answering the question 'What are the odds of winning the lottery?' is inevitability a *quantitative* question. Expectation probability is not like this, for you can compare the degree to which evidence warrants several beliefs *without*_using number ratios.

Math was first used in probability and was justified to the extent that they matched the prevailing interpretations and fields of application in legal, medical, and scientific settings. Later, the situation became reversed. The justification within these systems was first sanctioned to the degree it satisfied statistics and the law of large numbers.

Daston argues that certain passages in Aristotle could be construed as an embryonic version of statistical correlation or a scale of subjective probability. More clear-cut elements of math probability, such as enumeration of all possible outcomes for the throw of several dice, was in play as early as the tenth century. In the early modern period, mathematical probability had been sought in astronomy, gambling, medicine, and in the insurance trade. They continued to include other sorts of legal problems, such as credibility of testimony and the design of tribunals. But none of these applications suggest notions of stable statistical frequencies or combinational derivatives of probabilities until the sixteenth century. *Mathematical* probabilities did not emerge until the middle of the seventeenth century. The first formulations were heavily indebted to seventeenth-century legal notions of contract. *These granted late seventeenth-century probability a reprieve from the difficult task of justification.*

<u>Types of direct and indirect probability among the quantitative empiricists</u>

What is the difference between comparing these two probabilities?

- How much more likely is it that a seven rather than a eight will result from tossing two dice?
- How much more likely is it that a young man of twenty years will survive an old one of sixty?

In the first example, since we know the possible combinations that would produce a seven or an eight, we know the ratio of these to the total number of possible outcomes. We can determine the probabilities *a priori*. In the second example, because we don't know all the possible combinations beforehand, we have to find out by drawing on statistics and figure out the probabilities *a posteriori*—that is, after the fact.

Bernouli

Bernouli's theorem and the Urn model of causation suggested the same two types of questions:

- If the number of balls of each type is known a priori than how do we determine the probable results of the drawing? This is called direct probabilities or rationalizing from known causes to effects.

- If only the *results* of the drawings are known a posteriori, how do we determine the probable mixture of the balls? This involves indirect probabilities or rationalizing from known effects to questionable causes.

The early probabilists were interested in the first question. They had enlisted assumptions about physical symmetry and equity to justify equi-possible outcomes and had been unconcerned (with the exception of Cardano) with testing the extent to which these a priori probabilities were borne out by a posteriori observation.

Bernouli was the first mathematician to attempt to address the second question. His theorem opened up a whole new realm of problems for classical probabilities. The art of conjecture needs no longer be restricted to games of chance where equi-possible outcomes could be assumed. Bernouli's theory was the first stepping-stone between theories of probability and statistics.

He addressed such questions such as to what extent assurance improved with the ever-greater number of observations of trials. His work also addressed whether the repeated number of trials indefinitely increased probability, so that the observed ratio of outcomes finally *exceeded* any given degree of certainty, or whether the probability is bounded by its own asymptote, where some degree of certainty is given which it can never exceed, no matter how many observations we accumulate.

The philosophical importance of Bernouli's theories had been *epistemology:* if nature is governed by determinate laws, patient observations will ultimately conform to those laws. Bernoulli's work justified the hope that *counting*, carried on long enough, would determine the proportions and, by degrees, the whole of nature.

Bayes

According to Daston, Bayes was the last great representative of the expectation tradition in mathematical probability until the twentieth century. Bayes addressed the problem where events were known and causes unknown by showing how, when a given event has happened a number of times (or failed to happen a number of times) the expectation of deviation is justified.

Bayes' theorem would show what expectations are warranted by an experiment, according to the different number of times in which they have succeeded and failed. Bayes' theorem was published as early as 1763 but wasn't known in France until 1780.

Thus far, Bayes had solved the problem of rationalizing after the fact for a particular case, namely the one in which every value of an event is assumed to be as probable as any other. Bayes justified this assumption by the properties of the physical model he had chosen: on a perfect table, there was good reason to believe, a priori, that all resting points for the ball were equi-probable.

Poisson

Poisson distrusted the convenient assumption made by Bayes that a priori probabilities of causes were *equal*. Unless inverse probabilities took stock of all relevant information (including that pertaining to *prior* probability distributions), its solutions would contradict observation.

Poisson knew of Quetelet's work (to be discussed shortly) which showed that the rates of marriages, crimes, suicides, and other phenomena remained constant from year to year. Poisson's claims for the law of large numbers differed from De Moivre's interpretation of Bernouli's theorem in two respects:

- Poisson emphasized that the law of large numbers applied to *all* phenomena, not just to the natural realm
- he denied that the law of large numbers implied providential design

The law of large numbers was built into the universe, but

it was a secondary cause. Statistical regularities are indicative of *physical* causes, not the veiled hand of God. At the same time, Poisson could not conceive of the universe as ruled by chance alone.

Quantitative probability applied to law

Leibniz argues that lawyers should have rules for degrees of assent. In law, my right to something may be absolutely true, absolutely void, or it may be conditional. In 1654, mathematicians and intellectuals in Paris met at a salon and began to develop a model for probability calculus for these problems.

By 1665 Leibniz was working on an arithmetic of probability for degrees of proof in law from a generalized theory of games. He wanted to use probability theory for making any quantitative decision in situations where one must act on inconclusive evidence. He published a paper using numbers to represent what he called 'degrees of probability.' He proposed to measure degrees of right in law on a scale between 0 and 1:

- Impossible—0, which corresponded to null
- Necessary—1
- Uncertain—a fraction in between

According to Hacking and Daston, Leibniz was the first to try to axiomatize probability as a pure inferential science and the first to insist that probability theory could serve in a branch of logic comparable to the theory of deduction. He believed that all knowledge should be organized on a Euclidean plan (in other words rationalized' as we described in chapters ten and eleven). In order to represent epistemic probability on a numerical scale, the Port Royal Logic also used gaming as its model.

Concordet's mathematical application to justice in the courts was unprecedented. His probability of judgments included:

- the *number* of judges deciding the case

- the size of the juries involved
- what percentage should count as a majority

For Poisson, the chances of conviction and acquittal varied from one trial to another, just as the chances for the two sides of coin vary from one coin toss to another. This meant that the number of acquittals and convictions would be almost invariable, given a large enough number of trails, just like the ratio of the occurrences of two sides of different coins.

Concordet and Laplace also applied this model to the politics of *legislative* and *electoral* assemblies. Concordet's contractual model saw justice as a kind of contract, in which the risks to the social order were pitted against individual liberty, and were balanced in the same way that risks and potential gains were balanced in a fair game of dice.

Mathematicians against the use of mathematics in court

Poinsot, a mathematician himself, felt that applying mathematics to probability in the courts was a bad move for the probability theory he defended. He thought that to represent *by a number* the truth of a witness; to equate human complexities to the sides of dice, with some designated for error and others for truth, was an aberration of the intellect. John Stuart Mill also condemned attempts to apply the calculus of probabilities to the credibilities of witnesses and the accuracy of judicial verdicts as an offense to good sense.

By the middle of the nineteenth century, the probabilities of testimony and judgment had largely disappeared from texts. Weighing historical and courtroom evidence and designing tribunals once again became *qualitative* matters. The deliberately anti-formal anti-analytic system of free proofs replaced that or legal proofs, substituting an intuitive appeal, the 'intimate conviction' which was a product of the French Revolution. However, statistical reasoning did not disappear; it simply changed its application. Table 13.1 contrasts the two types of quantitative probabilities.

Table 13.1 Types of Quantitative Probability

The relationship between effects and causes Timing of probability	Reasoning from causes to effects (probability a priori)	Reasoning effects to causes (probability a posteriori)
Urn example	If the number of balls of each type is known a priori, the task is to determine the probable results of the drawing (direct probabilities)	If only the results of the drawings are known, the task is to determine the probable mixture of the balls (Bayes, Prices and Laplace), a new set of mathematical probabilities (statistics)
Comparing dice and life insurance example	How much more likely is it that a seven rather than an eight will result from tossing two dice? (probability)	How much more likely is it that a young man of 20 years old will survive to be 60? (statistics) Testing the extent to which these a priori probabilities were borne out by a posteriori observations
Can equi-possible cases be posited?	Yes Equi-possible cases can be plausibly posited	No Probabilities to observed frequencies of events where equi-possible cases could not be plausibly posited; question of how much this assurance improves with the greater number of observations of trials; those probabilities that can only be estimated a posteriori from statistics about the frequency of events
Explanation of equi-possibility	Since we know the possible combinations that would produce a seven or an eight, we know the ratio of these to the total number of possible outcomes; we can determine the probabilities a priori	Since we don't know the possible combinations that a young man of 20 years will survive an old one of 60, we can only determine the probabilities a posteriori

Quantitative Probability in Games: Bernouli

The emergence of theories of randomness started by Leibniz is completed in Jakob Bernouli's book which he wrote between 1680 and 1705. This book both undertakes a self-conscious analysis of the concept of probability and proves to be its first limit theory. Hacking has this to say about him:

> Bernouli's *The Art of Conjecturing* presents the most decisive conceptual innovation in the early history of probability. Its mathematical profundity, its unbounded practical applications, and its constant invitation for philosophizing...(*Emergence of Probability*, 143)

Among other callings, Ian Hacking is a philosopher of science. In looking at the history of scientific method, he claims there are three characteristics of an extraordinary research program which have long-term effects for science:

- it does something almost completely new which was 'in the air' but has never before crystallized
- it epitomizes what everyone has known for a long time but have been unable to state succinctly
- it *ends* certain possible lines of development which until that node in history were perfectly open

Hacking claims Bernouli had fulfilled all three.

The Art of Conjecture comes in four parts. In Part I, Bernouli introduces an improved version of Huygens' book on games of chance. In Part II he develops a theory of combinations for different kinds of evidence. In Part III, a theory of combinations is applied to a sequence of further exercises on games of chance. But it is in the fourth part that he revolutionizes probability theory in the following ways:

- Frequency estimates were the domain of chance; this showed how *observed* frequencies were related to underlying chances. He advocated for specific limits for what constituted certainty and uncertainty. Infinitely, little certainty was the same as impossibility, just as modern statisticians use one to five percent as indicators of significance. The frequency function contains the objective elements of tendency.
- Confidence levels: probability; for the first time, a *scientific* conception of epistemological probability was

> specified. This new kind of probability was distinguished from two other kinds of epistemological uncertainty. One theory Hacking calls 'personalism,' where the basis of uncertainty was the failure to know *one's own mind.* The second kind of uncertainty was *logical* uncertainty where there is failure *to do the logic.* Neither of these kinds of uncertainty was of interest to Bernouli. The third type of uncertainty had to do with neither vagueness or ambiguity of mind or problems with deductive logic. When scientists faced epistemological uncertainty, they had set up an *experiment* to clarify their uncertainty. Further, the scientist had to investigate *how many* repetitions were required before being confident of their estimates.

Bernouli was able to give a fundamental probability set in cases where there were a number of finite possibilities, such as with rolling dice or drawing lots. In the case of dice, so long as each face of the dice were exactly the same shape, and they are made of material that is has a homogeneous distribution density, there was a finite number of possibilities that could be estimated. Given the laws of gravity, there was no reason why one face should by more likely to turn up than another.

In the case of lots, let's say we are drawing lots from an urn filled with black and white slips of paper. All the lots are equally possible, because the number of papers of each kind are determinant and known. Hacking says that Bernouli discovered the weak law of large numbers. This means that in the case of the lots, the numbers of black and white faces that would turn up would be the same if there was a sufficient number of repeated trails. It was due to Bernouli's work that the distinction between aleatory and epistemic concepts of randomness became important.

The problem with knowing the laws of large numbers is that it does not make a prediction of what the *next* roll of the dice or lot drawn will be. Bernouli was not interested in this problem. He was not interested in the mathematics of predicting every trial. Nor was he interested in evaluating the problems of irregular dice, or games whose outcome depend in part on the skill of the players. His problem was one of estimating unknown aleatory possibilities, or chance *in general.*

Quantitative probability in annuities

As we saw earlier, there were good reasons to examine statistics other than for gambling. One reason to deal with chance in a systematic way was the practical problem of the increasing danger to merchants involved in long-distance trade in the sixteenth century. Statistics can be used to determine whether it was profitable for merchants or for the state to own stock. Naturally either choice is effective only when there is some statistical *data* with which to back up either choice. It comes as no surprise that these numbers would show up first in the Netherlands, the great capitalist sea-power of the seventeenth century. Dutch towns sold annuities to raise capital. The problem was how to figure out a method for determining a fair rate.

In simplest terms, if I loan you a thousand dollars, we can agree that you will pay me the lump sum by a certain date with interest. But with an annuity, I propose that you pay me a secure income *as we go*, for an assigned period. Hacking points out that if we disregard the impact of inflation, there are two parameters for determining a fair rate for simple life annuities:

- the mortality curve for the part of the population that buys annuities
- the prevailing rate of interest on long-term loans

What was lacking at the time was a theory of the relation between *the age* of the purchaser and annual payments.

The British attempted to set up an annuity system as early as in 1692, as they tried to raise a million pounds by contracting annuities over a period of fourteen years. The problem was they failed to consider the age of the purchasers. As we know, younger people care far less about annuities than older people do. This meant that although the state was selling annuities at the same rate to young and old, in fact those who bought annuities were disproportionately older and they naturally had more health problems. For the Dutch, the problem was how to sell life and joint annuities. Dutch towns sold and paid annuities in six-month units. If they knew the half-year mortality rate and the rate of interest, they could work out how much an annuity would cost.

Groping for Solutions: De Witt and Huddel

In 1671, John De Witt made a proposal to the Estates General of Holland. He invited them to imagine that there was some physically-determined device which gave us equal chances, such as drawing lots. Second, De Witt argued for a uniform mortality curve limited to *the time when a man is in full vigor.* Full vigor spans from the third or fourth year of life to fifty-three or fifty-four years. Third, De Witt claimed it wasn't more likely that a man should die in the second half of the year than for the first. One finds an equality of chances similar to the case of a tossed penny. So far, De Witt argued only *within a single year.*

Then de Witt used his audience's experience with dice and coins to show that that they should not expect equal distribution every year. Deaths, like dice or coins, sometimes have long aberrant runs.

> So De Witt has to urge that the lottery may combine irregularity within the random. We must not expect every year to have about the same number of deaths; we are to demand only that there is a discernable trend. (*Emergence of Proability*,116)

Huddle argued against De Witt for a uniform death rate. He was more sensitive to the problem of who bought and didn't buy annuities. It was not the death rate of the whole population that should have been considered, but *the death rate of those who are most likely to buy them.* Huddle constructed a mortality curve for that part of the population which is rich enough to buy annuities.

Together, Huddle and De Witt used Dutch annuity records to infer a mortality curve on which to work out the fair price for an annuity. Later, in 1725, de Moivre, whom Hacking characterizes as the finest probabilist of the age, says that from time of birth to the age of twelve, the probabilities of life increase rather than decrease. This accounts for the apparent irregularity of the tables at the beginning.

Summarizing:

- Granunt devised a mortality table on the simple assumption of uniform mortality;
- De Witt imagined that we have uniform mortality up to the prime of life, but that the death rate increases after age fifty-four;
- Huddle narrowed the focus of the analysis by introducing social class; The rich should be the base of the population drawn from, since they are the most likely to buy the annuities.

Transitions away from expectancy in annuities: Bernoulli, d'Alembert, Laplace

Bernoulli argued that the choice facing the average Parisian in 1750 was between a one-in-seven chance of dying of smallpox spread over the long term as opposed to a one-in-200 chance of dying of the inoculation over the short term (one or two months). How do you judge each prospect?

How did the risk for a thirty-year-old, who might have expected to live thirty additional years naturally and thirty-four with inoculation compare to that of an older person who stood to gain the same increment in life expectancy? How would this problem be solved? According to Bernouli's method, the average life expectancy was the same for both curves. Leibniz's argued against Bernouli's brand of reasoning from past observation because:

- in cases as complex as the diseases which beset the human body, the causes *might evolve with time*, discrediting earlier observation
- the number of human diseases could conceivably be infinite, thus rendering comparative ratios of Bernoulli meaningless

D'Alembert continued the criticism of Bernoulli. D'Alembert's list of requirements of a mathematical theory of inoculation depended on:

- accurate mortality tables
- a more sensitive method for computing life expectancies
- a mathematical way of weighing small short-term risks against large long-term ones

For d'Alembert, social mathematics would be a mathematical model of the way reasonable men made decisions and took risks. Laplace proposed a radical simplification in 1774. He said that the probabilistic treatments of social phenomena, no less than coin tosses, should follow observed *frequencies* of events. He complained that conventional probability theory confused *mathematical* with *physical* possibility and he wanted to modify probabilities in the light of physical experience.

The separation of gambling from life insurance in the nineteenth century

Earlier we said that by the nineteenth century the criteria for judging gambling and annuities was interchangeable. Daston points out that in order to develop a more sophisticated understanding of annuities, a change in values was required. These values would break the link between gambling and insurance. Insurance sellers had to be persuaded that:

- long-term regularities counted *more* than short-term ups and downs in order to calculate premiums using the mortality tables
- they had to put their faith and money in *general* rules rather than individual cases
- they had to extend the virtues of prudence and foresight from provision for self to the provision of family which made life insurance preferable to annuities
- they had to dread a sudden *catastrophe* more than they hoped for an unforeseen windfall
- calculations of self-interest had to become a *daily* habit rather than an episodic event
- they had to understand chance did not mean unforeseen exceptional circumstances, but rather *standard deviations that could be averaged*

Were there objective conditions in the nineteenth century that could make people feel less fearful? Daston identifies five positive conditions:

- longer periods of political peace
- the disappearance of pirates from many sea-routes
- improvements in navigation which made sea voyaging a more secure business
- a decrease of fires in cities because more buildings were made of stone and brick than wood and thatch
- mortality on the whole decreased

On the other hand, new risks included:

- smallpox
- malaria
- bad harvests (that made the average gain in years lived not as obvious)

There were good economic reasons for supporting the separation between gambling and annuity. For one thing, annuities provided security against misfortune *without discouraging either industry or activity,* as gambling did. Social scientists feared gambling undermined trust within families and led to the neglect of families. Economists predicted it would decrease productivity by destroying the link between hard work and gain. Among merchants, critics feared gambling would soon lead to a neglect of business projects and loss of reputation. Recurring themes were that gambling was a waste of time and money. Moralists proclaimed that it inflamed greed and destroyed the normal checks and balances between virtues and vices. According to them, the gambler was racked by uncontrollable passions. Probabilists joined forces with the *opponents* of gambling to attack fortune (luck, chance) as a superstition. By 1826, state lotteries were abandoned. Please see Table 13.2 for a summary comparison of attitudes towards risk-taking from Early Modern Europe to the most of the nineteenth century.

Table 13.2 Risk-taking Attitudes in Gambling, Annuities, and Life Insurance

Category of comparison	Sixteenth-seventeenth centuries Chance	Nineteenth century to 1840—Probabilists
Type of insurance	Annuities The sudden appearance of pirates on a sea route to Alexandria	Life insurance Possible death from inoculation
Method of assessment	Prudent judgment based on the particulars of the individual case; the rise of the price of maritime insurance from one day to the next based on: a) nature of the cargo b) the season of the year c) the route taken d) experience of the captain	General rules to determine the fair price of the risk Tables of life expectancies and compound interest; the seller of annuities need not personally interview the annuitant
Scale of social application	Individual cases	General population
Time frame	Short-term, immediate; buyers and sellers of annuities reluctant to substitute general rules for judgments about the individual case where the option existed	Long-term
Type of thinking involved in assessment	Seasoned judgment (reason); anti-statistical	Reckoning (rationality); stability of averages
What does time produce?	Unforeseen accidents; exceptions to the rule	Regularities; laws of Large numbers; time brought large numbers that reveal regularity; deviations from an average cancel each other out
What is the relationship between gambling and insurance?	Gambling and insurance used interchangeably	Gambling and insurance separated
Differentiation of groups?	None; gamblers and insurers (particularly life insurers) often the same people; insurance offices doubled as betting centers	Yes; gambling and insurances were different groups
Are distinctions made between necessary and unnecessary risks?	None	Yes; gamblers pay to take unnecessary risks (irrational, immoral); buyers of insurance pay to avoid the consequences of necessary risk (rational)
Control over the future?	Insurance more reckless; insurance offices and their customers were for the most part betting on the future	Insurance was prudential; planning for the future
Attitudes towards gambling	Acceptable (state lotteries)	Condemned by sociologists, economists, religious authorities; state lotteries abolished (1826)
What is fortune?	A blind force or goddess at once impartial and unfair, who is the champion of equality or the spoiler of just deserts	Probabilists claim fortune to be a superstition
Coping mechanisms for dealing with uncertainty	Rituals, lucky charms, belief in lucky and bad streaks	Ideology of meritocracy

Quantitative rationality and the state

Annuities also made it possible for the state raise money

for wars and expand nationalist loyalty by building monumental architecture. The state did this by selling capitalists military protection in exchange for a steady cash flow. For the state, annuities (as opposed to loans) were a standard way to raise public revenue.

Statistics are necessary in the field of annuities by making judgments based on averages rather than on individual cases. But the state needed statistics on its population for other reasons. It was the absolutist state in England that made it a priority to track the current state of the plague by keeping better records of births and deaths of its population. As early as 1603, the City of London kept bills of mortality and weekly tallies of christenings and burials. It also began to classify deaths according to disease.

The problem, however, was how to *gather* the statistics. Demographic records were less valuable in a feudal society than in a budding capitalist one. When *land* cultivation was the basis of taxation, the king or the nobles did not care exactly how many people there were. Furthermore, because the records of mortality rates first emerged during the worst plagues, they were unreliable.

In spite of these problems, the number of births could be known. In 1662, John Graunt took the number of births known and from this he developed rough idea of the fertility of women. He allowed for the effect of the plague not only through its ravages but also because of the exodus from the city by those who could afford to escape by moving to the country. Graunt could plot the rapid growth of the city and also prove that much of the increase was due to *migration*, not procreation.

William Petty wanted to put statistics to the service of political arithmetic. This included tax collection, military recruitment, the velocity of ships, and the strength of timbers. While Graunt drew the first detailed statistical inferences from the bills of mortality for the city of London, Petty urged the need for a central statistical office.

Once it became possible for Graunt to look at the data *as data*, rather than as a spiritual sign, it was now possible to draw a great many inferences. As we saw in the last chapter, only when the numbers could be grasped independently of their apparent signature can the use of statistics emerge. Inference from statistics, however, evolved slowly because there was not much data.

Accumulation of statistics

In the eighteenth century, amateurs and academics gathered numerical facts accessible to the public, but the facts were not organized systematically. As we saw earlier, eighteenth-century officials collected statistical data for taxation and conscription into the military. However, the information gathered was kept secret from the public. Before 1815, statistical generalizations about populations were largely restricted to births, deaths, and marriages. After 1815, Europeans states established offices to collect and publish statistics on vaccination, schooling, and occupation.

Between 1820 and 1840, states also created new institutions to gather and disseminate this information. They churned out reams of printed statistics and tables. In the case of Prussia, after Napoleon defeated Germany in 1806, statistics were crucial to building up the Prussian state in the nineteenth century.

By the 1830s, innumerable regularities about crime and suicide seemed strange and troubling to statisticians. There were patterns about their relative frequency by month, sex, region, and by nation. Year after year, within one or two units, the same number of suicides turned up by means of drowning, hanging, guns, or poisoning. These statistics varied predictably with the seasons. Then as now, Europeans of every nation were more suicidal in the summer than in the winter. Lord Kelvin's dictum that you knew little about something if you cannot measure it was true for the whole of the nineteenth century. As it turned out, the number of criminals in a given year was constant. We knew in advance how many individuals would be forgerers or murders. In a gruesome way, these numbers allowed the state to project its budget. As Hacking says, 'a budget for the scaffold, the galleys and the prisons.'

By 1837 Poisson proved the law of large numbers. This meant that if one observed a very considerable number of events of the same kind, even though causes of that distribution may vary irregularly, in the long run, the *ratios between the numbers of events* were very nearly constant. The law of large numbers stated that absolute regularity emerged in the long run. From this arose a conception of *pure irregularity*. This type of chance was something wilder and, at the same time, more domesticated than the kinds of chance most Enlightenment theories were willing to tolerate. Remember that Enlightenment theories of chance posited that chance was either subjective or obbective; and if it *was* objective, chance events in nature were *accidental, lawless, unique*. It was a kind of foam on an ocean of determinism.

From wild to domesticated chance in the nineteenth century

God from watchmaker to dice player

Up until now, the Deists' conception of God as a watchmaker who wound up the world and then walked away worked well in a world which seemed determined by natural laws. However, as the theory of chances spread beyond its application in games to the real world, it undermined determinism, whether materialist or spiritualist. If, in the long run, events in the universe had an equal chance of occurring, could long-run statistical stability be the effect of chance itself? De Moivre argued that the statistical regularity required a *divine hand* in order to work. The presence of chance in the universe was seen as evidence of design. God did not merely wind up the clock of the universe; He was also constantly pushing all the objects together according to certain fixed laws.

The English conception of probability in the early eighteenth century, guided by Newton, interpreted the stability of chance processes proven by the limit theorems as evidence of divine design. Newton's idea was of an omnipresent deity who maintains mean statistical values. The Royal society attempted to relate Newtonian science to natural religion. The new science, they hoped, was itself a witness to the deity's handiwork. Royal society theologians made a great deal of the notion that the laws of gravity were merely devices for *computation, prediction and description* of constant regularities. They do not state the *efficient causes* by which bodies attract each other. Those are merely constant conjunctions based on experience. For Moivre, the efficient cause was the regular action of divine energy. Like gravity, the laws of chance are merely description. Statistical laws do not get at efficient causes. God has been smuggled back into the picture. From being once depicted as mechanical clockmaker, God was now understood as the dice thrower.

Quetelet objectifies chance

Laplace and Poisson marked the transition from the eighteenth-century probabilist program to the more statistic orientation of Quetelet. Laplace did not wholly abandon probability hopes for a social mathematics, but rather directed probability towards a different measure of social experience: statistics. Instead of making the conduct and opinions of *reasonable* men their subject, the new breed of probablitists focused on compilations of averages about aspects of society, such as the annual rates of conviction in civil and criminal courts. When Quetelet and his followers abandoned the classical theory around 1840, they abandoned one whole area of application. Projects that Bernoulli and Laplace had considered respectable and central to their theory like probabilities of *causes* and *testimony* struck later probabilities as ridiculously ambitious.

The greatest advocate of the statistical movement of the century was Adolphe Quetelet. An astronomer by profession, by the start of the nineteenth century, he had recognized a law of errors that had been developed in observational astronomy. Whether we think of the normal distribution as an error curve or as a limit of a coin-tossing game, we are concerned with what we think of as real quantities—coins and the celestial position of stars. The coin has a real objective tendency to fall heads in a certain proportion of tosses. So too, the celestial position being measured is a real point in space. The distribution of error is an objective feature of the measuring device *and* of the measurer.

Quetelet's social physics united Laplace's vision of a societal mechanics with the featureless regularity of Poisson's law of large numbers. According to Daston, his conceptual innovations were few. His real contribution lay in his campaign for massive compilations of statistical data.

> Quetelet marks both the end of the classical interpretation and the beginning of a new statistical view of probability. Although he adhered to the Laplacean view of probability as a measure of ignorance...(*Classical Probability Theory in the Enlightenment*, 384)

He was preoccupied with statistics and distributions just as the frequentists were.

Quetelet's conjecture was that human attributes—mental and physical— are distributed just like the tosses of a coin. In his social physics, individuals were the equivalent of variable, accidental causes. He suggested that a great many human attributes had a graph or distribution curve just like that which had long been associated with coin-tossing. In 1844, he applied the same curve to biological and social phenomena. He thought that if social laws existed, they were like laws of physics. This led him to an astronomical conception of society in which forces acting on people were like cosmic forces of gravity. He saw in the behavior of fellow citizens a regularity like the stars.

Quetelet insisted that probability theory sanctioned the *neglect* of individuals who exerted little or no force on the mass. His nineteenth-century successors understood society as an aggregate of all behavior, reasonable or not. Within this mass of data, probability theory would uncover macroscopic regularities about social processes like population growth and the crime rate directly from what seem like microscopic chaos.

Quetelet transformed the theory of measuring unknown physical quantities with a definite probable error into a theory of measuring ideal or abstract properties of a population. He transformed the mean into a *real* quantity. He had made mean structure such as eye color, artistic skill, or disease into real quantities. This was a crucial step in the 'taming of chance' to which Hacking referred. It began to turn statistical laws that were merely *descriptive* of large-scale regularities into laws of nature and society that dealt with underlying truths and causes.

Are statistical regularities fate?

By the 1830s, human behavior was lumped under new probabilistic laws that were constantly grasped as if they were laws of gravity. In 1830, laws of society were seen as akin to physics and determinism. If statistically every year so many people would kill themselves in a given region, then it appeared that no matter what social laws are enacted, a certain amount of people would commit suicide. If there were statistical laws of crime and suicide, then is it fair to say criminals were just victims of circumstance? The answer is no.

Statistics isn't just about tracking normalcy in people. It had fewer abstract applications in the exercise of political power. Quetelet wanted to use statistics as a tool for reform. Statistics revealed not only regularities but *exceptions* to the rule, a law of variation. In the service of utilitarian 'greatest good for the greatest number,' social laws could be used as a basis for reform. For example, the knowledge of these numbers could be used in legislation in favor of improving the status of cultural minorities such as the Jews.

From the political right wing, statistics about Jews in 1880 led to anti-Semitism in Prussia. But from the liberal wing, Neumann and Virchow used statistics to implement sanitation reforms. Neumann was concerned about the uneven distribution of healthcare across the kingdom. He hoped these reforms could change whole districts. It is not a 'law' that Germans die sooner than the English. These phenomena are a product of society, and can be altered by political reform.

What's Normal?

In the nineteenth century, the idea of 'human nature' prevalent in the Enlightenment was replaced by a model of 'normal' people with statistical laws of dispersion. For a foundation for normalcy to be built, the researcher needed law-like statistical regularities of large populations. Yet to call someone 'normal' raises a complicated question.

If I ask you whether or not you are normal, you probably have mixed feelings about your answer. As your reference, you will probably think about how your characteristics relate to other people, but at the same time, the word implies an evaluation: you are not abnormal or pathological. In the early nineteenth-century medical terminology, 'normal' was the *opposite* of pathological.

Until Broussais, the pathological state was understood to obey laws *completely different* from those governing the normal state, so that observation of one could say little about the existence of the other. Broussiais established that the phenomena of illness are essentially the same kind as those of health, from which they differed only in *intensity*, not in kind. Before the nineteenth century, the number of suicides was tracked, but before the nineteenth century it was considered the domain of moralists or priests. By the nineteenth century, doctors began to have a right to guard, treat, control, and judge suicides. Statistically-minded doctors did not think that suicide was uniformly identical with madness. However, to use normal to mean *usual* or *typical* emerged only in the 1820s. It soon spread from medical diagnosis to states of domestic political climate, diplomatic relations and even the behavior of molecules.

Why did Galton and not Quetelet invent the theory of regression and correction?

In England, Quetelet's bell-shaped curve came to be named the 'Normal Law.' It was taken to be true of a vast range of phenomena, and showed how regularity arose within what first appeared disorderly. While Quetelet was preoccupied with averages, Galton was interested in the exceptional. Galton wanted to explain law-like phenomena about the distribution of hereditary genius in gifted families. So when each looked at the Bell curve, they focused on different things. Quetelet looked at the central tendency (the average) whereas Galton looked at the *tails* of distribution, that is the 'deviation from the mean' and the dispersion. The concentration on dispersion led to correlation coefficients. Whereas Quetelet made average height into something real, Galton added another tier of reality. He made correlations as real as causes. A was not the sole cause of B, but it contributed to the production of B. There may be other, many or few causes at work, some of which we do not know and may never know.

Table 13.3 summarizes the differences between conceptions of chance as 'wild' in the Enlightenment compared to "domesticated" in the nineteenth century. These comparisons are applied to state census, crime, and normalcy.

Table 13.3 From Wild to Domesticated Chance

Eighteenth-century Enlightenment 'wild' chance 1650-1840 classical probability	Category of comparison	Early nineteenth century 'domesticated' chance
Objective world determined by inexorable laws: Hobbes, Locke, Hume, Laplace	**Place of determinism**	Determinism eroded; Hamilton distinguished (1846) between determinism (having to do with motives) and necessitarianism (driven by efficient causes, which is fate)
Occasional irregularity; fortune, lawlessness, accidents	**What is chance in nature?**	Elimination of accidents; pure irregularity; every year the same number of crimes
Dominated by Laplacean subjectivism; probability due to superstition, laziness, ignorance of human minds	**What is probability?**	Poisson overturns Laplace (1837) using statistical inferences, proving the law of large numbers
De Morgan: probability is a feeling in the mind and not circumstances; it is the sister science of formal logic	**Theorists**	Venn: invented the frequency account, which combines individual irregularity with aggregate regularity
?	**How quickly do the relative frequencies tend to stabilize?**	Bernoulli trials: drawing with replacement from a single urn Poisson trials: drawing with replacement from multiple urns
Table of measurable properties of a physical object, such as the weight of the earth	**What are statistics?**	Abstract fundamental constants, which fix parameters, then boundary conditions Poggendorf's constants: solar system, force of gravity, atomic weights
Measuring unknown physical qualities with a definite probability error	**What is being measured?**	Measured ideal or abstract properties of a population which become real qualities
Counting (by census)	**How is it measured?**	1826-1829: from counting to minute classification of people counted
Condorcet (dies in 1795): social mathematics stirred by Newtonian ambitions of laws of society	**What social processes govern individuals?**	Social averages; law of large numbers
Taxation, recruitment, and tracking births, deaths and marriages; information was private with the state	**How the state uses statistics**	Avalanche of printed numbers Between 1820-1840; used for crime (including prostitution), suicide, madness, disease, vagrancy; Information is public
Human nature	**What is normal?**	Normal is average (Quetelet); normal people as usual and typical and associated with laws of dispersion brought order out of chaos; normal is mediocre (Galton); deviation from the mean
Pathologies obeys laws different from those of a normal state	**What are pathologies?**	Diseases are of the same kind as those of health and differ only in intensity
Suicides the domains of moralists or priests	**Who presides over pathology?**	Wards of doctors who directed asylums; they have a right to guard, treat, control and judge suicides

CHAPTER 14

Cognitive Evolution: Amplification of Concrete Operations in Early Modern Europe

Orientation

Are rationality, epistemological probability, and the laws of chance related?

In chapters ten and eleven, I described a process by which two forms of thinking—reason and rationality—competed with each other, with rationality being predominant among scientists in the seventeenth century and then being challenged in the nineteenth and twentieth centuries. At the same time the rational mode of thinking among scientists was in its heyday, another form of thinking arose alongside it which we discussed in chapter twelve and thirteen. As a result of the need for merchants to develop insurance policies as well as the state's desire to keep track of its population, an appreciation of statistical thinking arose. But how are reason (qualitative thinking) and rationality (quantitative thinking) related? In this chapter and the next, I argue that there is a way of thinking that combines qualitative and quantitative cognition that represented a new stage of thinking. This occurred initially among scientists, merchants, and lawyers, and then later, to a lesser degree, among the lower classes. This way of thinking was called formal operations by Piaget.

The controversy over cognitive evolution in history

Anthropologists and biologists agree that neither cultural nor physical evolution stopped with the coming of Homo Sapiens. Biologists will point to the physical changes in body types and skin color based on whether people live in hot or cold climates and the amount of sunlight they can count on. But what happens when we come to *cognitive* evolution?

Sociologists such as Durkheim and anthropologists like Levi-Strauss argue against any cognitive differences in how cultures process information. Most anthropologists today (cultural relativists) still hold that how adults reason is the same regardless of the type of society, the point in history, and the social class an individual is born into.

However, between 1100 CE through the High Middle Ages, long before the scientific revolution, let alone the development of industrial capitalism, there were the following revolutionary changes in mathematics, painting, musical notations, record keeping, mapmaking and image-making:

- from Roman numerals to the use of Hindu-Arabic numbers
- from counting and simple arithmetic to the use of algebra
- from no accounts receivable or payable to double-entry bookkeeping
- from spiritual sites where mythological beings are mixed with land and sea, to secular, objective, cartographic maps
- from painting two-dimensionally to painting in three dimensional perspectival illusions
- from using Gregorian chants to written scores and polyphonic singing

How could these extraordinary innovations in math, accounting, mapmaking, and music occur *without* a significant change in mental processes? How could mental processes of cultures remain the same despite vast changes. Please see Table 14.3 at the end of the chapter for an overview.

<u>In defense of neo-cognitive evolution</u>

Anthropologist Jack Goody (1977,1986, 1987) argued that the development of literacy within societies encourages the development of new processes of classification and memory in the mind. Another anthropologist C.R. Hallpike argued similarly about the ancient world and suggested further that the scientific revolution in the seventeenth century initiated a new stage of mental development. Attempts at categorizing stages of mentality, the 'primitive / civilization divide' were been made by Levi-Bruhl, Levi-Strauss, G.R. Lloyd, Alexander Luria (see Lerro, 2000 for more in depth summaries).

However, what these anthropologists and historians lacked was scientific research into the *psychology* of how human beings mentally develop *as individuals* from childhood to adulthood as a starting point. One exception among anthropologists and historians is C.R. Hallpike. Hallpike poses a whole other challenge to cultural relativist anthropology because he was both an anthropologist and very knowledgeable about Piaget's stages of development.

Hallpike's argument is that Piaget's four stages of cognitive development—sensory-motor, preoperational, concrete operational, and formal operational—will be amplified or muted depending on the presence or absence of certain social institutions. Like Goody and Luria, Hallpike thinks that the emergence of the state, the division from labor between mental and manual labor and the invention of coined money in the Bronze and Iron Ages allowed mental workers to both adapt to and create writing and numbering systems. These new inventions helped to advance *concrete operational cognition*. Hallpike also thought that the scientific revolution and the experimental method in the seventeenth century lead to a corresponding cognitive revolution in the amplification of *formal* operational thinking itself.

There are at least three other texts other than Hallpike's work that root Piaget's stages of development in technological, economic, and political changes that have occurred in history. Charles Radding, in his book A *World Made By Man*, uses Piaget's stages of cognitive development to explain a clear change in the thinking processes in Europeans between the early and late Middle Ages in the areas of spirituality, politics, and criminal justice. Radding argues that people in the early Middle Ages practiced a form of pre-operational thinking which was different from the operational thinking of the central Middle Ages.

The second text is a work by Don Le Pan, *The Cognitive Revolution in Western Culture*. Le Pan uses Piaget's stages to explain historical changes that occurred in play-writing and theatrical presentations between the Middle Ages and the time of Shakespeare in early modern Europe. Le Pan argues that pre-operational thinking characterized playwriting in the Middle Ages. This included plot construction, character development, and the relationship between the stage and the audience. Le Pan's point is that playwrights and audiences had to begin to use concrete operational thinking to understand these plays. Then they took these skills with them in their work settings and these new skills helped to revolutionize other social institutions.

The third text is by art historian Suzi Gablik. In her book *Progress in Art* she argues that art in the ancient world corresponds to Piaget's preoperational thinking. Concrete operations can be seen European artwork from the thirteenth century Renaissance through the nineteenth century. She argues that formal operations in art begins in the late nineteenth century with the impressionists and into the twentieth with the work of the cubists and Russian formalists.

In my work *From Earth Spirits to Skygods* (2000) I attempted to show how, prior to the rise of the state, the general mode of thinking was pre-operational. With the rise of the state, there was a division of labor between mental and physical labor which allowed mental workers to develop the cognitive skills of concrete operational thinking. Lastly the invention of the alphabet and coined money in Greece encouraged more people to develop a more abstract form of thinking which I characterized as early formal operational thinking. The changeover from earth-spirits to sky gods, from magic to monotheism, is inseparable from changes in cognition.

Just as complexity in social evolution is an adaptive response to rapidly changing ecological and demographic pressures, so we follow Piaget and claim that cognitive evolution is an adaption of problem-solving skills for increasingly complex social problems of cooperation in occupational settings, politics, economics, and child-rearing. To qualify, cognitive evolution is neither about changes in the *physical structure* of the brain, the quality of *content* in the mind, or a specific set of mental skills you possess such as reading, writing, or math. Cognitive evolution is about cognitive *processes* that take place in the adaptation process.

Can Piaget and Vygotsky Be Synthesized?

Piaget and Vygotsky had important similarities. They both opposed the behaviorists reduction of consciousness to 'behavior'. So too, they opposed nativists reduction of human consciousness to 'instincts'. At the other end, while both were sympathetic to the Gestalt theory of perception where human consciousness was a whole which was more than the sum of its parts, they both criticized it as being static rather than *developing*. Both Vygotsky and Piaget believed that there were qualitative leaps between levels of development.

The second commonality was they both agreed that cognitive development was rooted in *actions* and could not be simply something that goes on inside the body and mind of the individual. Furthermore, both agreed that actions were driven by goals, unlike the behaviorists whose behavior was driven by associations and consequences, both of which came from external forces. Third, they were both dialectical. They explained development processes as a result of multiple causation where what was once a cause becomes an effect. This was opposed to looking for a single cause. Fourth, each was skeptical of what research on human beings could be achieved in a lab. Both used interviewing techniques. Fifth, both did not think much of intelligence testing in formal settings for different reasons. Lastly, both were interdisciplinary. Piaget started as biologist and a philosopher before he came to psychology and he never put these disciplines aside in his psychological work. As for Vygotsky, before becoming a psychologist, Vygotsky was an art critic, producer of plays, and a Marxist.

Vygotsky and Piaget had many differences. For one thing, each came out of radically different philosophical influences. Piaget was most influenced by Kant and Ernst Mach, while Vygotsky's influences were Spinoza, Hegel, and, of course, Marx and Engels. They also disagreed over the nature of human beings. Piaget saw human beings as primarily bio-psychological creatures. He once said that prior to the ages of seven or eight, children didn't have much of a social life. Vygotsky saw human beings as primarily socio-historical beings right from birth, with biology only setting the necessary conditions.

The third difference has to do with the relationship between language and thought. Piaget argued that language was a *product* of cognitive maturation, an add-on *after* thinking is completed. Vygotsky saw language as a *mediator* for the completion of thought. Fourth, Vygotsky and Piaget saw the role of adults and schooling very differently. Piaget trusted children to spontaneously learn new things and argued that adults were just background sources who provided a setting in which children learned. The same function was played out in schools. Vygotsky argued that, left to their own devices, children are not spontaneously curious. It takes adults to get the ball rolling. Children only sustain curiosity when adults take center stage first. In the case of schooling, Vygotsky argued that without school scientific concepts cannot be learned. Children do not naturally learn to think more scientifically as a product of maturation.

Fifth, in the relationship between learning and development, Piaget emphasized that maturation leads learning. For him, learning is a secondary process which occurs later in time. For Vygotsky, cooperative learning through the zone of proximal development is the leading edge of maturation. Our biological nature becomes background, and the older we get the more our social learning takes over.

Each had theories of cognitive development. Piaget's stages, as we will see in detail shortly, were sensory-motor, pre-operational, concrete operational, and formal operational. Vygotsky, in his book *Thought and Language*, argued that children go through four cognitive stages: syncretism, complexification, graphic-functional, and categorical deductive. A comparison of these stages shows considerable overlap.

There are many other differences, but these differences center around child development, not history. For our purposes, the most important difference between Piaget and Vygotsky centers around whether the stages of cognitive development are affected by history. Piaget argues in *Psychogenesis and the History of Science* that his four cognitive stages of development are not affected by social evolution. All four of his stages will unfold inside the individual, regardless of whether the society is composed of hunter-gatherers, horticulturalists, agriculturalists, herders, or industrial-capitalists. Vygotsky and his colleagues Luria and Leontiev disagreed. Luria did research on the impact on peasants of the Russian revolution. In the late 1920s, he found that peasants underwent profound changes in perception, how they categorize, their concepts of self, and cognition. He found changes in cognition from thinking complexes to the graphic-functional to categorical-deductive as peasants moved from the countryside to the cities.

As a Vygotskyan, why am I using Piaget's stages as a foundation for cognitive evolution in history and not Vygotsky and Luria's model? For one thing, though rightly criticized for some shortcomings, Piaget's four stages have stood the test of time. While the ages children and adolescents go through his stages are not what Piaget originally proposed, the sequence of the stages as well as their contents have held up. As for Vygotsky and Luria's work, the work of a group in Russia whom Yurily Karpov calls "Neo-Vygotskians" (*The Neo-Vygotskian Approach to Child Development)* does not follow up on Vygotsky's and Luria's stages of cognitive development. In addition, it is far more difficult to find research from Russia, where most of his Marxian followers are likely to be. Many of the books have not been translated from Russian to English. In addition, if the books have been published, they are extremely expensive for an author no longer affiliated with an educational institution. Lastly, Vygotsky and his colleagues were in and out of trouble with Stalin and it is hard to know how much their research has been lost, suppressed, or marginalized.

Purposes of this chapter

In the first section of this chapter, my purpose is to define what abstraction is and then to contract Piaget's preoperational to operational cognition. I begin with how space, time, and number were understood in the Middle Ages. Then I do the same for early modern Europe. The bulk of the chapter is to show that between the High Middle Ages and the Renaissance, the emergence of algebra, the invention of clocks, double-entry bookkeeping, mapmaking, musical scores, and military strategies help produce an expansion of concrete operational thinking.

My intention is to show that that thinking processes are not initially *internal* processes which unfold inside individuals regardless of the kind of society they exist in. I propose that Piaget's stages are either amplified or muffled based on the type of society they occur in, their point in world history, and the class location of the people being examined. Following Vygotsky and Luria, the whole point here and in the next chapter is to show how the skill of abstraction, like all higher psychological processes:

- begins as a *social relation* between people, specifically the invention of the new symbol-systems, technology, economy and politics
- these social relations became internalized in the form of new levels of cognition
- these internalized thinking processes lead to the maintenance of existing social systems and the discoveries of new social tools which challenge the existing social order

Let's begin with a brief understanding of Piaget's stages of development.

What drives higher forms of cognition?

What is abstraction and what are its phases?

Abstract thinking is common to all human beings as a result of the cultivation of language, which allows us to think beyond the here-and-now. The process of abstraction can be broken down into three moments: extraction, deliberation, and generalization. Extraction is the process in which I pull out the essentials from the inessentials of a situation. It allows me to keep from being buried by the present situation in all its endless detail, or as William James once said, a blooming, buzzing confusion. As a college teacher I am subjected to sounds coming from other classrooms, a fly buzzing around in my classroom, or the temperature in the room being a bit too warm or too cold. However, I do not abandon my lecture to chase the fly. Extraction is the moment I extract my responsibilities as a lecturer and tell myself that my lecture overrides my sense data.

The second moment of abstraction is deliberation which occurs when I compare what a situation I just extracted has to do with previous situations in classrooms that I have already lived through. So, even though the state of my classroom is not ideal, I deliberate. I compare it to other classroom situations at this time of year. Deliberation also involves what I have learned from past mistakes and how I incorporate them into the present. The third moment of abstraction is generalization. This is when I evaluate whether what I have learned in my deliberation has worked relative to future teaching situations. Generalization comes in when I debate whether my current classroom strategies of closing the doors, shutting the windows, and turning the temperature up or down are adequate in future teacher settings. If not, I need to contact the administration to make adjustments.

Conversely, a person thinking in a concrete way would have trouble distinguishing the essential from inessential properties of things and would be lost in the accidental properties of situations such as a dim lighting or the smell of food in the next room. Having little sense of what was important in the present situation, they would have difficulty comparing the present to the past because there is too much undifferentiated material to compare. The same would be true in generalizing about the future. On the whole, a person who thought more concretely would not learn much from one situation to another. They would repeat the same actions regardless of time, place, and circumstance. A concrete thinker is buried in the present. An abstract thinker uses the present to learn about the past and then project new interventions into the future.

Piaget's stages in general

The movement from concrete to increasingly abstract thinking is beautifully described in Jean Piaget's stages of cognitive development.
Piaget discovered that the average child that he studied in France from infancy to adolescence went through four stages of cognitive development. The characterizations of them as body, action, mind combinations are my own.

> Sensory-motor—from birth to to age 2—body-action intelligence
> Pre-operational—2 to 7 years of age—body-action-mind intelligence
> Concrete operational—7 to 11—mind-body-action intelligence
> Formal Operation—12 through adulthood—mind-mind intelligence

What drives these stages forward is an increasingly complex environment the individual is faced with as he grows into adulthood. This environment requires an increase in problem-solving skills. Each of the four stages are a distinct and complete worldview which contain specific answers to questions of how time, space, causality, chance, and number are organized in the objective world. In addition, within the mind, there are changes in how to classify and construct language and how even the mind *itself* is understood. There is, then, a sensory-motor understanding of space, time, cause, a preoperational comprehension of space, time cause, et cetera.

After describing the differences between pre-operational and operational cognition in the next section, we will go on to name technologies that developed between 1250 to 1600 CE that supported the amplification of concrete operational thinking. Then in the next chapter we'll be ready for the next phase in cognitive evolution: formal operations which begins in the seventeenth century.

Table 14.1 Piaget's Stages of Cognitive Development

Preoperational thought	Category of comparison	Operational thought
Pre-objective and pre-subjective Properties of matter are fused with sensations	**Relationship between the outer world and inner world**	**Objectivity and subjectivity** Properties of matter, size, and motion (primary qualities) are distinguished from sensation and perceptions (secondary characteristics)
Dreams and reality are unstable and sometimes confused	Relationship between dreams and reality	Dreams and reality are clearly distinguished
Objective reality is teeming with symbolic meaning Names have power Magical symbols and numbers **Conceptual realism**	Names and symbols	Objective reality is independent of how it is symbolized and named. Names and symbols are understood as conventions
Actions are confused with images and thinking	Relationship between objective actions, images and thinking	Actions are independent of images and thinking
Mind is fused with the body and not understood as a mediator between the internal world and the external world Mind is described as breath or smoke	**Relationship between the mind and the body within the inner world**	**Mind is distinguished from the body** and is understood as an invisible mediator which has closed integrative relations which are autonomous from the body
Contextual time Time is mixed up with concrete events and cannot be separated from them	**How is time perceived?**	**Absolute time** Time is independent of events
Contextual space Space is inseparable from human projections: left, right, up, down, above below; Four directions have psychic properties **Perceptual space** Cannot represent the world spatially—lacks objective perspective independent of where they are **Topographical space** Just an extension of human scale	**How is space perceived?**	**Absolute space** Space is independent of human projections Four directions have no psychic properties **Conceptual space** Capacity to represent the world in drawing, modeling perspective drawing cartography **Euclidean space** Conservation of straight lines, parallels, and angles
Animistic causality **Projection** of human psychological properties onto objective reality **Introjection** of physical processes on to the operations of the mind **Sympathetic magic**	Causality	**Physical Causality** Physical events can be explained through the interaction with other physical objects independently of internal essences, will or purpose
Irreversible operations which mimic and narrate the temporal flow of events in local place and time **Enslaved to Appearances** Difficulty distinguishing illusions from reality	**Relationship between physical events in nature and thinking operations**	**Reversible operations** in which the mind reverses the flow of natural events in order to create logical coherency and draws from global space and past and future time **Appearances can be illusions** Can conserve, length, quantity, weight, volume and number
Hypostatization. Nature consists of unrelated **qualitative essences which cannot be measured mathematically**	**Quantities and Qualities in nature**	Laws of nature **can be quantified and measured mathematically**
Complexive classification Objects are grouped based on perceptual **proximity, functionality and situational** considerations	Classification systems	**Taxonomic classification** Objects are decontextualized and grouped based on **similarity of categories**
Transductive Confusion when moving from the whole to the parts and moving from the parts to the whole (composition and division fallacies)	Type of reasoning	**Inductive and deductive** Can clearly distinguish between moving from whole to the parts and from parts to the whole

Preoperational versus operational cognition

The literature on the work of Piaget is vast. I will be using the Flavell book (1968) to summarize along with Hallpike's text *Foundations of Primitive Thought*. Space does not permit us to go into depth, but Table 14.1 does categorize many of the difference between pre-Operational and operational cognition. Please take a few minutes to allow the differences in thinking to seep in. Understanding this table is crucial because I will be claiming that many of the social institutions that were built in the early modern world are expressions of the transition from pre-operational thinking in the Middle Ages to operational thinking in the early modern age.

At this point it is necessary to describe two global differences between pre-operational thinking and operational thinking simply in terms of an individual's development. The two most important global differences are that in preoperational thinking the boundaries between the objective world and the subjective world of psychology are porous. In operational thinking, we find the beginnings of hard boundaries between the objective world and the psychological world. The second difference is that in preoperational thinking the mental processes in the mind and the physical processes of the body are fused with each other. It isn't until the individual develops operational thinking that the mind is understood as a mediator between the external world on the one hand and the body on the other. From these two global differences flow differences in how time, space, causality, classification systems, and reasoning processes flow.

.

The passion for quantifying in early modern Europe

<u>The passion for quantifying</u>

Between 1250 and 1600 CE, Western society when through several changes in how time and space was perceived, and this impacted the disciplines of astronomy, mathematics, painting, music, commercial exchange, accounting, and military technology. What do the use of Hindu-Arabic numbers, linear perspective painting, polyphonic singing ,and double-entry bookkeeping have in common? These are just some of the questions Alfred Crosby attempts to answer in his clear and ambitious book *The Measure of Reality.* Crosby argues that the mania for quantification was behind all these inventions. I will add that all these inventions required operational cognition to be carried out.

Quanta means breaking things down into parts that are uniform and then counting them. The four steps in quantification include (this could be prices at a fair or the course of a planet through outer space):

- reducing what you are measuring to the minimum required by its definition
- visualizing it on paper
- dividing it into equal quanta
- measuring it—count the quanta

Spatially, material objects are broken into leagues, miles, degrees, and angles. Astronomically, quantification breaks planets down into orbits. Paintings are quantified into geometrical lines, squares, and circles. Music is quantified by musical staffs, and commerce is broken down into the ledgers and columns of accountants. Time is broken down on clocks which have hours and minutes.

According to Crosby, by the fifteenth century, the West had a greater proportion of individuals who understood wheels, levers, and gears than any other region on earth. According to Jane Gleeson-White (2011), this led to the following innovations:

- spectacles to correct eyesight
- written marine charts for navigation
- the first frescoes painted using artificial perspective
- clocks that began to regulate daily life in the city

- military weapons and protections such as citadels of the state, towers, trenches, and ramparts.

An overview of time, space, and number in the Middle Ages

Space

Time and space in the Middle Ages was easy to understand. Space was perceived to be a plenum (rather than a void), a closed system with the earth in the center. Through this space, qualitatively different objects moved. Space in this time consisted of an outer layer which held fixed stars. Closer to home, the planets, sun, and moon moved in perfect circles. Motion in a straight line was antithetical to the nature of the heavens. Everything below the moon was changeable and consisted of four elements, descending from fire and air to water and earth. The cardinal directions, instead of being neutral indicators, embodied spiritual qualities or correspondences that were a macro-interpretation of Galen's temperament theory.

Maps were a hodge-podge mixture of mythology and spiritual sites weaved in between actual depictions of land and sea. As Crosby says, maps were more like expressionist portraits than a geographical survey. Either people in the Middle Ages did not have translations of Ptolemy or Euclid, or they studiously ignored the measurement sections of their work. Medieval maps had nothing like inches, degrees of arc or indicators of heat and cold in various geographical areas.

Time

Sacred Time had a beginning (Creation) and an end (Last Judgment), and it was directed teleologically by God. Infinity is an attribute of God (not the world). At a macro level of history, the crucifixion of Christ was the axis of history. Sacred time was divided into three blocks: from creation to the giving of the ten commandments, then from commandments to the Incarnation of Christ, and, lastly, from incarnation to the second coming.

Time was envisioned not as a straight line marked off in equal quanta but a stage for the enactment of a cosmic salvation verses damnation drama.

In terms of everyday life, most people relied on a system of time proclaimed by *church bells* rather than clocks. These church bells were synchronized throughout the day as the seven canonical hours when prayers were to be said. In terms of secular history, people in the Middle Ages, like all people living in a predominately agricultural society, believed in patterns of *cyclic* time in its rounds of seasons.

Numbers: life without quantities

We tend to think of numbers as having nothing to do with spirituality. They are simply the names we use to count things. The number one has no spiritual meaning any more than two, three, or four. For those living in the Middle Ages, however, their most important application of numbers was as indicators of spiritual realms. For example, the Catholic symbol the trinity. Even today, we have the vestiges of the supernatural in numbers in the number thirteen being an unlucky number. In the early Middle Ages, people were reaching not for a handle on material reality, but for a clue as to what lay *beyond* reality. In such a world, the balance scale and the yardstick were just devices used halfheartedly for immediate convenience.

Crosby argues that we are most different from the Medieval world in designations of quantity. Whether it is in religious stories of the lives of saints, in historiography, technology, military history or civic oratory, description was never precise. Description was either vague or it was exaggerated. For example, in the lives of the saints, there is no date given as to when the saint was born or died. When it came to recipes used, whether in mixing paint, glassmaking, or smelting iron for blacksmithing, the units of measurement were not numbers. They are nails, fingers, hands, arms feet, thumbs, and straws. Instead of a numerically precise amount of an ingredient we find 'a bit more' or a 'medium size piece'.

In battle causalities, metaphors are used for the numbers of people killed such as 'died off like locusts' rather than a precise number. There was a scorn for numerical accuracy. When they used numbers they exaggerated, using them for psychological effect, not for accuracy.

Middle Agers were interested in the general and impressionistic rather than specific and concrete. Mathematically, they had no signs for plus and minus, divide, equal, or square root. They did not know about place value or zero. Most of the mathematics that went beyond counting and simple arithmetic was still expressed verbally. Their system of numeral expression was adequate enough for the weekly market or for local tax collection. For more difficult problems they used the abacus or counting board, but these had their problems as we shall see. Their sub-Euclidean understanding of geometry explains a large part of their ineptness in reasoning about quantities.

In the first period of the Middle Ages, major preoccupation with numbering was calendar reckoning for anticipating the end of the world. Though Charlemagne showed interest in math and wanted math rather than grammar taught in monastic schools, the monasteries were against it. Arithmetic was not a subject for school boys, rather only for a handful of mature students. Of the leading ancient literate cultures, Latin has been the least numerate. As late as 1130, we find the Church prevented subordinates from counting provisions during a crisis, claiming that this indicated that you mistrusted God. The limit of clear numerical consciousness for most of the literate people was arithmetic in using Roman numerals. People who did math in the Middle Ages learned enough arithmetic to keep accounts, do geometry for land surveying, and use astrology to calculate the dates of Christina feasts and fasts.

Inventions in early Modern Europe that invited concrete operational cognition

Growth of commerce, church,sand State the High Middle Ages

Crosby points out that the West's population doubled and may even have tripled between 1000 and 1340 CE. An expanding population, a growth in the Catholic church, the threat of various heresies, the centralization of the state, and expanding mercantile markets together produced a demand for more teachers, scholars, bureaucrats, and preachers. The new public were buyers, sellers, money changers, merchants, lawyers, scribes, and civil servants. Le Goff called this entire period an atmosphere of calculation with a growing emphasis on the precision and quantification of physical phenomena. These social conditions invited humans to think more *operationally* about nature and society. The idea that a person's thoughts could be used to control things in the world outside him through science was just beginning in 1100 CE to 1300 CE.

Economic stagnation ended in the last quarter of the tenth century and with it the reign of literacy over numeracy was coming to an end. A shift can be seen even in the mental habits of the literate, beginning with the introduction of the abacus in the late tenth century and at its end with the transition to the use of Arabic numerals in the middle of the twelfth century.

Absolute time: clocks

Just as numbers became quantified as independent of spiritual meaning, so time became unhinged from physical and spiritual activities. During the Middle Ages time was inseparable from the changing of the seasons and the waxing and waning of the agricultural cycles. In the cities, as was mentioned, time was regulated by church bells. As Crosby quotes Rabelais, "a city without bells is like a blind man without a stick". The problem was there were too few bell-tolls per day to provide a suitable tempo for urban schedules.

Previous attempts to measure time were not consistent because the material they used to measure time was uneven:

> Time had seemed to most people an unsegmented flow. Therefore, experimenters and tinkerers

> wasted centuries attempting to measure time by imitating its flowing passage, that is, the flow of water, sand, mercury, ground porcelain... or the slow and steady burning of a candle out of the wind. But no one has ever devised a practical way of measuring long periods by such means. The substance in motion grows, gelid, freezes evaporation or the candle perversely burns too fast or too slow. (*The Measure of Reality*, 80)

The clock changed all that. Westerners were not the first to have mechanical clocks. The Chinese had several, as early as the tenth century. The early mechanical clocks were large and expensive. Clocks were probably invented in northern Europe rather than south because seasonal differences are greater. When were clocks invented? Crosby thinks somewhere in the last decade of thirteenth century, just before or soon after the invention of spectacles. The smallest unit of the clock, the hour, was significant to city dwellers because it was in the merchant capitalist economy. Time was first extracted from agricultural work and religious holidays and then reintegrated as a unit of economic exchange. Time *was* money. The first specific reference to the universe running like clockwork first appears in the fourteenth century. Eventually, for Newton, mathematical, absolute time flows equably without relation to anything external.

Double entry bookkeeping and capitalist rationality

The adjectives that are usually linked to business are terms such as efficient, concise, direct, systematic, thorough, careful, and meticulous. These qualities hardly describe merchants in the late Middle Ages or even the Renaissance. According to Crosby, these merchants lived in a blizzard of transactions—bills of exchange along with promissory papers from barges, ships, and the mule trains which connected the biggest cities. They did not possess tools which would allow them to predict long and short-term trends. Without some precise record-keeping, the lack of quantity and variety of products in the Middle Ages can at least partly be explained by the difficulty merchants had in balancing their books and their capacity to loan money. The key technique in achieving organization was double-entry bookkeeping.

According to Gleeson-White, historians agree that the first surviving accounts date double entry bookkeeping to around 1300 CE. The father of double-entry bookkeeping was Luca Pacioli, a Franciscan monk who was the greatest mathematical encyclopedist of the Renaissance, having taught mathematics to Leonardo da Vinci. He spent six years as a merchant's assistant in one of the busiest trading centers in Europe. His achievements reflect the coming together of the printing press, the popularization of Hindu-Arabic numerals and the rise of merchant capitalism. His mathematical reach was not limited to double-entry bookkeeping. His work made possible Brunelleschi's great dome of the Cathedral of Santa Marie in the 1430s.

The first step towards an accurate set of books was to be able to take an inventory of stock. This included items which were the most valuable as well as those which were most likely to be lost. Once the inventory was made, the merchant needed to keep three types of books:

- A temporary record (diary) of the merchant's transactions as they take place day by day, hour by hour. Everything he sells or buys including the currency used
- A journal in which the raw data was interpreted. In this, all the transactions were grouped together into categories and all recordings needed to be in a single currency. A journal would be kept where the merchant could interpret the raw data
- A ledger page in which the credits and debits were compared out of which a profit and loss statement emerged

Even into the fourteenth century, many merchants recorded receipts in the front sections of their books and expenditures in the rear *but not on the same page*. This makes it difficult to compare debits and credits to see where they stood. Double entry bookkeeping encouraged merchants to see things in stark contrast. They encouraged dividing everything into black or red: accounts receivable and accounts payable.

Pacioli promised merchants that if they followed his system, the merchant would always know exactly whether the business was doing well or badly. Rather than mingle debit and credit entries *under* each other down a single column, debits and credits were placed *next* to each other. This also allowed him to find *mistakes* in his bookkeeping.

Double-entry bookkeeping was a means for *holding in suspension* the flow of commerce and then arranging and making sense out of masses of data that previously had been misplaced or lost. This allowed merchants to loan more money or go into debt *consciously* understanding what they were getting into. Double-entry bookkeeping made it easier calculate interest, expand the quantity and variety of products, to form partnerships to pool their money in order to hedge against failure. Merchants could extract themselves from immediate buying and selling at fairs and send representatives. As Gleeson-White argues, if the mechanical clock enabled Europeans to measure time, double-entry bookkeeping enabled them to *stop it*, at least on paper. It was this type of capitalist rationality that allowed the merchant class to triumph over the aristocrats for whom the handling and calculating of money was dirty business.

Absolute numbers: Arabic-Hindu numbers and algebra

In Medieval operations of number there were only the operations of addition and subtraction. The use of Roman numerals did not easily lend itself to learning of multiplication, and multiplication is a key operation for higher mathematics.

Limitations of the abacus

One of the inventions that broke the stranglehold written culture had over arithmetic as a cultural activity was the use of visual aids. The drudgery of numerical calculation shifted from the written page to a device: the abacus. Using the abacus was faster than doing numerical calculations by hand. This speed must have improved the mental operations of those using it. However, a problem was the *impermanence* of operations done on it. Written arithmetic was commonly done on *slates* because paper was too expensive. The speed of the abacus was weakened by lack of permanence. It could not handle very large numbers and very small numbers at the same time. The abacus was a device for computing, *not recording*.

What does it mean to not record something? At the most practical level, it was not possible to locate mistakes in addition, subtraction, multiplication, or division because your work process was erased. A calculator would have to go back to the beginning and repeat the whole process. The *steps* taken to come up with the right answer vanished in the process of solving the problem. At a deeper level, this also meant that the steps in calculation could not themselves be reflected on. At a still higher level, the characteristics of numbers themselves and their relationship to other numbers was muffled by the practicality of the problems the abacus was designed to solve. The differences between real, imaginary, rational, and irrational numbers would be buried in the process of everyday calculation.

A further problem was the fragility of the abacus. Unlike the counting boards of the east with beads on wires that mathematicians could flick back and forth, western counting boards had to be picked up, moved, and shoved from place to place. Any bump or careless brush count disorganize the board and ruin a long calculation.

Emergence of an arithmetical mentality: Arabic numerals

What changed this? Crosby says that it was the very inadequacies of the kind of counting board Europeans had to operate with that forced them to come up with something new. Arabic-Hindu numbers resolved many of these problems.

An Italian merchant known ib posterity as Fibonacci (1170-1240 CE) spent many days in local bazaars where he watched in awe at the stream of writing numbers developed by Arab merchants. The numbers used by the Arabs (our 1, 2, 3) could be used to multiply numbers which Fibonacci had never seen before. According to Gleeson-White, the Arab merchants learned their number system in India and had been using if for centuries to calculate interest rates and convert currencies. Fibonacci brought this Arabic number system to Italy. While scholars in Europe rejected and even outlawed Hindu-Arab learning, the merchants of Italy embraced it. It gave rules for adding, subtracting, multiplying, and dividing, and these solved commercial problems such as discounting, partnership start-ups, and partnerships dissolving. It was also used for bartering and currency exchange.

What were some of the advantages of using Arabic-Hindu numbering over Roman numerals? For one thing, there were only ten Arabic symbols which could be combined and manipulated far more easily than the awkwardness of manipulating Roman numerals. For another, calculating and recording could be done with *the same symbols*. Fibonacci used the new numerals with greater skill in the thirteenth century but had to express their relationship and operations *with words*.

Soon to follow the Arabic-Hindu numbering system came a change in operational notations themselves with signs for addition, subtraction, and equality. This was essential for the development of science. One of the problems with use of Arabic-Hindu system was they still used specific words to express unknowns in a problem. With the algebraic symbol of 'x' as a general unknown, by a feat of abstraction, they could forget the specific unknown of the problem they were working on and they could focus on the manipulation of numbers and operations in general. Money changers had found it more convenient to reckon in Arabic numerals by 1299. Eager to avoid being accused of usury, they used the numerals at all stages of accounting, including records of payment and receipt. Even at the bottom of the Medieval order, it might have been that even some peasants learned elementary math in working out in land-division, sheep-rearing and the measurement of arable produce. In sum, as Medieval society grew in population, towns and social stratification loosened a crucial way to move up commercially or politically was to develop mathematical skill.

Use of math in astrology

In these early years, Arabic numeracy and Latin literacy consciously avoided each together. The numerals in their early users appear to have been relatively indifferent to a literary education. A person could learn to reckon without ever learning to read and write. At this point, it may be tempting to think of literacy as connecting to religion or spirituality, while numeracy might be linked to the secular world. While this is largely true, it is important not to overstate it.

For example, Murray (*Reason in the Middle Ages*) claims that astrology involved the most complex arithmetic its epoch had known. In the twelfth century, interest in the skies turned increasingly from calendars to horoscopes. The new technique of Arabic numerals was indispensable to this project. Padua's chair of astrology had a vigorous, largely invisible tradition of mathematical calculation by the time Galileo held the position. Regardless of its failure to predict events, astrology was well-fitted to *rehearse* the principle of applied science. It had to deal with everyday events, and it had to defend itself against criticism. It had to be built on a strong theoretical basis. Even if it was not helpful in actually predicting events, it helped people get used to the idea of *preparing* for events. Farmers planned their harvests better and predictions of natural disasters would inspire people to build better houses and plan their future. Even though theologians cautioned that the power of the stars were limited by God's omnipotence, foreknowledge of configurations could make prayer more effective.

Importance of commerce on math

Math originated in the counting house needs of moneychangers. In thirteenth century Italy, learning the times table was part of schooling. In Florence, pupils flocked by the hundreds to schools for algorism. A merchant's son had to count and measure. In fact, it was considered as coming of age. Even ecclesiastical literature concerns sums of money paid for church office by Simonists. Pacioli wrote standard handbooks on pure and commercial arithmetic.

The financiers of the Renaissance Popes, the Medici, belonged to a city and profession that was on the front line of accounting innovations. Throughout the late Middle Ages, Italy's universities fought a battle against Arabic numerals as used by the stationarii (the booksellers and publishers attached to universities). By 1300, thousands of mathematically inclined people in any of the main European monarchies used Arabic numerals for calculation.

In thirteenth-century Italy, when they spoke of years of famine and plenty, lists of food prices, the costs of the war and the numbers killed were offered. In Milan, its population, buildings, trades, churches, natural, and artificial amenities were counted: 6000 fountains, 1000 retail shops, 150 hotels, ten hospitals, 120 lawyers, 100 armories, 200 shires, 200 church bells and fourteen monasteries. Murray comments that the work reads like a store inventory or account. Even lists of employees with their salaries and debts are listed beside each name.

*Limits of commerce in developing mathematics_*

While there is no question that commerce moved the development of math along, Murray cautions us from thinking that commerce alone was responsible for its development, citing three reasons:

- no known medieval specialist mathematician can be shown to have been a merchant

- historians of mathematics are agreed that merchant arithmetics were inferior branch of the subject
- The best mathematicians stood at a distinct distance from practical commerce
- Pacioli was a friar whose voluntary poverty was a deliberate *repudiation* of trader's preoccupations.

Mathematical implications for science

Crosby's argument is that the West's distinctive intellectual accomplishment was to bring mathematics and measurement together and then apply them to things and processes that had before been understood as qualitative and unmeasurable, such as velocity, temperature, and acceleration. For the measurement of phenomena of continuous quantity such as motion or heat, it is necessary that points, lines, and surfaces be imagined. Oresme charted the progression of time with a horizontal line and the variable intensity of a quality with vertical lines of various heights. This geometrical depiction of a physical phenomenon varying through time was the basis for the work done by Galileo, Pascal, Newton, and Leibnitz.

Linear perspective in painting: Medieval versus Renaissance

If you've ever gone into a European art museum, taken an art history class, or just glanced at an art history text, you will notice something very different when you examine the paintings of the Middle Ages compared to the Italian Renaissance. While the subject matter continues to be primarily religious, there is significant change in how the picture plane is organized.

The picture plane in Medieval art is flat. There is little attempt to order the objects clearly as foreground, mid-ground, and background. While Medieval art has a clear sense of what is most important and least important, they did not demonstrate this through the receding and advancing forward of objects on the picture plane. Importance is demonstrated by the disproportionate *size* of the figure and the *placement in the center* of the picture.

Furthermore, walls, ceilings, steps, the modeling of buildings, rooms, and altars are drawn *parallel* to the picture plane and vaguely converging toward the center. In order to create the illusion of the third dimension with parallel lines, receding Euclidian geometry would need to be applied. Crosby says that while medievalist scholars respected math, they did not apply very much. While not applying geometry himself, Dante says that perspective is the handmaiden of geometry, being the division of geometry pertaining to light. In addition, Medieval art does not use negative space as part of its message. In part, because Medieval philosophy understood the nature of the world as a *plenum,* in their art they do not recognize the negative space as having any creative potential.

As an expression of the weakly developed individualism in the Middle Ages, the emphasis of human subjects in Medieval pictures was their *rank* membership—kings, aristocrats, priests, or saints—not the unique characteristics of this or that particular individual. Thus, the idiosyncratic shapes of an individual face or the color of their eyes was not a serious consideration. In fourteenth century France, by contrast, portraitures actually looked like specific people.

Lastly, the sense of time in Medieval pictures was a nebulous cross between spiritual or allegorical time and secular time. Crosby puts this nicely:

> Today we usually think of pictures as depictions of what existed and what is happening at a knife-edge instant; that is, the now of a 16th century fresco of the Holy Family's flight to Egypt...The Medieval now...is not a knife-edge, but a saddle-back, with a certain breath of its own on which we sit perched...(166-168)

In Medieval art, the viewer can look in more than one direction of time. In the same picture, we will see several scenes. Crosby describes how in one picture St. Paul's ship might go aground, in another he may struggle to get to the shore, and in a third he might preach. That is, there are three separate nows. In contrast to this, Giotto painted his frescoes as if each were a scene viewed at a single moment by a single observer, with the illusion of the third dimension. But even Giotto straddled both worlds in terms of perspective. It is sometimes difficult to tell how far back in space Giotto's figures really go. Crosby compares them to portolani maps, which we touched on earlier. These pictures were like maps that indicated direction better than they did distance.

Causes of the changes to linear perspective

Migration of Byzantine artists to the West

In the 13th century, Byzantine art came to the West when the Ottoman empire drove sculptors from the North to the West. These artists brought with them more naturalistic style of sculpturing.

City planning, architecture and the carpentered world

What brought about this change in painting style? According to Crosby, one contributing factor was the emergence of city planning. Of course, there were cities long before the Renaissance, but most of these cities were not planned. Buildings were erected gradually over the years without an overall plan. However, these Renaissance architects would apply geometry to their city planning. Many of the age's greatest painters, from Brunelleschi to Michelangelo, were architects and several of them were city planners. By the turn of the fourteenth century, architects, engineers, artisans, mathematicians, and painters were very enthusiastic about perspective and optical theory.

Once these buildings were completed, the site lines of individuals would have to make visual adjustments to this carpentered world. The carpentered world hypothesis was an unconscious process of training of the eye to see long distances as shorter than they actually are because the buildings appear as receding rectangles or squares. This included long lines of market stalls and towers so tall they seemed to rear back from the viewer.

Perspective theory was not limited to architecture or city planning. Ptolemy's revolution in spatial navigation had its earliest impact on *painters* before cartographers. Brunelleschi and Alberti were the first painters to apply Ptolemy's rules for depicting with geometric rigor the curved surface on a flat surface via grid-work of latitudes and longitudes.

The use of coined money as a universal equivalent to homogenous space

In his book *The Social and Cultural Roots of Linear Perspective,* Leonard Goldstein points out (via art historian, Edgerton) that Panofsky said he thought the reason perspective was not developed in the Middle Ages was that its artists still accepted Aristotelian space: finite and discontinuous. On the other hand, Edgerton says that for linear perspective to win the day, a mathematically ordered space must be:

- Infinite
- Homogenous
- Isotropic

A new mechanistic worldview was the foundation of linear perspective and this perspective was applied to science as well as to art. The same homogenous space that was necessary for perspective in art was necessary in the work of Copernicus, Brahe, and Galileo in Astronomy. But where did this mechanistic world view come from? According to Franz Borkenau, it came from merchant capitalism:

> It is the transition from immovable property in land to the moveable property (money, tools, commodities) that generated the new conceptions

> of time and space...Since the individual as a property owner has greater potential for movement, his sense of his own movement changes. The potential for free movement of the individual among freely competing individuals is duplicated abstractly as the freed movement of body atoms in absolute space and time (*Social and Cultural Foundations of Linear Perspective*, 74)

Simple commodity production was a product of merchant capital. This required a universal equivalent that enabled people to exchange commodities. This universal equivalent would have to level qualitative differences between products and reduce them to a price. That universal equivalent was coined money. Exchanging products using coined money required a homogenous *economic* space. This economic space was a void within which commodities moved and extended in all directions without end. As people began to trade under conditions of merchant capitalism, the homogenous space required in this realm began to be projected onto other fields outside the economy. Economic homogeneity in capitalists in economic affairs became a prototype for homogenous space that was the foundation for mechanistic science and perspective theory in the arts on the other.

Furthermore, just as commodity relations were expanding eastward during the Renaissance, this proto-globalization expansion could seem theoretically infinite. Astronomical space and artistic space might also be seen as infinite.

Development of simple machines

Henryk Grossman argues that was that the mechanistic view originated in the invention of simple machines.

> It is the application of machines as motors in which human labor is replaced by water power that gives the impulse to deepen theoretic mechanics—in

> mining, metallurgy, and paper manufacturing. (*The Social and Cultural Roots of Linear Perspective*, 40)

Richard Hadden (*On the Shoulders of Merchants)* points out that

> Da Vinci, Tartagia, Cardano Benedett and Stevin developed experimental and mathematical mechanics. (6)
>
> In Descartes work one finds reference to lifting machines, ballistics and clocks. (23)

How Renaissance painters made sense of linear perspective

In his book *The Mirror, the Window, and the Telescope*, Edgerton argues that artists in the Renaissance were not motivated by a desire to break away from the medieval, religious realm. Rather, he says, these artists were devoted Christians who wanted to inspire fellow Christians to feel a divine presence in the world at a time when it was questionable after two centuries of church schisms and frustration with the failure of the Crusades. He points out they wanted to show how God created the universe at genesis according to the natural laws of Euclid. Far from wanting to represent *real life* in illusional form, they wanted to create the illusion of stage settings from contemporary *miracle plays*.

For Brunelleschi, the mirror was essential to the perspective of simulating in his audiences the same process by which the prophets saw God behind the images and likenesses of material objects. Alberti's window, on the other hand, introduced a secular alternative to perspective's original religious purposes. Alberti intended that his perspective should enhance the *moral* view of the ancients, as opposed to the *mystical* message of Christian stories. Please see Table 14.2 for a summary of the differences between Medieval and Renaissance painting.

Table 14.2 Comparison of Medieval to Early Modern Painting

Medieval painting	Painting	Renaissance
Flat	**Dimensionality of the picture plane**	Illusion of the third dimension
No application of geometry	**Application of mathematics**	Application of geometry
Nature is a plenum No use of negative space	**Use of negative space**	Nature is partly a void Use of negative space
The rank of kings, popes, priests, saints as a group	**Who is represented in pictures?**	kings, popes, priests, saints as individuals
Different times, places, and circumstances	**How is time represented?**	Immediate present—this particular time, place, and circumstances
Heterogeneous and qualitative	**How is space understood?**	Homogeneity and quantitative
Many observers	**Point-of-view**	One observer

Musical scores produce polyphonic singing

Victor Zucherkandl author of *Sound and Symbol Music and the External World* says that:

> for most peoples and most eras, musical time is of the nature of poetic rhythm, free rhythm in the sense that it is not constrained to *keep* time. Except for the special ease of dance music, which is self-explanatory, only Western music of the second millennium has imposed the shackles of time, meter upon itself. (160-161)

Let's see what this means.

How reading music impacts singing

If we return to Bruegel's *Temperance* painting, we see the artists are performing by *reading* music. How might reading music effect their kind of singing? Polyphonic music involves singing several independent lines with dramatic contrasts in pitch and volume which requires *time control* that is metered and measured. How might musical notion aid this process and how possible would it be to make polyphonic music without it?

Crosby notes that polyphonic music was unknown to the ancients. In the early Middle Ages, Europeans performed liturgical music from memory. The problem was that without any musical notation, the unevenness of memory from person to person would undermine the precision of the performance. Unless the sounds are remembered *precisely*, they perish because they cannot be written down. There was nothing the musician could do to recover it except to start again and become a better listener. This problem included not only words, but pitch, volume and rests. It would be more than enough of a challenge to sing the same song monophonically, let alone subgroups singing independent variations of a musical piece.

The earliest written music of Western Europe was the monophonic Gregorian chants, a sung version of the Roman Catholic liturgy. Gregorian chants lack dramatic contrasts in pitch, volume, and timed silences. Sound is not quantified, with no note an exact unit or division of any other note. Time is measured solely by the content of the words and the flow of Latin. Monks came up with something called a pneumatic notation which tracked pitch rather than time using dots and curlicues to indicate surges and trills.

> Neumes at first were written...in the open field... without staff lines. Their position, high or low, offered a hint as to whether a given note or phrase was higher or lower than the one preceding or following. After a while the monks lightly traced one and then two or more horizontal lines across the page to make the highs and lows easier to

> recognize. They were on their way to the musical staff, originally four and then five horizontal lines. (*Measure of Reality*, 144)

The musical staff was Europe's first graph. It measures the passage of time from left to right and pitch according to position from top to bottom. Some even *color-coded* the lines of the staff to minimize confusion about intervals.

How would written musical notations impact the kinds of singing that were possible? An individual can see on a page several minutes of music *at once*. You cannot hear it, but you can see it and instantly gain knowledge of its entire arc through time. The human ear had something to match up with what the eye saw as it looked at the musical notations. One music teacher bragged that his methods reduced the time required to turn out a good singer of an ecclesiastical chant from ten years to no more than one or two. Not only had the body of ecclesiastical music expanded in quantity and precision beyond the capacity of memory, but it was changing in kind as well, from monophony to polyphony.

If a group intends to sing in unison, then starting and stopping singing are not difficult. If we intend to sing polyphonically in several independent lines, staring together will be easy but introducing variation within subgroups will tend to slide into confusion. We need the guidance of sturdy forms and temporal dictates. We need to know where we are going and the pace at which we are to go. To an extent, the liturgy supplied the forms. Leonin, Perotine, and street minstrels supplied what was lacking in chant: a time-control, a rhythmic measure. The first masters of polyphony, Leonin and Perotine, were the first musical composers to introduce variations in words, content, pitch volume, and timed silences. Paris in the twelfth through the fourteenth century were centers for the development of Western polyphony.

Music, mathematics, and merchants

Musical scores, organized as a matter of pitches and durations is highly susceptible to mathematical analysis. In fact, Galileo, Descartes, Kepler, and Huygens were all trained musicians who wrote on musical subjects, sometimes extensively. Medieval philosophers like Boethius added a great deal of mathematical analysis of harmonics, intervals, and proportions. Johannes de Garlandia devoted more consideration to rhythmical time arrangement problems. He introduced notions for rests of various lengths. Rests were not signs for sounds but for the absence of sound. Not only was Galileo a mathematician and musician, but his work on perspective painting was formidable enough to get him elected to the Academy of Drawing in Florence!

In the city, musicians rubbed elbows with merchants and money changers, which had practical and intellectual effects. The rise of a cash economy meant that good singers of a chant and polyphony could count on exact fees and possibly eke out a living as professional musicians. Musicians cultivated their lives as individuals and proceeded self-consciously, proclaiming they were making intentional changes. Johannnes Boen claimed that the possibility of perpetual change was normal. Perhaps *new* sounds and techniques would become audible using new instruments and vocal skills. The opening up of space and time in astronomy had its musical expression in the incessant movement of polyphonic variation.

Crosby sums up:

> Between the 6th and 14th centuries something unique happened in Western Europe: the writer of music achieved control over the fine detail of sound. The composer learned how to extract music from actual time, put it on parchment or paper. (157)

They could also develop it. The composer was no longer imprisoned in the actual time of a musical performance but could abstract himself from it and study the arrangement independent of musicians.

Impact of Early Modern Inventions on Concrete Operational Cognition

What I would like you to do now is to compare Table 14.1 on the differences between pre-operational and operational cognition to Table 14.3 on the power of measurement. Table 14.3 includes changes in cartography, mathematics, painting, music, and accounting, as well as time and space categorizing which occurred in early modern Europe.

Economic objectivity

As we have seen, the emergence of simple commodity production made coined money into a universal equivalent for the exchange of commodities. In order to use money, the merchant must see the home currencies objectively:

- as independent of all commodities rather than something that could be consumed, the way bags of barley and might be used as both money and as edible commodities in the ancient world
- as relative to the other currencies which must be translated

Economic objectivity also requires moving beyond the personal taste of the merchant in order to anticipate the desires of an objective market for the commodities the merchant has to offer.

Double-entry bookkeeping requires the separation of the objective world into accounts payable and accounts receivable. These are separate from the subjective impulses of the merchant to buy something immediately or the subjective anxiety that comes from worry about his financial situation.

Astronomical and geographical objectivity

The same objectivity is true for the astronomical findings of Copernicus and Kepler. They had to have superseded animistic causality for physical causality, or efficient rather than formal or final causes in order to understand the heavens. It takes objectivity to overcome the comforting belief that the earth is the center of the solar system. The case of map-making necessitates giving up the old belief than that geographical locations are divided into the haunted places of ghosts or the home of deities. Instead, geographers learned to plot the longitude and latitude of the globe independent of their wishes or their spiritual beliefs.

To treat the geography this way requires the concrete operational belief in absolute space which is the foundation of homogeneous space. In Piaget's terminology, these astronomers and geographers must be able to 'conserve' light, quantity, weight, and volume in order to perform these operations.

Mathematical objectivity

In the Middle Ages, there might have been some operational thinking, but it was muffled. People used simple arithmetic for counting. But in early modern Europe, they began to use Hindu-Arabic numbers instead of Roman numerals. This made it made it possible to use the operational signs of addition, subtraction, and equal which led to the invention of algebra and the solving of quadradic equations. In addition, mathematicians freed themselves from the topical space of the Middle Ages to use Euclidean geometry.

Objectivity in theatre

It was not just economics and science which required a new kind of operational thinking. As I discussed in depth in *Forging Promethean Psychology,* Don Le Pan has discussed revolutionary changes in the theatre that occurred in the sixteenth century. The transition from pre-operational to operational thinking occurred in types of plot, character development, quality of character interaction, audience expectations, the relationship between stage and audience, the necessity of creating illusions, and techniques for creating altered states of consciousness in the audience. As it turns out, Shakespeare was inviting us to think in a concrete operational manner and leave behind the preoperational thinking about the way theatre and literature were presented in the Middle Ages. The theatrical audiences in Shakespeare's time were expected to be quiet and stay in their seats and treat the stage and the actors and actresses as objective. In the Middle Ages people yelled out at the performers and even got on the stage and acted the parts, especially when they didn't like a performance.

Objectivity in painting

In the case of painting, it requires objectivity for the artist to abstract from the qualities of real objects in the actual landscape, in order to place them in an order that will bring out the illusion of the third dimension on the picture plane. This involves reversibility in changing one's thinking from what is actually before one in the landscape, to reordering it on the picture plane. So, for example, in order to maximally bring out the three dimensionalities of deep space, foreground, mid-ground and background need to be organized at 45-degree angles as the Dutch masters taught us. For the foreground of a picture to come forward, the objects in the foreground:

- ought to be complimentary colors
- have highest contrast between darks and lights
- have the most explicit detail up front
- have the largest objects up close

Conversely in order to maximize deep space, the colors in the background should be analogous, low in contrast of lights and darks, have as little detail as possible and be small. All this requires reversing what our eyes may show us in real life and, as an art teacher once informed me, 'we have to correct nature'.

Perspective drawing requires the artist to overcome the natural eye's resistance to foreshortening. In other words, if a person is lying down on a bed and you are looking at them from the foot of the bed, that person's foot will appear much larger than the head at the other end of the bed. The person's head will be disproportionately smaller than it is in real life. To see this perspective objectively, we must resist making the head roughly the size of the feet and make it smaller than it actually is, because that is what the eye sees.

Lastly, one of the qualities Edgerton claims for perspective drawing is the subjectivity involved. Renaissance linear perspective converges on the view of a single individual at a particular time and place, not the divergent perspective of the Middle Ages.

Objectivity in music

Reading music allows for time control and the freeing of musical harmony from oral memory. The problem of oral memory involves not just words, but pitch volume and rests. Because individuals can see on a page several minutes before at a glance before a song has begun, singers are more able to anticipate what they are singing, when to enter, and when to leave the harmonics. This shortened the time of rehearsal and the learning time of groups.

Whether the markings on a page are algebraic equations, musical scores, perspective lines, or latitude and longitudinal lines in navigation, all require the mind to *reverse* its operations from the experiential flow of events so those events can be reinterpreted on paper. Irreversible, preoperational thinking is imprisoned in solving problems in present time.

I hope you see the connection between the use of Hindu-Arabic mathematics, musical notations, linear perspective, and double-entry bookkeeping that require many of the characteristics of operational thinking. All of them require that the world of reality and the world of the mind need to become separated before each can be reflected upon.

In the next chapter, we will see how the scientific revolution of the seventeenth century and the emergence of industrial and finance capital in the nineteenth and twentieth century helped produce the amplification of Piaget's fourth stage of cognitive development, formal operational thinking.

Table 14.3 The Power of Measurement*

Middle Ages	Category of comparison	Early modern period
Relative—finite, spherical, and qualitative Cardinal directions had qualities **Plenum with no void**	Characteristics of space	**Absolute, infinite, quantitative** Cardinal directions are neutral **Void**
Earth centered cosmos Fixed stars, planets in circular rotations	Astronomy	**Copernicus:** earth revolves around the sun Stars have a birth and death **Kepler:** planets rotate elliptically
Maps inseparable from deities and sacred places	**Cartography**	Maritime chart "Portolano"—Utilitarian drawing for enclosed waters like Mediterranean and North and Baltic seas.
Contextual Time Inseparable from the seasons, human events **Church bells**	**Time and timing**	**Absolute Time** Independent of seasons, human events. **Clocks**
Little loaning of currency Little debts or loans **Peddlers**	**Commerce**	More loaning of currency Calculation of interest **Merchants**
No accounts receivable or payable Difficulty tracking bills of exchange, promissory notes, tracking inventory, loans, debts, or economic trends **No annuities**	**Accounting**	**Double entry bookkeeping** Allowed for tracking bills of exchange, promissory notes, inventory, loans, debts, balancing accounts, and projecting trends **Taking out annuities.**
Lack of precision—general and impressionistic or exaggeration	**Mathematics**	**Precision:** specific and concrete Used of balance scale, yardstick
Roman numerals	Number systems	**Use of Hindu-Arabic numbers**
Counting and simple arithmetic The rest expressed verbally No operations of addition, subtraction, equal signs	Operations	**Algebra** Operations signs of addition, subtraction, and equals
Use of abacus—could not handle very large or very small numbers Computing not recording	Devices	Computing *and* recording
Numbers mixed with qualities of spiritual meaning	Secularization or spiritualization of numbers	Numbers separated from spiritual meaning— specific quantities specific qualities: Fibonacci
No written musical texts Gregorian chants	**Music**	**Written musical scores** Polyphonic singing
No serious planning Horseback: collisions of aristocrats	**Military operations**	**Strategic Planning** Foot soldiers who performed as automatons who marched in step
Proximate senses—touch, smell, taste, hearing	**Sense ratios**	**Predominance of sight**

- Adapted from Crosby, *the Measure of Reality*

CHAPTER 15

Cognitive Evolution: the Amplification of Formal Operations from the Seventeenth Century Through the Gilded Age

Orientation

Now that I have examined how concrete operational thinking was expanded through changes in art, music, mathematics, and physics through the sixteenth century, I will now examine how operational thinking has fared from the seventeenth century forward. In the previous chapter, we have referred to the changes in the *content* of scientific discoverers. In this chapter I consider how the research *methods* of science helped to catalyze a new 'formal operational' cognition. In addition, I probe the impact of capitalism has had in the development of formal operations in two ways:

- in the movement from merchant to industrial and to finance capital, social relations became increasingly abstract and expansive, as would be expected in formal operations
- in the evolution of currencies, from coins to bank notes to paper money, checks and credit cards also become more abstract and expansive

As a reminder, my purpose is to show a few key points:

- Western society had first gone through two *social* operational stages which are catalyzed by changes in institutions. These institutions required people to do mental work in new ways in order to reproduce those institutions, whether it in be art, music, science or economics.

- As a result of working in these institutions, individuals *internalized* this operational thinking,
- They learned to use formal operational thinking in *new* social situations not involving work, such as religious worship, child-rearing, and game playing.

The chapter begins by comparing concrete operational thinking to formal operations. From there I will show how the new procedures of scientific methodology produced formal operational thinking. In the second half of the chapter I'll turn to the history of the ways is which capitalism invited formal operational cognition, for better and for worse. The last section draws up the theoretical implications from a Vygotskian point of view.

Early science is inseparable from magic and craft

Back in chapter six we saw that the belief that social evolution is 'progress' is a relatively recent development, and that the fruits of progress largely depends one's social class membership. The Enlightenment picture of the scientific revolution as a linear, heroic success story of uncompromised intellectuals who overcame religious superstitions to help give birth to an independent secular culture is seriously flawed. From the Renaissance all the way into the eighteenth century, many of the greatest scientists of the period including Copernicus, Kepler, and even Newton saw themselves as part of a Neo-Platonic, magical and alchemical tradition. These magical and alchemical traditions—far from being ignorant superstitions—helped to guide scientific discoveries, at least early on.

For example, the alchemists produced how-to books on metallurgy, glass making, ceramics, dyeing, and painting. Two of the first disciplines to be impacted by the scientific revolution were astronomy and biology. The tools that were necessary for both—the telescope and the microscope—were provided not by astronomers or biologists but craftsman who were lens-grinders and spectacle makers. Turning from alchemy to astrology,

astrology was used not just by ignorant peasants but by courts of kings who hoped to predict the future. In the process, astrologers such as John Dee helped to develop mathematics.

Hallpike (2008) points out that the development of experimental science in the West would not have fully blossomed until scientists engaged *with* craftsmen whose work necessitated accurate physical measurement. The expertise of these 'artist-engineers' lay in the control of the materials themselves, the process of making them, and the practices of finding out what worked and what didn't work. These areas included clock-making, navigation, surveying, printing, bronze casting, masonry, canal-building, fortification, and gunpowder.

Hallpike further points out one of the major differences between the science of Western Europe and other great civilizations. In the West, forums were developed where craftsmen, scientists and artists worked on projects *jointly*. The merchant and artisan guilds were far more independent of the upper classes in Europe than elsewhere. By 1700, a number of colleges emerged to promote collaboration between craftsmen and scientists. Hallpike points to the activity of the Luna society in the late eighteenth century as just one example:

> Its members were a group of friends who met every month...and included James Watt and Mathew Boulton (steam power) William Murdock (gaslight) Joseph Priestley (chemistry) John Baskerville (printing) Josiah Wedgwood (pottery) Erasmus Darwin (botany and evolutionary theory) James Keir (chemistry and glassmaking) Richard Edgeworth (electricity and the telegraph)...(393)

From concrete to formal operations

Before proceeding to the implications for cognitive evolution as a result of the scientific revolution and the emergence of industrial capitalism, I want to make explicit some differences I see between concrete and formal operations. In formal operations:

- *Symbols* (whether letters, math notations or coins) become *more autonomous* from experiences and sensory data of goods, people and places
- symbols are *built upon* symbols, and acquire a 'life of their own' (they 'square' themselves)
- there is more powerful *manipulation* of the objective world (whether it be in the service of accumulating capital, the study of nature, or in inventing tools)
- the manipulation of the world occurs across a *greater range of space and over a shorter period of time*
- the mind becomes more *self*-reflective and *critical* of its own processes

Concrete operations exist in two forms:

- simple concrete; the way peasants and artisans might have used them in in early modern Europe (which might not have been tied to symbol systems)

- complex; amplified use of concrete operations in early modern Europe (discussed in the previous chapter); people in the arts and sciences (for the most part, middle and upper-middle classes)—painters, map-makers, astronomers, mathematicians, and musicians—might have used them

When we compare concrete operations to formal operations in the next section, we will be comparing *simple* concrete operations to formal operations for purposes of high contrast. The differences between complex concrete operations and formal operations is subtler and would take us too far afield to tease out the differences.

Comparing concrete to formal operations in scientific method

The process of scientific reasoning is the first *institutionalized* example of formal operational thinking in action in Western history. What I will do now is contrast how formal operational thinking is different from concrete operations. In an earlier section, we contrasted pre-operational thinking to operational thinking. When I was doing this, I was using 'operational' thinking as a general category which included both concrete and formal operations. Now we are in a position to clarify the difference between these two forms of operational thinking. As we saw in the last chapter, concrete operations are used in science before the seventeenth century. In this chapter we will see that formal operations began to be used as part of the scientific revolution in the seventeenth century and beyond. Keep in mind the five global differences between the two forms cognition from section two of this chapter.

Increasing expansion of time and space perception

When thinking in a concrete operational manner, the mind abstracts from sensory data and it reorganizes (reverses) its operations in a logical way, but it operates closer to the proximate space and time conditions in which it originated. In the formal operations used by seventeenth-century scientists, modern science applied the thinking process to objective conditions far from the original context in which the problem was posed.

For example, Newton discovered gravity through the observations of the free fall of bodies, the orbits of the planets, and the ebb and flow of the tides. These were hardly processes that were happening at one time and in his local area. Furthermore, not all sensory data that was immediately available to Newton was used. Only what Newton saw as *essential* about gravity was taken into account. The rest were considered 'accidents' and not worth attending to. Furthermore, his data was drawn from past times and other places, which he then shaped into an idealized model. Finally, using formal operations in science, whatever the results of the experiment were, results were systematically tested at different times and different places, to see if the experiment could be replicated.

In concrete operational thinking, whatever is found to be

true in the present is not systematically tested in varying the times and settings to try and replicate the results. In concrete operations, if the same procedure works in a new setting it continues to be used. If it doesn't, it is replaced by some other process in a trial-and-error way. What is missing in concrete operations is the *systematic process of elimination* by which one hypothesis is stands while another is eliminated.

In concrete operations an individual can clearly distinguish the symbols used from the objects in the world. However, symbols are mostly used for practical purposes in everyday life. There is no attempt to make a study of *the symbol system itself*. Mathematical notations are used in building architecture, paint marks making paintings or in writing poetry. There isn't a separate study of trigonometry, calculus, or the study of rational, irrational, or imaginary numbers. Nor are there treatises on perspective theory or the study of language (linguistics) itself.

Increasing reflection on symbol systems

In the case of science from the seventeenth century on, any hypothesis that emerged as true was a result of an experiment, and was incorporated into theories. These theories were built into laws that are expressed mathematically, and were hierarchically organized. These laws may *not* have had any reference to locally-experienced conditions. In formal operational science, theories and laws are studied autonomously from experiments. In concrete operations, successful experiments are immediately applied to practice and little thought is given to developing theories or laws.

The taming of perceptions about chance

Another distinction between concrete and formal operations is how to make sense of chance. In pre-operational thinking, the difference between what was and was not lawful was not considered. There was an underestimation of chance events, and these events were often given mystical meanings, as in divination practices. In concrete operations there is a distinction between what can be predicted and what cannot. However, as we saw in chapter fourteen, chance was understood as *accidents* or events that were unintended. Chance was understood as lawless. There was no sense of the laws of large numbers that were developed in the nineteenth century, or systematic combinations of possibilities which were independent of personal experience.

As we saw in the previous chapters, while the study of probabilities predated the seventeenth century, the study of chance came into being not just in the service of scientific investigation, but in the policies of absolutist states attempting to carry out a census, track taxes, and conscript its population. It also occurred in the annuity policies of merchants calculating the risks of trade.

From reason to rationality

Concrete operational thinking corresponds roughly to what we called 'reasoning' processes in an earlier chapter and connects up with what is called 'informal' logic in the field of critical thinking. This means that a claim is tested on the basis of evidence in the real world with the understanding that the world is too complicated to know anything with absolute certainty. In addition, in concrete operations the distinction between the *form* of an argument and its content can be mixed together. They will tend to slur over the distinctions between what is formally valid from what is informally probable in terms of content. For example, people using concrete operations will have a difficult time accepting that a syllogism can have formal validity, even though the statements will be false in terms of how the world really works. As I said in that chapter ten, formalist cognition goes with rationality which began with the Greeks, continued in the high Middle Ages with the schoolmen, and spread to science in the seventeenth century.

Dualistic understanding of opposites

To conclude this section, we come to the differences in how opposites are understood. People using pre-operational or concrete operational thinking use 'contraries' and 'complimentaries' but don't organize opposites as mutually exclusive. In in formal operations, opposites such as contraries, complimentaries, and contradictions are made explicit as in the logical square of opposition. Formal operationalists organize contradictions as mutually exclusive contradictions, as Aristotle does in his law of the excluded middle.

The mind reflects critically on its own processes

Let us turn to the ontological question of what the mind itself is. We said earlier that in pre-operational thinking the mind is understood either as a physical or spiritual substance. On the other hand, in both forms of operational thinking, the mind is understood not as a substance but as a *mediator* between the real world on the one hand, and the body on the other. Furthermore, another difference between concrete and formal operations is *what* the mind is operating on. As Piaget says, in concrete operations the mind is mostly operating in the service of *reacting* to problems in the physical world and *planning* actions on the world. Concrete operational thinking is less involved in self-reflection on how the mind itself works, especially in relation to the mind's typical predispositions, biases, and weaknesses.

In the early formal operations of the Greeks, the mind reflected on its *own* thinking process, not just in performing formal logical operations. Aristotle and the Sophists crafted the science of rhetoric which required showing the human mind reflecting on the thinking processes of others in terms of making an effective argument. The mind was reflecting on the timing, setting, and types of evidence necessary to persuade audiences in speech-making. But for full formal operations in scientific method in the seventeenth century, even more self-reflection was involved. Here scientists exposed the weaknesses and biases of the mind in how it set up and interpreted the results of experiments. For example, in relation to interpreting statistics, fallacies included base-rate neglect in estimating probabilities; inversion of conditional probabilities; small sampling; unrepresentative sampling; and the gamblers fallacy.

Movement from the real to the hypothetically possible

In concrete operations, the starting point of operation is the real situation. What is possible are the realistic strategies the mind might employ to resolve the problem in an adequate way. What is possible is a *special case* of reality that is taken as given. However, in formal operational thinking, the starting point is not a particular situation in real life, but a *possible* situation that the scientist constructs in setting up an experiment. In this case, the real is not a starting point, but only one of a number of possibilities. The scientist then tries to impose the best possibility on reality, rather than accepting reality as it is. In applied science, the results of an experiment are ideally applied in the form of technological advances or new energy harnessing systems.

In concrete operational thinking, not *all* the possibilities for a situation are considered before action is taken. Trial and error is used, and the first possibility that works is implemented without bothering to test and compare all other possibilities before settling on one. In concrete operations, people act before testing not just all *likely* outcomes but all *possible* outcomes. Identifying the conditions and reasons why the strategy works are limited in their rigor. They are like unskilled tool users that try different tools to fix a clogged piping system, picking up or discarding the tools as they become useful or useless. The reasons for choosing the initial strategy include convenience, economy of cost and benefits, and habit, not abstract concern for the truth.

In formal operations, all possibilities are tested in a planned and systematic way. But the most serious test for the truth of a proposition is its ability to predict the future under *controlled conditions*. People that think in a concrete operational way are not that ambitious. They simply want to solve immediate problems.

Criteria for a good theory: verification and replication

In formal operational procedures, the key to a good experiment is that the evidence used can be verified and that the experiment itself can be replicated by other scientists. This will allow these scientists to check the quality of the experiment as well as offering different interpretations of the same data. People using concrete operations may not leave a trace of the sources they've used to come to their conclusion. Their thinking is problem-focused and they are not necessarily responsible to a scientific body for either the quality of the evidence or their skill in revealing to anyone else their intellectual process. A motto for concrete operations is that the proof of the pudding is in the eating.

Making predictions, disconfirming alternative hypotheses

In formal operations, a good hypothesis tries to state as clearly and quantitatively as possible the conditions under which a prediction is likely to come to pass. This is done by operationalizing definitions of key terms. It makes predictions *before* rather than after whatever it has claimed to study. A good hypothesis acts efficiently, meaning it not only tries to show it is the best explanation, but it also disconfirms competing hypotheses. Disconfirming competing hypotheses allows others to test the new hypothesis or test the hypothesis that has worked so far, and test it and apply it to new realms. Being able to *eliminate competing hypotheses* is an important and underrated scientific activity.

Occam's razor

Furthermore, modern science insists that new solid hypotheses must not only explain new facts but also not violate facts that have been already established. This is referred to as Occam's razor. If a new hypothesis disrupts as much or more of an accumulated body of knowledge than it explains, it does not advance knowledge. It must conserve what already exists as well as expand upon it.

Statistics are the best evidence

In concrete operations, evidence that is typically allowed is personal experience (case studies), experience of friends (testimonials), cultural common sense, or expert authorities. In formal operations, this type of evidence is too unreliable because cases can be atypical. The motives of friends or witnesses are always mixed. Likewise, some cultural common sense can later be found to be illusory, thereby creating controversy between authorities. The evidence of choice for formal operations is research based on statistics which are verifiable and can be replicated, to ensure that the results are not a fluke.

Knowledge is public and independent of individuals

Lastly, in concrete operational thinking a body of knowledge is often inseparable from a particular person who has the knowledge. When individuals die, the knowledge dies with them. Secondly, this knowledge is often hoarded, used, or released as it serves the self-interest of individuals. In formal operations, knowledge gained is *independent* of the individuals with their unique skill or charisma. In the application of formal operations to scientific reasoning, modern scientific method is public rather than secret. This lessens the chances of its being corrupted or derailed. A body of knowledge is added to and reorganized *publicly*, independent of who said it or when or where it was said. Furthermore, after an experiment is reported, peers criticize it. Before a finding reaches the public, it has been filtered through a specialized scientific body of practitioners who have self-correcting mechanisms built in. This means that good science is a collective practice that *evolves over time*. Table 15.1 summarizes the differences between concrete and formal operational thinking as it applies to seventeenth-century science and beyond.

Table 15.1 Concrete and Formal Operations and the Scientific Revolution

Concrete Operations **Pre-17th century science**	**Category of Comparison**	**Formal Operations** **17th century and examples**
Closer proximity in time and space from experience, sense data of goods, people.	**1) What is the relationship between symbols and reality?** (Symbols include letters, math notions, music notions, painting or coins)	Greater distance from local space and present time from experience, sense data, goods and people. **Newton's experiment with gravity.** **Experimental replication in different times and places is attempted.**
Symbols are distinguished from objects (not magically enmeshed) but they are still **used reactively in relationship to objects.**	**2)To what extent do symbols act on symbols?**	**Symbols "square" themselves** Symbols are built on each other take on a life of their own. **Algebra, trigonometry, calculus, music theory, theories of painting perspective**
Reversible operations **on sense data and planned action**	**3) What does the mind operate?**	Reversible operation **on systems of ideas**
Taxonomic Objects grouped into classes but have close spatial and temporal locations.	**4) How are objects classified?**	**Taxonomic** Objects grouped into classes which have no spatial no temporal relations with each other. **Linnaeus system**
Instrumental, episodic manipulation in local contexts	**5)Extent of manipulation of the objective world**	**Systematic manipulation in inventing tools, study of nature as a global system.**
Chance is the result of uncaused accidents, unintended results. Likelihood estimations based on personal experience	**6) How are chance occurrences and likelihoods understood?**	**Chance is the result of lawful combinations which have regularity, whether they are intended or not.** Likelihood estimates may violate personal experience. **Galileo. Pascal, Port Royal Logic** Used by state for census collection, taxes, conscription. Annuity calculation by merchants
Informal logic Form (validity) of an argument is embedded in content (truth). Truth derives from personal experience and it cannot be counter to personal or human experience.	**7)Form of reasoning**	**Formal logic (deduction)** **Euclidian Geometry—Descartes, Spinoza** **Separation between validity and truth.** A proposition can be valid based on no experience as well as being empirically impossible **Induction** - physical evidence independent of authorities and testimonies of others.
Concrete Operations **Pre-17th century science**	**Category of Comparison**	**Formal Operations** **17th century**
Mind in the service of reactions to the problems of the world and planning what to do.	**8) Self-reflexiveness of the mind**	**Mind reflecting on itself, Self-critical.** **In statistics, being sensitive to cognitive mistakes such as** base rate neglect; small sample, unrepresentative sample, gamblers fallacy. **Experimental design in science**
Revelations of the authorities or personal experiences of a particular person. informal dialogue with friends	**9) What are sources of evidence?**	**Truth through experiment and dialogue.** Authorities, testimonies and personal experience are less trusted.
The real situation.	**10)What is the starting point in thinking?**	**The possible situation.** **Applied to new technology which improves productivity**
The possible is a special case of the real.	**11)What is the relationship between the real and the possible?**	**The real is a special case of the possible.** Reality is a special subset within a totality of possible things which the data will admit as a hypothesis.
Does not consider all possibilities before starting (trial and error, improvisation) Acting before complete testing not just all *likely* outcomes, but all *possible* outcomes.	**12)What kind of planning?**	**Considers exhaustively all possibilities in a situation and formed into a plan before acting** **Experimental design in science**
Ideas are embodied with individual thinker, particular time, place and circumstance.	**13) What is the relationship between knowledge and thinker?**	Ideas are independent of any particular thinker. Time and place and are part of a **scientific collective practice.**
No. Whatever works is the proof.	**14) Are predictions made?**	**Makes data verifiable and makes experiments replica table.**

Capitalism and formal operations

Phases of capitalism: merchant, industrial, and financial

The emergence of scientific institutions is not the only arena that will invite formal operational thinking. Another of these institutions exists under capitalism. Institutions such as banks and the stock exchange force everyone to use and cultivate formal operations to some extent because we simultaneously handle coins, paper money, checks, and credit cards (all various forms of increasing abstraction). To use any of these currencies requires many of the characteristics of formal operations. In order to draw out the full implications of formal operations, we must show how the structure of social institutions invited it. I am going to violate the stated historical parameters of this book and take us well into the twentieth century in order to show the full trajectory.

Using formal operational thinking becomes a greater possibility after the seventeenth century for those classes who do mental work. This means that middle and upper middle-class people engaged in the hard sciences, along with most professional fields including architecture, engineering, surveying, medicine, law, and education. These practices are likely to have required learning formal operations in order to do their job.

When coined money arose in the first-millennium Common Era, money was simply used as a medium to exchange commodities. Profit was made by selling goods at a price that exceeded the costs of the goods produced or purchased. The important point is that money was used instrumentally, as a *means* to accumulate more goods. But with the rise of industrial capitalism in the nineteenth century, this process was joined by another process by which money was not just a mediator for the buying and selling of goods and services but took on a life of its own. Money was invested in commodities as a means to *make more money*. 'Capital' is simply money made on money. In terms of formal operational thinking, capitalists and all those who accumulate capital are moving from the use of symbols (money) as a means (concrete operations) to allowing symbols to build on themselves (money made on money).

To be sure, in the case of industrial capitalism, some profits are poured back and invested in the social infrastructure, including the transformation of roads, the building of railroads, investment in communications systems, investment in research and development, and the investment in workers in the form of education and wages. However, this infrastructure is a means to accumulate more symbolic currency. The intention is less to produce more commodities or social infrastructure, and more to accumulate capital. This is the classic Marxian definition of the fetishization of money: money becomes unhinged from the circulation of production process and appears to develop an independent existence.

In its extreme form of finance, capital profits (most prevalent after World War I) are less derived from goods or equipment. Now profits are made on betting on the assumption that companies will be successful. Stocks, bonds, and (closer to the present time) derivatives are claimed as profits.

The way Marxists formulated the evolution of the forms of circulation of exchange value went from:

Exchange Relation	**Type of society**
Commodity A – Commodity B	Complex horticulture societies
Commodity A – Coins – Commodity B	High Middle Ages—Italy Merchant capital
Coins – Commodity A – Capital	Industrial capitalism—nineteenth- century England
Capital A – Capital B	Finance capitalism—twentieth-century United States

Over the course of the last 500 years, there has been an

increase in the accumulation of industrial and financial capital the later in the history of capitalism we go. For our purposes, the point is that there is a definite movement of capital from a more 'material' profit (based on trade in commodities or and investment in tools, equipment, and people) to more abstract investment in stocks and bonds.

In the industrial phases of the stock market, an investor was 'investing liquid assets' in *companies* that produced commodities, constructed machines, built roads and set up communications and transport systems. This investment in the stock market was a more abstract investment in symbols because they were no longer investing directly in products and services but in the *institutions* that made them. These investors were betting that these companies would make a profit on these products in the future. It was not a claim for profits *already* made.

At some point, moneylenders found it more convenient, efficient, and ultimately profitable to substitute their own bills-of-exchange for those of individual producers, forming institutions known as banks. The rise of banks in the twentieth century was inseparable from the rise of credit. Aside from making a profit, banks were institutions that emerged in order to manage credit. Their job was to connect the various forms of credit to each other as well as lines of credit to real money in the form of gold or legal tender. Banks used their own money to provide a centralized discounting function for many bills-of-exchange that originated, and then circulated them among individual commodity buyers and sellers. Bank notes replaced bills-of-exchange. When banks issued their own notes or allow checks to be drawn from them, they substituted their own warranty for particular capitalists who borrowed from them. In exchange, banks in part derived a profit from the interest charged to capitalists for providing this service.

However, this seemingly stabilizing function that banks provided was only temporary, since banks also competed with each other. Competition between banks drove forward a still more ethereal symbolic abstraction in an attempt to stabilize the circulation of capital. This resulted in the creation of a central bank. The job of a central bank was to convert the various forms of bank notes into each other in order to balance accounts of clients, without risking the danger of transporting more concrete forms of currency (like gold) from bank to bank. A central bank guaranteed the trustworthiness of private banks, just as private banks guaranteed the trustworthiness of individual capitalists. Typically, central banks did not compete with each other as they appeared to be somewhat limited by the geographical boundary of the nation-state. With the current wave of globalization that occurred in the twentieth century there was a need for a *world* bank to guarantee the quality of currency of central banks within nation-states.

To say that capital 'grows' is an example of how the symbolic forms of exchange have become unhinged from the relations of production that underlie them. As David Harvey argues (*The Limits of Capital*,1999) capital increases interest because capitalist enterprises have managed to produce enough surplus value within the banking period to cover their interest payment. Harvey identifies three functions of the credit system of banks:

- *the mobilization of money as capital* through the credit system which can convert the flow of monetary transactions into loan capital by bank drafts for cash; they do this by counting on deposits to furnish a permanent balance that underwrites this loan's capital
- *reductions of the cost time of circulation;* commodities which require extra-long production periods are paid for in installments
- *facilitating the quickening of the circulation of fixed capital* (for example, investments in the built environment have a much slower profit return than the more 'liquid' forms); existence of banks means capitalists do not have to wait for the circulating and fixed capital flows to complete their cycles before accumulating more capital

In an idealized capitalist world, the interest-bearing capital can best fulfill its function of coordination if it can be as flexible as possible and remain as separate as possible from a commitment to the more concrete forms of investment: plants, tools, products, or workers. This is where capitalism runs into contradictions, because without some investment in the real world there are no workers and institutions to generate the profit. (More on this in the next section.)

One temporary and very dangerous solution is for banks to issue fictitious capital—a flow of money *not* backed by any commodity transaction. This is when a capitalist receives credit on a commodity that hasn't even been sold yet. The bank holds the warranty that is backed by an unsold commodity. If these warrants begin to circulate, it is *fictitious* value that is circulating. A gap is opened up between capital accumulation based on already-sold commodities and capital based on commodities that have not been sold. Too much of the accumulation of fictitious capital, too much 'betting ahead' on unsold commodities is the stuff of economic depressions.

In short, with the rise in the power of banks in the twentieth century, profits are made less from concrete goods and services and more on profits derived from making loans to capitalists. Profits are made with less and less return to the social body. Social abstractions on paper are piled on top of each other. Betting on the stock market and all the paper options offered is a feat of mind-boggling abstraction which many of us don't comprehend. My suspicion is that most people that invest in the stock market invest without understanding it. They simply trust that their broker does understand it.

Class composition in the use of formal operations

Describing the movement of capitalism through various institutions is not saying that that once capitalism emerged all social classes were engaged in these institutions equally. Industrial and financial capitalist relations are entered into primarily by capitalists and their brokers. These classes are far more likely to have capital, and in the process of investing they get used to using formal operational thinking. Of course, there are capitalists that have inherited their wealth, and don't have to think in a formal operational way, because they don't do the work. However, their brokers do have to work, and use formal operations to do their jobs.

Among the middle classes, not only does the kind of work they do (supervising, planning) encourage their use of formal operational thinking on the job; but as the stock market opened up to the middle classes in the twentieth century, they had to learn to think like capitalists about their investments.

Initially, for the working classes, the primacy of the commodity-money-commodity relation was predominant as producers in the 'Commodity A—money—Commodity B' circuit. Their work itself, their labor power, was a commodity owned by the capitalist (Commodity A); they received a wage (money) from the capitalist which these workers in turn bought subsistence commodities (Commodity B). As consumers, the working classes are still in this circuit. Workers use money as an instrument to buy goods and services. They do not use goods and services to make more money.

However, as the industrial phase of capitalism unfolded, even working- class people (unlike serfs in the Middle Ages) had to grow accustomed to the following more abstract, decontextualized, taxonomic classification of relations that resemble formal operations:

- They did not own any portion of what they produced. Unlike a peasant, they could not claim any of *the product* of their labor (however small) as their own whether it be food, clothing or shelter.
- They did not own or make the *tools* they used; they 'rented' them.
- The products and tools were available to them in the form of a standardized *price* as opposed to bargaining and haggling.

And how did they acquire these products and tools? They paid for them with *wages*. Rather than being entitled to goods and services as part of either generalized reciprocity and/ or a redistribution system as under feudalism, their labor itself became a commodity that was sold at a price.

Summing up formal operations and the phases of capitalism

What I now want to show is how the movement across these phases of capitalism affected how people think. I will show that in order to participate in a capitalist economy people's thinking had to resemble formal operational thinking, at least some of the time. Examine the characteristics of formal operational thinking on Table 15.2. Ignore their application to science, and just examine the general characteristics. If you match these characteristics up with the capitalist institutions like banks, the stock exchange and all the various forms of currency, I think you'll agree that use of formal operations is necessary in many of our categories, including at least the following:

- the relationship between symbols and reality
- the extent to which symbols act upon other symbols
- extent of manipulation of the objective world
- impact on space and time (Harvey's globalization and space-time compression)
- understanding of chance (at least among stock brokers)
- reversible thinking operations between ideas (currency symbols)
- epistemology—betting on fictitious capital
- taxonomic classification—investment in wealth with no space-time referents
- relationship between ideas (symbols) and thinker—commodities exchanged for a price independent of who the people are
- starting point is the hypothetical not the real (fictitious capital)

Table 15.2 Application of formal operation to the evolution of modern science and capitalism

Categorical question addressed	Formal operational thinking	Scientific revolution	Industrial and finance capital
What is the relationship between symbols and reality? (Symbols include letters, math notations, music notations, painting or coins)	Greater distance from local space and present time from experience, sense data, goods and people	Newton's equations Newton's experiment with gravity Experimental replication by other scientists in different times and places	Prices of commodities unified into a price which independent of the quality of the particular product; where it was made or who the buyer or seller were From coins to paper money: extracting the principle of social approval from material value of coin Greater trust in invisible relations between strangers (the state and capitalists that stand beside them)
To what extent do symbols act on other symbols?	Symbols "square" themselves; they're built on and into each other, taking on a life of their own	Algebra, trigonometry, calculus	Extraction of self-expanding exchange value from circulation of commodities (time alone adds value) Accumulation of financial capital process; sources of profit change from money made on circulation and production to profit made on paper—interest, stocks, bonds, derivatives Symbols of money "square themselves" into coins to paper money to checks to credit cards
What does the mind operate on?	Reversible operations, but operates on systems of ideas (rather than on concrete problem solving)	Development of epistemology in philosophy; theories of probability	Creation of systems of abstract currency
How are classification systems grouped?	Taxonomic; objects are grouped into classes which have no spatial no temporal relations with each other	Chemical, plant and animal classification systems by Linnaeus	Objects grouped as commodities independent of who, where, or when they were produced
What is the extent of manipulation of the objective world?	Global; systematic manipulation of the objective world	Harnessing of inanimate sources of energy; global study of nature—land, sea and air	Penetration of capital into greater areas of life within core countries and spreading to the periphery; 'everything's for sale'
What is the understanding of chance occurrences and likelihoods?	Chance is the result of lawful combinations which have regularity, whether they are intended or not	Likelihood estimates may violate personal experience Work of Cardano, Galileo. Pascal, *Port Royal Logic* Bernoulli	Annuities; policies of merchants used by the state in the seventeenth century for census collection, taxes, conscription; insurance policies in twentieth century; polling predictions for political elections; financial 'instruments'
What is the Mind for? (Solving everyday problems, or studying the world objectively and self-reflection?)	Studying the world objectively and self-reflection, on the thinking process itself	'Organized skepticism': peer review Statistical fallacies Reliability, and validity tests	
What are the sources of evidence? (Revelation of the authorities and personal experience, informal dialogue with friends, or truth through experiment?)	Truth through experiment and dialogue	Scientific experiment Scientific community (Royal society)	Irrational: rate of profit; makes things people don't want and does not make what people say they want
What is the starting point in thinking?	The possible situation over the real situation	Starting point may be advanced mathematical theory possibilities, but eventually applied to solve problems and invent new technology, which improves productivity	
What is the degree of foresight? (Design rather than trial-and-error and improvisation?)	Considers exhaustively all possibilities in a situation, and formed into a plan	Extensive planning in research review of literature, and setting up experiments Long-term planning in research grants	Irrational: will not systematically invest in building and repairing infrastructures; invests in institutions that destroys what it has built: prisons, wars
What is the relationship between the real and the possible?	Reality a special subset within a totality of possible things, which the data will admit as a hypothesis	The real is a special case of the possible Scientific theory starts with the real, invents a possible hypothesis and then tests the hypothesis against the real	Irrational: derivatives; betting on the future independently of anything that is produced
What is the relationship between knowledge and thinker?	Knowledge independent of any particular thinker, time or place	Discoveries of individuals are pooled, criticized and stored within the scientific community and available as public knowledge	Capitalist system operates independently of any particular capitalist 'Money talks' independently of who owns the money
How are predictions made?	Identifies conditions under which something could be proven wrong	Makes predictions which must compete with alternative predictions	Irrational: capitalists do not learn from past panics and depressions; represses its own part and resumes polices that have already proven to be failures

How capitalists fail to use formal operations under their system

Do capitalists seek to find out what is true (for its consumers)?

On the whole, the capitalist economic system falls far short of the discipline of science in terms of the full use of 'social' formal operations in how the system actually operates. In terms of the sources of knowledge, there is no equivalent in capitalism in the early twentieth century to performing a scientific experiment to find out what is true. If a capitalist wanted to discover whether people wanted his product, there is no social mechanism in place by which he could find out. Capitalists compete with each other producing commodities that people *don't* want. Furthermore, products sit on the shelves when advertising campaigns fail. At the same time, capitalists do not produce commodities that people say they *do* want if the rate of profit on those products is potentially too low.

Capitalists do not use the full power of science to build cars or make clothes that are long-lasting. In fact, they have been known to repress or destroy technologies that undermine its resource base. Rockefeller bought up and then destroyed trolley cars as a means of public transportation at the turn to the twentieth century. Why? To make way for buses and cars powered by oil. For the products they do make, capitalists plan for their products to wear out sooner rather than later. Whereas in a scientific experiment all possibilities are exhausted in the search for knowledge, capitalism does not exhaust all possibilities but picks selectively those investments which will maximize profit. Whether these investments are risky, whether they produce goods that are deadening or have no redeeming social value, is irrelevant to capitalists.

Do capitalists plan with foresight?

In research designs of a scientific community, the experiment is constructed with an overall plan, where short-term and long-term consequences are considered. This means research and development programs invest in new equipment and repair old equipment. As most of us are painfully aware, especially under finance capitalism, capitalists

- neglect building infrastructures;
- strive to minimize paying health benefits to workers;
- will not invest seriously in education;
- pollute the biophysical environment; and
- resist paying the cost of cleaning up their messes (these messes are dismissed as 'externalities')

When capitalists invest in building prisons rather than schools, they undermine their own resource base. How can you buy the products of capitalism if you are in prison? When capitalists invest in war, they tear down the very buildings, transport systems, communication systems that they helped to build. This is not a moral argument. I am trying to show how capitalists fail to see that infrastructure and workers are the foundation that makes his profit possible. Capitalists are the most powerful economic class in the world and have the most responsibility for determining how goods and services are exchanged. Not only is there no social plan beyond this generation but, at least in the United States, there is no plan beyond a business quarter.

<u>Is the hypothetical situation applied to the real world</u>?

In science, mathematical systems create hypothetical scenarios that may not exist in nature. Science begins with the hypothetical situation and sees real life as a special case. At the same time, science wants to apply mathematics to the real world with more powerful tools to solve problems. Mathematical symbol systems in the long run come back to reality in the form of new bridges or rocket ships that land or circulate around other planets. Capitalists, on the other hand, invent financial 'instruments' (derivatives, stock options to name a couple) that also have a basis in mathematics. But the application of these instruments loses its base in the real world. Real, in this sense, means one that profits on goods and services. Capitalists draw sources of profit on hypothetical scenarios that have no basis in reality, because no real goods or services have to be created. This is fictitious capital.

<u>Can capitalists make predictions through self-reflection on its own process</u>?

Lastly, in science there is an *accumulating* body of

knowledge which includes not just what we know works, but what we know *doesn't* work. A new hypothesis must explain new facts while continuing to be grounded in what has already been proven. In other words, science is self-reflective about its own process *and* its history.

Do capitalists actually *learn* from past mistakes? Are they self-reflective on their own historical processes, including the depressions which have rocked the world in the last 150 years? After the depression in the 1930s, capitalists made some adjustments by introducing Keynesian economic policies. These policies had their own limits and did not solve capitalism's most basic problems. Still, Keynesianism was used for forty years afterward, and helped to catalyze a recovery after World War II. Then, beginning in the middle of the 1970s, when Keynesian system ran into difficulties, capitalist strategists reverted to pre-Keynesian policies (headed by Von Hayek and Friedman), as if the depression of the 1930s never occurred.

Most economists are apologists for capitalism. They do not set up verifying and replicating conditions for admitting serious problems within the system. No mainstream economist predicted the economic crisis which began in 2008 and has continued to the present. Alan Greenspan, head of the Federal Reserve for many years, admitted he was completely stunned by what happened. Did the presence of this crisis (euphemistically known as a recession) make capitalists question the viability of the system? No. Instead, they attempted to explain systematic problems away by looking for individual or small-group scapegoats, such as:

- the greediness of individual businessmen (a few 'bad apples')
- poor people who shouldn't have taken out a home loan
- a bloated state bureaucracy, spending too freely and needing regulation

To summarize, in at least these four categories of formal operations, capitalism *discourages* individuals thinking about *social* problems using formal operations. The use of formal operations at this institutional level would require at least a social democratic economic system where collective reasoning were operating. Table 15.2 summarizes the application of formal operational categories to the two modern institutions we discussed: the scientific revolution and capitalism. The section on science largely repeats what was in Table 15.1, but I think it is valuable to see where scientists have commonalities and differences with capitalists in how formal operations is applied.

Theoretical implications: the socio-historical nature of formal operations

Qualifications

The way I have presented cognitive evolution so far might be misunderstood as being automatic, rigid, and linear. To minimize this misunderstanding, I think the following qualifications are in order:

- **Formal operations are not necessarily more progressive or better than concrete operations or pre-operational thinking.** If Piaget argues that intelligence is adaptation to the environment, then for adults that means adaptation by creating technological, political and economic systems that are adaptive to work, play and home situations. The presence of concrete or formal operations simply means that people living in those societies have built up a *complex* social environment of institutions that require a higher proportion of abstract thinking to work and live in them.

- **Formal operational thinking is not automatically adaptive.** The fruits of the scientific revolution that was part of building formal operations were used to increase the scope and depth of war from the sixteenth to the end of the nineteenth century. The institutions of science have presided over ecological degradation. As we have just seen in the case of formal operations applied to capitalism, the wheeling and dealing of the stock markets is highly questionable as an adaptation strategy for at least eighty percent of the population.

- **Concrete or pre-operational thinking does not disappear.** Just as coin or paper money does not disappear once checks and credit cards emerge, so preoperational thinking or concrete operational thinking continue to exist among members of society when they switch to more hands-on problems or problems they are unfamiliar with. An adult may use formal operations when playing chess with another adult. However, when the same adult plays 'king of the hill' with his four-year-old, formal operations are nowhere to be found.

- **Formal operational thinking exists in a more muted form, even in the Middle Ages.** All social classes living in the Middle Ages could still use formal operational thinking. However, without the development of economic capitalist markets with their currencies; without political centralized states with their administrators, civil servants, lawyers and other mental workers, most people will not have a reason to use formal operations. Thinking in a formal operational way was not spontaneously enjoyable prospect for most people. People in the Middle Ages would not spontaneously teach themselves the statistical laws of probability when playing games of chance even if statistical laws had been invented in the Middle Ages. In fact, people in industrial capitalist societies don't learn these laws when they go to the racetrack or play the lottery. While concrete operations might exist in the Middle Ages for those being numerate or literate, I am cynical that formal operational thinking is possible without being able to write and read.

- **Formal operational thinking is not used by at least half the population in Industrial capitalist societies.** I am not suggesting that all or even most people used formal operational thinking by the end of the nineteenth century. At most, a minority of social classes (mostly the middle and upper middle classes) will use them; and even if they do, this does not mean they will use this skill in settings outside of work. I am only claiming that if, when or whether formal operations emerge, science, capitalism, and a centralized state are necessary for their cultivation.

A Vygotskian overlay of Piaget

In the last two chapters we have seen how various forms of technology (such as double entry bookkeeping, algebra, cartographic maps, the printing press) and the scientific and capitalist revolutions invited two forms of cognition: concrete and formal operations. But by what process did the technology, economics, sciences actually get *inside* the operational cognition of the individual? In other words, we need a *mechanism* which mediates between social institutions and psychological processes.

According to the socio-historical school of psychology, cooperative learning goes through three phases: first, local interpersonal learning is social; next, internalization of learning is psychological; finally, 'global' interpersonal interaction is social again. If Vygotsky was right, that all higher psychological processes are first social before that became internalized, than this applies to abstraction as well. That means that the processes of abstraction discussed in the previous chapter—extraction, deliberation and generalization—were first social abstract processes *before* they became private. This means that when a new tool, a means of exchanging goods and services, or political institution emerges, *society as a whole* goes through a Vygotsky's three phases:

- local interpersonal corresponds to the moment of *social* extraction
- internalization corresponds to *social* deliberation
- global interpersonal corresponds to *social* generalization

What is interesting is that the need for social abstraction starts with a social reaction to a situation—a social problem that needs resolution—and it ends with a need for social abstraction to apply the results of abstraction to a new social situation. Every time we enter a new occupation, we must learn a new language, master a new set of tools, learn to role-take and role-make. Thus, the alpha and omega of abstraction is social, *not* psychological. It is only as individuals who do mental work in these fields and develop expertise in their work that these social abstractions become internalized into their psychology. Then, inside the minds, they go through process of individually abstracting—extraction, deliberation, generalization. For now, we will focus on how social abstraction occurs.

To summarize:

- historical inventions—double entry bookkeeping, algebra, mapmaking, scientific method, paper money
- socio-cultural mediations—three phases of cooperative learning
    - local interpersonal (social extraction)
    - internalization (social deliberation)
    - global interpersonal (social generalization)

The consequences in 'social' operational cognition results in

- psychological processes
    - concrete operations
    - formal operations

These psychological processes, in turn, can lead to new historical inventions.

Our aim now is to show more precisely how this kind of 'social' formal operational thinking was necessary to shape the formation of institutions of the capitalist system.

How the three phases of abstraction manifest in the history of capitalism

What I am going to do now is to show how formal operational thinking is first a *socio-historical* process of building capitalist institutions as we take those institutions through the three phases of social abstraction: extraction, deliberation and generalization. As people on the job built these institutions as they worked, they began to internalize formal operations so that it became a normal part of their cognitive processes independent of work. Then they applied it what they've learned to social situations outside of work, for example, child rearing, religious practices or game playing. First, I will trace the phases of social abstraction through the evolution from merchant

Figure 15.3 Formal operations through the three stages of abstraction

ECONOMIC EXCHANGE	TYPE OF ABSTRACTION USED	STAGES OF ABSTRACTION
Mercantile capital; industrial capital	Concrete operations Formal operations	Social Extraction Extraction of self-expanding exchange value from circulation of commodities
Industrial capital to finance capital	Formal operations	Extraction of exchange value from either circulation or production; immediate expansion of exchange value (time alone adds value)
Coined money; bank notes	Concrete operations Formal operations	Social Extraction Extraction of 'principle of approval' from the material value of the coin
Bank notes to paper money	Formal operations	Extraction of principle of approval from a particular individual
Paper money to checks	Formal operations	Extracting the principle of signification from denomination
		Extraction of the principle of trust from present time-space to the future
Checks to credit cards	Formal operations	Extraction of denomination; variability from collateral not limited to present assets

to industrial to finance capital. Then I will trace the three movements of abstraction through the use of coined money, bank notes, paper money checks and credit cards. If you prefer an overview of where we are going before you begin, check out Table 15.3.

Circulation of merchant, industrial, and finance capital

We will begin with the movement from mercantile to industrial capital. The *social extraction phase of abstraction* began when the self-expanding exchange value was separated from the circulation of commodities. This means that merchants began to track their costs and benefits more systematically using double entry bookkeeping. But this had its limitations.

Cognitive Evolution: the Amplification of Formal Operations applied to the history of capitalism

STAGES OF ABSTRACTION	STAGES OF ABSTRACTION
Social Deliberation Systematic accumulation of capital by a more rational cost-benefit analysis.	Social Generalization Expansion from circulation to production—reorganization of land, labor, infrastructure
Rationalized system of increasing benefits' risk ratio. Minimize risk of techno-depreciation of fixed capital.	Unsecured lending bank notes, credit cards, bonds, emergence of local, central and world banks; spreads from core countries (industry) to the semi-periphery and periphery
Social Deliberation Realizing that medium of currency can be *any* medium, and can be applied to other institutions besides the state	Social Generalization Application to private institutions (banks) of bank notes
Realizing the state can issue its own promissory notes	Issuing paper money by the state to groups, not just individuals
Seeing past problems with arbitrary fixed denomination; potential time-space bottlenecks	Specified variable denomination; checks issued and backed by banks
Increased trust in invisible relations with strangers and institutions that stand behind them	Banks issue checks
Recognizing timeless availability of loans	Allows borrowing into the future from realm of assets to the realm of liability (credit cards)

When mercantile capitalists weighed costs against the benefits of buying and selling, they were subjected to time and place contingencies. For example, a merchant's timing might have been right as to *when* to sell a product, but the *place* he was delivering the goods to may have had a famine or an epidemic. So too, the merchant may have delivered his goods to a society that wanted them, but another merchant had arrived before him. In this case, the place was right, but the timing was wrong. In other words, the degree of control a merchant had over his accumulation of capital was significantly limited.

The social deliberation phase involved the planning process of turning merchant capital to industrial capital. This included the planning involved in the building of railroads, coal mining, and the building of factories. All these projects involved long-term planning that was considerably beyond the scope of the merchant capitalist. The social generalization phase occurred in the application of profits to the reorganization of land and labor across expanding social space.

Of course, the industrial period also had its risks. When the industrial capitalist invested in a particular technology or energy source, his investment could be undermined if another invention or energy source was found which can render obsolete his investments. So too, when the capitalist invested in upgrading the skills of the working and middle classes, providing them training and education, there was no guarantee that they wouldn't oppose the interests of the capitalist by forming unions or opposing profitable wars. Still, because of the increase in concentration of capital and the intervention of the state compared to the state in the mercantile phase, new technologies, energy sources, and workers could now be more easily repressed, but only temporarily.

The movement from industrial to financial capital was even more extreme, but it could still be broken into the three phases of abstraction. In the social extraction phase of industrial capital, exchange value was separated from *both the* circulation and the production phases and became immediately expanded into more exchange value. In other words, it was not the investment in goods and services, but *the passage of time* alone that added value. This means money 'grew' in banks in the form of interests and dividends. The social deliberation occurred with the invention of credit systems, bank notes, the stock market, local banks, central banks, and world banks to increase the rate of profit. The generalization phase occurred when banks and their paper currencies spread from nation-states of core countries across the entire globe. Stock markets no longer existed just in New York or London, but in every industrialized country.

The basis for investing in unsecured loans was various bank notes and financial instruments like credit cards. Since banks invested less in concrete processes, capital was much freer to move across unsecured lending possibilities, because the capitalist was not demanding that his debtors pay up immediately. He just kept loaning, and made a profit off the interest.

How the three phases of abstraction manifest in changes in the forms of economic currency

The three phases of social abstraction can be applied not only to the historical phases of capitalist accumulation. It can also be used to track historical changes within the material forms of currency—from coins to notes to paper money to checks and to credit cards.

The material value of coined money rests with a long and trusted metal medium: gold, silver, and copper. This means the metal *itself* has value independent of whatever social agreements transpire to make it legal tender. At least in the early days of capitalism, in an economic crisis, the metal content of the currency could be reconverted by smelting back into usable items such as tools or cups.

In the movement from coined money to bank notes, we will find the same three stages of social abstraction operating. The social extraction phase occurred when the principle of *social approval* of the coin was separated from the *material value* of the coin itself as a use-value. What matters now is less the coin itself, but the social institution, the bank, that stands behind it.

The social deliberation moment was the recognition that, at least in state societies, the medium of currency could be made of almost *any* material. Whatever the material the currency was made of the banks would stand behind it. The social generalization phase occurred when *banks* issued notes. This was a generalization because banks were institutions that, through centralization, could spread the use of bank notes across the land.

Notice that once notes replaced coins, there could no longer be a conversion back to some socially useful item, the way metal could be converted to jewelry or goblets. To be able to accept this form of transaction (notes) required new confidence by the population in a more abstract social relationship than was required with coins, because no reconversion is possible. The population had to have faith that the bank stood behind the currency with real gold which stood behind the bank notes, even though the bank notes are 'only paper.'

The movement from bank notes to paper money was not so much an intensification of abstraction as much a converse movement at the same level. In the movement from bank notes to paper money, the principle of approval was separated from the particular individual and expanded to *groups*. The moment of social deliberation occurred when the state operated with the collective understanding that it could issue its own 'bank notes' (promissory notes) just like the banks. The social generalization occurred when the state issued paper money to *everyone*, not just to individual investors the way banks did. In other words, the state 'learned' from the banks about bank notes and applied it to the issuing of currency the way it did with coined money *but at a higher level of abstraction.*

What happened when we moved from paper money to checks? The social extraction movement occurred when the principle of signification was separated from any particular denomination of currency. In other words, paper money was issued in denominations of one dollar, five dollars, ten dollars, twenty dollars, et cetera. When we separated the principle of approval from fixed denominations, we allowed both buyer and seller more freedom. How so?

The social deliberation movement occurred when the problems of fixed denominations were exposed to collective analysis. The problem with operating with fixed denominations of paper caused some time-space problems that could reduce rate of circulation of goods and services. For example, let's say a consumer wanted to buy an object and only had a one-hundred-dollar bill. The commodity was being sold for, say, sixty dollars. The buyer was not likely to part with a hundred-dollar bill and pay forty dollars more than the cost. If the seller did not have the right change, he might not make the sale at all.

Conversely, if the buyer only had two twenty-dollar bills, the seller was not likely to sell the commodity for twenty dollars less. In other words, in some transactions involving fixed denominations, being in the wrong place or wrong time could slow down commercial exchange. Being able to write checks would correct for this by writing an IOU statement for the exact amount which could be cashed in later.

The phase of social generalization involved in using checks occurred when the principle of signification (or approval) was preserved, while the check was not tied to the concrete constellation of paper money the consumer had on them at the time. *Checks bypassed the problem of making change* and allowed transactions to proceed more smoothly. Checks opened up the range of spatial transactions in which they could occur, as well as the times they could occur.

We will close this section by applying the three stages of social abstraction to the movement from checks to credit cards. In the stage of social extraction, denominational variability (checks) was separated from collateral and *not limited to present assets*. The social deliberation stage was the recognition by banking planners that the availability of loans could extend far into the future. From the point of view of the capitalist loaning money so far into the future, long-term profit could be made by keeping people in more or less permanent debt. The social generalization occurred when borrowing into the future had been moved from the realm of assets to the realm of liability. The social generalization also occurred when credit cards used spreads to the middle class, working class and even the poor.

<u>How past, present, and future are perceived in using currency</u>

Now we will turn our attention to how the *perception of time* changed with changes in the currency. Like coins, paper money is liquid *on the spot*. No identification cards or driver's licenses are necessary to make a transaction. Furthermore, when you give someone paper money you know that you are parting with something 'real' (that you now have less of). From the viewpoint of the owner of currency, checks began the process of creating a distance between the present and the future. Although checks were not as 'concrete' as paper money, one still had to consider how much money was in their checking account before purchasing something. Because checks (at least when they are first used) did not seems as 'real' as ten- or twenty-dollar bills, it seemed easier to spend. It appeared that one was buying something for nothing. However, in another sense, the balance must cover the product bought.

If a checking account did not have the money to cover what was being bought, a small gamble had to be made on the hope that money would be in the account to cover the purchase before the check bounces. On the other hand, the seller was well aware of the increasing abstraction of currency as well as the increasing trust that was necessary in accepting a check. To help the seller feel more secure, he may want to check the name of the bank on the check and/or write down a license number. One could not go into a store and say 'my checking account cannot cover this but I'll put some cash into it right away. Give me the product and I'll come back soon with the check.' However, one could give the seller a check and buy something even without money in my checking account. provided that a quick deposit is made in the *near* future.

With the emergence of the credit card, economic exchanges became even more abstracted from present time. With a credit card, many products could be purchased without the liquid assets available to cover the prices. When using a credit card, how much liquid savings one had currently on hand became even less relevant than in operating with checks. With credit cards, one could now buy large amounts of goods and bet that they'd be be able to produce income to back up the purchase *even if it wasn't yet earned.* The individual began betting on his *future* labor power. This of course required a much more elaborate tracking system because the stakes were higher. Above and beyond the interest rates of credit cards, if you didn't pay the bill at the end of the month, many people went into what seemed to be permanent debt or even bankruptcy. In part, this was because they couldn't track and keep up with their present and projected future earnings against what they had actually spent.

Whether we discuss mental coins, bank notes, paper money, checks or credit cards, these currency forms involve the use by increasing numbers of people regardless of their class location. This means the phases of capitalist accumulation, the currency used, and changes in the perception of time are first housed in the 'social' mind as the three phases of social abstraction, social deliberation and social generalization. Then this social mind cultivates the cognitive psychological thinking process known as formal operations. Then the individuals who are first the products of these social institutions become the co-producers of these institutions as they work in the ensuing years. Some may co-create new social institutions.

CONCLUSION

The Perils and the Promise of Lucifer's Labyrinth

Orientation

The major thrust of this book is to argue that higher psychological states originate as *social* processes people learn at work. These skills become internalized psychologically and then become social again as they are applied outside of work. New kinds of work based on new technologies, economic production, and political innovations affect the middle social classes first and then the working classes a little later. Since it is the middle classes who occupy powerful positions as scientists, artists, lawyers, merchants, architects, and the like, they will be the first to test the new tools and the new work practices.

In the first part of this conclusion, we will be explicit about what these macro-social forces are. In the second section, we will discuss how the psychological processes expand and amplify each other. We will ask:

- how individualism is connected to a spatial sense of geography
- How individualism is connected to a linear sense of time
- how individualism is connected to the process of becoming civilized
- How individualism is connected to the process of romanticism
- How individualism is connected to rationality
- How individualism is connected to probability and chance
- How individualism is connected to formal operational thinking

In section three, I will ask about how the pros and cons of *Lucifer's Labyrinth* has affected western society as a whole, as it impacts all social stratified groups. Lastly, we evaluate the pros and cons of Lucifer's Labyrinth using relative standards. This means I ask how included was the working class in this process? I also ask how women as a group, in and out of the working class, were impacted.

Impact of macro-social structures on psychology

Impact of technology, politics, and science

One important technological innovation crucial to the rise of a linear, quantitative time was the invention of clocks. One the one hand, clocks sliced time into quantitative increments setting the temporal parameters for what eventually became 'factory' time in the nineteenth century. As more and more people moved from rural farms to cities, tracking time according to the seasons of planting and harvesting made less and less sense. The cyclical time of agriculture was 'straightened' into the linear time with the Industrial Revolution. A linear tracking of time was grounded in the need for the industrial bourgeoisie to develop and monitor a work schedule in industrial factories. Part of a linear sense of time is that an individual tends to do one thing at a time rather than what anthropologist Edward Hall called 'polychronic' time, which means doing many things at once. A linear sense of time is crucial for the specialization of labor, which comes about from factory work. Polychronic time would not support capitalist production because it undermines specialization of tasks.

As we discussed in chapter five, the technology of the railroads impacted the individual's sense of space, time, and sense-ratios. Railroads created flat, predictable routes across the countryside, somewhat akin to the grid pattern that was developed in cities. As hills, marshes and gorges were modified, tunnels and bridges were built, which diminished the qualitative differences between places. For train passengers, the speed of the trains made any sensual *experience* of the terrain impossible. 'Sights and vistas' were the only thing left for passengers to behold. By the end of the nineteenth century factory time was matched by a railroad time schedule, which was synchronized across time zones.

In the areas of the sciences, what I call 'promethean' cognition is impacted by the scientific method on human cognition. In chapter ten we saw that in Dewey's 'quest for certainty,' scientists in the seventeenth century developed mathematical models of understanding, first astronomy and then physics. In the same century, scientists began to distinguish probability from chance, and by the nineteenth century the rise of statistics (quantitative reasoning) emerged. Rationality was defined in chapters ten and eleven as *qualitative* rationality (deductive logic). In chapters twelve and thirteen, probability and chance were defined as *quantitative* rationality. These types of rationality are joined by qualitative reasoning, also in chapters ten and eleven. These kinds of rationality are joined by qualitative reason (also in chapters ten and eleven) to form the foundation for formal operational cognition of among scientists, merchants, and state bureaucrats in the eighteenth, nineteenth, and early twentieth centuries. It is hard to imagine how formal operational thinking could have developed inside of individuals without first the presence of social institutions that required it among its mental workers.

Lastly, the development of capitalism was a global component for cultivating so many of Lucifer's elements. Capitalism invites individualism by promising a better life for all, so long as individuals compete successfully against each other. The bodies of the middle class must be controlled by becoming civilized just as the bodies of working-class people become disciplined under the rule of capitalists. The fact that human development (childhood, adolescence, and adulthood) becomes increasingly conflicted by the end of the nineteenth century is directly related to the increase of options open to people with the expansion of a greater variety of occupations under capitalism. City life being nerve-racking is directly related to an increase in the pace of life due to the uptick in turnaround time necessary to make a profit. As we saw in chapter fifteen, capitalism promoted the amplification of formal operations in the forms of currency developed, as well as in the emergence of finance capital.

Impact of the arts

Where the Renaissance intersected with promethean psychology was in the kind of space that was introduced by three-dimensional perspective. Linear perspective not only created an illusion of the third dimension, but it *linearized* space. This linearized space, with the eye trained to a central vanishing point, suppressed the actual existence of objects in real nature, and replaced them with idealized objects that conformed to the rules of perspective composition. The actual local color in nature that occurs in places was suppressed in favor of optical color which conformed to other spatial rules. These rules specify that in terms of how the eyes perceives, complementary colors should be the foreground, and analogous colors in the middle ground or background. The purpose of this arrangement is to maximize the illusion of the third dimension on a flat picture-plane. Just as actual objects in nature were reshuffled in Renaissance perspective painting, so too city planners during the modern era cleared out local places to make room for commercialized city-spaces.

How luciferian elements magnify and expand each other

Individualism and geographical space

In our first chapter we saw how there were seven characteristics of individualism: equality at birth, autonomy, privacy, self-development; self-reflection, self-control, and uniqueness. Individualism, whether in Europe or in the United States, accepted an absolute separation between the inner world and the outer world. The characteristics of this outer world included seeing the objective world as 'spaces' which supported qualitative change, innovation, and what was unknown. Spaces were subjectively thrilling, and the emphasis was on the future (whereas in places highlight what is past). Inhabiting spaces induced wonder, delirium and amusement.

All these characteristics went nicely with how individualists related to the life in the cities and the consumption of products under capitalism, especially in the 'expressive' individualism in Yankeedom at the end of the nineteenth century.

The characteristics of industrialized cities as gridded systems of streets allowed capitalists speedier production and circulation of goods. It also allowed for individualists, especially in coastal cities, experience exotic foods, and culture of people from all over the world. The pace of cities created a thrilling experience for individuals who operated under geographical and class mobility. Both mass transportation and mass communication in cities produced individualist engagement with strangers rather than kinship. The specialization of spaces in houses with specialized functions continued the division of labor at work with rooms serving one rather than many functions. Once commodities were housed in large buildings, these became 'spaces' themselves. This is most easily seen in the rise of department stores in the second half of the nineteenth century.

Individualism, space and time displacement

What does it mean to say that time has been displaced? What is its relationship to individualism? Time is displaced when the present is lived with a knowledge of the deep past and future trends which embody it. This results in what Anthony Giddens has called 'space-time instantiation.' To some extent human beings have always had to do this because seeing long-term patterns was crucial in our success in competing with other animals for resources. But in the modern era, the emergence of the discipline of history that is tracked in books and state records has allowed us to examine a much deeper human *historical* past. In addition, as we saw in chapter six, the discovery of deep time by geologists and then biological evolutionists gave us a deep *natural* history of time. The emergence of clock time, speed of the railroads and the invention of the telegraph accelerated time up so that to be *in the present* we had to be *on the move*.

By the end of the nineteenth century, the invention of the telephone was one of many instances of time-space compression. The telephone undermined the appreciation of the past which characterized letter-writing with the expectation of 'catching up' in real time. The telephone also expanded space to include people hundreds of miles way. It encouraged self-reflectiveness in individualists because they had to prepare themselves for conversations, but it heightened the sense of alertness or nervousness for individualists because a phone call could occur at any time.

Individualists and a linear sense of time

We saw in chapter six that perception of the shape of time had changed in the West from cycles based on turning agricultural seasons to a linear sense of time. As the self-confidence of science grew, the exploration of the macro and micro worlds spread from astronomy to physics to biology. The scientific revolution was integrated by the Enlightenment into depiction of the sweep of social evolution as 'progress.' Progress was the application of linear time—past-present and future—into human history. The theory of progress was instrumental in justifying the rise to power of the bourgeoisie.

As we saw in chapter two, for most of western history, individuals were defined as having a temperament, i.e. a predisposition that was the result of a blending of the four elements in nature: fire, air, earth and water inside the body. A temperament was the identity we were born with, and about which nothing could be done. But contrasting to this, unlike temperament, the individualist quality self-development meant that individuals had *potential* that could only be realized *over the life span* of the individual. The individual had the right to develop this potential by harnessing their skills. In other words, the notion of self-development is the *application of the social theory of progress* to the lifespan of the individual. Time displacement helps individuals reflect on the present moment by examining their past and making plans for their future in order to realize their potential. Individualists had to be patient, adaptable to unusual changes in temporal trends and retain confidence they could realize their potential in spite the various migrations, famines and economic depressions and recoveries.

From an individualist point of view, progress in ontogenesis means that the future is better than the past and that personal past doesn't matter much. This is because the past cannot repeat itself, while the future is open. This suits the individualist just fine because they like to imagine that freedom consists in no rules, roles or temporal constraints. While Erikson's and Freud's theories of individual development both have conflict and competition built into them, and have regressive components, in the best of all possible worlds the healthy person is the older, mature person. The later in the individual lifetime we go, the more mature they become.

Just as in social evolution, the process of improvement is slow, and the stages of society are built on the foundation of previous ones. So too, in the psycho-social stages individual development of Erikson, stages are irreversible and accumulate. Just as social progress takes place through hard work and sacrifice, developmental psychologists imagine that improvement of the individual happens because of hard work and sacrifice, not because of luck or inheritance. In Yankeedom, this can be seen in the utilitarian individualism in the early nineteenth century.

Individualism and the process of becoming civilized

So far it might seem that individualism is simply a tendency of an individual to ignore other people, and simply do with they want. But the process of individuals becoming civilized means that the individualist must learn social graces in navigating in dense social situations. The individualist element that most reflects what it means to be civilized is self-reflection. The individualist must have foresight, hindsight and insight about they have done to others and what they intend to do. Being civilized does not mean conformity. Conformity is often blind and unconscious, whereas becoming civilized is the essence of being conscious and calculating moves. When the individualist becomes civilized, they delay or renounce emotional expressiveness and sensual gratification. They not only learn how to play roles but how to switch roles and manage intra-role, inter-role conflicts along with role strain.

By the late eighteenth century, marshes were drained, diseases were less lethal, and agricultural production seemed more predictable with a warming climatic period. The bourgeoisie, flush with the hopes of the Enlightenment, blew the roof off of aristocratic pretension and pessimism. It proclaimed happiness and serenity was possible in the modern world. As Elias points out, in the Enlightenment, aspirations to being civilized (what they called "cultured") were not the privilege of a few, but open to all. Emotional life became more sensitive towards others. Animals were taken as pets. What remained uncivilized—bodily functions and psychological abnormalities—was buried in the unconscious or subjected to etiquette books and manners. A sense of adventure was introduced into marriages where romance was a criterion for judging suitability. As the pace of life quickened, the elderly seemed to have less to teach. My point is that promethean individualism was far from the romantic notion of breaking out of the collectivist chains of the villages, king and church while standing alone. Individualism was constrained externally by nationalism and internally by civility.

Individualism and romanticism

As a result of the industrial revolution, with its problems of crowded city-life, smokestack factories and horrible working conditions, by the middle of the nineteenth century all was not well for the vision of the Enlightenment. Romanticism developed in Germany and in France in which artists championed a *retreat* from modern life into pastoral fancies of the countryside. Uncivilized individuals were held up as heroes and the unconscious was explored as a motivation of individualist behavior. The search for origins in primitive life—whether in tribal societies, feudalism or in childhood—became the ideal as romantics rebelled against civilization. This rebellion against civilization reached its peak with the crypto-romantics at the end of the nineteenth century. At this point, the rebellion was directed at the bourgeoisie rather than at aristocrats. As we saw in chapter eight, aristocrats were now emulated by dandies, anesthetists, and bohemians.

Also, as we saw in chapter eight, romanticism was a direct reaction against both the theory of progress in both society and the individual. The characteristics of individualism that most easily fit with romanticism were autonomy and uniqueness. Both the old romantics and the crypto-romantics championed primitive societies at the macro-level and children at the micro-level. The old romantic individual rebelled against both the aristocracy politically and capitalism economically in the name of the arts. They rejected the mechanistic nature of science for organic theories of nature. They dabbled in the occult and searched for an earthly pan-spirituality while rejecting organized religion. While they sought lost communities in pre-state societies or the Middle Ages, the actual communities of romantics were in were other lower middle-class artists and teachers. Their rejection of what the west had built did not turn them into collectivists. Rather, they became another kind of individualist.

In the United States, there were two kinds of civilization championed: the civilized nature of New England and New York on the one hand, and the culture of the South on the other. The culture in the south had a mixture of another kind of feudalism, along with some tinges of romanticism. The real hothouse for romanticism in the United States was in the culture of the frontier and the American west. Pioneers such as Daniel Boone and Davy Crockett became legions and fed the romantic individualism, which was critical of both the civilizations of the East and the South. Frontiersman were still individualists in that they sought autonomy.

Individualism and qualitative rationality

Unlike reason, rationality operates within a closed system of information. It is individualistic because it isolates the thinking process from a changing, objective world, as individualists reflect on the relationships of internal logical relationships. Rationality is also individualist in its separation between the validity of an argument and its soundness. In testing the validity of the proposition: all women are immortal; Sarah is a woman; Sarah is immortal, it does not matter at all that in real life, women are not immortal. What matters is the logical structure of this chain argument. Even within the individual, cognition is isolated into components—the skill at rational calculation is separate from relying on the senses or the emotions. Another way in which rationality is individualistic is in its denial and contempt of rhetoric. Aristotle said rhetoric is the science of persuasion. Persuasion involves stepping out of the self and accessing who the audience is as well as the time, place and circumstance. Rational calculation cares nothing for the audience or its setting.

When these rationalists turn to religion, they project an image of God as a watchmaker who winds up the world once and then walks away. God cannot evolve or tinker with the workings of nature. God is a macro-reflection of a mechanical engineer, Himself an individualist, who builds the world out of his head. Just as emotions and the senses are excluded from the cognition of the individualist, the God of rationalists has neither emotions nor senses.

In our first chapter we saw how Thomas Hobbes was the main architect of possessive individualism. For him, individuals are isolated monads, blindly crashing into each other as they live a life that is short, brutal and nasty. Not surprisingly, when Hobbes attempts to describe human societies, they become projections of the state of individuals. Society is an aggregate, a whole which is no more than the sum of its parts. In the nineteenth century, the individualist nature of rationality can be seen in the economic theories of Merger, Walras, and Bohm-Bawerk, who were the precursors of the rational choice school of economics today.

Individualism and quantitative rationality (probability)

Within the field of quantitative rationality, we said that probability is assessing reasonable *degrees of belief* which is warranted by evidence. The field of philosophy that assessed how we can know what is true is called epistemology. Unlike the qualitative rationalists like Descartes or Leibniz, quantitative rationalists believe that the mind is not trustworthy because it is enslaved to conventions, habits, prejudices, and superstitious. But whether the mind is considered trustworthy or not is its confidence in the level of beliefs. What it is important to note is that the epistemology *starts and ends with the individual* (rather than the social). In fact, is wasn't until well into the twentieth century in the West that philosophers began to consider that epistemology could be social. Stephen Lukas makes this point in his book *Individualism*.

Individualism and Formal Operations and space

Lastly, as we saw in the previous chapter, the development of formal operations was crucial for upper management in learning to supervise and plan; for capitalists to manage their budgets; for bankers to manipulate credit; and for investors to play the stock market. Later in the twentieth century, formal operations were developed and spread at least partly among the working class.

As we also saw in the last chapter, for collectivist selves in the Middle Ages their identity was immediately grounded in the roles and situations in the villages. In addition, these roles and situations were rooted in definite meeting 'places' at particular times of the year (cyclic time). It follows that in this pre-operational cognition, the classification systems that collectivists use are complexive—that is, objects are grouped based on *perceptual proximity, functional and situational considerations*. But since the Renaissance, we can see a gradual loosening of individual loyalty to the roles being played. Soon after, thanks to the printing press, newspapers, and the railroad, new connections were made with strangers—whether as merchants, scientists or artists. Concurrently, as relations between people were changing, individualists questioned their 'stations' in life (class mobility) along with the cyclic time and its foundation in agriculture. All these material changes are reflected in how individualists classify information.

In formal operational thinking, there is a move away from the merging of people, places and times towards a differentiation of all three. In formal operations, thanks to Newton, physical space became absolute and separated from matter. So too, social space was organized like Euclidean space as much as possible into grids in cites and on maps. Furthermore, as we saw in chapter six, as time sped up it became independent and separate from events. Just as the individualist leaves behind the animistic causality of the magical traditions for the efficient causality of modern science, so too, in formal operational thinking, natural events are explained as occurring because of *other physical causes* rather than the will of demons or gods. As people, events, time and space are separated out, the classification systems reflect these changes. Instead of a complexive classification system, objects are subject to *taxonomic classification* based on the similarity of objects to each other, independently of the function or situation in which they are found.

As we saw in chapter one, in the Middle Ages the boundaries between the collectivist self, society, and nature were porous. The person did not imagine they had an identity that had autonomy from society or the realm of the spirits. But slowly, the individualist self gradually came to see oneself as fundamentally separate from society and nature, at least at the end of the nineteenth century. In formal operations, this roughly corresponds to the mind understanding itself not as a substance but as a process. The mind is no longer imagined as another physical substance operating in the workings of nature, such as smoke or wind. Neither is it connected to the physiology if the individual is in the form of breath or the heart. The mind is an invisible mediator between nature and our bodies, but being reduced to neither.

As the individualist self-worked on their self-development, they were able to analyze critically the events that had occurred in their life. Instead of imagining that events just happened to them because of luck, bad magic or God's will, they had to look at the consequences and causes for why things happened. Some events were accidents, while others were not, and connected to each other by causes that may not follow immediately. This corresponds in formal operations to the mind performing reversible operations in their thinking rather than being enslaved to appearances. In formal operations, the chronology of events is reorganized is the service of underlying causes.

As we saw in chapter twelve, for collectivists in the Middle Ages there were no accidents. Every event was chock full of meaning. But as part of the individualist self's navigation through the world, there emerged an understanding of chance and probability. Living in a capitalist world, he must understand likelihoods and probabilities. If he was a capitalist living in the seventeenth century, he needed to judge what was the best bet for shipping his goods overseas. If he was a wage-worker selling his labor, the worker had to guess where to place himself in the labor market. The individualist skill of asking what the odds were corresponds to Piagetian description of the understanding of chance in formal operations. Here chance is not understood as the result of sorcery, demons or an angry God. Neither is it understood as a result of the weaknesses in human reasoning. Chance is understood as an objective property of the real world.

As I said earlier, a major component of individualist self-development is self-reflection on his own past actions as well as his future plans. So too, in formal operations, the mind does not limit itself to operating on real world problems, as concrete operations might. In formal operations, a body of ideas in a discipline and their relationships to other ideas is examined independent of real world problem-solving. This means the mind examines deductive relationships of syllogisms and common fallacious reasoning. The most important result of this is formal operational thinking tests by systematically organizing all possible relationships in a problem, *even hypothetical ones*. In the concrete operations thinking, this flight into rationalist heaven appears to be impractical and silly. But for individualists out to change the world, examining systematically all possibilities, even hypothetical ones, is a foundation for imagining new interventions into society or the biophysical nature.

Geographical Space, linear time and becoming civilized

Up until now we have treated these psychological elements as if they all emerged at the same time within an 800-year period. But this wasn't always the case. For example, individualism in Europe was developing as early as the thirteenth century in England, while in the United States it developed in the early nineteenth century. Another case is when we think about the relationship between becoming civilized, geographical space and linear time. People became civilized in both Europe and the United States in the seventeenth century, but theories of progress (linear time) did not emerge until the eighteenth and nineteenth centuries. The same is true for the geographical space that emerges in European cities in the eighteenth and nineteenth centuries.

The first wave of becoming civilized in the century did not require a linear sense of time or geographical space. In fact, the manners of the court aristocracy had little to do with either. But once linear time and geographical space emerged, it changed what it meant to be civilized. In Europe (France), the home of the civilizational process was the courts. In the United States, the equivalence of being civilized was on the plantation between aristocrats.

But in the nineteenth century, the location where adults were civilized moved to the cities in both Europe and the United States. But once city life emerged, becoming civilized spread beyond the aristocrats to include the middle classes. Now becoming civilized was a more unstable undertaking, because of the pace of life and the unpredictability of public encounters with complete strangers.

The relationship between becoming civilized, geographical space and a linear theory of progress is not an interdependent relationship. Classes can and did become civilized without a linear sense of time or geographical space but once these emerge, they become interdependent. The construction of geographical space in cities can be achieved without a theory of progress, but something like a civilized process would need to be in place to govern the relationship between strangers exchanging goods and services under capitalism.

Chance, space, and romanticism

The 'wild' chance prior to the nineteenth century was based on exceptions to the rule of a deterministic nature and society. But by the nineteenth century, determinism was eroded, and what was once thought of as already determined was now seen as subject to the laws of either large numbers or pure irregularity. This change in how chance was understood was inseparable from the increase in the pace of life among uprooted individualists. The law of large numbers would never have occurred when geographical locates were conceived of as 'places' as they were in the Middle Ages. It takes a time-space compression in order for the law of large numbers to even be conceivable.

The true enemy of romanticism was a mechanically-determined nature and society. For a time, the early romantics would seize on any accidents or lawlessness as proof that there was still freedom. But as the realm of what counted as chance spread, and as space became more commercialized, the early romantics saw this as a new kind of coldness, cities with a lack of heart. The 'law of averages' appeared to ignore individual choice or will. So once again, the early romantics were lost at sea. However, the crypto-romantics at the end of the nineteenth century had celebrated the chance nature of social life as proof that all was lost and the best we could do was to live well on the slopes of Vesuvius. Either that or they escaped the chance nature of city life in Gothic novels, the artistic process (art for art's sake) or theosophy, which all gave comfort in different ways.

Value of Lucifer's Labyrinth material culture using absolute standards of society as a whole

Individualism vs collectivism

Collectivism in the Middle Ages in Europe and in the

United States was not as extreme as the collectivism that arose out of the bureaucratic agricultural states in other parts of the world such as China or India. Still, in Europe and the United States the collectivizing forces of the family, the Church and neighbors were constraining individuals. As I said earlier, the rise of individualism was a slower and smoother process in Europe than in the United States. In Europe, individualism had been 'cooking' in England since the thirteenth century. Though individualism was expressed in different countries, in different ways in different historical periods, the most important thing was that individualism had 600 years to develop. In the United States individualism didn't emerge until the beginning of the nineteenth century. The four different types of individualism arose there in only a hundred years' time, making it less cooked. This might partly explain the more extreme individualism that appeared in the United States.

But what about the value of individualism itself? I think it is fair to say that it was a good thing for society to challenge the conformity and obedience that was prevalent in the Middle Ages. I say this because society needs innovation and initiative if we are to adapt to a changing nature. If not taken too far, certain kinds of individualism do contribute to the social whole in the way of inventions, geographical discoverers, new artistic techniques and new political visions. In Europe, Renaissance and Enlightenment individualism provided most of this. In the United states, the utilitarian self provided a similar foundation. The revolution of the merchants against the trade monopolies of mercantile capitalism opened up a greater variety of products available and gave merchants and opportunity to sell their wares without being under the tutelages of these monopolies.

But in Europe in the nineteenth century, individualism was thrown into crisis by the industrial revolution and the rapid transformation of space and time. The result was that individualism became unhinged from society, and was experienced as if it has a life of its own. In the United States this alienated individualism took the form of:

- a spiritual withdrawal of the transcendentalists

- a greedy entrepreneurial individualism of the social Darwinists
- a backward-looking romanticism of frontier individualism

In Europe at the end of the nineteenth century, there arose an anemic, insecure crypto-romantic self with was self-indulgent and drunk on revelry as a way of life. This I see as degeneration.

An undervalued characteristic of individualism is its connection to universalism. When we talk about collectivism, we are talking about the power of intermediate groups including not only the family, church and neighbors but regional and provincial loyalties. The forces of Protestantism, the printing press, capitalism and the industrial revolution fracture and then marginalize these intermediate forces while creating another kind of loyalty—a loyalty to the state (nationalism). At the same time, printing, centralized transportation such as the railroad and mass communication creates a new voluntary social relationship with that other individualist artists and scientists from around the world. A loyalty to scientific associations, artistic clubs and political movements benefit both society and the individual.

Geographical space vs place

As we saw in chapter five, in the Middle Ages, with the exception of trading areas, and travel across locales, geography was organized as 'places'. Places are physical locales which support habit, sacred ritual, community building and belonging. Places are locations in which to physically to root memories and provide comfort. The rise of 'spaces' such as city-grids, the railroad, the expansion of trade routes and capitalist markets either drove people from their places, or hollowed those places out. Since spaces supported novelty, risk, danger and adventure, it both attracted and repelled those living in modern Europe.

The problem with spaces is the same as our problem with the accumulation of commodities. On the one hand, we need spaces, arenas in which we take initiative, try new roles, new occupations and we seek new thrills. The problem is that, thanks mostly to capitalism, the *proportion* of spaces compared to places has become lopsided, so that it is difficult even for middle-class people not to be 'lost in space'.

The other problem with spaces is the *content* of what is in them. What capitalism does not deliver real adventure, thrills and novelty but the *vicarious living* though the accumulation of commodities bought at departments stores in the second half of the nineteenth century. Space in cities was impoverished and became runways for commerce. It also promotes vicarious living through entertainment at sports stadiums, at movie theaters and mass musical concerts. The vicarious living here is through identifiable with celebrities in sports, movies and music.

Yet plenty of spaces have delivered adventure, thrills and exotic exploration without being commercialized. Revolutionary situations in the nineteenth century were examples of social exploration of new spatial realm with the building of barricades and the taking over or public space. Public meetings of scientific clubs, as well as gatherings in cafes by artistic movements like the impressionists are other examples. As I pointed out in my introduction, the book *St. Petersburg* describes city life in 1905 that shows city-life as its most exotic.

Linear social time (progress) vs cyclical time

The intellectuals in the eighteenth and nineteenth century who championed temporal notions of progress invited individuals into to step into a breathtaking macro-world in which different kinds of societies were organized and ranked according to their economic systems, political systems and religious evolution. Theories of progress also provided comfort to the people who believed in it that the industrial capitalist society they were living in was the latest and the greatest. They also provided the individual with hope for our social futures.

The problem with the theory of progress is that its theorists had little appreciation that the Middle Ages were not simply barbaric, superstitious and violent. There were religious heretical movements which championed mystical spiritual experience and the most extreme of these movement (Anabaptists) wanted to create a spiritual heaven on earth. Lastly, the theorists of progress understated the conflicts between social classes that capitalism produced, as well as the ecological deterioration, as capitalists looked at biophysical nature as 'externalities'.

Linear individual time: ontogenesis

Just as historians had organized human societies as a temporal chain in which societies evolved from 'immaturity to maturity', so psychologists became more dynamic in their approach to the individual. As we saw in chapter two, temperament theory categorized individuals as having essences based on the proportions of liquids in the body. Temperaments didn't change. But as temperament theory declined, John Locke proposed that the individual was born with a blank slate on which anything could be written. This led psychologists at the end of the nineteenth century such as James Mark Baldwin and Freud to suggest that the individual "progresses" through identifiable stages.

In chapter seven we identified one such psychological developmental theory: Erikson's stages of psycho social development. To be fair to Erikson, his theory cannot easily be characterized as 'progress' because it contains conflict at every stage. He also suggests that if a stage does not go well, the problems which result are not dissolved, but brought into the next stage. Erikson's weakness is that his stages for individuals don't hold up very well prior to the nineteenth century. (See Table 7.4)

For example, children in the Middle Ages were considerably more mature in the first six years of life than children in industrial capitalist because they were thrown into adult life much sooner---working, gambling, and witnessing sexual activity. It is not until the eighteenth century that children were really protected and seen more as individuals. As for adolescence prior to industrialization, they were able to be independent sooner, as they worked outside the home.

Adolescents in the second half of the nineteenth century were more sheltered at home. They were in a state of limbo, as new middle-class jobs were opening up, but required training. Eventually public-school systems opened up more possibilities for adolescence but that occurred after the Gilded Age. So, in neither childhood or adolescence can we see "progress" in any kind of straightforward way.

As for adulthood, it is problematic to say that the lives of adults improved. It is clear that adults began to live longer. By the end of the nineteenth century, the average life span had risen from thirty-five to forty years of age. In addition, the variety of occupations for adults expanded. Adults did spend more time reflecting on their lives, but this started with Puritan diary-keeping long before the industrialization process. Romantic love began to be considered part of a marriage, thus development intimacy in marriages was present. However, when historical social psychologist Roy Baumeister compared life stages across nine-dimensions, most of the time by the nineteenth century, individual life was either destabilized or trivialized. These are hardly indicators of progress.

Civilization vs uncivilized

As we saw in chapter eight, the civilizational processes varied between Europe and the United States. In the Eastern the United States people were more literate, obsessed with cleanliness, more informal and more violent as the state did not disarm its population as much as European states did. In Europe, becoming civilized was less dispersed across classes and concentrated in the aristocracy.

In the Middle Ages, aristocrats had a code of honor governing how they engaged each other when meeting. But for the most part, aristocrats lived on different manors and did not have to develop a coding system for ongoing relationships, as far as I know. This changed when the noble's land was bought off by the merchants. Because kings did not trust aristocrats to offer reliable military protection, only choice open to aristocrats was to join the king's court. What is valuable for western civilization is that aristocrats had to develop the social psychological skills of hindsight, foresight and insight for dealing with situations which:

- were densely populated
- necessitated playing multiple roles
- engaged with strangers
- had intra-class problems that had to be conducted non-violently

Gradually this skill spread in the eighteenth and nineteenth centuries to the middle classes and civilized behavior spread from the courts to the public. But at the same time, as feudal relations faded and representational political bodies became the norm, there was less deference between social classes when they did engage each other. On the whole I think becoming civilized, in spite of its degeneration into phoniness and triviality, was an advance, in terms of small groups and mass psychology.

Romanticism

Just as individualism developed in Europe for over six hundred years before it came to the United States in the nineteenth century, so romanticism emerged in Europe with Rousseau in the second half of the eighteenth century and only in the United States towards the end of the nineteenth century. The early romanticism in Europe, in my estimation, was a healthy reaction against the stifling obsession with manners and appearances that governed court society. The work of Rousseau in emphasizing sincerity, emotional expression and self-reflection gave individualist civil servants, teachers and artists hope in overcoming the perceived mechanization of nature and science

However, the late-nineteenth century crypto-romantics lost their appreciation of content and substance in art (art-for- art's sake). They took the expressive cult of individuality towards a darker side with its flight to the occult; its excessive use of the drugs; its interest in decadence; it's championing of mental illness as an ideal and the sadistic and masochistic side of sex were processes that were not inevitable and certainly not something which brought out the best in people.

Meanwhile in Yankeedom, romanticism had neither of these extremes of old nor the crypto-romanticism. It played itself out in the formation and sustaining of the frontier. Frontiersman and pioneers were anything but romantics. It was American writers and painters who noticed the contrast between the civilized Eastern coast, the plantation culture decadence. Both were compared unfavorably against the Indian fighting, rustic gunslinging characters like Daniel Boone and Davy Crocket. Western novels dramatized in stories about Jesse James, Kit Carson and Billy the Kid. The painters of the American Renaissance—Moran, Remington and Church—sanctified the pristine American West.

Rationality vs reason

Rationality as a cognitive process has been very good for the West. The process of comparing proportions in closed systems had brought the West systems of perspective painting, and higher mathematics that allowed scientific breakthroughs in astronomy and physics. The invention of musical notational systems allowed people to harmonize more clearly, at a larger scale and for longer durations.

Where rationality went wrong was in its application to *open* systems with uncertain outcomes, its 'quest for certainty,' into the areas of history, sociology and psychology. Rationalism led to the extreme dualities such as:

- otherworldly idealism vs mechanical materialism
- mysticism vs hedonism
- aesthetic mind and a mechanical body
- disembodied theory and mindless action

It was the *reasoning* process which accepts probably rather than certainty that dissolves these dualities. It wasn't until the fanaticism of the seventeenth century waned that reason began to be used again among the higher classes. Reason challenged rationalistic assumption that nature was stable, matter was inert, mental activities were all conscious, objectivity meant detachment and economic activity was rational. Rationality has its place, as the saying goes, 'within reason.'

Quantitative rationality: chance

As we saw in chapter twelve, in the Middle Ages the search for knowledge was imagined dualistically. One the one hand, the criteria for truth was certainty, or demonstration and based on the judgment of judges or ecclesiastical authorities. On the other hand, probability was understood as an inferior form of knowledge, not much better than opinions. The big transition from this in the seventeenth century was the transformation of signs to circumstantial evidence. This opened the door to inductive logic and making predictions (Table 12.6).

This new understanding was partly driven by the need to create insurance policies for merchants and for the state to gather statistics for crowd control.

Chance in the sixteenth and seventeenth century was understood as unforeseen accidents, exceptions to the rule. Most everything else was governed by determinism. But by the nineteenth century, chance had expanded to cover most all natural and social phenomenon driven by the law of large numbers. This included life-insurance policies. What was now possible was to differentiate between foolish risks and calculated risks. By the late nineteenth century, determinism, once scientists' pride and joy was being undermined even in the house of physics. Irregularity had won the day.

What are the pros and cons of understanding the laws of chance and laws of large numbers? For one thing, it directly challenges spiritual notions of deism or of God having a plan for every individual. Chance also undermines the work of the devil because, like it or not, the devil wants to control things and would prefer not to roll the dice. Therefore, understanding the laws of large numbers is not for the spiritually faint of heart. On the other hand, for scientists it created problems. At the heart of science is the search for causes. But if everything was to be explained by the laws of chance, then the ground that science starts from seems to be undermined. A solution to this is to recognize that the law of large numbers operates within a causal body of knowledge which varies from physics to biology to society.

The danger of understanding the laws of large numbers is twofold. One to weaken the will and to assume that there is no use planning and then executing one's will. On the other hand, there is a misunderstanding of chance as meaning that *anything* is possible and that knowledge of chance is somehow connected to a lawless kind of freedom.

Formal Operational thinking

In the Middle Ages, a combination of preoperational thinking and concrete operational thinking engaged people's minds when they thought about local, particular problems on their farms or in their workshops. One shortcoming of preoperational and concrete operational thinking is that they do not encourage thinking about problems beyond everyday life. It does not it encourage deliberation about the deep past and deep future.

Formal operational thinking promoted an expansion of the mind beyond everyday life that would encourage people to think about the objectively expanding horizons of the world they lived in. These worlds could be foreign lands in the case of commerce. As we saw in the last chapter, formal operations were both the product and co-producer of increasingly abstract forms of currency which facilitated trade over wider regions and nation-states. Other expanding horizons included the astronomical world of other planets or the micro-world of biology. Formal operations promoted looking at the world objectively through the mind of the scientist. At the same time, formal operations invited the mind to reflect on its own depths, analyzing the thinking process itself, that is, thinking about thinking.

This 'thinking squared' meant that the mind could

deliberate on its own symbol-making systems of music, art and mathematics, developing each. Through scientific methodology, formal operations helped scientists to systematically analyze its most common errors in the experimental processes, expanding Aristotle's fallacies. The fruits of formal operational thinking will be most likely to operate in professional work in which people are paid to think—doctors, lawyers, architects, city planners, librarians and managers.

Piaget argued that intelligence is adapting to environments. The danger of formal operations might come in its application in situations where a less complex form of thinking would be more intelligent. For example, dancing, singing or any disciplined moving in space requires a sophisticated version of sensorimotor intelligence. Using formal operational thinking to dance risks being labeled a klutz or spastic by others. Another danger of formal operations is that it can be used in the service of social processes that are fundamentally irrational such those discussed on under capitalism in the 'dark side of formal operational thinking' section.

Value of Lucifer's Labyrinth material culture using absolute standards of class and gender

Painting with very broad brushstrokes, we can say that all of Lucifer's elements impacted middle class and upper middles classes more than the lower classes both for better and for worse. Poor and working-class people were either:

- untouched by these elements;
- they participated in their benefits marginally; or
- the elements were used against them so their life deteriorated as a result

When it comes to gender, both the virtues and the vices of Lucifer's Elements impacted men more than women. We can say that the same three possibilities-were in place when it came to women.

Individualism relative to class and gender

Whether in Europe or in Yankeedom, individualism helped the lives of the upper-middle class and the middle class. For these social classes, autonomy, privacy, individual rights, self-reflectiveness and self-development were real advances from life in the Middle Ages.

For the working class, they dream of autonomy and privacy of the middle classes, but the material conditions of working-class people is such as to work against this value. Psychologically, this worked against working class people because under capitalism, the individual is seen responsible for success and failure. Therefore, many working-class people believed there was something wrong with them for not rising in their social class. The exception to the rule is workers who because socialists, because socialism has a systematic way of unmasking individualism as ideological propaganda to mask class exploitation. American workers were more subject to this 'hidden injury of class' because of the onslaught of individualism in one century must have been overwhelming.

In the case of women, we can say that a few upper middle-class women, mostly in the arts, had autonomy, privacy and were self-reflective. But for the most part, individualism was not a dream for most women because so much of their life was both working at semi-skilled jobs and managing the domestic household. There was no time, place or circumstance for anything else.

Geographical space in relation to class and gender

For working-class people, the transformation of places into spaces was a loss of their physical attachment to neighborhoods, play haunts, and what has been called 'third places' by Ray Oldenberg in his book, *Third Places*. These third places are public, physical sites (indoors or outdoors) which are attended regularly. A working-class person goes to be with "regulars" where they play games, (pool, darts, cards, chess) or banter about politics or sports. What makes it a third place is that they are encouraged by the owners of the place to stay as long as they liked.

At the end of the nineteenth century, Metropolitan cities were beginning to promote vicarious living through entertainment with sports teams at ballparks, at movie houses and musical clubs. Movie stars and musicians seem to be living the life the working class wants. In addition to unions, all these outlets form a new working-class loyalty to that comes from a deterioration of working-class neighborhoods.

Meanwhile in his real work-life, the grid system of transportation is set up for capitalists to speed up the process and expansion of production. The creation of geographical space in cities makes working class people work faster and faster to while staying in the same space. At the same time, as Richard Sennett had pointed out, urban planner's Haussman's reorganization of cities intentionally fractured the connection between working class neighborhoods to make revolutions more difficult.

While amusement parks, state lotteries and casinos provide spatial thrills, at least in the case of lotteries and gambling establishments, these institutions empty his pockets of the little cash he has. Nineteenth century railroads were no scenic opportunities for them to reflect on as they were for the middle and upper-middle class people. Working class people rode in crowded, windowless box cars when they did travel, which was mostly work-related.

Broadly speaking, most women did not find their primary identity in spaces, but in places such as the home and the neighborhoods. Upper middle-class women were certainly present in the space of public salons and middle-class women began to work in cities by the end of the nineteenth century, taking clerical jobs. However, a vicarious outlet for middle-class women were department stores because they were safe public spaces to inhabit while having access to a seeming cornucopia of goods. To a lesser extent, variety stores served the same function for working class women.

Linear time (social progress) in relation to class and gender

For the professional classes, doctors, lawyers, architects, merchants and those in state administration, the theory of social progress was no dream, but a reality when compared to their lives before the seventeenth century. The same was true, to a lesser extent, for the middle classes. For the working class, this depends on the century. By the eighteenth century, class mobility for them was real. In the early and mid-nineteenth century, work for those trapped in factories, work became worse than it was for them as artisans before the industrial revolution. Then, after 1870 thanks to their organization into unions and the presence of socialism, life improved for working class people.

As for upper-class and upper-middle class women, the eighteenth-century salons allowed women as a group to have a public identity. The nineteenth century continued improvement for these women in the arts, especially as writers. It would be a stretch to say that for working-class women, the eighteenth and nineteenth centuries could be characterized as progress. However, working class women made a place for themselves in social revolutionary situations and in some cases made themselves into revolutionaries. The names Louise Michel, Vera Figner, Vera Zazulich and Rosa Luxenberg are just the tip of the iceberg. However, this stepping forward for women was not 'progress' as it was defined because according to the theory of progress, there are social improvements that happen gradually, not through revolutionary activity.

Childhoods, adolescence, and adulthood in term of class and gender

The eighteenth and nineteenth centuries were less harrowing for all social classes, as most disease was under control and family life, at least for the middle classes became more privatized and cozier. Upper middle-class children and adolescence had tutors and, according to Phillipe Aries, childhood was seen as a distinct period in life (rather than seeing children as 'little adults'). Children were seen more as individuals in part because as mortality rates decreased it paid for adults to give more attention to them. Thanks to the work of John Locke, children were seen as blank slates, rather than little demons and parents were held more responsible for socializing their children.

In a way, teenage life was worse in the nineteenth century as families no longer sent their teenagers away to work. In living and working with other adults, boys and girls had more freedom. In the nineteenth century, they lived at home and then either were trained professionally or, in the case of working class, they went to work in factories. In terms of adulthood, the lives of working-class men deteriorated as factory work became or specialized and they lost control of the work process to middle managers and as machines took over the creative part of their work. The lives of working-class women throughout the nineteenth century did not improve and a good case could be made that it got worse.

In terms of female ontogenesis, female children were generally treated as less valuable than boys and they spent less time in school than boys. In addition, unless girls were from the middle and upper-middle classes, they were not taught to read and write, or study in the sciences or philosophy. What training they had was in domestic economics or in the arts. After the middle of the seventeenth century, women began to come out from under the oppressive hand of the patriarchal father, as Lawrence Stone has point out. Another advance was that marriages became more companionate, and for the first time, romance was expected *inside* a marriage rather than something to be found outside of marriage.

Becoming civilized according to class and gender

In my book *Forging Promethean Psychology*, I argued that the working-class in Europe and the United States was never civilized. Being civilized was strictly first an upper-middle class project and then, in the eighteenth and nineteenth century, a middle class phenomenon. What was done to the working class was to *discipline* them. This was done in Churches (standing, kneeling) in the military socialization (drilling), when working within state bureaucracies (in following bureaucratic rules) and lastly factories (in the time-and-motion applications of Fredrich Taylor). Mostly discipline was used to tame working class men to internalize being obedient to the authorities.

In the case of woman, if part of becoming civilized meant cultivating hindsight, foresight and insight; if it meant knowing when to be embarrassed and ashamed; if it meant monitoring the behavior of others and knowing when to be quiet and when to speak up without escalating, women, even working-class women have been trained to be civilized in ways that are foreign to men. The difference is that women performed these skills in *domestic* households rather than in the courts and in public.

Becoming a romantic according to class and gender

Romanticism was essentially a lower middle-class movement which never caught on among the working class. This is understandable, given that working classes have struggled to get more of a piece of the capitalist pie. Generally, the working class does not rise above daily life and muse over span the last three centuries and identify historical trends. It does not study languages of old or consider the virtues of peasant life before the capitalist revolution. Working class people generally prefer religion to the occult, hard and soft liquor to drugs and likes its art representational rather than expressive. At least by the end of the ninettenth century, working class men and women prefer their sex in a straightforward way without the additions of sadomasochism. In this, working class women are pretty much on the same page has their men.

Rationality according to class and gender

Working-class men are reasonable, not rational. Setting up rational systems of philosophy (Descartes), law (Grotius), mathematics (Leibniz), or physics (Galileo, Newton) is the work of the professional classes used to handling symbolic linguistic and numerical systems. Rational systematizing for manipulation is an expansion of the mental work that goes with their work. The kind of reason the working class engages is not the high reasoning that Toulmin describes in his argumentation studies, but reason either through experience or artisan experiment (Table 10.1). While both rationality and reason benefit from literacy and numeracy, it is possible for working class people to reason well and be illiterate and ill numerate. It is not possible to be rational without having mastered literacy and/or numeracy. With the exception of some skilled working-class jobs, most jobs often require neither. Middle and upper middle-class work require at least literacy and, in some cases, both literacy and numeracy.

Chance among the working class and women

Gambling goes all the way back into human history as we saw in chapter twelve. It cuts across all social classes, since predictability about nature and society is a very important skill. Gambling is especially important to working class people since gambling is often seen as a fast way to make money and to change fates when the normal channels of success have been blocked or are too slow to materialize. However, this does not mean that working class people ever explored any of the theories of probability or chance that we've covered in chapters twelve and thirteen. In fact, they might have good reason to *avoid* them, at least in relation to gambling. To the extent that these theories spell out what the real chances of winning the lottery are, working class people would ignore them because they would see how far-fetched their hopes really are.

In the other fields in which it paid to understand theories of probability and the law of large numbers, these were the areas for the middle and upper-middle class people. The calculation of annuities were tools for merchant capitalists defending themselves against piracy. For purposes of crowd control, calculating the census were important for state administrators. The fields of statistical rationality in the scientific method were also important for physicists and astronomers. As for working class women they are less likely than their men to gamble for evolutionary reasons.

Formal operational thinking in the working class and women

As we discussed in chapter fifteen, formal operations is the kind of thinking most consistent with the work the middle and upper middle classes do. With the exception of skilled working class, such as electricians or carpenters, much working-class work is body work. In most working-class jobs, workers are paid to follow orders and do physical labor more than they are paid to think. As we saw in chapter fifteen, the working class must develop some skills in formal operational thinking in order to participate in a capitalist economy just by receiving a wage, renting rather than owning their tools, buying commodities on installment (end of the nineteenth century) or depositing or withdrawing cash. However, they will rarely be trained in the full use of formal operations as long as their work involves primarily physical actions and taking orders.

As for women, upper-class and upper-middle class women certainly learned to write and possibly read music more than learn mathematics. However, the fields that they might practice writing are limited. The fields of the sciences, including scientific method, law, engineering, architecture was pretty much closed to them. While the nunnery was a haven for smart women to contemplate God or have mystical experiences, it was the priests and bishops that developed the theoretical systems that might resemble formal operational thinking.

Please see Table 16.2 which summarizes the pros and cons of the Lucifer's Labyrinth both for society as a whole and relatively according to class and gender.

Table 16.1 The Amplification of Lucifer's Psychological Elements

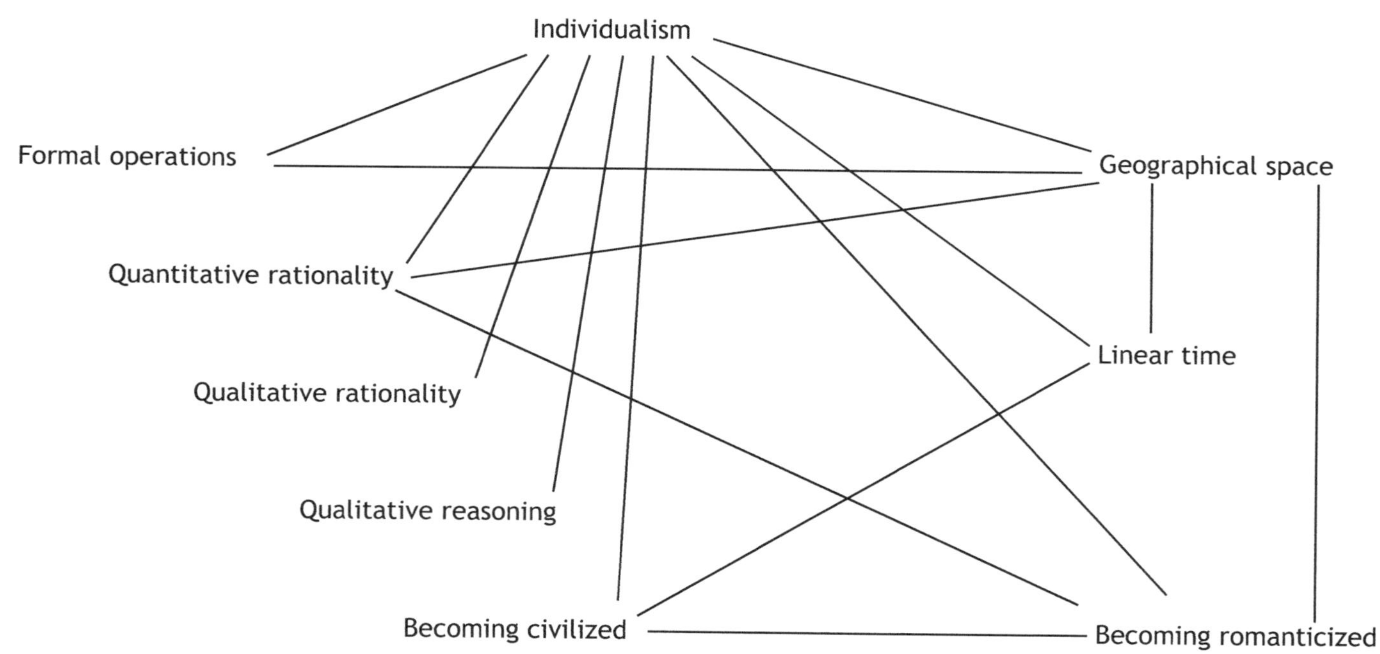

Table 16.2 The Perils and Promise of Lucifer's Elements

Element of Lucifer's Labyrinth	Evaluation based on society as a whole	Evaluation based on class (working class and gender)
Individualism	Challenged conformity and obedience and monopoly of trading companies.	*Working class people conflicted between aspiring to be individuals but their objective situation discourages it. Causes psychological problems except for to a lesser extent for socialists.*
	Promoted seafaring discoveries, science, the arts, political visions. Renaissance, Reformation and Enlightenment individualism in Europe. Utilitarian self in the US Promoted universalist—de-sensualized communities of strangers.	*Loss of "places"*
	Spiritual withdrawal of transcendentalists. Entrepreneurial individualist and romantic individualism are liabilities for different reasons. Universalism leads to nationalism	
Geographical "space"	Exotic city-life provides arena to try new identities. Café's for artistic movements. Taking over cities in revolutionary situations.	*Amusement parks, state lotteries empty the pockets of working-class.*
	Cities become "runways for commerce". Needs of commerce determine city planning.	*Grid system of cities makes working class people work faster and harder.* Department stores provide middle- class and working-class women with an outlet through shopping.
	Vicarious entertainment through sports, stadiums, movie houses and musical concerts	*Vicarious entertainment as a substitute living from alienated existence.*
Linear time (social)	Progress helps to order and rank different kinds of societies and provides hope for the future.	There was improvement for upper middle and middle-class men and some women. Improvement for working class in 18th century.
	Understates the Middle Ages which had heretics and invited mystical experience.	*Understates the misery of the lower classes in the 19th century.*
Linear time (ontogenesis)	Self-development of personality replaces temperament.	*Adolescence had less freedom as they lived at home and worked in factories.*
	Both childhood and adolescence become more protected and dependent than prior to the 18th century.	*Female children treated not as valuable as boys and had with less schooling.* Marriages of adult women become more companionate.
	Increase in variety of work in 19th century	*Factory work for men is more specialized and creative part of job taken over by managers or machines.*
	People begin to live longer after 1875	

Becoming civilized	Cultivation of hindsight, foresight and insight based in dense social situations in multiple roles with acquaintances.	*Working class men become disciplined not civilized.* Women had elements of being civilized but in domestic settings rather than in courts or in cities.
Becoming romantic	Being sincere, emotional expressiveness and selfreflection.	Working class men and women did not become romantics.
	Expressive individualism loses touch with the objective world. Art for art's sake, occultism, drugs.	
Qualitative Rationality	Perspective painting in the arts. Higher mathematics; musical notions allow for longer and larger scale harmonies.	Neither working class men or women become rational. They remain reasonable in everyday life
	Application of rationality to open systems leads to problems in understanding history, sociology, and psychology	
Quantitative rationality (chance)	Insurance policies for merchants against piracy. Statistics for the population of cities.	Did not use systematic chance in their gambling because it would reveal how far-fetched their chances of winning were.
Formal operational thinking	Expansion in the abstractness of the natural and social worlds. Expansion in depth of the inner world of self-reflection (doctors, lawyers, architects and merchants).	*Most working-class men and women do not do the mental work that requires formal operational thinking.*
	Learning about common fallacies in scientific thinking.	
	Application to creation of fictitious capital.	
Element of Lucifer's Labyrinth	**Evaluation based on society as a whole**	**Evaluation based on class (working class and gender)**

Works Cited

Introduction

Barbu, Zevedei. 1960. *Problems of Historical Psychology.* Greenwood Press.
Berman, Marshall. 1988. *All That is Solid Melts into Air.* Penguin.
Blunden, Andy. 2010. *An Interdisciplinary Theory of Activity.* Haymarket Books.
Ratner, Carl. 2002. *Cultural Psychology.* Plenum.
Ratner, Carl. 1991. *Vygotsky's Sociohistorical Psychology and its Contemporary Applications*. Plenum.
Ratner, Carl. 2012. *Macro Cultural Psychology.* Oxford University Press.
Stannard, David. 1980. *Shrinking History.* Oxford University Press.
Szaluta, Jacques. 2000. *Psychohistory: Theory and Practice.* American University Studies.
Tulviste, Peeter. 1991. *The Cultural-Historical Development of Verbal Thinking*. Nova Science Publishers Inc.
Vygotsky, Lev. 1988. *Thought and Language*. MIT Press.

Chapter 1 The Promethean Self: Individualism from the Middle Ages to the Reformation

Bond, Michael Harris and Bevington Smith. 1999. *Social Psychology Across Cultures*. Allyn and Bacon.
Burke, Peter. 1987. *The Italian Renaissance*. Princeton University.
Cassirer, Ernst. 1963. *The Individual and the Cosmos in Renaissance Philosophy.* Harper Torchbooks.
Gurevich, Aaron. 1995. *Origins of European Individualism.* Blackwell.
Heller, Agnes. 1978. *Renaissance Man*. Schocken Books.
Lukes, Steven. 1978. *Individualism*. Blackwell.
Lyon, John. 1978. *Invention of the Self*. Southern University

Press.
MacFarlane, Alan. 1978. *Origins of English Individualism.* Cambridge University Press.
MacPherson, *Crawford Brough.* 1962. *The Political Theory of Possessive Individualism.* Oxford University Press.
Martin, John. 2004. *Myths of Renaissance Individualism.* Palgrave.
Martines, Lauro. 1979. *Power and Imagination.* Alfred Knopf.
Morris, Colin. 2000. *Discovery of the Individual 1000-1250.* University of Toronto Press.
Trilling, Lionel. 1971. *Sincerity and Authenticity.* Harvard University Press.
Triandis, Harry. 1995. *Individualism and Collectivism.* Westview.
Ullmann, Walter. *1963. Individualism and Society in the Middle Ages.* Johns Hopkins University Press.
Weintraub, Karl. 1978. *The Value of the Individual.* University of Chicago.

Chapter 2 The Promethean Self: From the capitalist revolution to Proto-Romanticism

Arikha, Noga. 2007. *Passions and Tempers.* Harper Perennial.
Berman, Marshall. 1970. *The Politics of Authenticity.* Verso.
Dumont, Louis. 1986. *Essays on Individualism.* University of Chicago Press.
Hirschman, Albert. 2013. *The Passions and the Interests.* Princeton University Press.
Murray, Alexander. 1978. *Reason in the Middle Ages.* Clarendon Press.
Lindholm, Charles. 2001. *Culture and Identity.* McGraw Hill.
Taylor, Charles. 1989. *Sources of the Self.* Harvard University Press.

Chapter 3 Yankee Individualism: Its Spiritual and Economic Foundations

Arieli, Yehoshua. 1966. *Individualism and Nationalism in American Ideology.* Penguin.
Crowley, John E. 1974. *This Sheba Self.* Johns Hopkins University Press.
Cushman, Philip. 1995. *Constructing the Self, Constructing America.* Addison-Wesley.
Curry, Richard Orr and Lawrence B. Goodheart. 1991. *American Chameleon.* Kent State University Press.
Shlain, Barry Alan. 1994. *Myth of American Individualism.* Princeton University Press.

Chapter 4 The Varieties of Yankee Individualism: From the Early Nineteenth Century through the Gilded Age

Anderson, Quentin. 1971. *The Imperial Self.* Alfred A. Knopf.
Berger, Peter and Brigitte Berger and Hansfried Kellner. 1973. *The Homeless Mind.* Vintage.
Braverman, Harry. 1974. *Labor and Monopoly Capital.* Monthly Review.
Fromm, Erich. 1955. *The Sane Society.* Holt Reinhart and Winston.
Hewitt, James. 1989. *Dilemmas of the American Self.* Temple University Press.
Hofstadter, Richard. 1967. *Social Darwinism in American Thought.* Beacon Press.
Horsman, Reginald. 1981. *Race and Manifest Destiny.* Harvard University Press.
Lasch, Christopher. 1978. *The Culture of Narcissism.* Norton.
Melchior-Bonnet, Sabine. 2001. *The Mirror: A History.* Routledge.
Reisman, David. 1961. *The Lonely Crowd.* Yale University Press.
Sennett, Richard. 1998. *The Corrosion of Character.* Norton.
Wheelis, Allen. 1958. *The Quest for Identity.* Norton.

Chapter 5 Promethean Geography: Households, Theatre and Metropolitan Life

Bell, Paul and Jeffrey D. Fisher and A. Baum and Thomas C. Greene. 1996. *Environmental Psychology.* Harcourt Brace.
Berman, Marshall. 1988. *All That is Solid Melts into Air.* Penguin.
Biddiss, Michael. 1977. *Age of the Masses.* Harper and Row.
Briggs, Asa and Peter Burke. 2005. *Social History of Media.* Polity.
Cipolla, Carlo. 1978. *Clocks and Culture.* Norton.
Hobsbawm, Eric. 1989. *Age of Empire.* Vintage.
Hughes, Stuart. 1958. *Consciousness and Society 1890-1930.* Vintage.
Kern, Stephen. 1983. *Culture of Time and Space 1880-1914.* Harvard University Press.
Lofland, Lyn. 1998. *Public Realm.* Aldine De Gruyter.
Pirenne, Henri. 2014. *Medieval Cities.* Princeton University Press.
Sacks, Robert. 1992. *Place Modernity and the Consumer's World.* Johns Hopkins University Press.
Sacks, Robert. 1997. *Homo Geographicus.* Johns Hopkins University Press.
Sennett, Richard. 1990. *Consciousness of the Eye.* Alfred A. Knopf.
Sennett, Richard. 1977. *Fall of Public Man.* Vintage.
Sennett, Richard. 1994. *Flesh and Stone.* Norton.
Schivelbusch, Wolfgang. 1986. *The Railway Journey.* University of California Press.
Schivelbusch, Wolfgang. 1995. *Disenchanted Night.* University of California Press.
Shattuck, Roger. 1968. *The Banquet Years.* Vintage.
Sjgoberg, Gideon. 1965. *The Pre-Industrial City.* Free Press.
Starr, Paul. 2004. *Creation of Media.* Basic Books.
Sternberger, Dolf. 1955. *The Panorama of the Nineteenth Century.* Urizen Books.
Tuan, Yi-Fu. 1982. *Segmented Worlds and the Self.* University of Minnesota Press.
Tuan, Yi-Fu. 1977. *Space and Place.* University of Minnesota Press.

Chapter 6 Promethean Temporality: From Cyclic to Linear Time

Jones, Richard. 1961. *Ancients and Moderns*. Dover.

Kern, Stephen. 1983. *Culture of Time and Space 1880-1914*. Harvard University Press.

Nisbet, Richard. 1970. *History of the Idea of Progress*. Basic Books.

Toulmin, Stephen and June Goodfield. 1965. *The Discovery of Time*. Harper and Row.

Chapter 7 Ontogenesis: The Evolution of Childhoods Adolescence and Adulthood

Aries, Phillipe. 1962. *Centuries of Childhood*. Vintage.

Bock, Philip. 1999. *Rethinking Psychological Anthropology*. Waveland Press.

Baumeister, Roy. 1986. *Identity, Cultural Change and the Struggle for Self*. Oxford University Press.

Friedman, Lawrence. 1999. *Identity's Architect*. Scribner.

Gauvain, Mary. 2001. *The Social Context of Cognitive Development*. Guilford Press.

Karpov, Yurily. 2006. *The Neo-Vygotskian Approach to Child Development*. Cambridge University Press.

Langer, Jonas. 1969. *Theories of Development*. Holt Rinehart and Winston, Inc.

Meyrowitz, Joshua. 1985. *No Sense of Place*. Oxford University Press.

Richardson, Ken. 1988. *Models of Cognitive Development*. Psychology Press.

Werner, Han. 1957. *Comparative Psychology of Mental Development*. International Universities Press.

Valsiner, Jaan. 2005. *Heinz Werner and Developmental Science*. Plenum Publishers.

Houston, R. A. 1988. *Literacy in Early Modern Europe*. Longman.

Stone, Lawrence. 1977. *The Family Sex and Marriage in England 1500-1800*. Weidenfeld and Nicolson.
Riegal, Klaus. 1978. *Psychology, Mon Amour.* Houghton Mifflin Company.

Chapter 8 Becoming Civilized in Europe: How the Upper Classes Got Class

Burke, Peter. 1978. *Popular Culture in Early Modern Europe*. Harper Torchbooks.
Campbell, Colin. 1987. *Protestant Ethic and the Spirit of Consumerism*. Writers Printshop.
Mennell, Stephen. 1992. *Norbert Elias: An Introduction*. University College Dublin Press.
Ranulf, Svend. 1964. *Moral Indignation and Middle Class Psychology*. Schocken Books.
Spiereburg, Pieter. 1991. *The Broken Spell*. Rutgers University Press.
Van Krieken, Robert. 1998. *Norbert Elias*. Routledge.

Chapter 9 Becoming Civilized in America: How the Upper Classes Got Class

Mennell, Stephen. 2007. *The American Civilization Process*. Polity Press.
Merchant, Carolyn. 1989. *Ecological Revolutions*. University of North Carolina.
Woodard, Colin. 2012. *American Nations*. Penguin Books.
Smith, Henry Nash. 1950. *Virgin Land*. Harvard University Press.
Zelinsky, Wilbur. 1992. *The Cultural Geography of the United States*. Prentice Hall.
Slotkin, Richard. 1973. *Regeneration Through Violence*. Harper Perennial.
Turner, Fredrick. 1983. *Beyond Geography.* Rutgers University Press.

Chapter 10 and 11 Promethean Qualitative Thinking from Reason to Rationality and **How Reason Lost and Regained its Balance**

Bernal, John Desmond. 1965. *Science in History: Volume II*. MIT Press.
Dewey, John. 1960. *Quest for Certainty*. Capricorn Books.
Janik, Ailan and Stephen Toumlin. 1973. *Wittgenstein's Vienna*. Simon and Schuster.
Jowlett, Garth and Victoria O'Donnell. 1999. *Propaganda and Persuasion*. Sage.
Maravall, Jose. 1986. *Culture of the Baroque*. University of Minnesota Press.
Parker, Geoffrey and Lesley M. Smith, Editors. 1978. *The General Crisis of the Seventeenth Century*. Routledge.
Popkin, Richard. 1979. *History of Skepticism*. University of California Press.
Rabb, Theodore. 1975. *The Struggle for Stability in Early Modern Europe*.
Oxford University Press.
Toulmin, Stephen. 1992. *Cosmopolis*. University of Chicago Press.
Toulmin, Stephen. 2001. *Return to Reason*. Harvard University Press.
Toulmin, Stephen and June Goodfield. 1962. *Architecture of Matter*. Harper and Row.
Tuck, Richard. 1993. *Philosophy and Government*. Cambridge University Press.
Westfall, Richard. 1977. *Construction of Modern Science*. Cambridge University Press.
Whitehead, Alfred North. 1925. *Science and the Modern World*. The Free Press.

Chapter 12 and 13 Promethean Quantitative Reasoning and

The Two Faces of Randomness—Probability and Chance

Datson, Lorraine. 1988. *Classical Probability in the Enlightenment*. Princeton University Press.

David, Florence Nightengale. 1962. *Games, Gods and Gambling*. Dover.

Hacking, Ian. 1975. *Emergence of Probability Theory*. Cambridge University Press.

Hacking, Ian. 1990. *The Taming of Chance*. Cambridge University Press.

Shapiro, Barbara. 1983. *Probability and Certainty in Seventeenth-Century England*. Princeton.

Porter, Theodore. 2004. *Karl Pearson*. Princeton University Press.

Chapters 14 and **15 Promethean Cognitive Evolution** and **The Amplification of Formal Operational Reasoning**

Crosby, David. 1997. *The Measure of Reality*. Cambridge University Press.

Gablik, Suzi. 1976. *Progress in Art*. Rizzoli.

Gleeson-White, Jane. 2011. *Double Entry*. Norton.

Goldstein, Leonard. 1988. *The Social and Cultural Roots of Linear Perspective*. MEP Publications.

Hadden, Richard. 1994 *On the Shoulder of Merchants*. State University of New York.

Hallpike, Christopher Robert. 2008. *How We Got Here*. Authorhouse UK.

Harvey, David. 2018. *The Limits of Capital*. Verso.

Levi-Bruhl, Lucien. 1985. *How Natives Think*. Princeton University Press.

Levi-Bruhl, Lucien. 1966. *The Soul of the Primitive*. Gateway.

Nye, Andrea. 1990. *Words of Power*. Routledge.

Olson, David. 1994. *World on Paper*. Cambridge University Press.

Olson, David. 2016. *The Mind on Paper*. Cambridge University Press.

Ong, Walter. 1983. *Ramus Method and the Decay of Dialogue.* Harvard University Press.
Piaget, Jean and Garcia Rolando. 1983. *Psychogenesis and the History of Science.* Columbia University Press.
Radding, Charles. 1985. *A World Made by Men.* University of North Carolina Press.
Shenefelt, Michael and Heidi White. 2013. *If A, Then B.* Columbia University Press.
Swetz, Frank. 1987. *Capitalism and Arithmetic.* Open Court.

Chapter 16 Conclusion

Heard, Gerald. 1963. *The Five Ages of Man.* The Julian Press.
Kahler, Erich. 1943. *Man the Measure.* Meridian Books.
Kahler, Erich. 1957. *The Tower and the Abyss.* George Braziller Inc.
Perelman, Fredy. 1983. *Against History, Against Leviathan.* Black and Red.

www.ingramcontent.com/pod-product-compliance
Lightning Source LLC
Chambersburg PA
CBHW031421270326
41930CB00007B/531

* 9 7 8 0 9 9 7 4 6 7 0 3 1 *